BASIC RESEARCH METHODS
FOR LIBRARIANS

Recent Titles in Library and Information Science Text Series

BASIC RESEARCH METHODS
FOR LIBRARIANS
Fourth Edition

Ronald R. Powell and Lynn Silipigni Connaway

Library and Information Science Text Series

A Member of the Greenwood Publishing Group

Westport, Connecticut, and London

Library of Congress Cataloging-in-Publication Data

Powell, Ronald R.
 Basic research methods for librarians. — 4th ed. / Ronald R. Powell and Lynn Silipigni Connaway.
  p. cm. — (Library and information science text series)
 Includes bibliographical references and index.
 ISBN 1-59158-103-6 (alk. paper) — ISBN 1-59158-112-5 (pbk. : alk. paper)
 1. Library science—Research—Methodology. I. Connaway, Lynn Silipigni. II. Title.
III. Series.
Z669.7.P68   2004
020'.72—dc22   2004048772

British Library Cataloguing in Publication Data is available.

Library of Congress Catalog Card Number: 2004048772
ISBN: 1-59158-103-6
       1-59158-112-5(pbk)

First published in 2004

Libraries Unlimited, 88 Post Road West, Westport, CT 06881
A member of the Greenwood Publishing Group, Inc.
www.lu.com

Printed in the United States of America

The paper used in this book complies with the
Permanent Paper Standard issued by the National
Information Standards Organization (Z39.48-1984).

10 9 8 7 6 5 4 3 2

Contents

Preface

This text is addressed to the practicing librarian and other information professionals who need to conduct research and publish. It is intended to provide guidance for any librarian who must be able to read and evaluate research reports critically and assist others with their research. It also is designed to be of benefit to the graduate library and information science student.

The book almost exclusively considers basic research methods, as opposed to applied and action research methods. Its primary purpose is to help teach the skills necessary for a librarian to conduct rigorous, basic research. Yet many of the methods, techniques, and tenets of basic research are relevant for applied research, and a person conducting applied research should benefit from a solid understanding of basic research methods. The librarian wishing to carry out a cost study, evaluate the performance of his or her library, or survey the library's users will need to be able to apply many of the principles and techniques treated in this book to his or her specific project. The more rigorous the research, the more useful its results, whether it be basic or applied in nature.

The perspective of this work is that library-related research should be as sound as any scientific research, and basic concepts are presented accordingly. A second viewpoint is that the conceptual development of a study is as crucial to its success as are the specific techniques employed in its conduct. That too is reflected in the contents of the text. The methods presented are applicable to most social science research, but the illustrations and applications presented throughout the text are specific to library settings. With the exception of the seventh chapter, quantitative, rather than qualitative, methods are generally emphasized; however, a number of the techniques covered are noted as having applications to qualitative research.

The book first addresses the role of research in librarianship and then considers the major steps in the development of a research study. Following that, it focuses on four major research methodologies—survey, experimental, qualitative, and historical—with extra attention given to sampling procedures. Chapters on data analysis, research proposals, and research reports conclude the text.

This text is not intended to be a cookbook for conducting basic research in library and information science, but it does attempt to introduce the researcher to the major issues involved in conducting original research and to present the basic information needed to design effective research. Neither is the text meant to stand alone. There are a variety of textbooks and other resources which the reader should consult, and referral to standard texts on statistical analysis is recommended. This book is an introductory presentation of basic research methods, and the reader wishing to become an accomplished researcher should not stop here.

The fourth edition of *Basic Research Methods for Librarians* represents a general revision and some reorganization of the third edition. References to other sources were updated, and additional works are cited where appropriate. (A limited number of Web site URLs were added, but their inherent instability should be kept in mind.) Additions to the text include expanded sections on ethics in research and focus group interviews, a section on sampling in-library use, an appendix addressing how to get published, and more consideration of research about and utilizing electronic technology.

We added a new author, Lynn Silipigni Connaway, who brought her relevant background and expertise to bear on the revision of this book. The authors would like to thank the many students who have made helpful comments over the years and Lynn Westbrook, Jack Glazier, and Sebastian Mundt for their contributions to the text. They also are indebted to Lisa Newton and Larry Olszewski, Terry Butterworth, and Anya Dyer of OCLC Online Computer Library Center for their assistance in the preparation of the fourth edition; and to Regina K. Manning and Katherine E. Seeburger for preparing the index.

It is not a simple matter to conduct rigorous research, but it can be interesting, enlightening, and rewarding. Hopefully, this book will help and encourage librarians and others to become more active and productive researchers.

Chapter 1

Research and Librarianship

THE RESEARCH RECORD

Those who have assessed the previous research of librarians have been of a consensus that the quantity and quality have left something to be desired. For example, "Ennis described library research as 'noncumulative, fragmentary, generally weak and relentlessly oriented to immediate practice.'"[1] But that is not to say that there has not been a substantial amount of good library-related research. In addition, most observers seem to be of the opinion that library-related research of late has shown improvement with regard to its rigorousness, sophistication, and incorporation of multiple methods and statistical analysis. Yet they also seem to agree that there continues to be room for improvement.

This chapter will concern itself only with the relatively recent record of library research. Readers wishing to learn more about the history of library science research may wish to consult Jackson's brief history of research in librarianship in the United States and Canada, or Busha's review of the past status of library science research.[2, 3]

1

Definition of Research

There is no one definition of research, in part because there is more than one kind of research. Considering research in the general sense, *Webster's Seventh New Collegiate Dictionary* defined it as "studious inquiry or examination; especially: investigation or experimentation aimed at the discovery and interpretation of facts, revision of accepted theories or laws in the light of new facts, or practical applications of such new or revised theories or laws." Hillway, in his introductory text on research methods, defined research as "a method of study by which, through the careful and exhaustive investigation of all the ascertainable evidence bearing upon a definable problem, we reach a solution to that problem."[4] Mouly stated that "Research is best conceived as the process of arriving at dependable solutions to problems through the planned and systematic collection, analysis, and interpretation of data."[5]

These general definitions suggest that there are at least two major types of research, one of which is *basic research*. Basic research, also referred to as pure, theoretical, or scientific research, is primarily interested in deriving new knowledge and is, at most, only indirectly involved with how that knowledge will be applied to specific, practical, or real problems. Or, as Vickery stated, "Scientific research . . . is concerned with elucidating concepts and their relations, hypotheses and theories, and is not necessarily and certainly not directly related to technical and practical problems."[6] It is sometimes labeled as research conducted in order to acquire knowledge for its own sake, but, as will be argued later, that probably is a simplistic viewpoint. Basic research, particularly if quantitative in nature, is usually designed so as to produce new knowledge that is generalizable.

The second major type of research is usually known as *applied research*, and it encompasses a variety of specific research techniques such as systems analysis and operations research. In contrast to pure or basic research, applied research emphasizes the solving of specific problems in real situations. Much of the library-related research has been applied research dealing with everything from evaluating book collections to adopting automated circulation systems. (See Chapter 3 for additional information on applied and action research.)

But in spite of the fact that basic and applied research have tended to be conducted in isolation from one another, they are not necessarily dichotomous. As Shera noted, "Research is no less 'pure' for leading to useful results, though it most certainly does not have to possess immediate applicability to qualify as research."[7] In other words, basic research often leads to practical applications, while applied research frequently acts as a foundation for subsequent theoretical or basic research. According to Mouly, "the distinction between pure and applied research is not very clear. All research findings will be useful and practical—sooner or later—no matter how disinterested in immediate utilitarian goals the pure researcher might be. Both pure and applied research are oriented toward the discovery of scientific truth, and both are practical in the sense that they lead to the solution of man's problems."[8] Perhaps, as Muller argued, the crucial factor is not whether the research is pure or applied but whether it is relevant.[9]

Research also can be dichotomized as quantitative and qualitative. *"Quantitative research* methods involve a problem-solving approach that is highly structured in nature and that relies on the quantification of concepts, where possible, for purposes of measurement and evaluation."[10] *Qualitative research* methods focus on observing events from the perspective of those involved and attempt to understand why individuals behave as they do. They take a more natural approach to the resolution of research problems. Some research projects utilize both quantitative and qualitative research methods to study and report behaviors and events. This book emphasizes quantitative methods; however, Chapter 7 is devoted to qualitative methods, and a number of the procedures covered elsewhere have qualitative applications.

Types of Previous Library Research

According to Shera, Beals once categorized library literature into the tripartite classification of Glad Tidings, Testimony, and Research, and noted that there was little of the last.[11] Goldhor, in his text on library research, categorized library literature with regard to research as including: one, a relatively small body of published research as defined in the narrow sense; two, a larger amount of published and unpublished services studies, or applied research; three, an even larger number of reports or descriptions of specific situations, or simply opinions; and four, original data.[12] Losee and Worley stated, "There is a tendency among information professionals to write and publish in the 'How I done it good' genre, a genre that is very situation-specific."[13] In short, as was noted earlier, and as Busha and Harter indicated in their textbook, the preponderance of library-related research has been applied in nature.[14]

A 1984 issue of *Library Trends* was devoted to research in librarianship, and it reviewed research as related to the history of library and information science, economics of libraries, political science, sociology, psychology of information use, organization theory, public administration, and operations research. This work thus provided a categorization of library research in terms of both methodology and subject. In the first chapter of this issue of *Library Trends,* Lynch identified her own general categories for describing different research activities as practical research, bibliographical research, scholarly research, and scientific research.[15] She characterized practical research as problem solving with information; bibliographical research as reordering the thoughts of others; scholarly research as the systematic collecting, organizing, and analyzing of data; and scientific research as discovering new knowledge.

Mathews described research performed by the U.S. Department of Education from 1977 to 1988.[16] Along with analyzing the products of the research, she discussed recent research agenda efforts of the department and implications for future research. McClure and Bishop provided a useful summary of reports published from 1976 to 1988 related to the status of research in librarianship.[17] Several of the reports contained analyses of the types of research methods utilized during various time periods. Powell summarized some methodological studies ranging from an analysis of dissertations dating back to 1925 to an examination of research articles published in 1984.[18] He also characterized more recent trends including qualitative, interdisciplinary, and technology-based research. Buttlar analyzed library and information science (LIS) dissertations to identify the authors' gender, the nature of the most highly cited materials, the most highly cited journals, the literature cited in disciplines other than LIS, the countries of origin of publications cited, and the currency of the cited literature.[19] She did not identify the types of methodologies used but did report that the literature from the LIS field is cited about 50% of the time, and she identified education, computer science, health and medicine, psychology, communications, and business as disciplines that impact LIS research.

Bao analyzed the articles published in *College & Research Libraries* (*C&RL*) and *Journal of Academic Librarianship* (*JAL*) between 1990 and 1999.[20] The majority of the refereed articles addressed collections, services, staffing, and the Internet, indicating that some of the research areas identified by the College Library Section of the Association of College and Research Libraries (ACRL) had not been studied by the authors included in the sample. Bao could not identify any research patterns or trends for the journals, except that Internet technology has been a popular research topic since 1994.[21]

Crawford reported research patterns represented by the articles published in *C&RL* and *JAL* for 1996 and 1997.[22] He identified more than 65% of the articles published in *C&RL* as quantitative empirical studies, while less than 25% of the articles published in *JAL* during this same time period were categorized as quantitative empirical studies. How-to, model and issue discussions, project reports, and other non-empirical papers represented 29.6% of the articles published in *JAL*, while 14.3% of the articles published in *C&RL* were categorized as nonempirical.

Limitations of Previous Library Research

Unfortunately, the past research record for library and information science is not exemplary. It has been easier to find criticism of library research than praise. In 1976, Zweizig called for improvements in research methodologies, especially as they related to users of library services.[23] Busha and Harter stated, "a large proportion of librarianship's research has been uneven in quality and demonstrably weak methodologically . . ."[24] Shaughnessy was even more critical in contending that traditionally the field has permitted much of what is not actually research to be called research.[25] In an article, Converse identified shortcomings in library and information science research so far as purpose is concerned. He noted "a failure to ask the right questions and to establish a proper theoretical foundation for later research or application."[26]

On what else do these writers and others base their rather negative evaluations of much of the previous library research? Martyn and Lancaster pointed out that much of the earlier literature of library science was too heavily based on opinion, as opposed to investigation, to be considered research.[27] Shera noted that, because of library research's "excessive dependence upon local observations and limited data, more frequently than not it is provincial and parochial rather than general in applicability."[28] Van House observed that "much of the research in LIS is episodic. Rarely do researchers build a continuing series of projects so that their own work is a coherent whole. Nor do they often build on one another's work."[29]

Garrison, while acknowledging that considerable advances had been made in public library research in the previous decade, went on to itemize several shortcomings of research, including the following:

1. Researchers have not disseminated their results adequately;
2. Practitioners have not kept up with research results that have been reported;
3. The profession has been too content with nonresearch reports;
4. The audiences for research journals have been too limited;
5. Dissertations have seldom had any relationship to previous or subsequent research;
6. The impact of reported research has been weakened due to poor bibliographic control and inadequate availability of copies.[30]

Goodall reported that a variety of topics were being investigated by public librarians in England, yet the methodologies used for the studies were limited.[31] Survey methodology was employed for the majority of the studies. Although new and varied methodologies are being demonstrated in the library and information science literature, survey methodology continues to dominate.[32]

Gatten criticized library science research for failing to draw upon the research literature and methods of other disciplines and for too often utilizing unsophisticated analytical techniques and limited theoretical frameworks.[33] Trahan stated that library research "is at a relatively primitive stage in its development when compared to the research literature of other disciplines" and that "there has been little, if any, increase in research activity in librarianship."[34] In an editorial, Hernon expressed his concern for the poor quality of research published in library and information science journals.[35] Although Fisher concluded that the professional literature represented in six LIS journals in 1993 validates the results of prior studies in regard to author demographics, he recommended the continued publication of both applied and "rigorous empirical/theoretical research" to meet our professional needs.[36]

In short, in spite of some progress, there continues to be a need for more and better library-related research. The limitations of earlier research are not the only reasons for calling for better conducted research. There are a number of positive justifications that can be made for more rigorous research and, in particular, basic research.

THE RATIONALE FOR BASIC RESEARCH IN LIBRARY SCIENCE

Growth of the Profession

As indicated earlier, one of the major purposes of basic research is to create new knowledge. Or, as stated by Mouly, "it is the purpose of science [scientific research] to go beyond experience and common sense, which frequently are quite limited and inadequate—and often quite incorrect . . . for advancing knowledge, for promoting progress, and for enabling man to relate more effectively to his environment, to accomplish his purposes, and to resolve his conflicts."[37] As Kunge has written, "Learning to master theoretically and in practical application, the ground rules of re-search creates the best foundation for continuing growth in a profession."[38]

But perhaps even more basic to the advancement of the profession "is the need for the field to test the various myths, assumptions, rules-of-thumb, and other conventions by which it has operated for so long a time, to link concepts which have been proven through testing to be valid, and thereby establish theories in-digenous to the field itself."[39] In addition, the profession needs to advance be-yond its heavy dependence on descriptive data and establish principles and theo-ries on which libraries and information systems and services can be based.[40] "One of the hallmarks of a profession is the ability of its members to give advice to clientele derived from a body of generalized and systematic knowledge that comprises its theoretical core."[41]

Those concerned about the status of the LIS profession have commented on the need for more and better basic research. Shaughnessy noted, "Of the two primary marks of a profession—a service ideal and a body of theoretical knowledge—it has been suggested that librarianship possesses the first, but not the second. Theo-retical knowledge, as distinguished from knowledge based on practice, is gener-ally developed or discovered through the process of research; a process in which librarianship has not had much of a tradition."[42] Busha and Harter argued that "If librarianship is to merit the coveted designation 'science,' a significant number of scholars and research workers must regularly apply scientific method to analyze relationships among the problems which librarians are obligated to explore and which they are qualified to serve."[43] In other words, "A profession that would know itself—that would anticipate or, to use Gabor's phrase, 'invent the future'—must support and engage in productive research."[44]

In 2001, the Special Library Association (SLA) published a research state-ment, "Putting OUR Knowledge to Work," defining library and information science research as not well developed, with few peer-reviewed journals and grant-funded research in comparison to other disciplines.[45] The statement identi-fies ways in which special librarians, researchers, and the SLA can work together to contribute to the library and information profession and to build a foundation for evidence-based practice.

In short, basic research is crucial if the field of library and information science is "to solve professional problems, develop tools and methods for analysis of organization, services, and behavior, to determine costs and benefits of our services, and most importantly, to establish or develop a body of theory on which to base our practice."[46] LIS students and professionals must not only be able to "read, understand, and value the LIS research literature," but "they must also be able to locate it within its cultural context." A commitment to understanding and applying research is also essential if the field is to continue to advance."[47] Unfortunately, as Busha and others have noted, the development of new knowledge within the library and information science profession has traditionally received a relatively low priority.[48]

Management

As has been indicated earlier, basic research has more to offer than the expansion and refinement of the profession's theoretical underpinnings. Much of the knowledge created as the result of basic research is likely to have practical applications for the improvement of practices in actual library operations.[49] Swisher argued that "there is no more important activity than acquiring new information that may now or someday assist in the goal of improving our professional decision making. Assuming the responsibility of practical research is probably the most important role a librarian can accept."[50] The application of research findings should result in "improved decision making, more knowledgeable insights into a wealth of library issues, better and more accountable services and programs, and the continued maturation of LIS as a discipline/profession."[51] "Thus, there is the need for academic librarians to possess an understanding of data-gathering techniques, which are informed by an understanding of the nature of the research methodologies available and an understanding of the nature of the statistical analysis techniques available."[52] The American Library Association (ALA) promotes the need for the dissemination of research findings for support of professional practice and has published "recommendations related to the effective dissemination of research."[53]

While most research for decision making takes the form of applied research, it typically draws upon the tenets of basic research. McClure observed that "applied research takes the theory and concepts from basic research and by formal methods of inquiry; investigates 'real world' phenomenon."[54] In other words, a solid understanding of the basic research process should better enable one to conduct sound applied research. As Goldhor pointed out, "Once one has learned this method [scientific research] he can understand and use any of the less rigorous methods, but learning the latter will not prepare one really to use the former."[55]

ACRL established the Focus on the Future Task Force in the fall of 2001 to identify the issues facing academic librarians to assist with developing "services to further improve learning and research."[56] After extensive interviews and open forum discussions, seven top issues were identified. These issues provide a research agenda that can guide and direct research projects that will enable library managers to make intelligent decisions.

Reading Research Reports

Another benefit of having a reasonable mastery of basic research methods is that it should allow one to understand and evaluate critically the research reports of others. According to Swisher, "the reader who understands the process of research will question much more about the literature in general, and correctly identify the working limitations of the literature."[57] Some librarians, particularly special librarians, are expected to evaluate or screen research reports (i.e., serve as research intermediaries) for their clientele. Unfortunately, as Sullivan has contended, not only do librarians who are practitioners tend to be too busy and unskilled to conduct their own research, but, more seriously, "they are also either uninformed or unwilling to accept or unable to judge critically the research of others in the field of librarianship."[58] Until a majority of the field's practitioners can understand and apply the research results of others, the profession is not likely to realize much benefit from its research efforts. Numerous writers, including Busha and Harter and Grazier have argued for the need to evaluate and apply published research.[59, 60] As Williams and Winston stated, "the research literature in any discipline can serve to further the scholarly discussion, advance the theoretical base of the profession, and inform practice."[61]

A study by Powell, Baker, and Mika provides a more hopeful perspective on the profession's use of research.[62] Members of the ALA, the American Society for Information Science and Technology (ASIST), the Medical Library Association, and the SLA were surveyed to identify their involvement in reading, applying, and conducting research. The findings revealed that "almost 90% of LIS practitioners in the United States and Canada regularly read at least one research journal, nearly 62% regularly read research-based articles, approximately 50% occasionally apply research results to professional practices, and 42% occasionally or frequently perform research related to their job or to the LIS profession."[63] Only 15% of those surveyed indicated that they read more than four research journals, and research activity varied by membership in the professional associations represented in the study. Research methods master's degree courses were found "to be significantly related to conducting, as well as reading, research."[64]

Improved Service to Researchers

Yet another advantage to having a basic knowledge of research methods, at least for those librarians who serve researchers, is the greater understanding of the needs of researchers provided by this awareness. Only when the librarian knows the basic process which a researcher utilizes, can he or she fully anticipate and meet those research needs. Or as Engle stated, "A thorough and continuing personal grounding in the experience of learning and research in an academic setting prepares us to join students and faculty in the creative act which bibliographic research can be."[65] In addition, the librarian's status is likely to benefit from being knowledgeable about the researchers' techniques and from being able to discuss them intelligently with his or her clientele. Grover and Hale argued that librarians should assume a proactive role in faculty research and be viewed as key players in the process.[66]

Personal Benefits

Perhaps most important among the benefits one could expect to realize from a study of research methods is the ability to conduct research. For many librarians, especially in academic settings, research activities are not only desirable but necessary. A number of academic institutions expect their professional librarians to meet the same requirements for promotion and tenure as do their regular teaching faculty, and these usually include research and publishing. If these librarians, and others, are to conduct the kind of rigorous research that they and their profession need, a thorough understanding of basic research methods is absolutely essential.

An awareness of research methods and design also should prove helpful for those preparing research proposals in order to obtain financial support for their research activities. In addition, it has been pointed out that the study of research methods can improve one's ability to think critically and analytically—competencies associated with leadership. A library's involvement in research can even improve staff morale and enhance the library's status in its community.

THE FUTURE OF LIBRARY RESEARCH

As Busha noted, past weaknesses of library-related research can at least partially be explained by the fact "that research in librarianship is still relatively young. Clear conceptions of the goals, objectives, and methodologies of library science research are only now beginning to be solidly formulated."[67] It does appear clear, however, that it will become more and more "necessary to use the methodology of other disciplines—in particular, those of sociology, psychology, economics, linguistics, history—and to employ more generally applicable methodologies" in order to study the many problems facing librarianship today.[68]

But who is going to be qualified to conduct the kinds of research needed, how will they be trained, and how will practitioners be equipped to read and utilize their research? Shera provided at least one answer to these questions when he wrote, "Research is too important to be left to dilettantes and amateurs, and its pursuit should be reserved for those who are qualified for it by aptitude, education, and motivation."[69] In short, education appears to be one key to solving the problem. Not only can education provide the basic skills needed for conducting research, but it can help to shape attitudes and supply motivations.

Logically, the major responsibility for imparting research skills to librarians must belong to the LIS education programs. As Shera stated, "A specific part of the course of study for a graduate student in librarianship should be the acquiring of 'a knowledge of the principles and methods of research as applied to the investigation of library problems, together with the ability to evaluate research results, especially research in librarianship.'"[70] As Muller wrote, "Students should learn to appreciate the contribution of research and be urged to rid themselves of the notion that research is something esoteric, remote, or impractical."[71] Yet most students view LIS programs as primarily concerned with providing professional, not academic, training[72] and "too few practitioners have education in the research or knowledge creating process."[73] Only 47% of the practitioners responding to a survey conducted in 2000 reported that they had taken a course on research methods at the master's degree level, and 59% of them reported that their master's degree programs had not adequately prepared them to conduct research.[74]

The track record of LIS programs regarding the teaching of research skills is not outstanding.[75] O'Connor and Park reported that a research methods course was not required in 38.5% of the ALA-accredited LIS programs and that "only half of the twenty-four top-rated programs required Master of Library Science (MLS) students to take research methods."[76] Hernon and Schwartz refer to this as a crisis that should not be allowed to continue.[77] In a study she conducted, Dimitroff reported that special librarians identified the following as the top barriers to their involvement in research activities: the lack of management support of research, the lack of money/funding for research, the lack of personal interest in research, an insecurity of research skills, and a lack of research ideas.[78]

However, LIS programs do not have the entire responsibility for training competent researchers. It is also the responsibility of professional associations and, in some cases, research organizations, to provide appropriate continuing education opportunities. If libraries and other employers are going to expect librarians to equip themselves to do research, then they must be prepared to provide appropriate incentives, support, and rewards. For example, released time, special leaves, and sabbaticals can be arranged to allow more time for research. Administrative support can be provided through salary raises, in-house training, and financial and clerical support for research projects. Relevant courses such as those in statistical analysis can be taken in departments outside the LIS program when desirable or necessary. Ultimately, of course, it is the responsibility of the would-be researcher to take advantage of continuing education and staff development programs and to commit himself or herself to a substantial program of self-study.

Goldhor's statement made more than three decades ago still rings true: "Librarianship today is particularly in need of the generalized truths which scientific research is designed to uncover."[79] And the research problems ultimately will direct the methodologies employed, which justifies the sustained development of research theories and models described by Glazier and Grover in their multidisciplinary framework for theory building.[80] In other words, if we are to realize the professional growth needed by the field of library and information science, "Our attention must increasingly be devoted to research which is more basic and less applied."[81] "We must all raise our expectations and challenge the profession to value and use research."[82]

Fortunately, there are promising signs. In a 1986 editorial in *Research Strategies*, the authors stated that "a new strain of thought has sprung up in the field of librarianship . . . an interest on the part of practicing librarians in conducting serious research."[83] The professional associations continue to establish more and more units concerned with research. As of 2002–2003, ALA's Research and Statistics Assembly had 29 member units. At the annual conferences of the ALA, a considerable number of programs and committee meetings deal directly with research and statistics. The ACRL recently established a Research Mentoring Program to help members with various aspects of the research process. ALA's Committee on Research and Statistics is charged with promoting research to answer questions regarding library services.

SLA's Research Statement calls for evidence-based practice, which is decision making "based on the strongest evidence" of what will work best for the libraries' clients.[84] With the expanding role of library and information professionals and the widespread accessibility of information, SLA advocates for the selection, acquisition, organization, and management of information resources to be based on research findings.

The creation and dissemination of research is central to the Vision Statement of the ASIST. The vision of the society includes, "advancing knowledge about information, its creation, properties, and use; providing analysis of ideas, practices, and technologies; valuing theory, research, applications, and service; nurturing new perspectives, interests, and ideas; and increasing public awareness of the information sciences and technologies and their benefits to society."[85]

McClure and Bishop asked 23 leading researchers in library and information science about the status of research in the field.[86] They concluded that it had improved somewhat in the 1980s and expressed "guarded optimism" about the future status of research in library and information science. At least two studies indicated that the number of published research articles is increasing (though there is some evidence that the proportion of research articles in the core journals has declined since 1975).[87, 88] A 1991 book, edited by McClure and Hernon, was dedicated to the improvement of library and information science research. It provided an overview of LIS research, considered its practical context, and discussed issues and concerns related to research in library and information science.[89]

The annual reports of ALA's Office for Research and Statistics continue to show considerable activity in the research arena. Eisenberg wrote in 1993[90] that we can take pride in the research that has been conducted in the area of school library media programs. In three editorials, Hernon and Hernon and Schwartz argued that some of the indictments of library research are supported by few references to the LIS literature, LIS researchers have drawn on procedures developed in other disciplines, and LIS researchers have contributed to the development of innovative methods.[91, 92, 93] Two national Library Research Seminars, one in November 1996 and one in November 2000, received numerous proposals for papers representing a wide range of methodologies including content analysis, historiography, path analysis, discourse analysis, transaction log analysis, protocol analysis, survey, modeling, and metaanalysis. The research topics were equally diverse and often interdisciplinary. These two research seminars provided an effective forum solely devoted to research ideas and methodologies. The third Library Research Seminar is in the planning stages and is scheduled for October 2004.

It is always difficult to predict the future, but research in LIS will probably continue to incorporate more multidisciplinary and qualitative methods.[94] Studies addressing the impacts and use of digital resources and technology are currently represented in the literature and will probably continue to pique interest in researchers and practitioners as the resources and technologies evolve and library users become more sophisticated in their demands for and use of these resources. Hernon and Schwartz support this assessment and add, "the problems, research designs, the tool chest of methodologies, and data analysis techniques and software are richer today than ever before."[95]

In conclusion, there is mounting evidence that the quality, if not the quantity, of LIS research is improving. And, hopefully, there is increasing recognition "that the results of research in a broad spectrum of effort extending well beyond librarianship will, in large measure, determine the future directions of library services and the nature of the profession itself."[96]

NOTES

[1]Laurel Grotzinger, "Methodology of Library Science Inquiry—Past and Present," in *A Library Science Research Reader and Bibliographic Guide*, edited by Charles H. Busha (Littleton, CO: Libraries Unlimited, 1981): 44.

[2]S. L. Jackson, "Environment: Research," in *A Century of Service: Librarianship in the United States and Canada,* edited by S. L. Jackson, E. B. Herling, and E. J. Josey (Chicago, IL: American Library Association, 1976): 341–54.

[3]Charles A. Busha, "Library Science Research: The Path to Progress," in *A Library Science Research Reader and Bibliographic Guide,* edited by Charles A. Busha (Littleton, CO: Libraries Unlimited, 1981).

[4]Tyrus Hillway, *Introduction to Research*, 2nd ed. (Boston, MA: Houghton Mifflin, 1964): 5.

[5]George J. Mouly, *Educational Research: The Art and Science of Investigation* (Boston, MA: Allyn and Bacon, 1978): 12.

[6]B. C. Vickery, "Academic Research in Library and Information Studies," *Journal of Librarianship* 7 (July 1975): 153–60.

[7]Jesse H. Shera, "Darwin, Bacon, and Research in Librarianship," *Library Trends* 3 (July 1964): 143.

[8]Mouly, *Educational Research*, 43.

[9]Robert H. Muller, "The Research Mind in Library Education and Practice," *Library Journal* 92 (March 15, 1967): 1129.

[10]Jack D. Glazier and Ronald R. Powell, eds. *Qualitative Research in Information Management* (Englewood, CO: Libraries Unlimited, 1992): xi.

[11]Shera, "Darwin, Bacon, and Research," 145.

[12]Herbert Goldhor, *An Introduction to Scientific Research in Librarianship* (Urbana, IL: University of Illinois, Graduate School of Library Science, 1972).

[13]Robert M. Losee, Jr. and Karen A. Worley, *Research and Evaluation for Information Professionals* (San Diego: Academic Press, 1993): ix.

[14]Charles A. Busha and Stephen P. Harter, *Research Methods in Librarianship: Techniques and Interpretations* (New York: Academic Press, 1980): 8.

[15]Mary Jo Lynch, "Research and Librarianship: An Uneasy Connection," *Library Trends* 32 (Spring 1984): 367.

[16]Anne J. Mathews, "An Overview of Issues, Proposals, and Products in Library/Information Research," *Journal of Education for Library and Information Science* 29 (Spring 1989): 251–61.

[17]Charles R. McClure and Ann Bishop, "The Status of Research in Library/Information Science: Guarded Optimism," *College & Research Libraries* 50 (March 1989): 127–43.

[18]Ronald R. Powell, "Research Competence for Ph.D. Students in Library and Information Science," *Journal of Education for Library and Information Science* 36 (Fall 1995): 319–29.

[19]Lois Buttlar, "Information Sources in Library and Information Science Doctoral Research," *Library & Information Science Research* 21 (1999): 227–45.

[20]Xue-Ming Bao, "An Analysis of the Research Areas of the Articles Published in *C&RL* and *JAL* between 1990 and 1999," *College & Research Libraries* 66 (2000): 536–44.

[21]Ibid., 543.

[22]Gregory A. Crawford, "The Research Literature of Academic Librarianship: A Comparison of College & Research Libraries and Journal of Academic Librarianship," *College & Research Libraries* 60 (May 1999): 224–30.

[23]Douglas L. Zweizig, "With Our Eye on the User: Needed Research for Information and Referral in the Public Library," *Drexel Library Quarterly* 13 (1976): 48–58.

[24]Busha and Harter, *Research Methods in Librarianship*, 7.

[25]Thomas W. Shaughnessy, "Library Research in the 70's: Problems and Prospects," *California Librarian* 37 (July 1976): 44–52.

[26]W. R. Converse, "Research: What We Need, and What We Get," *Canadian Library Journal* 41 (October 1984): 236.

[27]John Martyn and F. Wilfrid Lancaster, *Investigative Methods in Library and Information Science: An Introduction* (Arlington, VA: Information Resources Press, 1981): 193.

[28]Shera, "Darwin, Bacon, and Research", 147.

[29]Nancy A. Van House, "Assessing the Quantity, Quality, and Impact of LIS Research," in *Library and Information Science Research: Perspectives and Strategies for Improvement* (Norwood, NJ: Ablex, 1991).

[30]Guy Garrison, "A Look at Research on Public Library Problems in the 1970's," *Public Libraries* 19 (Spring 1980): 4–8.

[31]Deborah Goodall, "It Ain't What You Do, It's the Way That You Do It: A Review of Public Library Research with Special Reference to Methodology," *Public Library Journal* 11 (1996): 69–76.

[32]Ronald R. Powell, "Recent Trends in Research: A Methodological Essay," *Library & Information Science Research* 21 (1999): 91–119.

[33]Jeffery N. Gatten, "Paradigm Restrictions on Interdisciplinary Research into Librarianship," *College & Research Libraries* 52 (November 1991): 575–84.

[34]Eric Trahan, "Applying Meta-Analysis to Library Research and Information Science Research," *Library Quarterly* 63 (January 1993): 73.

[35]Peter Hernon, "Editorial: Research in Library and Information Science-Reflections on the Journal Literature," *Journal of Academic Librarianship* 25 (July 1999): 263–66.

[36]William Fisher, "When Write Is Wrong: Is All Our Professional Literature on the Same Page?" *Library Collections, Acquisitions, & Technical Services* 23 (Spring 1999): 61–72.

[37]George J. Mouly, *Educational Research*, 12.

[38]Busha and Harter, *Research Methods in Librarianship*, 6.

[39]Grotzinger, "Methodology of Library Science Inquiry," 45.

[40]Vickery, "Academic Research in Library and Information Studies," 155.

[41]Carolyn E. Poole, "Guest Editorial: Importance of Research and Publication by Community College Librarians," *College & Research Libraries* (2000): 486.

[42]Shaughnessy, "Library Research in the 70's," 44.

[43]Busha and Harter, *Research Methods in Librarianship*, 4.

[44]Shera, "Darwin, Bacon, and Research," 148–9.

[45]"Putting OUR Knowledge to Work: A New SLA Research Statement," Available, [http://www.sla.org/content/resources/research/rschstatement.cfm.] 2001 June.

[46]Shaughnessy, "Library Research in the 70's," 51.

[47]Prudence W. Dalrymple, "A Quarter Century of User-Centered Study: The Impact of Zweizig and Dervin on LIS Research," *Library & Information Science Research* 23 (2001): 163.

[48]Busha, "Library Science Research," 2.

[49]Busha and Harter, *Research Methods in Librarianship*, 8.

[50]Robert Swisher, "Focus on Research, "*Top of the News* 42 (Winter 1986): 176.

[51]Peter Hernon and Candy Schwartz, "Can Research Be Assimilated into the Soul of Library and Information Science?" *Library and Information Science Research* 17 (Spring 1995): 101.

[52]James F. Williams II and Mark D. Winston, "Leadership Competencies and the Importance of Research Methods and Statistical Analysis in Decision Making and Research and Publication: A Study of Citation Patterns," *Library & Information Science Research* 25 (2003): 390.

[53]"Dissemination of Research in LIS: A statement by the American Library Association Committee on Research and Statistics." Available, [http://www.ala.org/Content/NavigationMenu/Our_Association/Offices/Research_and_Statistics/Committee_on_Research_and_Statistics/Dissemination_of_Research_in_LIS/Dissemination_of_Research_in_LIS.htm.] 2001 June.

[54]Charles R. McClure, "Management Data for Library Decision Making: The Role of the Researcher," in *Library Lectures* edited by Robert S. Martin, vol. 12, (Baton Rouge, LA: LSU Libraries, 1988).

[55]Goldhor, *An Introduction to Scientific Research,* 1–2.

[56]W. Lee Hisle, "Top Issues Facing Academic Libraries: A Report of the Focus on the Future Task Force," *C&RL News* 63 (November 2002): 714.

[57]Swisher, "Focus on Research," 175.

[58]Peggy A. Sullivan, "Research in Librarianship: Achievements, Needs, and Prospects" *Illinois Libraries* 60 (May 1978): 511.

[59]Busha and Harter, *Research Methods in Librarianship.*

[60]Margaret H. Grazier, "Critically Reading and Applying Research in School Library Media Centers," *School Library Media Quarterly* 10 (Winter 1982): 135–46.

[61]Williams and Winston, "Leadership Competencies and the Importance of Research Methods," 401.

[62]Ronald R. Powell, Lynda M. Baker, and Joseph J. Mika, "Library and Information Science Practitioners and Research," *Library & Information Science Research* 24 (2002):49–72.

[63]Ibid., 55–61.

[64]Ibid., 70.

[65]Michael Engle, "Creativity and the Research Process in Academic Libraries," *College & Research Libraries News* 48 (November 1987): 629.

[66]Robert Grover and Martha L. Hale, "The Role of the Librarian in Faculty Research," *College & Research Libraries* 49 (January 1988): 9–15.

[67]Busha, "Library Science Research," 2.

[68]Vickery, "Academic Research in Library and Information Studies," 158.

[69]Shera, "Darwin, Bacon, and Research," 149.

[70]Grotzinger, "Methodology of Library Science Inquiry," 45–6.

[71]Muller, "The Research Mind In Library Education and Practice," 1129.

[72]Converse, "Research: What We Need, and What We Get," 238.

[73]Jane B. Robbins, "Research in Information Service Practice," *Library and Information Science Research* 12 (April 1990): 127.

[74]Powell, Baker, and Mika, "Library and Information Science Practitioners and Research," 49–72.

[75]Busha and Harter, *Research Methods in Librarianship*, 5, 8.

[76]Daniel O. O'Connor and Soyeon Park, "Guest Editorial: Crisis in LIS Research Capacity," *Library & Information Science Research* 23 (2001): 105.

[77]Peter Hernon and Candy Schwartz, "Editorial: We Will Not Rest on Our Laurels! " *Library & Information Science Research* 25 (2003): 125–6.

[78]Alexandra Dimitroff, "Research Knowledge and Activities of Special Librarians: Results of a Survey," *Special Libraries* 87 (Winter 1996): 1–9.

[79]Goldhor, *An Introduction to Scientific Research,* 2.

[80]Jack D. Glazier and Robert Grover, "A Multidisciplinary Framework for Theory Building," *Library Trends* 50 (Winter 2002): 317–29.

[81]Shaughnessy, "Library Research in the 70's," 52.

[82]Peter Hernon, "Editorial: Components of the Research Process: Where Do We Need to Focus Attention?" *Journal of Academic Librarianship* 27 (March 2001): 88.

[83]Sharon A. Hogan and Mary W. George, "Cropping Up: Librarians' Desire to Conduct Serious Research," *Research Strategies* 4 (Spring 1986): 58.

[84]"Putting OUR Knowledge to Work: A New SLA Research Statement," Available, [http://www.sla.org/content/memberserviceresearchforum/rschstatement.cfm] 2001 June.

[85]"Vision," Available, [http://www.asis.org/AboutASIS/asis-mission.html] 2001.

[86]McClure and Bishop, "The Status of Research in Library/Information Science," 127–43.

[87]Bluma C. Peritz, "Research in Library Science as Reflected in the Core Journals of the Profession: A Quantitative Analysis (1950–1975)," (Berkeley: University of California, 1977).

[88]Martyvonne M. Nour, "A Quantitative Analysis of the Research Articles Published in Core Library Journals of 1980," *Library and Information Science Research* 7 (July 1985): 261–73.

[89]Charles R. McClure and Peter Hernon, eds. *Library and Information Science Research: Perspectives and Strategies for Improvement* (Norwood, NJ: Ablex Press, 1991).

[90]Michael B. Eisenberg, "The State of Research Today," *School Library Media Quarterly* 21 (Summer 1993): 241.

[91]Peter Hernon, "Library and Information Science Research: Not an Island unto Itself," *Library and Information Science Research* 14 (January-March 1992): 1-3.

[92]Peter Hernon, "LIS Extends to the Research Frontier," *College & Research Libraries* 53 (January 1992): 3–5.

[93]Peter Hernon and Candy Schwartz, "Library and Information Science Research: Is It Misunderstood?" *Library and Information Science Research* 15 (Summer 1993): 215–7.

[94]Powell, "Recent Trends in Research," 91–119.

[95]Hernon and Schwartz, "Editorial: We Will Not Rest on Our Laurels!" 125.

[96]American Library association. "Policy Statement on the Role of Research in the American Library Association." (Chicago: ALA, 1970).

Chapter 2

Developing the Research Study

More research effort is wasted by going off half prepared, with only a vague set of ideas and procedures, than in any other way.[1]

PLANNING FOR RESEARCH

The first question that a researcher may well ask is, "Where do I begin?" In other words, where does the planning begin? Leedy suggests that "it begins with an understanding of the manner in which knowledge is discovered."[2] After all, as we learned earlier, the major purpose of basic research is to discover new knowledge.

Historically, new knowledge has been sought either by means of deductive logic or through the use of inductive reasoning. Deductive or systematic logic, which was developed by Aristotle, is characterized by use of the syllogism. A syllogism starts with a basic premise, which is then logically applied to a particular case; for example: "All men are mortal; John Doe is a man; therefore John Doe is mortal." The truth of the conclusion obviously depends upon the truth of the basic premise, which in this example was "All men are mortal."

In contrast to the deductive method, inductive reasoning proceeds from particular instances to general principles, or from facts to theories. Using inductive logic, one might note that John Doe is mortal and then observe a number of other men as well. One might next decide that all of the *observed* men were mortals and arrive at the conclusion that *all* men are mortal. The obvious limitation to this method is that it is virtually impossible to observe all of the instances supporting the inductive generalization.

Let us consider one more example which may help to illustrate the distinction between deductive and inductive logic. Suppose we are interested in the possible relationship between the amount of library instruction received by certain college students and their subsequent academic performance. Using the deductive method, we could hypothesize that library instruction improves academic performance. We could then specify that library instruction would be represented by the number of hours spent receiving library instruction in an English literature course, and that academic performance would be represented by the final grade for the course. If we were to observe that, as the hours of instruction increase, grades improve, we could then conclude that our hypothesis describes the relationship that exists.

Using inductive reasoning, we could start with an observation that the students in a particular English literature class who had received library instruction seemed to do quite well in the course. We might then wonder if most library instruction methods have a positive effect on the academic performance of college students. We could proceed to make a variety of observations related to both library instruction and academic performance. Next, we would look for a pattern that best represents or summarizes our observations. In other words, we would attempt to generalize that, based on our observations, library instruction of all types tends to improve academic performance. As Babbie has pointed out, with the deductive method we would have reasoned *toward* observations; with the inductive method we would have reasoned *from* observations.[3]

THE SCIENTIFIC METHOD OF INQUIRY

Inductive reasoning contributed to the development of what is known as the scientific method or the scientific method of inquiry (SMI). This approach to the discovery of knowledge, which arose during the Renaissance, gained major support in the sixteenth century. It has long been considered to be "the most valid method for problem solving and the resolution of unanswered questions."[4] There are other viewpoints, however. Budd, for example, argues that the SMI is too positivist in nature, and that LIS needs more research that is based on a different epistemological foundation—one that is less concerned with universal laws and invariant relationships.[5]

There is a general consensus among researchers regarding the basic pattern of the scientific method of inquiry, but specific elements do sometimes vary. Leedy describes the scientific method of inquiry as a means by which insight into an undiscovered truth is sought by (a) identifying the problem that will provide the goal of the research, (b) gathering the data needed to resolve the problem, (c) developing a tentative hypothesis, and (d) empirically testing the hypothesis by analyzing the data.[6]

Babbie, who sees the scientific method of inquiry as a combination of the inductive and deductive methods, depending upon the research phase, summarizes the basic steps of the scientific method as (a) theory construction, (b) derivation of theoretical hypotheses, (c) operationalization of concepts, and (d) testing of hypotheses.[7] Frankfort-Nachmias and Nachmias state that the scientific process consists of seven principal stages: problem, hypothesis, research design, measurement, data collection, data analysis, and generalization. They point out that "Each stage affects **theory** and is affected by it as well."[8]

Some believe that LIS has little formal theory[9, 10]; others call for more LIS research to advance practice and theory.[11, 12] Budd reminds us that "general progress only occurs when there has been deep critical investigation into the workings of our field."[13] This means that we must study the intellectual foundations of the LIS field. This type of reflection will influence not only our research but also the development of systems and services for the practice of LIS. Glazier (see Appendix A) argues that, before we begin the research process, we should consider our basic epistemological and ontological assumptions and presuppositions. They influence how we approach and carry out research in the social and behavioral sciences.

A General Outline for Research

Given differences in subject disciplines and/or the types of data to be collected, researchers find it necessary to employ a variety of specific methodologies, but most true research does follow the same general outline and exhibits similar characteristics. In developing a research study, the investigator typically begins with a question about something of interest. For example, a college librarian may wonder why the use of his or her library seems to be declining or, better yet, increasing. As early as this point, and throughout the development of the research study, the investigator is likely to benefit from a thorough review of the literature (see Chapter 10 for tips on reviewing the related literature).

The next important, logical step would be for the librarian to identify the problem that this question represents. He or she may have a hunch that library use is low because the majority of the students do not have adequate library skills. In other words, the actual problem facing the librarian may be poor library skills, which ultimately tend to be evidenced by low library use. The librarian may also conclude that he or she is actually confronted with several problems, or at least subproblems of the main problem. For example, the librarian turned researcher may need to consider specific types of library skills or different class levels.

Having identified the specific research problem, the researcher should then attempt to place the problem in its broader theoretical framework. An adequate theory might have been articulated already, or it may be necessary to develop one.

Keeping in mind the main problem, subproblems if any, and the relevant theory, the librarian should consider developing one or more hypotheses to guide the future investigation or study. In this case, the librarian may wish to hypothesize that library skills have a positive effect on library use. This hypothesis may be based on obvious assumptions, such as "library instruction will in fact be reasonably effective at teaching certain library skills," or "students will be able to transfer skills learned as a result of an instructional program to actual use of a library."

Throughout this process, but perhaps particularly at this point, the librarian will need to develop a plan for attempting to resolve the problem. In other words, he or she will need to decide what methodology and data collection techniques, among other procedures, to utilize in the investigation. He or she could elect to conduct an experiment during which a particular type of library instruction would be given, and after which the students' library skills would be post-tested. Or a survey could be conducted in which students would, for example, be asked about their library use and/or skills. Stephenson provides a Web site that includes links to many full-text articles, book chapters, and conference papers on various research methodologies. She updates the site, which makes it a useful resource for learning about the methodologies and how they have been used in actual research studies.[14]

Another characteristic of research inherent to most of the process is the necessity to deal with facts and their meanings. This activity is particularly crucial during the data collection and analysis stages. It is here that the researcher must attempt to gather information needed to solve the problem, organize it in meaningful categories, and analyze its significance. Data collected during the library instruction study could include scores on tests, attitudes toward the library, and self-perceptions of library skills.

And last, but not least, the librarian should keep in mind that this process is almost always circular in nature. The researcher's analysis and interpretation of the results of his or her study may well lead to new questions, or fail to answer the original question, thereby starting the research process again. Leedy and Ormrod developed a diagram, reproduced below as Figure 2.1, which helps to illustrate the circular nature of research.[15] As they state, "Every researcher soon learns that genuine research yields as many problems as it resolves. Such is the nature of the discovery of knowledge."[16]

General Criteria for Basic Research

In addition to adhering to a general outline, basic research studies generally should meet certain criteria to qualify as basic or pure research:

1. Universality, which means that the study should be researchable by any other qualified investigator. In other words, another researcher should be able to conduct the study as designed and get essentially the same results as the original researcher would have obtained and should be able to generalize the results to a comparable situation.

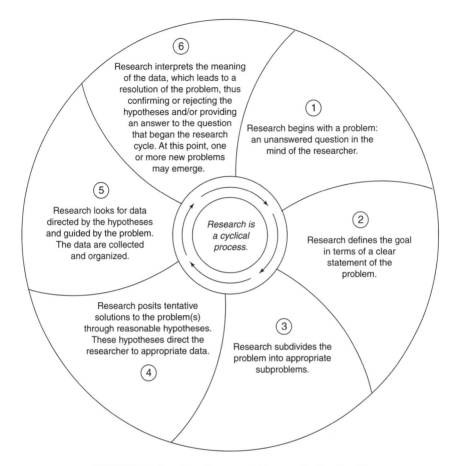

FIGURE 2.1. The Research Process Is Cyclical*

*From *Practical Research; Planning and Design*, 7th edition, by Paul D. Leedy and Jeanne E. Ormrod. © 2001. Reprinted with permission of Pearson Education, Inc., Upper Saddle River, NJ.

2. Replication, which is related to the criterion of universality. It means that the research study is repeatable. Not only should another competent researcher be able to conduct the study and get essentially the same results, but he or she also should be able to do so time and time again.

3. Control, which relates to the parameters of the research study. This criterion is important for isolating the critical factors and for facilitating replication. As will be emphasized later, control is relatively easy to realize in experimental research and much more difficult, if not impossible, to realize in survey and historical research.

4. Measurement, which constitutes the observation and recording of phenomena. This activity requires, of course, that the data be susceptible to measurement.

Measurement (and control) generally is easier to accomplish in physical science research than in humanistic and social research. The latter typically require more comparative and subjective judgments. Consequently, measurement in the humanities and social sciences is seldom as precise as in the physical and natural sciences.

Hernon categorizes the criteria for basic research into the following five components:.

1. Reflective inquiry, which includes problem statement, literature review, theoretical framework, logical structure, objectives, research questions, and hypotheses (if appropriate)
2. Procedures or research design and data collection methods
3. Data gathering, processing, and analysis
4. Reliability and validity, for quantitative studies, and credibility, trustworthiness, transferability, dependability, and confirmability for qualitative studies
5. Presentation of the research findings.[17]

More specific criteria for basic research are contained in the checklist reproduced below as Table 2.1. This checklist refers specifically to research in educational psychology, but most of the criteria can be applied to any basic research in the social sciences. As can be seen, some of the criteria presented here also relate to the feasibility of a research study. For example, the third question asks, "Have you sufficiently limited your problem?" Leedy and Ormrod, in their textbook on research, provide the reader with an Estimation Sheet to Determine the Feasibility of the Research Project (see Figure 2.2 on p. 25).[18] Feasibility is one of the most important questions that the researcher can raise before initiating a study. Consequently, the estimation sheet is reproduced below.

This estimation inventory represents a useful exercise, and it is highly recommended that the would-be researcher work through this, or a similar exercise, before undertaking a research study of any magnitude. Some particularly important practical concerns raised by the feasibility exercise are represented by the questions asking about the aptitudes of the researcher, the availability of data, and the data collection techniques to be used. No matter how worthwhile a research study is potentially, if it cannot be managed, it is not likely to be of any value.

IDENTIFICATION OF THE PROBLEM

The research problem is essentially the topic to be investigated or what needs to be known. It is assumed that one plans a research study because he or she has identified some problem worthy of investigation. In fact, Einstein and Infield have been quoted as saying, "The formulation of a problem is often more essential than its solution."[19] Or as Leedy and Ormrod stated, "The heart of every

TABLE 2.1
A Check List for Planning a Research Study*

A. Scope and Definition of Study
    1. Is your study related to an educational problem?
    2. Is your problem being considered broadly enough?
    3. Have you sufficiently limited your problem?
    4. Have you made the educational implications of the study clear?
    5. Have your decisions benefited by the experiences of investigators who have preceded you?
    6. Have you consulted the *Encyclopedia of Educational Research*, the *Handbook of Research on Teaching*, the *Review of Educational Research*, and other background sources?
B. Hypotheses or Questions to Be Answered
    1. Are the hypotheses clearly and precisely stated?
    2. Are the hypotheses stated in a form that permits them to be tested?
C. Definitions
    1. Are concepts adequately and accurately defined?
    2. Are your sample and experimental procedures sufficiently described so that another investigator would be able to replicate the study?
    3. Do the measurements of variables in the study have validity and reliability?
D. Method of Study
    1. Is there a direct relation between the question which the study is trying to answer and the data to be collected?
    2. Do you have a plan for securing the data necessary for your study?
    3. When more than one investigational approach is available, is it worthwhile to compare the results using different criteria?
    4. Can you draw conclusions as to cause and effect from evidence as to relationships from the design employed?
    5. How do you propose to select your subjects for study?
E. Design
    1. Have you conferred with the persons and/or agencies involved?
    2. Is the design of your study clearly formulated?
    3. Do you have a PERT chart or a systematic schedule of procedures for the study?
    4. Is it feasible to assign subjects randomly to treatment groups?
    5. Have you considered the possibility of statistically equating groups on relevant factors?
    6. Have you included the most relevant variables in a factorial design so that you can detect interaction between variables?
    7. Is your choice of statistical methods the most efficient for the intended purposes?
    8. Have you consulted statistics, measurements, and research specialists in the design and analysis of your study?
    9. Are there standard library computer programs available for your purposes?
    10. Have you determined limitations of time, cost, materials, manpower, instrumentation, and other facilities and extraneous conditions?
    11. Have you given consideration to the human and personal relations "side effects?"
F. Sampling
    1. Is your sample representative of the group to which you wish to generalize your findings?
    2. What factors may be biasing the selection of subjects?
    3. Are you taking into account the subgroups in your total sample?

(Continued)

TABLE 2.1
(*Continued*)

G. Criteria Factors
1. How do you propose to measure achievement, intelligence, attitudes, and interests you plan to investigate?
2. Have you purchased or developed the tests, instruments, and materials needed?
3. Are you going to attempt to ensure that your subjects or judges express their true feelings and attitudes?
4. Have you given sufficient study to determine the best criteria for your study?
5. Have you taken into account the difficulty level and readability of your test for your subjects?
6. If you are using a nonstandardized test, how are you determining its reliability and validity?
7. Have you consulted Buros' *Mental Measurements Yearbook* for critical reviews of standardized measures to be employed in your study?
8. If you plan to use judgments, have you specified the basis on which your judgments would be made?
9. If you plan to use judgments, are you sure your judges have the necessary intelligence, information, background, and other qualifications to permit them to make the judgments?
10. To what extent will bias enter into judgments that you propose to make (or use), and how can these be avoided?

H. Interpretation of Results
1. Have you confined your conclusions to the evidence at hand?
2. Have you tempered your conclusions with the practical meaning of the results as well as with their statistical significance?
3. Have you pointed out implications of the findings for application and for further study?
4. Have you accounted for any inconsistencies and limitations imposed by the methods used?
5. Have you interpreted findings in light of *operational* definitions of variables investigated?

I. Preparing the Report
1. Have you described your work clearly in order that, if necessary, it could be replicated by a later investigator?
2. Have you used tabular and graphic methods for presenting the results where possible?
3. Have you supplied sufficient information to permit the reader to verify results and draw his own conclusions?
4. Have you plans for publishing your study?

*Adapted from P. M. Symonds, "A Research Checklist in Educational Psychology," *Journal of Educational Psychology* 47 (1959): 101–109; Charles A. Bieking, "Some Uses of Statistics in the Planning of Experiments," *Industrial Quantity Control,* 10 (1954): 23.

research project is the problem. It is paramount in importance to the success of the research effort. To see the problem with unwavering clarity and to state it in precise and unmistakable terms is the first requirement in the research process."[20]

But given the primary importance of identifying a problem before conducting research, where and how are problems found? The answer to the first part of this question is that problems are all around us. In response to the second part of the

The Problem

1. With what area(s) will the problem deal?

   Your problem may involve more   ____ People
   than one of these areas. A study   ____ Things
   of the philosophic viewpoints in   ____ Records
   the poetry of Robert Frost would deal   ____ Thoughts and ideas
   both with people and with thoughts and ideas.   ____ Dynamics or energy

2. Are data that relate directly to the problem available for each of the categories you've just checked?   Yes ____   No ____.

3. What academic discipline is primarily concerned with the problem? _____

4. What other academic disciplines are possibly also related to the problem? _____

5. What special aptitude do you have as a researcher for this problem?
      ____ Interest in the problem   ____ Education and/or training
      ____ Experience in the problem area   ____ Other: Specify _____

The Data

6. How available are the data to you?   ____ Readily available   ____ Available, with permission   ____ Available with great difficulty or rarely available   ____ Unavailable

7. How frequently are you personally in contact with the source of the data?   ____ Once a day   ____ Once a week   ____ Once a month   ____ Once a year   ____ Never

8. Will the data arise directly out of the problem situation?   Yes ____   No ____   If your answer is no, where or how will you secure the data?

9. How do you plan to gather the data?   ____ Observation,   ____ Questionnaire,   ____ Tests or inventories,   ____ Photocopying of records,   ____ Interview and tape recording,   ____ Other, Explain:_____

10. Is special equipment or special conditions necessary for gathering or processing the data?   Yes ____   No ____   If your answer is "yes" specify: _____

11. If the answer to the preceding question was "yes," do you have access to such equipment and the skill to use it?
    Yes ____   No ____   If the answer is "no" how do you intend to overcome this difficulty? Explain:_____

12. What is the estimated cost in time and money to gather the data? _____

13. What evidence do you have that the data you gather will be valid and reliable indicators of the phenomena you wish to study? _____

Criterion-Based Evaluation

14. Does your research project meet the criteria proposed in the chapter as being applicable to all research?

Universality	____ Yes	____ No
Replication	____ Yes	____ No
Control	____ Yes	____ No
Measurement	____ Yes	____ No

15. As you review this estimation evaluation, might any of the factors you've just considered, or perhaps any other factors, hinder a successful completion of your research project?
    Yes ____   No ____
    If your answer is "yes," list those factors. _____

FIGURE 2.2.   Estimation Sheet to Determine the Feasibility of the Research Project*

*From *Practical Research; Planning and Design*, 7th edition, by Paul D. Leedy and Jeanne E. Ormrod. © 2001. Reprinted with permission of Pearson Education, Inc., Upper Saddle River, NJ.

question, we can take a variety of approaches. For example, one important, if not essential, approach toward identifying problems for research in a given field is to develop a thorough knowledge and understanding of that field. More specifically, the would-be researcher should be fully familiar with the known facts and accepted ideas in the field, be knowledgeable of previous, related research in the area, and be aware of gaps in knowledge in the field or unresearched areas.

These objectives can be met, at least in part, by reading published research, which often identifies needed research in the field. Doctoral dissertations are particularly good sources of suggestions for further research. Another potentially useful activity can be the checking of new bibliographies and other lists of related materials. Specific titles can suggest new topics for research.

Other "techniques" which can be used to identify research topics or problems include disagreeing with some previous research and developing a study to test its findings, becoming involved in the design and development of research tools and techniques relevant to some area of interest, and attempting to deal with actual problems in real work situations (this last approach is more likely to lead to applied research, however). Networking, or sharing ideas and information, with colleagues can be a very productive activity as well.

But perhaps the two best methods for identifying research topics or problems simply involve being curious about items of interest and being a clear and critical reader and thinker. For again, research problems abound and one simply needs to recognize them. And only by being a curious, critical observer is one likely to do so with any regularity.

Characteristics of a Problem Suitable for Basic Research

In order to be suitable for basic research, a problem should exhibit several characteristics. First, the problem should represent conceptual thinking, inquiry, and insight—not merely activity. For example, simply collecting data and making comparisons, are not activities representative of true research problems. Activities such as studying a subject field and reading earlier research are more likely to be indicative of a conceptually developed research problem.

Second, the variables related to the problem should represent some sort of meaningful relationship. The study of miscellaneous, unrelated facts is not likely to be true research, though it may lead to true research. For example, a tabulation of library circulation statistics is nothing more than a series of calculations, which at best may provide the basis for a thorough categorization of such statistics. On the other hand, if the circulation librarian wonders about the nature of the relationship between certain circulation statistics and certain user characteristics, he or she may in effect be conducting exploratory research and be well on the way to identifying a problem for more formal research.

Inherent in a problem representing some kind of relationship between two or more variables is consideration of the cause of the relationship. If evidence suggests, for example, a relationship between level of college library use and class level of student users, why does such a relationship exist? Why does a higher class level seem to "cause" greater use of the library? Again, what is the nature of the relationship, and does the problem incorporate this concern? Or, if there is not a causal relationship between the variables, how are they related, if at all? To answer this, the problem must reflect some interpretation of the relationship. For example, perhaps the variables are not related directly but indirectly, through the influence of yet another variable or variables. Only a problem represented by a conceptual, insightful development and statement will be able to lead to this kind of understanding.

There are also several more practical considerations that the researcher should make before settling on a specific problem. Among these is the researcher's interest in the problem. Does it represent a topic that he or she is likely to enjoy researching after several months, if not years, of study? This is a question that is particularly important for doctoral students to ask of themselves.

Does the problem represent an area of research that is reasonably new? Does anyone have a prior claim to the area? Again, this is of particular concern to doctoral students. However, a problem does not have to be entirely new and unresearched in order to be worthy of investigation. Some of the most important research builds on and improves or refines previous research. The degree of uniqueness desired will in part depend upon the purpose of the research.

More important, probably, is the question of whether the research will contribute to the knowledge of the field and ultimately have some impact, or does the problem represent a trivial question of no real importance? Again, whether the research should make a significant contribution to the field is in part determined by the purpose of the research. For example, if it is intended solely to meet the requirements for a doctoral. dissertation, perhaps some justification can be made for emphasizing the design and conduct of the research over its likely contribution to the field's knowledge.

Last, but not least, the problem should point to research that is manageable. In short, is the problem researchable? Due to real constraints, such as time and money, perfectly designed research is not always possible. The researcher typically is in the position of having to compromise what is ideal and what is practicable. This is particularly true of research, which is relatively applied in nature. As Martyn and Lancaster stated, "In any investigation within a library or information center, some compromises may be necessary between what is most desirable from the investigator's viewpoint and what appears feasible to the manager of the service."[21]

Statement of the Problem

Having identified a suitable problem for research, the next logical step is to write a statement of it for future reference. Perhaps it goes without saying, but the problem should be written in complete grammatical sentences, not as mere phrases. For example, "library instruction and library use" would be better as "The problem to be resolved is whether providing college students with library instruction will have some effect on their use of the library." The problem should be written as clearly as possible, and it should be stated in straightforward, unambiguous terms; vague terms and clichés are to be avoided.

In addition, the problem should be stated as precisely as possible. There should be no discrepancy between what the researcher writes and what he or she actually means. The problem statement should be both specific and explicit. In that the problem should guide all of the research that follows, it is essential that it be well developed and stated. In order to achieve an appropriately stated problem, it is a good idea to edit the problem as initially written, at least once, in order to eliminate needless and ambiguous words and to increase its precision and clarity.

As suggested by the characteristics of a researchable problem, it is also important that it be stated responsibly. It should not be so broad in scope that it will be unmanageable. For example, the problem statement just given was, "whether providing college students with library instruction will have some effect on their use of the library." While this was seen as an improvement on the preceding phrase, in light of our criteria for a suitable statement, it still needs work. Though it seems reasonably clear, it should be more precise or specific and thereby more manageable. An improved problem statement might be, "The problem to be resolved by this study is whether the frequency of library use of first-year college students given course-integrated library instruction is different than the frequency of library use of first-year college students not given course-integrated library instruction."

Some research methods textbooks indicate that the research problem may be written as a question and/or as a purpose statement.[22] The view of this textbook is that a research question is typically more precise and specific than a problem statement and that the purpose and problem for a research study are not interchangeable. As Hernon stated, "Many studies published in LIS do not contain a problem statement or confuse such a statement with a statement of purpose."[23] The *problem* is what the research is about and the *purpose* is why the research is conducted. For example, one might conduct research on the relationship between certain teaching methods and the effectiveness of bibliographic instruction (the problem) in order to increase the success of future bibliographic instruction programs (the purpose).

Identifying Subproblems

Virtually all problems comprise components or subproblems, which should be appropriate for study, if not solution. Subproblems can facilitate resolving a large problem piecemeal, as they are often more manageable or researchable than the general problem and can be investigated separately. They should be amenable to some realistic research method and suggest adequate data with which to resolve the problem. The interpretation of the data within each subproblem must be apparent. It should not be necessary to go outside the confines of the study as set by the subproblem in order to relate data to the subproblem.

In addition, the subproblems should, when combined, equal the whole of the main problem. On the other hand, the subproblems should not add up to more than the totality of the main problem. If they do, it is likely that the main problem actually represents more than one problem. While rules of thumb should be used with caution, most well-defined research problems can be broken down into from two to six subproblems. Many more than that may suggest that the main problem was too broadly or vaguely conceived.

Another possible explanation for an excess of subproblems may be that some of the subproblems are in fact what Leedy and Ormrod have labeled "pseudosubproblems."[24] While related to the study, pseudosubproblems are more procedural in nature and do not actually relate to the conceptual questions raised by the problem. They often arise from such questions as how to select the sample or how to observe certain phenomena. For example, the question of how to *measure* library use as included in the earlier example of a problem would be more of a pseudo than a true subproblem. It is more methodological than conceptual, though the distinction is sometimes fine, as is the case here.

Actually, identifying subproblems is generally a relatively straightforward process involving two basic, related steps: (a) the researcher should break the main problem down into its components, and (b) he or she should identify the words that indicate a need for the collection and interpretation of data. In order to illustrate this process, let us return to the last formulation of the problem. It was as follows:

> The problem to be resolved by this study is whether the frequency of library use of first-year college students given course-integrated library instruction is different than the frequency of library use of first-year college students not given course-integrated library instruction.

In analyzing this problem statement, one can see that there are three components that will require investigation before the main problem can be resolved. These three subproblems can be written as follows:

1. What is the frequency of library use of the first-year college students who did receive course-integrated library instruction?
2. What is the frequency of library use of the first-year college students who did *not* receive course-integrated library instruction?
3. What is the difference in the frequency of library use between the two groups of students?

As is commonly done, these subproblems have been posed as questions. Again, they are questions that must be answered before the main, more complex problem can be resolved. In many studies, the researcher will attempt to do no more than answer one or two subproblems or research questions; additional studies may be necessary to deal with the entire problem.

Having identified and stated what hopefully is a satisfactory research problem, the investigator must next turn his or her attention to providing further guidance for the study. For example, the researcher should indicate precisely the limitations of the problem, which in turn help to limit the goals of the study. Limitations implicit in the problem statement given above include the fact that it is concerned with the frequency of library use, not quality. It is concerned with course-integrated library instruction as opposed to the many other types that could have been considered.

The researcher should also consider providing both conceptual and operational definitions for important terms related to the study, particularly if they are used in an unusual sense or can be interpreted in more than one way. This procedure will be covered in more detail later, but, generally speaking, this step is necessary in order to indicate how certain terms are to be used by the researcher in relation to the study.

Further delineation of the problem can be achieved by stating assumptions, or what the researcher takes for granted. Returning to our problem on library instruction, the researcher appears to be assuming, for example, that those persons teaching the library instruction can in fact teach. The quality of their teaching is not something that will be tested in the study.

Finally, when feasible, the researcher should develop one or more hypotheses to further delimit the problem and project. Development of the hypothesis, as well as the identification of the basic assumptions, will be treated in greater depth later in the text.

THE ROLE OF THEORY IN THE DESIGN OF RESEARCH

Before taking up assumptions and hypotheses, we should consider the role of theory in the design of a research study. As was noted earlier, theory or theory construction is the first major component of the scientific method of inquiry. It tends to be the base from which the subsequent stages of the scientific method flow. But exactly how does theory fit into or affect this process? An understanding of how a field of knowledge develops should help to explain the role of theory in the design of research.

As Goldhor and others have explained, a field of knowledge usually develops in a logical sequence of three stages.[25] The first stage typically involves the accumulation of specific facts regarding a variety of isolated phenomena. These facts are derived from actual experience or the observation of certain activities. The specific facts are usually historical or descriptive in nature and are unlikely to be quantitative.

The second main stage typically involves the definition, review, and classification of these existing facts or data into a meaningful set of categories, a procedure that will be covered in more detail later. It is also worth noting that it is essential that the observations which produce the data be categorized as accurately as possible. The categorization can be improved or made more precise by quantifying the data to the greatest extent possible. For example, data relating to library use are difficult to classify if subjective in nature, but once they have been quantified in terms of frequency of use, number of books checked out, number of reference questions asked, and so on, it is a relatively simple, straightforward process to classify them.

Related to the simplification of complex phenomena, classification of the data can help to point out gaps in the existing knowledge. In attempting to observe and categorize all of the various activities that constitute library use, it is conceivable that the researcher may identify certain activities that represent heretofore unrecognized types of library use, or at least variants of already identified library use activities. For example, in studying the use of an academic library, the researcher may discover that part-time students use the library somewhat differently than do full-time students. Such knowledge could have important ramifications for the library's services and policies.

The classification of existing data can also help to identify relationships between various categories within the classification scheme. The formulation and testing of these groupings of data, or variables, make up the third main stage in the development of a field of knowledge. This stage can be considered the formal research stage of a discipline, and as Goldhor has stated, this is probably the stage at which library and information science is at present.[26]

But to return to the original question, how does theory fit into the scheme of things? In fact, theory plays a crucial role in the just-mentioned research stage, which in turn often utilizes the scientific method of inquiry. Theory helps to make research more productive in that it organizes a number of "unassorted facts, laws, concepts, constructs, and principles into a meaningful and manageable form."[27] Or, as Goldhor observed, theory can explain a group of phenomena, suggest relationships between facts, structure concepts, organize facts into a meaningful pattern, and provide logical explanations for facts.[28] If certain facts or variables appear to be causally related, theory can help to explain the nature of the relationship.

Theory also can act as a guide to discovering facts. It identifies gaps to be investigated, crucial aspects on which to focus, and major questions to be answered. In short, theory can stimulate research in areas that warrant study.[29] The research can, in turn, develop new theories or improve existing ones. Theory also can help to connect studies and facilitate the interpretation of the larger meaning of research findings.

In addition, theory helps to produce an economy of research effort. It can be used to identify the most important and/or manageable propositions for testing, define and limit the area of research, and relate the research to other relevant studies. Theory can provide an economical or simple summary of actual or anticipated research results.[30] In short, the main value of theory in research derives from its ability to "summarize existing knowledge, to provide an explanation for observed events and relationships, and to predict the occurrence of as yet unobserved events and relationships on the basis of the explanatory principles embodied in the theory."[31]

Definition of Theory

Having determined the role and value of theory in research, it should be relatively easy to define. Babbie defines theory "as a complex set of relationships among several variables."[32] It also has been defined as something which interrelates a set or sets of variables on the basis of the rules of logic. In a workshop for health science librarians, Marshall described a theory as "A set of related propositions that suggest why events occur in the manner that they do. The propositions that make up theories are of the same form as hypotheses; they consist of concepts and the linkages or relationships between them."[33] McGrath defines theory as "an explanation for a quantifiable phenomenon."[34] It can also be thought of as a unified explanation for discrete observations. Goldhor defines theory as "a deductively connected set of laws, in the logical form of an explanation and with all statements as generalizations."[35]

Goldhor goes on to point out that those laws (hypotheses whose validity is relatively established) that do the explaining are axioms, and those laws that are explained by or based on the axioms are theorems.[36] He also notes that the theorems usually are known first, and axioms must be identified in order to explain the theorems. On the other hand, axioms can be used to predict new laws not yet identified. If any axioms are found to be false, then the theory itself must be considered false.

The Formation of Theories

Suitable theories do not always already exist for the researcher in need of one. In many cases they must be developed or "built." Goldhor defines theory building as the accumulation of empirical findings and the development of a system of intermeshing hypotheses concerning their relationships.[37] He notes that this process requires the identification of the variables that are appropriate for a theoretical system and represent the relevant concepts. Theory construction also requires that the person developing the theory have a thorough understanding of the already accepted facts and theories of the field in question as well as of related fields.

Grover and Glazier propose a model for theory building, which displays relationships among phenomena and various levels of theory and research. Their taxonomy ranges from phenomena, or individual objects and events, through hypotheses, to a "world view" or general orientation.[38]

Mouly states that a good theory should meet the following criteria:

1. A theory, or theoretical system, should permit deductions that can be tested empirically; in other words, it should provide the means for its own testing.
2. A theory should be compatible with both observation and previously verified theories. It must be well grounded and should be able to explain the phenomena under study.
3. A theory should be stated as simply as possible. It should explain adequately the existing knowledge but should not be any more complex than necessary. This characteristic represents the so-called law of parsimony.[39]

At this point, based on previous research and recent observations, one could construct a theory related to the earlier stated problem involving the effect of library instruction on library use. Such a theory, even in an abbreviated version, might include the following:

> It has been observed, and previous research has indicated, that certain facts are related to student use of college libraries. Among these facts are (a) some students use their college library more than do others, (b) some students have better library skills than do others, and (c) appropriate library instruction is capable of teaching students how to use the college library. Based on these and other facts, one could formulate a theorem stating that some students use their college library more than do others because they have the necessary library skills (or at least more than the nonusers). At least one axiom which could help to explain the theorem might argue that students who know how to use the college library are more inclined to do so than those with fewer or no library skills because they are more aware of the library's resources, have more confidence in their abilities, and so on.

At this point, the theory already had identified several facts, laws, and variables (library instruction, library skills, library use, confidence, etc.). It also has identified possible relationships among some of the variables and has suggested how and why they are related. In short, it is helping to bring some order to what would otherwise be a less meaningful group of facts and concepts.

Published examples of theory building include works by Mellon and Poole. Based on data gathered from diaries and essays, Mellon constructed a grounded theory (a unique theory based on the event or situation studied) of library anxiety.[40] Poole, after analyzing 97 studies published in the *Annual Review of Information Science and Technology*, constructed three theoretical statements on the behavior of scientists and engineers in formal information systems.[41] McKechnie and Pettigrew did a content analysis of 1,160 LIS articles published between 1993 and 1998 and found that 34.2 percent of the articles incorporated theory in the title, abstract, or text.[42]

Testing the Theory

Having developed, or at least identified, a suitable theory, the next requisite step is to test it. Much of the rest of this text will directly or indirectly concern itself with testing procedures, but a brief indication of some of the implications of theory testing is in order here. For example, it should be kept in mind that, in order to test a theory, one must determine how well each of its theorems and related propositions agrees with the observed facts in one or more test situations.[43]

Second, it should be noted that a well-constructed, informative theory would provide specific hypotheses or statements of certain relationships by which the theory can be tested. In fact, a theory can be thought of as a large hypothesis comprising a number of more specific, more testable subhypotheses, though a theory typically rests on a more sophisticated basis than does an individual hypothesis. Consequently, the entire theory can be tested by testing each of the hypotheses individually.

FORMULATING HYPOTHESES

Definitions of Hypotheses

The second major step in the standard scientific method of inquiry is the formulation of one or more theoretical hypotheses. A variety of definitions of
hypotheses found in the literature reflect slightly different perspectives or emphases. Babbie defines the hypothesis as "an expectation about the nature of
things derived from a theory."[44] Leedy and Ormrod view hypotheses as "tentative
propositions set forth to assist in guiding the investigation of a problem or to provide possible explanations for the observations made."[45] Mouly considers a hypothesis to be "a tentative generalization concerning the relationship between
two or more variables of critical interest in the solution of a problem under investigation."[46] Finally, Selltiz, quoting Webster, defines a hypothesis as "a proposi-
tion, condition, or principle, which is assumed, perhaps without belief, in order to
draw out its logical consequences and by this method to test its accord with facts
which are known or may be determined."[47]

To complicate the picture a bit more, there are several types of hypotheses,
including the following:

1. Working or research hypothesis—the hypothesis with which a research
   study begins. It should help to delimit and guide the study.
2. Final hypothesis—the hypothesis that reflects the findings of the research
   study. It probably is almost synonymous with the study's final conclusion.
3. Particular hypothesis—a hypothesis which merely explains a specific fact or
   situation; for example, "not all college students are skilled library users."
4. Causal hypothesis—a hypothesis which states that there is a causal relationship between two or more variables (i.e., that a particular factor or condition
   determines or affects another factor or condition).
5. Alternative hypothesis—a rival hypothesis which provides a possible
   and plausible solution to the problem (i.e., a different explanation of the
   same facts). This is sometimes used interchangeably with a "minor" or
   "secondary" hypothesis, though the latter, which has less well-accepted
   concepts, seems to suggest something quite different.
6. Null hypothesis—a hypothesis which asserts that there is no real relationship between or among the variables in question. It involves the supposition
   that chance rather than an identifiable cause has produced some observed
   result. It is used primarily for purposes of statistical testing.
7. Inductive hypothesis—a hypothesis which moves from the particular to the
   general, or a generalization based on observation.
8. Deductive hypothesis—a hypothesis which shifts from the general to the
   particular, or a hypothesis derived from a theory.
9. Nondirectional hypothesis—a hypothesis which merely indicates that a relationship or difference exists. It says nothing about the nature or direction
   of the relationship. For example, one might hypothesize that a student's

grade point average and use of libraries are related without going so far as to argue that either factor causes the other.

10. Directional hypothesis—a hypothesis which indicates the nature of the relationship between or among variables. For example, it could logically be hypothesized that the assignment of term papers results in more library use by certain students.
11. Multivariate hypothesis—a hypothesis proposing a relationship among more than two phenomena.
12. Bivariate hypothesis—a hypothesis proposing a relationship between two phenomena.
13. Univariate hypothesis—a hypothesis concerned with only one phenomenon or variable. In that no relationship is involved, one could argue that this kind of statement does not meet the minimal criteria for a hypothesis. It might better be termed a research question.

Not all of these hypotheses are mutually exclusive. For example, one might begin a study with a research hypothesis that proposes a causal relationship between two variables and indicates which variable affects which variable.

To complicate the picture yet again, Hillway states that "the terms hypothesis, theory, law, generalization, and conclusion all mean much the same thing in relation to a study."[48] He argues that what differences do exist are slight and relative. Other writers would disagree, however. It also may be worth noting here that the term "model" is often used interchangeably with hypothesis, as well as with theory, but in fact it has a slightly different meaning. Mouly defines a model as "a descriptive analogy designed to help visualize a complex phenomenon."[49]

Sources of Hypotheses

As was suggested earlier, one of the most convenient and logical sources of hypotheses is a theory, in that it can be considered to be a broad hypothesis or a set of subhypotheses. However, theories seldom, if ever, simply appear when needed. They are a result of one's being thoroughly knowledgeable about a field, staying abreast of the literature, and so on. Indeed, the findings of other studies reported in the literature are excellent sources of hypotheses. Existing and assumed relationships reported in research results often provide the basis for formulating hypotheses. Similarly, certain relationships often can be observed in a work setting; such observations or hunches frequently lead to more formal hypotheses.

Pilot or exploratory studies also are good sources of hypotheses. In fact, Mouly states that some amount of data gathering, such as the recall of past experience, the review of the literature, or a pilot study, must precede the formulation and refinement of the hypothesis.[50]

Mouly also argues that "reasoning by analogy" is an excellent source of hypotheses.[51] In other words, if two situations agree with one another in one or more respects relevant to the problem in question, they will probably agree in yet other respects. Such an assumption may then be restated as one or more hypotheses.

Developing the Hypothesis

Again, the formulation of a hypothesis ideally begins with consideration of a theory, and more specifically, one or more components of a theory. But at the very least, this process starts with a set of specific facts or observations, which the researcher is attempting to explain. Generally, this explanation, or hypothesis, will be written as a statement of a possible relationship between two or more variables.

The basis for the hypothesis almost always rests on one or more assumptions. The most closely related assumption and the hypothesis are considered to constitute the premises from which the facts to be explained must logically be implied. In some research only the most basic assumption is referred to as the premise. Basic assumptions are assumed, for the purposes of a particular research study, to be true and therefore are not tested during the research.

Basic assumptions should not be confused with methodological assumptions. The former help to support or explain the hypothesis. For example, a hypothesis which predicts that older people are less likely to use information technology than are younger people might be partially explained by the assumption that older people have more anxiety regarding the use of technology. In conducting a study on the use of information technology by different age groups, one might make the methodological assumption that adequate numbers of people of different ages will be willing to participate in the study.

Goldhor points out that, having identified the hypothesis and basic assumptions, it should then be possible to develop additional explanations of relationships between or among the variables in specific situations.[52] These additional explanations constitute, in effect, alternative hypotheses.

The most viable hypothesis must then be identified by evaluating the various alternative hypotheses and eliminating the less effective ones. As was noted earlier, one guiding principle is the law of parsimony, which dictates selecting the simplest explanation or hypothesis and the one requiring the fewest assumptions. The hypothesis selected should nevertheless explain the most facts. Other characteristics of good hypotheses will be identified later, but next let us consider the major components of the hypothesis'—the variables.

Variables

A *variable* may be thought of as "any property of a person, thing, event, setting, and so on that is not fixed."[53] Variables, or factors, can be perceived or labeled in a variety of ways depending on the nature of the relationship between or among them. For example, in a causal relationship the factor (or factors) typically identified first in the hypothesis is referred to as the *independent variable*. Other labels used for the independent variable include the predictor variable and the experimental variable. This is the variable that determines, influences, or produces the change in the other main factor.

The second main factor (or factors) in the causal hypothesis is usually referred to as the *dependent variable* or the subject variable. This variable is dependent on or influenced by the independent variable(s). The statement of the hypothesis should at least imply the nature of the relationship between the independent and dependent variables. For example, "the *more* library instruction a college student receives, the *more* he or she will use the college library."

However, hypotheses often take the form of conjectural statements. For example, "librarians are as assertive as other professional groups" or "the information needs of researchers are different from those of practitioners."[54] Thus, the independent and dependent variables are not always as easily identified as perhaps they should be. Given below are the titles of ten studies. The reader may wish to attempt to identify the independent and dependent variables within each title. For example, "assertiveness training" would appear to be the independent variable and "job satisfaction" the dependent variable in the title, "A note on the contribution of assertiveness training to job satisfaction of professional librarians."

1. A study of the relationship of role conflict, the need for role clarity, and job satisfaction for professional librarians.
2. Library design influences on user behavior and satisfaction.
3. An investigation of the relationships between quantifiable reference service variables and reference performance in public libraries.
4. The impact of differing orientations of librarians on the process of children's book selection: a case study of library tensions.
5. Book selection and book collection usage in academic libraries.
6. The effect of prime display location on public library circulation of selected adult titles.
7. Implications of title diversity and collection overlap for interlibrary loan among secondary schools.
8. The attitudes of adults toward the public library and their relationships to library use.
9. Early libraries in Louisiana: a study of the Creole influence.
10. The Great Depression: its impact on 46 large American public libraries; an inquiry based on a content analysis of published writings of their directors.*

*Title number 1: independent variable—role conflict, dependent variables—need for role clarity and job satisfaction; title number 2: independent variable—library design, dependent variables—user behavior and satisfaction; title number 3: independent variable—quantifiable reference service variables, dependent variable—reference performance; title number 4: independent variable—differing orientations of librarians, dependent variable—process of children's book selection; title number 5: independent variable—book selection, dependent variable—book collection usage; title number 6: independent variable—prime display location, dependent variable—circulation of selected adult titles, title number 7: independent variables—title diversity and collection overlap, dependent variable—interlibrary loan among secondary schools; title number 8: independent variable—attitudes of adults toward the public library, dependent variable—library use; title number 9: independent variable—Creole influence, dependent variable—early libraries in Louisiana; title number 10: independent variable—Great Depression, dependent variable—large American public libraries.

As can be seen from these examples, relationships between variables often are indicated by the use of such terms as "influence," "impact," and "effect." But such clues are not always present, and they do not always convey the specific nature of the relationship nor distinguish between independent and dependent variables. In fact, a hypothesized relationship may not even include independent and dependent variables as such. The researcher may not be knowledgeable enough to predict that one variable causes another. For example, does an increase in grade point average cause an increase in library use or vice versa? In a given study, a variable might logically be viewed as either an independent or a dependent variable, or neither. Other types of variables include the following:

1. Intervening variable—any variable which occurs in the causal chain between some independent variable and its dependent variable. It also serves as an independent variable for the dependent variable. For example, we might hypothesize that library instruction (the independent variable) causes more library use (the dependent variable) when in actuality, library instruction produces greater confidence (the intervening variable), which in turn, causes more library use.

2. Antecedent variable—a variable which occurs prior to some already identified or hypothesized independent variable. In the previous example, had confidence been initially identified as the independent variable, then library instruction could have been thought of as the antecedent variable.

3. Extraneous variable—a variable at first perceived as the real cause of some effect when, in fact, it was only a coincidental correlate of that effect. (Extraneous variables are discussed in more detail in the section on experimental research methods.)

4. Component variables—two or more variables which really represent the same variable. For example, reference questions and book loans are components of a variable called library use.

5. Conditioning or moderating variable—a variable which represents the conditions under which a hypothesized relationship between other variables holds true. For example, more library instruction might cause more library use *only if* the instruction is relevant to the interests or needs of the learner.

6. Confounding or interfering variable—another influence that may affect the dependent variable but one in which the researcher is not interested.

Concepts

A researcher, in order to organize his or her data so as to perceive relationships among variables, must first make use of concepts. A *concept* may be defined as an abstraction from observed events or a shorthand representation of a variety of facts. Its purpose is to simplify thinking by subsuming a number of events under one general heading.[55] Library use is a concept representing or abstracting the many characteristics and types of library use. As indicated in the earlier example, there are a variety of specific kinds of library use such as reading, browsing, and borrowing books.

Not only can concepts be broken down into more concrete elements, they can be elevated to more abstract levels. These higher level concepts, often referred to as *constructs*, generally represent such phenomena as attitudes, perceptions, roles, and so on. For a specific phenomenon, the conceptual hierarchy would thus range from the construct, at the most abstract level, to the concept, and finally to the variable at the most concrete level.

It should be noted at this point that the greater the distance between the concepts or constructs and the facts to which they are supposed to refer, the greater the possibility of their being misunderstood or carelessly used. In addition, constructs, due to their greater abstractedness, are more difficult to relate to the phenomena they are intended to represent. Therefore, it is important to define carefully the concepts and constructs, both in abstract terms and in terms of the operations by which they will be represented in the study. The former may be considered formal or *conceptual definitions*; the latter are referred to as working or *operational definitions*.

In providing a conceptual definition of a phenomenon such as "library use," the researcher would no doubt rely heavily on the already established definition as reflected in other studies. If a conceptual definition did not already exist, the researcher would need to develop his or her own, keeping it consistent, where possible, with present thought and attempting to link it to the existing body of knowledge using similar concepts or constructs.

In order to carry out the planned research, the investigator must translate the formal definitions of the concepts into observable or measurable events (i.e., variables) via working definitions. Most concepts cannot be directly observed, so they must be broken down into more concrete phenomena which can be measured.

Some argue that working definitions should state the means by which the concept will be measured and provide the appropriate categories. While this may not be a necessary part of the actual definition, at some point this step will be necessary, and the working definition should at least imply how the concept will be measured.

Returning to the example of library use, one could formally define library use, as did Zweizig, as "the output of libraries, the point at which the potential for service becomes kinetic."[56] While this may be a suitable conceptual definition, it does little to suggest how one would actually measure library use. Consequently, the researcher would need to develop one or more working definitions in order to operationalize "library use."

In fact, more than one working definition for a concept is generally considered to be desirable, if not necessary. A given concept may be too complex to be reduced to a single measurable phenomenon. In addition, having more than one working definition for a concept helps to increase the reliability of the findings, as the different measurements tend to serve as cross checks for one another. For example, if a person were found to own a library card, which could be one definition of library use, but were found never to use the library, then one would question the validity of using card ownership to represent library use. The researcher would be better advised to utilize a variety of working definitions, including borrowing books, asking reference questions, requesting interlibrary loans, and so on.

Again, at some point, the researcher would need to specify exactly how the activities specified by the working definitions would be measured. For example, will only substantive, as opposed to directional, reference questions be counted? What categories, such as research, bibliographic, and so on, will be used to organize the questions? It should be kept in mind that working definitions are usually considered adequate only to the extent that the instruments or procedures based on them gather data that constitute satisfactory indicators of the concepts they are intended to represent. So, if the asking of reference questions does not represent the kind of library use that the researcher had in mind, then obviously it should not be used.

One other note of caution—in developing both conceptual and working definitions, one should avoid so-called *spurious definitions*. These are circular definitions, which tend to define terms using those same terms. If one defined "library use" as "using the library," then one would be providing a circular definition of no real value to the researcher or reader.

Desirable Characteristics of Hypotheses

In addition to representing the simplest possible explanation of a specific phenomenon, an ideal hypothesis should possess several other characteristics, including the following:

1. Generalizability, or universality—a hypothesis with this trait should hold up in more than one situation. On the other hand, valid hypotheses can be formulated legitimately for specific situations.
2. Compatibility with existing knowledge—a hypothesis is more likely to be generalizable if it has been based on the findings of other studies. The hypothesis should not be isolated from the larger body of knowledge.
3. Testability—the suitability of the hypothesis for empirical testing may be its most important characteristic. Regardless of its other traits, if it cannot be tested adequately, it is of little or no value. It even can be argued that the hypothesis should imply how it can be tested.
4. Invariability—simply put, the relationship stated in the hypothesis should not vary over a reasonable period of time.
5. Causality—the ideal hypothesis states a relationship that is causal in nature (i.e., that the independent variable(s) actually causes or determines one or more dependent variables). Many researchers also argue that the hypothesis should be predictive. Hillway states that "the success of a theory [of which the hypothesis is a part] for predictive purposes constitutes one of the most useful criteria by which it may be judged."[57]

Unfortunately, it often is not possible in the social sciences to formulate hypotheses that are causal or predictive in nature. Social science researchers frequently have to settle for associative type hypotheses, or hypotheses which state a correlational but not causal relationship between two or more variables. For example, one may argue that, as a student's library use increases, his or her grades improve, without being prepared to contend that greater library use actually causes the improvement in grades. It could be that some other factor, such as an interest in reading, is causing both the library use and the high grades. The concept of causality will be discussed in greater detail in the section on experimental research.

Goldhor, among others, argues that a good hypothesis should contain a "causal element" that explains why it is thought that the hypothesized relationship holds true. An example of a causal element is provided by Goldhor in the following hypothesis (the causal element follows the word "because"):

> The more a person is interested in a hobby, the more he will read books about that hobby, because the intensive development of a hobby calls for knowledge and skills usually available only in print.[58]

It may well be that the causal element is synonymous with the hypothesis' most basic assumption, or premise. Regardless of the terminology used however, the process of identifying why the relationship exists is an important one, producing several benefits. For example, the researcher cannot hope to explain why a certain relationship exists without acquiring a thorough understanding of the phenomenon under study. Explaining why a relationship holds true forces the investigator to go beyond mere description of it. Consideration of causality also forces the researcher to distinguish between the independent and dependent variables. Otherwise, one cannot state which factor causes which. Finally, after specifying why a relationship exists, the researcher is more likely to be able to predict what the hypothesized relationship will produce.

Testing the Hypothesis

In testing the validity of a hypothesis, the researcher typically employs the deductive method in that he or she begins with a theoretical framework, formulates a hypothesis, and logically deduces what the results of the test should be if the hypothesis is correct. This is usually accomplished in two stages.

First, the researcher deductively develops certain logical implications (also known as logical consequences and criteria) which, when stated in operational terms, can help to reject or support the hypothesis. These logical implications should indicate evidence which must be collected and which must be valid for an adequate test. Considering our hypothesis regarding library instruction and library use, several criteria could logically represent library use or provide evidence of use. Operationally defined, such criteria could include the number of visits to the library, the number of books borrowed, and so on.

The second basic step in testing a hypothesis involves actually subjecting it to a trial by collecting and analyzing relevant data. For example, one would, at this point, collect data on the subjects' actual library use, as evidenced by criteria already established. This stage requires the use of one or more criterion measures in order to evaluate the evidence that has been collected. "The choice of the criterion measure is crucial: not only must it be reliable and valid, it must also be sufficiently sensitive to detect changes as they occur."[59] If one were using the number of visits to the library as evidence of library use, it would be important to detect all library visits, not just some of them. It might also be necessary to determine types of library visits—their purpose and duration, for example.

As was indicated earlier, in order to measure library use adequately, it probably would be necessary to measure it in more than one way (i. e., employ more than one operational definition). If more than one operational definition is considered, then it follows that more than one logical consequence can be expected and that more than one criterion measure must be employed. In fact, establishment of "the truth of an hypothesis in the absolute sense is not accomplished until all possible logical consequences have been tested and the hypothesis becomes a law."[60] Until a hypothesis is tested in every appropriate situation, the researcher is at best building support for the hypothesis, not proving it. In effect, each logical consequence can provide several different bases for testing the same hypothesis or relationship.

Causation also plays an important role in the testing of hypotheses. As Goldhor has noted, "The testing or verification of an hypothesis is strengthened or augmented by analysis of available relevant data so as to show (1) that they agree with predictions drawn logically from the one hypothesis, (2) that they do not also confirm the consequences of alternative hypotheses, and (3) that they involve points in a logical chain of cause and effect."[61] Consideration of the causal relationship (when it exists) forces the investigator to employ or measure consequences that will provide evidence of the nature of the hypothetical relationship. This usually can be accomplished by utilizing data collection procedures and criterion measures that have the ability to support or reject the hypothetical cause of the relationship. For example, if college students who had high grades and who were heavy users of the library were found to be using the library strictly for recreational reading, we probably would have to reject the hypothesis and consider some phenomenon other than library use to be the cause of high grades. Such a finding might well suggest other possible relationships.

At this point, two reminders appear to be in order. One, it should not be forgotten that the hypothesis should be related to existing knowledge as closely as possible. This caveat also applies to the findings resulting from the testing of the hypothesis. This process is crucial if research is to build on previous studies and not merely produce fragmentary, unrelated bits of data.

Two, it is important to remember that scientific research should produce a circular movement from facts to hypotheses, to laws, to theories, and back to facts as the basis for the testing and refinement of more adequate hypotheses. In other words, the research process should never end; it should merely continue to build on previous research, and to shape and reshape its findings.

An appropriate question to ask at this point is whether a hypothesis is always possible and/or helpful. In fact, it is not always possible, desirable, or justifiable to develop a formal hypothesis for a research study. This is particularly the case for exploratory research in areas too undeveloped to provide the basis for formally stated hypotheses and for most qualitative research. A formal research hypothesis can even be a hindrance to exploratory research, and the investigator may have more to gain by entering into an exploratory study with few preconceived ideas. It may not be possible, or at least not advisable, to predict relationships and outcomes of exploratory research in that doing so may bias the researcher and encourage neglect of potentially important information.

Also, when fact-finding alone is the purpose of the study, which is often the case with descriptive surveys, there may be little use for a hypothesis. At the very least, however, the researcher should have some "research questions" which he or she is attempting to answer and which will help, in lieu of a hypothesis, to guide the research. Some researchers distinguish between "descriptive research questions," which ask what is the amount or extent of a given variable, and "explanatory research questions," which ask how or whether certain variables are related. The following are examples of the former: How many students use their college library during specific time periods? What are the subject majors of the users of a college library? The following are examples of the latter: Is there a relationship between the subject majors of students and how often they use their college library? Is there a relationship between the subject majors of students and the types of reference questions that they ask? It is probably safe to say, however, that most major studies, particularly those involving some interpretation of facts, should incorporate a research hypothesis. "Not the facts alone, but the conclusions that we can draw from them must be regarded as the chief objective of research."[62] Without the rigorous testing of a valid hypothesis, generalizable conclusions are not possible.

VALIDITY AND RELIABILITY

As one develops, and conducts, a research study, one should always be concerned with its validity and reliability. Generally speaking, research is considered to be valid when the conclusions are true, and reliable when the findings are repeatable. But validity and reliability are actually requirements for both the design and the measurement of research. Regarding the design, the researcher should ask whether the conclusions are true (valid) and repeatable (reliable).[63] Measurement, of course, is the process of ascertaining the dimensions, quantity, or capacity of something, and it is closely related to the notion of operational definitions discussed earlier. "More specifically, measurement is a procedure in which one assigns numerals, numbers or other symbols, to empirical properties (variables) according to rules."[64] Research design is the plan and structure of the research framework. It is influenced by the nature of the hypothesis, the variables, the constraints of the real world, and so on. Research design must occur at the beginning of a research project, but it involves all of the steps that follow.

Validity of Research Design

There are at least three types of validity as it relates to the design of research. One is referred to as *internal validity*. Briefly stated, a research design is internally valid if it accurately identifies causal relationships, if any, and rules out rival explanations of the relationships. Internal validity is particularly crucial to experimental research design.

Research design is considered to have *construct validity* if the variables being investigated can be identified and labeled properly. The design should permit the specification of the actual cause and effect and the identification of the concepts or constructs involved. (A somewhat different view of construct validity will be considered later in the discussion of validity as it relates to the measurement process.)

The third kind of validity critical to the design of research is external validity. Research has *external validity* or generalizability when its conclusions are true or hold up beyond the confines of a particular study. In other words, the findings should be generally true for studies conducted under a variety of circumstances or conditions (e.g., other times, people, places). The quality of external validity can best be determined by replicating a study or retesting to see if the results will be repeated in another setting. (This aspect of validity is similar to the concept of reliability.)

Validity in Measurement

In brief, the extent to which an instrument measures what it is designed to measure indicates the level of validity of that measure. Data collection instruments may be high in reliability and low in validity, or vice versa. For example, a test intended to measure the effect of library skills on library use might actually be measuring the influence of instructors on library use, and it would therefore be low in validity. On the other hand, repeated applications of the test, in comparable circumstances, may produce essentially the same results, indicating high reliability. Ideally, the instrument would be high in both validity and reliability.

As is the case for reliability, correlation coefficients can be calculated for the validity of an instrument. Reliability coefficients are correlations between identical or similar methods, while validity coefficients are correlations between dissimilar methods based on dissimilar operational definitions but measuring the same concepts. In other words, the validity coefficient indicates the extent to which independent instruments or observations measure the same thing.

One example of a method for calculating the validity of an instrument involves the multitrait-multimethod matrix, which is a table of correlations for two or more traits measured by two or more methods. The matrix should produce relatively high correlations between scores that reflect the same trait measured by different methods, while the correlations obtained from measuring two different traits with different instruments or measuring traits with the same instrument should be low. If two separate tests, measuring two different concepts, are highly correlated, then the two concepts are probably not truly separate and distinct.

For some standardized tests, such as IQ and personality tests, reliability and validity scores have been calculated based on past applications and validation studies and are available in the literature. For many tests or instruments, and obviously for newly developed ones, however, scores are not available. Reliability scores can be calculated by correlating the scores for repeated tests. The method used to evaluate the validity of an instrument is determined by the type of validity with which one is concerned.

The standard texts on research methods do not evidence unanimity on their categorization of validity. A careful reading of several works, however, suggests that the terminology and classification schemes vary more than the types of validity themselves. What follows is hopefully at least a consensual overview of the basic types of validity as they relate to measurement.

Logical Validity

Logical validity is a type of validity generally based on expert judgment. It includes content validity and face validity. *Content* validity represents the degree to which an instrument measures a specific content area. For example, a test designed to measure a student's mastery of library skills must measure what the student was supposed to learn.

In order to be adequate, content validity must contain both item validity and sampling validity. *Item* validity reflects whether the items of the instrument or test actually represent measurement in the intended content area. Does a question about filing rules in fact measure a student's understanding of how records are arranged in a library's catalog? *Sampling* validity is concerned with how well the instrument samples the total content area. A test on library skills should not be limited to measuring library users' ability to check out books. The test should cover catalogue use, search strategy, and so on.

Face validity is similar to content validity, and the terms are sometimes used interchangeably. Face validity is a sort of catchall term often used rather loosely. It has been defined as "the degree to which a test *appears* to measure what it purports to measure."[65] Face validity is usually based on the opinion of subject experts who have been asked to evaluate an instrument. (This method of determining validity is quite subjective, but sometimes it is the only feasible one available.)

Empirical Validity

The second basic type of validity regarding measurement has been referred to as empirical and criterion-related validity. In contrast to logical validity, empirical validity is based on external, objective criteria. It includes concurrent validity and predictive validity.

Concurrent validity indicates the degree to which the scores on a test or other data collection instrument are related to the scores on another, already validated, test administered at the same time, or to some other valid criterion (e.g., grade point average) available at the same time. Concurrent validity also represents the ability of an instrument to discriminate among people (or whatever) who are known to differ. For instance, in developing an instrument to measure *how* people use a university library, one would expect it to distinguish between under-graduates and graduate students, as we already have evidence indicating that their library use differs. If members of these two groups "scored" the same on the test, then there would be a good chance that the test was actually measuring something other than types of library use—perhaps simply frequency.

Predictive validity has to do with the degree to which an instrument can identify differences that will evidence themselves in the future. If one were pre-dicting that frequent library users were more likely to go on to graduate school than were infrequent or nonusers, then subsequent observations should support that prediction. A greater proportion of the people who scored relatively high on an initial library use questionnaire should be found enrolled in graduate school at a later date.

Construct Validity

It is possible for validity of measurement to be based on both logical judgment and external criteria. Such validity is usually known as construct validity. The de-finition for construct validity sounds like the definition for face validity in that construct validity represents the extent to which an instrument measures the con-cept or construct that it is intended to measure. As is the case with face validity, when selecting a test or instrument to employ in a research study, one must take care to choose one that accurately measures the construct of interest. This selec-tion process should be based on the judgment of subject experts. Unlike face va-lidity, however, construct validity requires more than expert opinion for determi-nation. In order to ensure construct validity, it must be demonstrated that an instrument measures the construct in question and no other. In operational terms, construct validity requires that two or more measures of different constructs, using similar instruments, produce low correlations (i.e., *discriminant* validity) and that two or more measures of the same construct result in high correlations, even though different instruments are used (i.e., *convergent* validity). In other words, an instrument should be capable of measuring the construct (as repre-sented by appropriate variables) it is supposed to measure, of distinguishing the construct from others, and of measuring other constructs simultaneously. (The multitrait-multimethod matrix discussed earlier represents one method for deter-mining the convergent and discriminant validity of an instrument and thereby measuring its construct validity.)

Reliability of Research Design

If the design of a research study is reliable, then its findings should be repeatable or replicable and generalizable beyond the one study. Exact replications of the study, including specific procedures, can be made to assess the reliability of the design. (Conceptual replications of only the ideas or concepts can be used to evaluate the external validity of the design.)

Reliability in Measurement

As was stated earlier, research requires that one be able to measure concepts and constructs as represented by variables which often are translated into, or operationally defined as, a set of categories or a scale. Unfortunately, however, virtually all measurement is imperfect. Consequently, a measurement, or observed score, comprises the true score (which may never be known) and the error of measurement, or the discrepancy between the observed and the true scores. A measurement is generally considered to be reliable when the error component is reasonably small and does not fluctuate greatly from one observation to another. Thus reliability can be defined as the degree to which an instrument accurately *and* consistently measures whatever it measures. In short, a reliable data collection instrument is one that is relatively free from measurement error.

There are methods for assessing the reliability or *stability* of measurement techniques. One of the most commonly used methods results in what is known as a test-retest correlation. When the researcher employs this technique, he or she uses the same data collection instrument to observe or collect scores twice for the same group of subjects. (The instrument should be administered at different times but under equivalent conditions.) The two sets of scores are then correlated to see how consistent or reliable the instrument was in measuring the variables. The smaller the error of measurement, the more likely the correlation will be high.

If it is not feasible to repeat the measurement process, or if the *internal consistency* or homogeneity of the test is of concern, other methods can be used to determine the reliability of the instrument. For example, in utilizing the split-half method, the researcher splits the measuring instrument into two sets of questions or items after it is administered. The scores on the two halves are then correlated to provide an estimate of reliability. (The instrument should be split in equivalent halves, each of which is representative of the total. This can be done by assigning the odd-numbered items to one set and the even-numbered items to the other, or by using some random assignment technique. Keep in mind, however, that a data collection instrument may have been designed to measure one variable or several variables.)

Other methods for assessing the reliability of measurement include the average item-total correlation, in which each item's score is correlated with the total score, and the coefficients are averaged. With a technique called the average interitem correlation, each item is correlated with every other item, and the average of the coefficients represents a measure of internal consistency and indicates how well the items all measure the same construct. (If these conditions do exist, then the test-retest correlation of the total score will be higher than the test-retest correlation of the individual items.) When data are gathered by observers, it is important that their observations agree if they observed the same phenomena. *Interrater reliability* refers to the extent to which two or more observers agree.

Reliability also can be expressed in terms of the *standard error of measurement*, which is an estimate of how often one can expect errors of a given size. It is calculated with the following formula:

$$SE_m = SD\sqrt{1-r}$$

where

SE$_m$ = standard error of measurement
SD = standard deviation of scores
 r = reliability coefficient.

A small standard error of measurement indicates high reliability and vice versa.

In considering the reliability of the data collection tool, one must, as has been stated, be concerned with the amount of measurement error. It is also essential that the instrument measure only the constructs of interest, not a variety of others. Otherwise it is difficult, if not impossible, to know which construct, or variable, to credit for the magnitude of the score.

A reasonable question to ask at this point would be, what is a satisfactory reliability coefficient? Ideally, every score or observation should have a reasonably high correlation with the construct or variable measured, but the determination of what constitutes a "high" correlation must be somewhat subjective. This question is comparable to asking what constitutes a high correlation between two variables. Both answers depend on a variety of factors. Regarding measurement, it should be noted that the reliability is always contingent on the degree of uniformity of the given characteristics in the population. The more homogeneous the population with regard to the variable in question, the more reliable the instrument is likely to be. For example, if an instrument has been designed to measure library use, and library use varies little among the subjects being studied, the instrument should be able to measure use consistently.

The level of reliability needed by a researcher also will vary according to the desired degree of distinction among cases. High reliability is more important, or at least more difficult to achieve, when making fine discriminations among cases than when merely identifying extremes. If the latter is all that is desired, a relatively crude measurement device should suffice. If a librarian merely wished to know what proportion of the library's patrons were children, young adults, and adults, then users could be observed and assigned to one of the three broad categories. If it were important to know exact ages, then patrons would have to be asked for that information on a questionnaire or during an interview. The resultant set of categories or the measurement scale would contain the number of ages reported and would require a more reliable data collection instrument.

Scales

The level of discrimination is in large part a function of the measurement scale used by the research instrument. The *American Heritage Dictionary* defines scale as "a progressive classification, as of size, amount, importance, or rank; a relative level or degree." There are generally considered to be four types of measurement scales:[66]

1. Nominal scale—The nominal or categorical scale consists of two or more named categories into which objects, individuals, or responses are classified. For example, a survey of academic library users could employ a nominal scale for the purpose of categorizing users by subject major. The simplest nominal scale is the dichotomous scale, which has only two values, such as male-female, yes-no, and so on. The important characteristic of the nominal scale is that the categories are qualitative, not quantitative.

2. Ordinal scale—An ordinal scale defines the relative position of objects or individuals with respect to a characteristic, with no implication as to the distance between positions. This type of scale is also referred to as a "rank order." Attitude or Likert-type scales are examples of ordinal scales. (It should be noted, however, that some researchers do consider Likert-type scales to be interval level scales.) For example, one could rank order patrons' level of satisfaction on a scale such as the following:

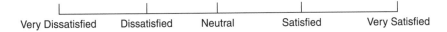

Very Dissatisfied   Dissatisfied   Neutral   Satisfied   Very Satisfied

But one could not assume that the distance from "Very Dissatisfied" to "Dissatisfied" is the same as the distance from "Neutral" to "Satisfied." In other words, the second range might represent a greater change than the first range.

3. Interval scale—The interval scale provides a ranking of positions, as does the ordinal scale, but the intervals of measurement are equal. In addition, the interval scale has a zero point below which scores are given a negative value if they occur. A temperature scale is an example of an interval scale. Interval level data are less common than ordinal in the social sciences.

4. Ratio scale—The ratio scale is comparable to the interval scale except that it has an absolute zero, below which values cannot occur. The ratio scale allows one to compare the magnitude of responses or measurements. Frequency of library use could be considered to be ratio level data, and, in analyzing such information, one would be able to correctly state, for example, that one person has used the library twice as often as another. Ratio level data are relatively rare in the social sciences because few scales actually have true zero points.

In considering the issue of measurement, it should be kept in mind that measurement presupposes theory. In order for any measurement to have meaning, one must have a solid understanding of the relationship between the variable and the underlying construct that it represents. Kidder refers to this relationship as "epistemic correlation."[67] To some extent, epistemic correlation can be established by developing an intuitive theory regarding the relationship and identifying a second variable that also meets the construct. If a significant epistemic correlation exists, then there should be a correlation between each variable and the construct, and between the two variables.

SUMMARY

As was stated earlier, a research project that adheres to the basic scientific method of inquiry consists of certain stages; this chapter has considered four of these stages: identification or development of the theory; identification of the problem; formulation of the hypothesis; and measurement as related to validity, reliability, and level. A research project is not likely to succeed unless careful attention has been paid to these steps. Yet it is tempting for the researcher to slight, if not ignore, these steps in order to get involved in the design of the study and the collection and analysis of data. Unfortunately, such research is generally inefficient and less productive and meaningful than it could be. Would-be researchers should realize that the time that goes into the conceptual development and planning of a research study is time well spent, and it will result in fewer problems in the later stages of the research. As has been written elsewhere, "A question well-stated is a question half answered."[68]

NOTES

[1]Paul D. Leedy and Jeanne E. Ormrod, *Practical Research: Planning and Design*, 7th ed. (Upper Saddle River, NJ: Merrill Prentice Hall, 2001): 91.

[2]Paul D. Leedy, *Practical Research: Planning and Design*, 2d ed. (New York: Macmillan, 1980): 41.

[3]Earl R. Babbie, *The Practice of Social Research*, 9th ed. (Belmont, CA: Wadsworth, 2001): 4–5.

[4]Leedy, *Practical Research*.

[5]John M. Budd, "An Epistemological Foundation for Library and Information Science," *Library Quarterly* 65, no. 3 (1995): 295–318.

[6]Leedy, *Practical Research*, 42.

[7]Babbie, *The Practice of Social Research*, 9th ed., 54–55.

[8]Chava Frankfort-Nachmias and David Nachmias, *Research Methods in the Social Sciences*, 4th ed. (New York: St. Martin's Press, 1992): 21.

[9]Karen E. Pettigrew and Lynne (E. F.) McKechnie, "The Use of Theory in Information Science Research," *Journal of the American Society for Information Science and Technology* 52 (2001): 62–73.

[10]William Ernest McGrath, "Current Theory in Library and Information Science," *Library Trends* 50 (Winter 2002): 309–569.

[11] Donald E. Riggs, "Losing the Foundation of Understanding," *American Libraries* 25 (May 1994): 449.

[12] Peter Hernon, "Editorial: Publishing Research," *Journal of Academic Librarianship* 22 (January 1996): 1–2.

[13] John M. Budd, *Knowledge and Knowing in Library and Information Science: A Philosophical Framework* (Lanham, MD: Scarecrow Press, 2001).

[14] Mary Sue Stephenson, Senior Instructor Chair of the MLIS Program, Coordinator of Information Technology, WELCOME TO RESEARCH METHODS RESOURCES ON THE WWW [Web page], Available, [http://www.slais.ubc.ca/resources/research_methods/index.htm]. Accessed 2003.

[15] Leedy and Ormrod, *Practical Research*, 9.

[16] Ibid., 8.

[17] Peter Hernon, "Editorial: Components of the Research Process: Where Do We Need to Focus Attention? " *Journal of Academic Librarianship* 27 (March 2001): 81–89.

[18] Leedy and Ormrod, *Practical Research*, 114–16.

[19] Claire Selltiz, Lawrence S. Wrightsman, and Stuart W. Cook, *Research Methods in Social Relations*, rev. ed. (New York: Holt, Rinehart and Winston, 1959): 26.

[20] Leedy and Ormrod, *Practical Research*, 46.

[21] John Martyn and F. Wilfrid Lancaster, *Investigative Methods in Library and Information Science: An Introduction* (Arlington, VA: Information Resources Press, 1981): 3.

[22] Peter Hernon and Cheryl Metoyer-Duran, "Problem Statements: An Exploratory Study of Their Function, Significance, and Form," *Library and Information Science Research* 15 (Winter 1993): 71–92.

[23] Hernon, "Components of the Research Process", 87.

[24] Leedy and Ormrod, *Practical Research*, 57.

[25] Herbert Goldhor, *An Introduction to Scientific Research in Librarianship* (Urbana: University of Illinois, Graduate School of Library Science, 1972).

[26] Ibid., 42.

[27] George J. Mouly, *Educational Research: The Art and Science of Investigation* (Boston, MA: Allyn and Bacon, 1978): 35.

[28] Goldhor, *An Introduction to Scientific Research*, 42.

[29] Mouly, *Educational Research*, 35.

[30] Goldhor, *An Introduction to Scientific Research*, 49.

[31] Selltiz, Wrightsman, and Cook, *Research Methods in Social Relations*, 481.

[32] Earl R. Babbie, *The Practice of Social Research*, 2d ed. (Belmont, CA: Wadsworth, 1979): 108.

[33] Joanne G. Marshall, *An Introduction to Research Methods for Health Sciences Librarians*, Chicago: Medical Library Association, Courses for Continuing Education, 1989:16.

[34] McGrath, "Current Theory," 310.

[35] Goldhor, *An Introduction to Scientific Research*, 43.

[36] Ibid.

[37] Ibid., 42.

[38] Robert J. Grover and Jack D. Glazier, "A Conceptual Framework for Theory Building in Library and Information Science ," *Library & Information Science Research* 8 (1986) : 227–42.

[39] Mouly, *Educational Research*, 35–36.

[40] Constance A. Mellon, "Library Anxiety: A Grounded Theory and Its Development," *College & Research Libraries* 47 (March 1986): 160–65.

[41] Herbert L. Poole, *Theories of the Middle Range* (Norwood, NJ: Ablex Publishing Corporation, 1985).

[42] Lynne (E. F.) McKechnie and Karen E. Pettigrew, "Surveying the Use of Theory in Library and Information Science Research: A Disciplinary Perspective," *Library Trends* 50; no. 3 (2002): 406–17.

[43] Goldhor, *An Introduction to Scientific Research*, 45.

[44] Babbie, *The Practice of Social Research*, 9th ed., 65.

[45] Leedy and Ormrod, *Practical Research*, 60.

[46] Mouly, *Educational Research*, 62.

[47]Selltiz, Wrightsman, and Cook, *Research Methods in Social Relations*, 35.

[48]Tyrus Hillway, *Introduction to Research*, 2d ed. (Boston, MA: Houghton Mifflin, 1964): 132.

[49]Mouly, *Educational Research*, 38.

[50]Ibid., 64.

[51]Ibid., 50.

[52]Goldhor, *An Introduction to Scientific Research*, 55.

[53]Marshall, *An Introduction to Research Methods*, 17.

[54]Ibid., 15.

[55]Selltiz, Wrightsman and Cook, *Research Methods in Social Relations*, 41.

[56]Douglas L. Zweizig, "Measuring Library Use," *Drexel Library Quarterly* 13 (July 1977): 3.

[57]Hillway, *Introduction to Research*, 128.

[58]Goldhor, *An Introduction to Scientific Research*, 59.

[59]Mouly, *Educational Research*, 69.

[60]Goldhor, *An Introduction to Scientific Research*, 81.

[61]Ibid., 86.

[62]Hillway, *Introduction to Research*, 131.

[63]Louise H. Kidder, *Research Methods in Social Relations*, 4th ed. (New York: Holt, Rinehart and Winston, 1981): 7.

[64]David Nachmias and Chava Nachmias, *Research Methods in the Social Sciences*, 2d ed. (New York: St. Martin's Press, 1981): 58.

[65]L. R. Gay, *Educational Research: Competencies for Analysis and Application*, 5th ed. (Englewood Cliffs, NJ: Charles E. Merrill, 1996): 111.

[66]*American Heritage Dictionary; Second College Edition* (Boston: Houghton Mifflin Co, 1982): 1095.

[67]Kidder, *Research Methods in Social Relations*, 139.

[68]Stephen Isaac and William B. Michael, *Handbook in Research and Evaluation*, 3d ed. (San Diego, CA: EdITS Publishers, 1995): 36.

Chapter 3

Selecting the Research Method

Having identified the research problem, identified or built a theory, and formulated a hypothesis (where appropriate), the researcher is ready to select a methodology for his or her study. The researcher must first decide whether the proposed research will be primarily applied or basic and quantitative or qualitative in nature. As was previously indicated, the emphases of this book are basic and quantitative approaches to research. The methods that fall into those categories will be given minimal attention in this section as they are treated more fully later in the text.

APPLIED RESEARCH

As was noted in Chapter 1, there is a distinction to be made between basic and applied research. Basic research tends to be theoretical in nature and concerns itself primarily with theory construction, hypothesis testing, and producing new, generalizable knowledge. Applied research tends to be more pragmatic and emphasizes providing information that is immediately usable in the resolution of actual problems, which may or may not have application beyond the immediate study.

53

On the other hand, both types of research ultimately should add to the existing body of knowledge within a field, and in doing so, they may utilize similar methods and techniques. Such utilization is nicely illustrated by the discussion of the evaluation of information storage and retrieval systems in *Guide to Information Science* by Davis and Rush.[1] Davis points out that "the interplay between academics [basic researchers] and practitioners [applied researchers] can be extremely valuable," and it should be encouraged.[2] There is no good reason to assume that basic and applied research are mutually exclusive. In fact, basic and applied research can be considered as two parts of a continuum. Furthermore, "although the criteria for merit vary somewhat along the continuum, there is more overlap than typically realized. For example, basic research is judged by its clarity of purpose and interpretation, by its ability to support or refute particular hypotheses, by the incisiveness of the new hypotheses it generates, by the generalizability of the results, and by its technical accuracy, but in addition by the degree to which the results can be utilized in developing a product, a process, or a policy, to mention just a few types of application."[3] Applied research, on the other hand, can validate theories and lead to the revision of theories. It "takes the theory and concepts from basic research and, by formal methods of inquiry, investigates 'real world' phenomena."[4]

Action Research

A major type of applied research, and one sometimes treated interchangeably with applied research, is action research. According to Wilson, "action research in the original sense is participative organizational research, focused on problem definition and resolution, which involves (usually) an external researcher who works with organizational members to arrive at workable solutions to their problems, within the framework of some theoretical perspective."[5] Action research differs from applied research in that "it has direct application to the immediate workplace of the researcher, whereas applied research may have the broader purpose of improving the profession at large."[6] Isaac and Michael, for example, state that the purpose of action research is "to develop new skills or new approaches and to solve problems with direct application to the classroom or working world setting."[7] They characterize action research as practical, orderly, flexible and adaptive, and empirical to a degree, but weak in internal and external validity.

Isaac and Michael identify the following basic steps in action research:

1. Defining the problem or setting the goal
2. Reviewing the literature
3. Formulating testable hypotheses
4. Arranging the research setting
5. Establishing measurement techniques and evaluation criteria
6. Analyzing the data and evaluating the results.[8]

As can be seen, these steps do not differ significantly from those typically followed in a basic research study. It is likely, however, that they would be carried out somewhat less rigorously than for basic research. Typically, the data are provided to library decision makers who in turn take some action, for example, improve a service, develop a new one, or discontinue a service.

Evaluative Research

Evaluative or evaluation research, as a specific type of applied research, has as its primary goal not the discovery of knowledge but rather a testing of the application of knowledge within a specific program or project. Thus it is usually practical or utilitarian in nature, and it is generally less useful than basic research for developing theoretical generalizations. In most evaluative hypotheses the dependent variable is a desired value, goal, or effect (for example, better library skills, higher circulation statistics, etc.), and the independent variable is often a program or service.

Evaluative research studies often have a relatively large number of uncontrolled variables, as they are carried out in real settings. They are usually limited in terms of time and space, and if the evaluative researcher has a vested interest in the project being evaluated, he or she is highly susceptible to bias.

With regard to design and measurement, evaluative research is much like basic research. Verification of the hypothesis requires a design that will show that the desired effect was more likely to occur in the presence of the program than in its absence. It conceivably can employ most of the same designs that are used in basic research. Evaluative researchers must be concerned with threats to validity, such as intervening variables, measurement techniques, and operational definitions.

The two general types of evaluative research are *summative evaluation* and *formative evaluation*. Summative, or *outcome*, research is concerned with the effects of a program. It tends to be quantitative in nature and often is used as the basis for deciding whether a program will be continued.

Formative, or *process*, evaluation, which is done during a program, not following its completion, examines how well the program is working. It is often more qualitative and typically is used for revising and improving programs. In both types, feedback from program participants is usually considered important.

Performance measurement is a more specific type of evaluative research. Performance or output measures are made in order to determine what was accomplished as a result of specific programs, services, and resources being available. Performance measures focus on indicators of library output and effectiveness, rather than merely on input (monetary support, number of books, etc.). They are clearly related to the impact of the library on the community, are often concerned with user satisfaction, and can be used with longitudinal as well as current data. Other examples of performance measures have included service area penetration, level of use of facilities and equipment, circulation statistics, availability of materials and staff, and reference service use. Lately, the LIS profession has been concerned with using performance measures to evaluate electronic resources and services, including networked services (see Bertot, McClure, and Ryan, for example[9]).

A variety of techniques can be used for measuring performance; they have included the collection of statistics, questionnaires, interviews, observations, unobtrusive reference questions, diaries, consumer panels, and document delivery tests. One of the more recent approaches to measuring the performance of libraries and other organizations is *benchmarking*. Benchmarking "represents a structured, proactive change effort designed to help achieve high performance through comparative assessment. It is a process that establishes an external standard to which intended operations can be compared."[10] "Benchmarking not only allows for the establishment of a systematic process to indicate the quality of outputs, but also allows for an organization to create its own definition of quality for any process or output."[11] It is critical to keep in mind, however, that whatever technique(s) is used to assess performance, it should be related to the organization's goals and objectives.

Other relatively recent attempts to evaluate the effectiveness of libraries have focused on their outcomes or actual *impact*. In other words, rather than stop with the measurement of output or performance, an increasing number of researchers are attempting to determine how the lives of individuals are actually affected by their use of libraries and other information resources. For example, an impact assessment of a university library would go beyond measures of reference activity and circulation statistics and attempt to determine how the borrowing of books and procurement of answers to reference questions ultimately affect a student's test scores, papers, course grades, and so on. Impact or effect may well be the most important indicator of a library's effectiveness and represents its most meaningful approach to accountability, but, unfortunately, impact is elusive and no doubt more difficult to measure than input and performance. Steffen, Lance, and Logan measured the impact of public library services in the lives of library users.[12] Lance has also completed studies for individual states to measure the impact of school libraries on student achievement.[13]

In the past several years there has been much discussion of assessing library service quality based on customer feedback.[14, 15] Hernon and Dugan argue that outcomes assessment must be linked to accountability, which can be measured by user satisfaction and service quality.[16] The economic environment, the convenience of the Internet, and the growing number of mega-book stores have encouraged librarians to view library users as customers and to develop library services accordingly. This approach, derived from the business world, "cannot adequately be conveyed by output and performance measures."[17] In an attempt to assess university library users' perceptions of services, the Association of Research Libraries has undertaken a research and development project now called LibQUAL+. The project attempts "to define and measure library service quality across institutions and to create useful quality-assessment tools for local planning, such as the evaluation of a library's collections-related services from the user's point of view."[18] "Impact" and "outcomes" are often used interchangeably in the literature.

King has identified ten different approaches to evaluative research, along with some of their characteristics, applications, strengths, and weaknesses.[19] Those approaches are presented in Table 3.1.

TABLE 3.1.   **Approaches to Evaluation**

Method	Emphasis	Application	Strengths	Weaknesses
Objectives-based evaluation	Assessment of student attainment of preestablished goals and objectives	Primarily summative	Relatively easy to understand and apply	Does not reveal unintended outcomes; tendency to over-simplify by measuring only what is easily measurable; concentrates on program content without means for determining the value of the content
Discrepancy evaluation	Assessment on the basis of performance standards for educational decision making	Formative and summative	Provides constant feedback on program progress; expands and improves on objectives-based methods	Does not reveal unintended outcomes; lengthy process requiring time and expertise
Responsive Evaluation	Description of program processes and outcomes according to values of key people	Formative and summative	Reveals unintended as well as intended results; Comprehensiveness of findings	Requires expertise in variety of formal methods; may be a lengthy and involved process
Decision-oriented evaluation	Collection and analysis of information for decision making	Formative and summative	Reveals unintended as well as intended results; comprehensiveness of findings	May concentrate too much on the value perspectives of decision makers; not all activities are clearly evaluated
Goal-free evaluation	Collection and analysis of information related to actual results rather than preestablished objectives	Formative and summative	Reveals unintended as well as intended results; reveals the value of the program as a whole	Requires expert evaluator of high credibility with a variety of skills

(Continued)

TABLE 3.1. *(Continued)*

Method	Emphasis	Application	Strengths	Weaknesses
Adversary evaluation	Evaluation should present two competing interpretations of a program's value	Primarily summative	Pros and cons of a program discussed in strongest manner	Requires more people with sufficient skills in both evaluation and presentations; may be too subjective; not all arguments may be based on true judgment
Illuminative evaluation	To illuminate the acceptability of program processes and content	Primarily formative	Relatively easy to implement	Kinds of information obtained may not address needs of all audiences; may be open to bias; may be too subjective for many audiences
Evaluation research	Assessment of educational effects for validity, reliability, and generalizability	Summative	Objectively demonstrated effects	Requires strict controls; only one or two effects can be evaluated at a time; little information provided for program improvement
Naturalistic evaluation	Use of case study and anthropological and sociological methods to describe program processes and results comprehensively	Formative and summative	Full expertise and sensitivities of evaluator employed; comprehensive-ness of results	Usually requires an expert evaluator from outside the program; highly subjective results which may not be acceptable to all audiences
Professional Judgment	Assessment of program on basis of normative and comparative standards	Formative and summative	Assures that minimum standards are met or that program has value comparable to similar programs	Consists almost entirely of judgments of merit; little attention to program performance or outcomes

QUALITATIVE RESEARCH

In addition to having to decide whether one's research will be primarily basic or applied, the researcher must determine whether it will be quantitative or qualitative in nature. Quantitative research, which is emphasized in this book, "is appropriate where quantifiable measures of variables of interest are possible, where hypotheses can be formulated and tested, and inferences drawn from samples to populations. Qualitative methods, on the other hand, are appropriate when the phenomena under study are complex, are social in nature, and do not lend themselves to quantification."[20] Qualitative research (field studies and ethnographic techniques are related terms) focuses on attempting to understand why participants react as they do.[21] Qualitative research tends to apply a more holistic and natural approach to the resolution of a problem than does quantitative research. It also tends to give more attention to the subjective aspects of human experience and behavior.

Qualitative researchers have used a variety of methods and techniques, many drawn from anthropology and sociology. They have ranged from ones tradition-ally used in quantitative research, such as observation and the interview, to less common ones, such as mechanical recording and photography. Gorman and Clayton have written an excellent guide to qualitative research methods, with a practical, how-to approach for information professionals.[22]

While the bulk of basic research in library science has taken the form of quan-titative research, which tends to adhere relatively closely to the scientific method of inquiry, qualitative methods have been employed to a greater degree in more recent years. In the report of a study utilizing structured observation, Grover and Glazier argue that qualitative research methods can be useful for gathering data about information users' behavior and information needs.[23] Qualitative methods can be especially useful in exploratory research. Chapter 7 of this book is de-voted to qualitative research methods.

SPECIFIC RESEARCH METHODS

Having decided on the general approach to be taken in the research study, the researcher must next identify one, or more, specific methods that he or she wishes to employ to gather the necessary data. As was indicated at the beginning of this chapter, what follows is a brief introduction to a number of research methods. Several of the methods are treated in some detail, others are merely identified with an indication that more information is to be provided elsewhere in the text. A number of additional related readings are provided at the end of the chapter.

Survey Research

Survey research has been defined as "the research strategy where one collects data from all or part of a population to assess the relative incidence, distribution, and interrelations of naturally occurring variables."[24] This methodology, which is most commonly used in descriptive studies, is dealt with in Chapters 4 and 5.

Experimental Research

Experimental research is "research in which at least one independent variable is manipulated, other relevant variables are controlled, and the effect on one or more dependent variables is observed."[25] This method is considered to be the best method for testing causal relationships and is treated more fully in Chapter 6.

Historical Research

Isaac and Michael describe the purpose of historical research as one of "reconstruct[ing] the past systematically and objectively by collecting, evaluating, verifying, and synthesizing evidence to establish facts and reach defensible conclusions, often in relation to particular hypotheses."[26] Gay defines it as "the systematic collection and objective evaluation of data related to past occurrences in order to test hypotheses concerning causes, effects, or trends of those events which may help to explain present events and anticipate future events."[27] These are useful definitions, but they both raise issues related to the role of hypotheses in historical research, the feasibility of determining cause and effect, and so on. Such issues, and others, are addressed in Chapter 8.

Operations Research

Operations research (OR) is the application of scientific method to management operations in an effort to aid managerial decision making. It is used to identify optimal solutions to real problems, utilizing analytical mathematical techniques. Some general types of operations research are resource allocation, sequencing, inventory, replacement, queuing theory, and competitive strategies.

According to O'Neill, the standard approach to applying operations research includes the following steps:

1. Formulating the problem
2. Constructing a mathematical model to represent the system under study
3. Deriving a solution from the model
4. Testing the model and the solution derived from it
5. Establishing controls over the solution
6. Putting the solution to work: implementation.[28]

Modeling

Modeling, which is sometimes used synonymously with simulation, is "at the heart of the operations research methodology. . . . A model is an abstraction, a mental framework for analysis of a system"[29]; modeling involves the use of simplified representations of real-world phenomena. Modeling is typically used to determine the performance of a real system (e.g., interlibrary loan) by observing the behavior of a representational or analogous system. Computers are often used in simulating complex problems.

Systems Analysis

Systems analysis is another process that might better be thought of as a management technique than a research method; it actually has characteristics of both. It is similar in concept to operations research but tends to place greater emphasis on the total system and how the various components of the system interact. Systems analysis often utilizes operations research type techniques. A systems analysis typically takes into consideration the objectives and performance, the environment, the resources, the components, and the management of the entire system. Libraries often conduct systems analyses before adding a new service or revising an existing one, such as an online catalog.

Case Study

The case study is a specific field or qualitative research method and thus is an investigation "of phenomena as they occur without any significant intervention of the investigators."[30] It seems to be appropriate for investigating phenomena when "(1) a large variety of factors and relationships are included, (2) no basic laws exist to determine which factors and relationships are important, and (3) when the factors and relationships can be directly observed."[31]

Yin[32] defines a case study as "an empirical inquiry that: 1) investigates a contemporary phenomenon within its real-life context; when 2) the boundaries between phenomenon and context are not clearly evident; and in which 3) multiple sources of evidence are used."[33] Leedy and Ormrod define case study research as "a type of qualitative research in which in-depth data are gathered relative to a single individual, program, or event, for the purpose of learning more about an unknown or poorly understood situation."[34] Harrison also recommends the case study method for investigating organizational structure and functions or organizational performance.[35] The case study is often useful as an exploratory technique. In contrast to most survey research, case studies involve intensive analyses of a small number of subjects rather than gathering data from a large sample or population. A number of data collection techniques are usually employed in case studies. For example, an investigation of staff burnout in a reference department might utilize questionnaires, interviews, observation, and the analysis of documents.

If several phenomena exist, a multiple case design may be desirable.[36] Leedy suggests that case after case be studied until continually recurring facts suggest certain conclusions.[37] Yin also stresses replication logic, rather than sampling logic, for multiple case studies. "Each case must be carefully selected so that it either a) predicts similar results (a literal replication) or b) produces contrary results but for predictable reasons (a theoretical replication)."[38] Multiple case studies were conducted, in conjunction with individual interviews and task log analyses, in dissertation research by Connaway to investigate academic technical services librarians' levels of decisions and involvement in decision making.[39]

Most researchers consider the case study to be relatively low in internal and external validity (see Paris,[40] for an alternative view), but it certainly has the potential to be a valuable research tool. As Paris points out, the nature of the problem is the major determinant of the most appropriate research methodology, and the case study is well suited to collecting descriptive data. "The detailed observations that case studies provide are especially useful in documenting phenomena occurring over a period of time or whose implications are complex."[41]

Delphi Study

The Delphi study or technique "is a procedure using sequential questionnaires by which the opinions of experts can be brought to bear on issues that are essentially non-factual."[42] It is designed to generate consensus by systematically refining prior responses of study participants. "This form of data gathering is effective when policy level decision making is necessary."[43] For example, a library administrator might be faced with developing a collection development policy for electronic resources. After reviewing the professional literature, networking with colleagues at conferences, and so on, the administrator would develop a list of experts on the acquisition of electronic resources and a list of relevant issues. The latter list would then be distributed to the experts for their reactions, which could be suggestions for revision of the list and/or possible resolutions of the issues. The administrator would revise the list based on the responses. The list would be sent back to the experts for further suggestions, if any. This process would continue for more rounds of polling until a consensus among the experts had been reached. This methodology is also useful when the participants are hostile toward one another, argumentative, or unable to meet easily in person.[44]

Content Analysis

The *ALA Glossary of Library and Information Science* defines content analysis as "Analysis of the manifest and latent content of a body of communicated material (as a book or film) through a classification, tabulation, and evaluation of its key symbols and themes in order to ascertain its meaning and probable effect."[45] Content analysis is essentially a systematic analysis of the occurrence of words, phrases, concepts, and so on in books, films, and other kinds of materials. Content analysis has been used, for example, to determine how frequently racist and sexist terms appear in certain books. Kracker and Peiling used content analysis to study students' research anxiety and their perceptions of research.[46] See Chapter 7 on qualitative research for more information about content analysis.

Bibliometrics

Bibliometrics is a special type of documentary research or inquiry into the tools of library and information science. It has been defined as "the application of mathematics and statistical methods to books and other media of communication."[47] It also has been referred to as "a series of techniques that seek to quantify the process of written communication"[48] and as "the quantification of bibliographical data."[49] Related terms are scientometrics, informetrics, and librametrics.

The early bibliometric studies produced three basic laws: (1) Bradford's Law of Scatter, which describes how the literature of a subject area is distributed in its journals and which forms the basis for calculating how many journals contain a certain percentage of the published articles; (2) Lotka's Law, a formula for measuring/predicting the productivity of scientific researchers; and (3) Zipf's Law, which describes the frequency of the appearance of certain words or, more specifically, suggests that people are more likely to select and use familiar, rather than unfamiliar, words. (See Wallace[50] and Osareh[51] for useful overviews of the origins of bibliometrics.)

Following early research, bibliometrics branched into quantitative analyses, qualitative studies, and most recently, studies combining quantitative and qualitative methods. Bibliometric research, especially if quantitative, involves the application of mathematical formulas and considerable counting and statistical analysis. Bibliometric analyses have greatly benefited from the availability of computerized bibliographic databases, citation indexes, and statistical programs.

Perhaps the most common type of bibliometric research is concerned with citations. *Citation analysis* is essentially concerned with "who cites whom."[52] The three basic concepts of citation analysis are (1) "direct citation, which establishes the relationship between documents and the researchers who use them"[53]; (2) bibliographic coupling, where the reference lists of two documents share one or more of the same cited documents[54]; and (3) co-citation, which occurs when two citations are cited together.[55]

Applications of bibliometric research identified by White,[56] von Ungern-Sternberg,[57] Wallace,[58] Osareh,[59] and others include

1. Improving the bibliographic control of a literature
2. Identifying a core literature, especially journals
3. Classifying a literature
4. Tracing the spread of ideas and growth of a literature
5. Designing more economic information systems and networks
6. Improving the efficiency of information handling services
7. Predicting publishing trends
8. Describing patterns of book use by patrons
9. Developing and evaluating library collections.

Bibliometric and informetric methods are being applied to Internet-based research. "Informetrics investigates characteristics and measurements of persons, groups, institutions, countries; publications and information sources; disciplines and fields; and information retrieval processes."[60] These methods are used to study Web documents, sites, information retrieval tools (such as search engines), and user studies. Webometrics, which focuses on the quantitative study of Web phenomena, encompasses a variety of types of research. Bertot, McClure, Moen, and Rubin, for example, considered the use of Web server-generated log files to evaluate the use of the Web.[61] A special issue of the *Journal of the American Society for Information Science and Technology*, scheduled for publication in 2004, is expected to cover such topics as structures, patterns, and topologies of hyperlinks on the Web; methodological issues related to the use of search engines; social, cultural, and linguistic factors in Web use; and Web impact measurements.

Bibliometric and citation analysis are not without their limitations and potential problems, however. For example, the three basic laws identified above have not held up in every situation where they have been applied; a number of researchers have concerns about using citation counts to evaluate the scholarship of researchers; sound bibliometric analysis can be followed by faulty interpretation; and quantity and quality are not necessarily related. Treating Web links as citations begs questions about validity because of variability in the search engines, the lack of quality control, the automatic replication of links, and so on.

Comparative Librarianship

Interestingly, there is a long-standing debate over whether comparative librarianship is a research method or a subject matter. As a subject, it deals with phenomena in librarianship that can be compared. As a research method, it provides the framework for conducting an appropriate comparative analysis. In either case, comparative librarianship often has an international element. A definition that nicely incorporates all of these aspects, which can be found in the *Encyclopedia of Library and Information Science*, reads as follows:

> The systematic analysis of library development, practices, or problems as they occur under different circumstances (most usually in different countries), considered in the context of the relevant historical, geographical, political, economic, social, cultural, and other determinant background factors found in the situations under study. Essentially it constitutes an important approach to the search for cause and effect in library development, and to the understanding of library problems.[62]

"It is commonly stressed in defining the term that (1) comparative librarianship involves two or more national, cultural, or societal environments; (2) the study includes a comparable comparison; and (3) it induces philosophical or theoretical concepts of librarianship through the analysis of similarities and differences of phenomena in various environments."[63] Danton and others have argued that the scientific method of inquiry is the most satisfactory method for comparative studies in librarianship while recognizing that history and comparison are essential elements of this process.[64] The four basic steps for research in comparative librarianship have been identified as description, interpretation, juxtaposition, and comparison. Specific data collection techniques have included case histories, personal interviews, observation, and documentary analysis.

Technology-Based Research Methods

As libraries and other information agencies embrace more and more technology and employ personnel with technological backgrounds, the profession is going to have to facilitate and encourage technology-based research. "One of the difficulties in doing so has to do with reconciling the scientific method with activities that are more similar to product development than to basic research."[65] A perusal of some of the information-related sections of *Dissertation Abstracts International*, for example, turns up titles such as "Multiplexing Traffic at the Entrance to Wide-Area Networks" and "The Design and Implementation of a Log-Structured File System." The creation of the Coalition for Networked Information (CNI) and the Digital Library Federation (DLF), as well as Mellon-sponsored projects, such as the Harvard Learning Management Systems/Library Repository Interface and D-Space projects, affirm the importance of developing new techniques for investigating the new methods for accessing information.

"Geographic information system (GIS) technology is a rapidly growing and powerful method for managing and analyzing spatial data and information for libraries. . . . A GIS is designed for the collection, storage, and analysis of objects and phenomena where geographic location is an important characteristic or critical to the analysis."[66] While not a basic research method itself, GIS technology certainly has the potential to be a data collection and analysis tool for research, especially applied research. "The basic operations for GIS spatial analysis are: retrieval, map generalization, map abstractions, map sheet manipulation, buffer generation, polygon overlay and dissolve, measurements, digital terrain analyses, and network analyses."[67] Ottensmann discusses how geographic information systems can be employed to analyze patterns of library utilization in public libraries with multiple branches.[68]

Libraries are particularly interested in utilizing appropriate methods to evaluate their new information technologies. Online catalog use, for example, has been evaluated with traditional research methods and techniques such as questionnaires, interviews, focus group interviews, observation, and experiments. A less common method, *protocol analysis*, has been found useful for studying the use of online catalogs. Protocol analysis has been called "the thinking aloud technique" because it represents an analysis of subject searchers' thoughts as they perform their subject searches at the catalog.[69] During a protocol analysis, the user verbalizes the decisions and behaviors that he or she is performing in order to search the catalog. A video camera may be used to record the activity being analyzed.[70] As a type of obtrusive observation, the process itself can affect the behavior being analyzed, but using a camera is likely to be less intrusive than direct human observation.

DLF members indicated that protocols were used when "previous research or anecdotal evidence indicated serious problems with a user interface."[71] It is often difficult to recruit subjects for protocol analysis research projects; therefore, only two or three subjects may be included for each user group. DLF respondents also indicated that researchers may have assumptions about user behaviors or preferences that skew the observations and reporting of the protocols. It is difficult to interpret and use the data generated by protocols unless behaviors are identified and defined, and quantitative metrics are developed prior to the initiation of the protocols.[72]

In contrast, *transaction log analysis* or transaction monitoring is a relatively new method that is not only unobtrusive but also takes advantage of the technology that is being evaluated. Online public access catalogs (OPACs) and Web search engines are able to record and monitor use of the catalog and site; transaction log analysis is the examination of those records. Transaction log analysis can take the form of macroanalysis and microanalysis. The former is concerned with aggregate use data and patterns, the latter with the dynamics of individual search patterns. The transaction log analysis methodology is used to help researchers understand the behaviors of users of online information retrieval systems. The rationale of the analyses is for the development of information retrieval systems that will better fulfill the needs of users, based on their actual search behaviors. Peters, however, believes that transaction log analysis has been underutilized in practice where it can provide data for library managers to develop systems and services for library users.[73] Banks suggests that practicing library managers could use OPAC usage transaction log data to schedule reference service staff based on the high and low usage patterns during a specified time period.[74, 75]

One of the most important online catalog use studies, begun in 1980, was sponsored by the Council on Library Resources (CLR) (now the Council on Library and Information Resources). This study utilized questionnaires, focus group interviews, and transaction log analysis as means to study use and users. Five organizations were involved in this research: (1) J. Matthews & Associates, (2) the Library of Congress, (3) Online Computer Library Center (OCLC), (4) Research Libraries Group, and (5) the University of California, Division of Library Automation and Library Research and Analysis Group.[76] A total of 29 academic, public, state, and federal libraries participated in the catalog study, represented by 16 online catalogs.[77] A questionnaire was developed and used by all five of the organizations involved in the CLR-funded research to examine patron and staff experiences with online public access catalogs. In addition to the questionnaire, OCLC conducted focus group interviews, and transaction logs were analyzed to study the use of online public access catalogs.

Since transaction logs provide a record of the search strategy employed by users without interfering with the searcher, an analysis of transaction logs can reflect users' actual online search experiences. This methodology clearly demonstrates how users actually employ search strategies rather than how users describe their search strategies. There is also no chance of the interference of interviewer bias in the data collection.

Among other studies of transaction logs, Norden and Lawrence,[78] Tolle,[79] Dickson,[80] Nielsen,[81] Peters,[82] Hunter,[83] Zink,[84] Kalin,[85] Nelson,[86] Cherry,[87] Wallace,[88] Lucas,[89] and Millsap and Ferl,[90] examined transaction logs to study the search methods used by OPAC users. These studies report failures and successes of online searches in regard to the improvement of OPAC capabilities and screen presentation and of OPAC user instruction. Kalin, Lucas, and Millsap and Ferl studied the search methods of remote users.[91, 92, 93] Ciliberti, Radford, and Radford studied the transaction logs of library users of the OPAC and CD-ROM journal indexes to verify the accuracy of user self-reports on the availability of the resources.[94] Mudrock describes how the University of Washington libraries used server usage statistics and e-mail reference queries to create a user-oriented ready reference Web site.[95] Simpson has provided an exhaustive review of the literature on transaction log analysis.[96]

In addition to the report of search type and failure and success rates and search method types, errors and problems are also calculated for most of the studies. Unfortunately the search types, failure or success rates, and errors or problems are not defined or calculated consistently throughout the published literature, and the data provided from each system are not standardized.[97] In addition to these disadvantages, the actual users are not identifiable from the transaction logs, and it is often difficult or impossible to determine when one searcher ends a session and another begins a search session. It is also impossible to discern from the transaction logs who is doing the search and why.

For these reasons, it is often useful to incorporate the transaction log analysis data collection method with other data collection methods. Nielsen linked transaction log analysis data with user demographic data,[98] as did Millsap and Ferl and Connaway, Budd, and Kochtanek.[99, 100] Connaway, Budd, and Kochtanek interviewed subjects, using a questionnaire, after the subjects completed their online searches.[101] This enabled the researchers to link the transaction logs (subjects' search behaviors) with demographic data. Structuring a study in this way allows for the search behaviors to be analyzed in relation to the searchers' experience with online systems, educational background, reason for the search, and so on, thus requiring the researcher to infer less about the nature of the search and maintaining the validity of the study.

With the popularity and high visibility of the Internet, many researchers have used transaction or Web log analysis to investigate information retrieval on the Web. Keily and Moukdad and Large analyzed queries from the search engine WebCrawler.[102, 103] Silverstein, Henzinger, Marais, and Moricz analyzed approximately one billion queries from Alta Vista during a 43-day period.[104] Smith, Ruocco and Jansen,[105] Xu,[106] Jansen, Spink and Saracevic,[107] Spink and Xu,[108] and Spink, Wolfram Jansen, and Saracevic[109] used queries from the search engine Excite to study information retrieval patterns on the Web. These studies have identified query characteristics submitted to several Internet search engines. Jansen and Pooch give an overview of the findings of several Web user studies.[110]

Covey provides an extensive overview of transaction log analysis. Her study of the methods used by the 24 DLF libraries "to assess the use and usability of their online collections and services" includes why and how these libraries used the transaction log analysis approach.[111] The problems and challenges associated with this methodology and information on the analysis, interpretation, and presentation of the data collected from transaction log analysis are outlined and discussed by Covey. The book also includes an excellent bibliography on the topic.

A special issue of *Library Hi Tech* provided a useful overview of transaction log analysis. Kaske's article in the issue addressed a number of issues and questions relevant to using transaction log analysis as a research method, including

1. Basic constraints
2. Proposed general model
3. Research or management
4. Quantitative or qualitative methods
5. Micro or macro evaluation
6. Sample or population
7. Controlled or uncontrolled experiments
8. Ethics and transaction logs.[112]

The next to last item in the list above reinforces that transaction log analysis may be used in conjunction with other research methods; for example, transaction logs can be matched with questionnaire data, as discussed above. The last item serves as a reminder that any research method that is unobtrusive, or does not inform the subjects they are being observed, raises ethical questions related to the invasion of privacy.

THE ETHICS OF RESEARCH

Ethics are in fact of importance to all kinds of social and behavioral research, especially when the research involves human subjects. Unfortunately, unethical practices seem to have become more common, or at least more difficult to detect, in recent years. An increasing number of research studies are conducted by large groups of researchers, making it more difficult to observe misconduct and attribute it to the appropriate person(s). Experimental replication, a traditional safeguard against unethical conduct, is more problematic given the size, cost, and complexity of many contemporary studies. The proliferation of journals has resulted in less stringent editing, and more of what is published is going unchallenged. Finally, what is ethical practice and what is not is not always clear-cut.

General Guidelines

A book by Sieber provides a reasonably comprehensive, but succinct, guide to planning ethical research. In her opening chapter, she commented that "the ethics of social research is not about etiquette; nor is it about considering the poor hapless subject at the expense of science or society. Rather, we study ethics to learn how to make social research 'work' for all concerned. The ethical researcher creates a mutually respectful, win-win relationship with the research population; this is a relationship in which subjects are pleased to participate candidly, and the community at large regards the conclusions as constructive."[113] Or as Judd, Smith, and Kidder noted, the issue of ethics often comes down to balancing the costs of questionable practices against the potential benefits of the research.[114]

Sieber's first chapter also includes a discussion of IRBs, or Institutional Review Boards (also known as Human Subjects Committees, Human Investigation Committees, and Human Subjects Review Boards). The U.S. government requires that all universities and other organizations that conduct research involving human subjects and that receive federal funding for research involving human subjects (virtually all universities granting doctoral degrees) must have an IRB. "The purpose of the IRB is to review all proposals for human research *before* the research is conducted to ascertain whether the research plan has adequately included the ethical dimensions of the project."[115] They are to help ensure that no harm will come to human subjects, that they are informed of and consent to the protocol of the research study, and that their confidentiality or anonymity will be provided. Miller's textbook on research design includes facsimiles of the IRB documents used by the University of Kansas.[116] Those documents address submission criteria, application forms, audio and video recording of subjects, payment to subjects, subject selection considerations, implied consent, inclusion of research instruments, deception of subjects, the review process, and so on. Readers wishing to know more about IRBs may wish to consult *The IRB Reference Book* (2001), edited by Russell-Einhorn and Puglisi.

Many professional associations have guidelines for ethical research. Miller and Salkind's book provides a reprint of the *Code of Ethics* published by the American Sociological Association. That code covers issues such as professional competence; integrity; respect for people's rights, dignity, and diversity; social responsibility; ethical standards; harassment; conflicts of interest; disclosure of financial support and relevant relationships; confidentiality; and the publication process.[117]

The other chapters in the book by Sieber cover the research protocol (proposal), general ethical principles, voluntary informed consent and debriefing (interaction with subjects immediately following their participation in the research), privacy, confidentiality, deception, elements of risk, benefits, research on children and adolescents, and community-based research on vulnerable urban populations and AIDS. Sieber's appendix includes sample consent and assent forms for use with older children.[118]

A number of other standard textbooks on research methods in the social and behavioral sciences devote space to ethics in research. Judd, Smith, and Kidder, for
example, give considerable attention to the ethical implications of research.[119]
Johanson stated, "It is impossible for any research to avoid ethics. They are inextri-
cably entwined."[120] He then proceeds to take a rather philosophical approach to
ethics in research in discussing social ideals and research and principles and ethical
codes, but he also addresses some of the more pragmatic concerns such as ethics
committees and the publishing of research results. Johanson provides several useful
examples or case studies relating to the links among practice, ethics, and research.
Chapter 7 of this book discusses ethics in the context of qualitative research.

Schutt deals with ethical issues in experimental research and in survey research separately. As he noted, "social science experiments often involve subject
deception [in order to increase the validity of the study]. Primarily because of
this feature, some experiments have prompted contentious debates about research
ethics."[121] He then discusses the issue of deception in more detail and next considers the question of how much subjects may be harmed by the way benefits are
distributed as part of a field experiment.

In his section on ethics in survey research, Schutt points out that if a "questionnaire includes questions about attitudes or behaviors that are socially stigmatized
or generally considered to be private or questions about actions that are illegal,
the researcher must proceed carefully and ensure that respondents' rights are protected."[122] He notes that many surveys employ questions that might prove damaging to the subjects if their answers were disclosed, and in such cases it is critical
to preserve subject confidentiality, if not anonymity. Schutt pointed out that the
cover letter included with a mailed questionnaire or the opening statement for an
interview should clearly explain the nature and purposes of the survey and inform respondents that their participation is voluntary.[123] The cover letter or opening statement should also disclose the researcher's affiliation and the project's
sponsors and identify any possible harm or benefits for subjects.

A book by Kimmel focuses on ethics in *applied* social research. Kimmel covers
many of the same topics treated by other textbooks, but there is a particularly useful chapter on special problems in applied settings. One section of that chapter
discusses some of the ethical issues in organizational research, which often deals
with issues such as personnel evaluation, program evaluation, and the implementation of interventions designed to improve employee performance and relations.
Such activities are quite susceptible to ethical abuse. He also addresses some of
the unanticipated consequences of prevention research. For example, a preventive
intervention designed to increase worker productivity might cause psychological
harm. Kimmel concludes the chapter with a consideration of ethical issues that
may arise after the research is completed related to possible consequences of
applying the results, misuse of the new knowledge, and responsibilities of the
applied social researcher.[124]

A brief consideration of ethical issues regarding the use of and reporting of the
results of statistical analysis is provided by Losee and Worley. Some of those

issues relate to the biased use and/or interpretation of statistical techniques and data. Others have to do with "the level of effort researchers should make to ensure that no errors in their research or in the writing up of their results will appear in print or in distributed electronic form."[125] Krathwohl raises two possible ethical issues related to ownership of the data: availability of the data to others for secondary analysis and apportionment of credit on publication.[126]

Guidelines for LIS Professionals

"Although LIS has imported [methodologies] from other disciplines, it has not turned its attention to 'research ethics' to the extent of the fields it borrows from."[127] However, a few books and articles have been concerned, at least in part, with ethical issues somewhat specific to LIS practitioners and researchers. Westbrook, for example, in her book on the analysis of community information needs, incorporates guidelines for ethical practices as appropriate. These guidelines stress that anonymity, or confidentiality, of everyone involved must be maintained; that library services should never appear to depend on patron participation in the study; and no harm should come to any subject.[128] She reminds the reader that, upon completion of the study, all confidential data should be destroyed, including interview transcripts, lists of subject names, and observation notes and that both electronic and paper files should be weeded as much as possible. Westbrook also stresses the importance of emphasizing ethical practices when training staff to conduct information needs analyses.

In his article on the ethical considerations of information professionals, Froehlich discusses the ethical issues that can arise when decisions are being made about who should publish research results and take the credit. Other issues related to the publication process can include plagiarism, falsification or fabrication of data, dual submissions of manuscripts to journals, and duplicate publication of identical or largely identical manuscripts without permission from the editors.[129] Losee and Worley, in their book about research for information professionals, also provide brief, but useful, information about ethics in the dissemination of research results.[130] They, too, deal with plagiarism and the submission of results to more than one journal or conference. Chapter 9 of a book by Hauptman includes a discussion of ethical issues related to research and publication by academic librarians.[131]

Smith, in her 1994 article, focuses on the ethics of research about the uses of information provided by librarians. In other words, to what extent are librarians justified in investigating the information use activities of patrons in order to improve information services provided to them? What are the ethics of user studies? Smith noted that there is a need for guidelines for research on user needs and information use, but one concludes that such guidelines should not scare practitioners away from "the serious evaluation and research that needs to be conducted if librarians are to serve the public and to preserve the profession."[132]

Carlin, while pointing out the need for more consideration of the place of ethics in LIS research, presents several cases and debates from other disciplines so as to raise the visibility of research ethics for researchers in LIS. He also discusses the possibility of an "ethics of interdisciplinarity" and stresses the importance of being accountable for the presentation of research strategies and accurately distinguishing between primary and secondary sources.[133]

Ethics for Research on the Internet

As Case indicated, a new ethical issue has to do with the uses of the Internet for research:

> The ubiquity of information exchange on the Internet, for example, has led to discussion among researchers regarding the ethics of collecting public submissions to mailing lists, discussion boards, and Web sites. Although chat rooms and individual e-mail exchanges are considered to be "private," some researchers maintain that postings to public channels like usenet and open mailing lists are fair game for analysis and reporting. Yet the increasingly common practice of collecting electronic discussions, particularly on controversial topics, raises the issue of whether the contributors are "fully informed" that they are subjects of study. Whatever individual investigators think about the ethicality of studying public discussions, institutional review boards typically ask for evidence that research subjects are informed of possible observation and its consequences. If the investigator is taking an active role in the discussion—posing questions to the list, for example—the issue becomes even more complex.

> As computer and biomedical technology provide increased monitoring capability of overt behavior and physical responses, we can expect more challenges to the boundaries of acceptable research. Witness the increased awareness of privacy brought about by use of the Internet. Many users gradually became aware that commercial entities were not only tracking the most obvious data—their demographic background (such as they were willing to supply voluntarily) and electronic purchases—but were even recording their visits to Web sites in which transactions were *not* conducted. The pervasive use of tracking cookies and of online forms and questionnaires, coupled with the ability to aggregate and cross-reference data by individual computer user, has led to massive collections of data on electronic information seeking. That much of this has been collected without the full consent and understanding of Internet users is an example of how far things can go if ethical data collection principles are not observed.[134]

Most existing guidelines for ethical research were not developed with such information technologies in mind. Jones pointed out, for example, that issues such as public versus private information and informed consent in an electronic environment are not adequately addressed by the guidelines provided by the typical research university. He cautioned researchers to recognize the limitations of existing guidelines and to take steps to ensure that research on the Internet is just as ethical as any other research.[135]

Scientific and Research Misconduct

As Krathwohl stated, ethical standards are, in effect, a constraint on research; and they can be divided "into two aspects: (1) the legal and institutional constraints designed to protect the people from whom data are gathered and (2) the responsibility of the individual researcher for proper conduct above and beyond legalities. The former, covered by U.S. federal regulations, ensures that the researcher's institution provides adequate safeguards for the protection of human subjects in all federally funded research."[136] Hence the Institutional Review Boards discussed earlier.

In addition to IRBs, many universities have policies and procedures regarding scientific misconduct. Wayne State University, in Michigan, for example, has a four-page policy that provides necessary definitions and procedures for handling allegations of scientific misconduct, initial inquiries, formal investigations, possible resolutions, and appeals. Other mechanisms for minimizing scientific misconduct have included (1) the mentor-apprentice relationship, in which the senior researcher imparts the importance of intellectual honesty; (2) the communal review of research results via scholarly communication; (3) the replication of research results; and (4) the review of proposals before the research is conducted.[137]

In spite of the guidelines and codes of ethics for research, scientific/research misconduct can and does still occur. In fact, "the Commission on Research Integrity, which was created as part of the National Institutes of Health Revitalization Act of 1993, proposed new procedures for addressing scientific misconduct"[138] "because, beyond the high-profile cases, widespread problems in the conduct of research remain."[139] "The lay public presumes that professions are self-regulating. . . . However, the effectiveness of self-regulation in the academic profession is currently being challenged."[140]

There is at least a perception that research misconduct in library and information science is less of a problem than it is in other fields, "principally because the stakes are not terribly high in LIS, as compared with fields such as biology, physics, medicine, and the like."[141] Or as Wiberley stated, "there is less of it than in other fields that have greater funding or greater prestige. The greater the stakes, the more incentive there is to cheat."[142]

But what is scientific or research misconduct; how is it defined? According to Wayne State University's policy, "scientific misconduct includes fabrication, falsification, plagiarism, or other practices that seriously deviate from commonly accepted practices within the scientific community for proposing, conducting, or reporting research. Misconduct does not include honest error or honest differences of interpretation in judgments of data. Nor does it include the innocent failure to comply with the terms of research grants."[143] Altman noted an agreement among professional organizations, governmental agencies, and scientists "that fabrication, falsification, or plagiarism in proposing, performing, or reporting research constitute scientific misconduct."[144]

Library and information professionals desiring more information about scientific and research misconduct are encouraged to consult a book edited by Altman and Hernon.[145] Chapters in that work address such issues as misconduct and the scholarly literature, implications of misconduct for bibliographic instruction, and implications of research misconduct for libraries and librarians. Also included are appendices with references to codes of ethics from professional societies, guidelines for instructions to authors, and sources helpful in finding out about cases of research misconduct.

Another useful resource is a special issue of the *Journal of Information Ethics* (1996) devoted to research misconduct. Articles treat, among other topics, information ethics in the workplace, the lure of scientific misconduct, the influence of academic departments/disciplines on misconduct, federal actions against plagiarism, misconduct involving digital imaging, and the legal aspects of scientific misconduct. Finally, readers interested in electronic guides to research ethics can consult the bibliography on Tom Wilson's Web site: InformationR.net (see the section *Electronic Resources for Information Research Methods*); and Sharon Stoerger's *Research Ethics Webliographies*, which include resources on research ethics in general (http:/www.web-miner.com/researchethics.htm), plagiarism, and research ethics in specific subject fields.

SUMMARY

This chapter pertains to the fifth stage of the basic scientific method of inquiry—the methodology. The reader is reminded that the researcher must first decide if his or her research will be quantitative and/or qualitative in nature, applied or basic. Then a number of specific research methods are introduced. The list and discussion of various methods and their uses in LIS is not, however, exhaustive. Nor are the descriptions detailed enough to provide adequate instruction in how to use the methods. Readers wishing to employ one or more of these methods should refer to the relevant sections of this work, other standard texts on research methods, and appropriate readings listed above. The last section addresses the important issue of ethics in research.

ADDITIONAL READINGS

Adeyami, Nat M. "Library Operations Research—Purpose, Tools, Utility, and Implications for Developing Libraries." *Libri* 27 (March 1977): 22–30.
Allen, G. G. "Management and the Conduct of In-House Library Research." *Library and Information Science Research* 8 (1986): 155–62.
Baker, Sharon, and F. Wilfrid Lancaster. *The Measurement and Evaluation of Library Services.* 2d ed. Arlington VA: Information Resources Press, 1991.
Bogdan, Robert C., and Sari K. Biklen. *Qualitative Research for Education: An Introduction to Theory and Methods.* 4th ed. Boston: Allyn and Bacon, 2003.

Boyce, Bert R., Charles T. Meadows, and Donald H. Kraft. *Measurement in Information Science.* San Diego: Academic Press, 1994.

Budd, Richard, Robert K. Thorp, and Lewis Donohew. *Content Analysis of Communication.* New York: Macmillan, 1967.

Burgess, Roben G. *Field Research: A Sourcebook and Field Manual.* London: George Allen and Unwin, 1982.

Busha, Charles H., and Stephen P. Harter. *Research Methods in Librarianship: Techniques and Interpretation.* New York: Academic Press, 1980.

Chen, Ching-Chih, ed. *Quantitative Measurement and Dynamic Library Service.* Phoenix, AZ: Oryx Press, 1978.

Childers, Thomas A., and Nancy A. Van House. *What's Good? Describing Your Public Library's Effectiveness.* Chicago: American Library Association, 1993.

Covey, Denise Troll. *Usage and Usability Assessment: Library Practices and Concerns.* Washington, D.C.: Digital Library Federation and Council on Library and Information Resources, 2002.

DeProspo, Ernest R., Ellen Altman, and Kenneth Beasley. *Performance Measures for Public Libraries.* Chicago: Public Library Association, 1973.

Diodato, Virgil. *Dictionary of Bibliometrics.* New York: Haworth Press, 1994.

Dougherty, Richard M., and Fred J. Heinritz. *Scientific Management of Library Operations.* 2d ed. Metuchen, NJ: Scarecrow Press, 1982.

Dugan, Robert E., and Peter Hernon. "Outcomes Assessment: Not Synonymous with Inputs and Outputs." *Journal of Academic Librarianship* 38 (November 2002): 376–80.

Dyer, Esther R. "The Delphi Technique in Library Research." *Library Research* 1 (Spring 1979): 41–52.

Hernon, Peter, and Charles McClure. *Evaluation and Library Decision Making.* Norwood, NJ: Ablex Publishing, 1990.

Hoadley, Irene Braden, and Alice S. Clark, eds. *Quantitative Methods in Librarianship: Standards, Research, Management.* Westport, CT: Greenwood Press, 1972.

Kantor, Paul B. *Objective Performance Measures for Academic and Research Libraries.* Washington, D.C: Association of Research Libraries, 1984.

Lancaster, F. W. *If You Want to Evaluate Your Library. . .* Champaign: University of Illinois, Graduate School of Library and Information Science, 1988.

Leimkuhler, F. F. "Operations Research." In *Encyclopedia of Library and Information Science,* vol. 20. edited by Allen Kent, Harold Lancour & J.E. Daily New York: Dekker, 1977, 412–39.

"LibQUAL+ General FAQ." Available, [http://www.arl.org/libqual/geninfo/faqgen.html.]

Lofland, J., and L. H. Lofland. *Analyzing Social Settings: A Guide to Qualitative Observation and Analysis.* 3rd ed. Belmont, CA: Wadsworth Publishing, 1995.

MacKee, Monique. *A Handbook of Comparative Librarianship.* 3d ed. London: Clive Bingley, 1983.

Nicholas, David, and Maureen Ritchie. *Literature and Bibliometrics.* London: Clive Bingley, 1984.

Orr, R. H. "Measuring the Goodness of Library Services: A General Framework for Considering Quantitative Measures." *Journal of Documentation* 29 (September 1973): 315–32.

Peritz, B. C. "On the Objectives of Citation Analysis: Problems of Theory and Method." *Journal of the American Society for Information Science* 43 (July 1992): 448–51.

Powell, Ronald R. "Impact Assessment of University Libraries." In *Encyclopedia of Library and Information Science,* edited by Allen Kent, vol. 55. New York: Marcel Dekker, 1994, 151–64.

Ravichandra Rao, I. K. *Quantitative Methods for Library and Information Science.* New York: John Wiley and Sons, 1983. (See the chapter on bibliometrics.)

Reilly, Kevin D. "The Delphi Technique: Fundamentals and Applications." In *Targets for Research in Library Education,* edited by Harold Borko. Chicago, American Library Association, 1973.

Simpson, I. S. *Basic Statistics for Librarians.* 3d ed. London: Library Association, 1988. (See the chapter on bibliometrics.)

Simsova, Sylva. *A Primer of Comparative Librarianship.* London: Clive Bingley, 1982.

Strauss, A. *Qualitative Analysis for Social Scientists.* New York: Cambridge University Press, 1987.

Suchman, Edward A. *Evaluative Research.* New York: Russell Sage Foundation, 1967.

Swisher, Robert, and Charles R. McClure. *Research for Decision Making: Methods for Librarians.* Chicago: American Library Association, 1984.

Taylor, Steven J., and Robert Bogdan. *Introduction to Qualitative Research Methods: A Guidebook and Resource.* 3d ed. New York: John Wiley & Sons, 1998.

Van House, N., B. Weil, and C. McClure. *Measuring Academic Library Performance: A Practical Approach.* Chicago: American Library Association, 1990.

Van House, Nancy A., and others. *Output Measures for Public Libraries.* 2d ed. Chicago: American Library Association, 1987.

Weiss, Carol H. *Evaluation Research.* Englewood Cliffs, NJ: Prentice-Hall, 1972.

Wilson, Concepcion S. "Informetrics." In *Annual Review of Information Science and Technology,* edited by Martha E. Williams, vol. 34. Medford, NJ: American Society for Information Science, 1999.

Zweizig, Douglas L. "Measuring Library Use." *Drexel Library Quarterly* 13 (July 1977): 3–15.

Zweizig, Douglas, and Eleanor Jo Rodger. *Output Measures for Public Libraries: A Manual of Standardized Procedures.* Chicago: American Library Association, 1982.

Zweizig, Douglas, Debra Wilcox Johnson, and Jane Robbins with Michele Besant. *The Tell It! Manual: The Complete Program for Evaluating Library Performance.* Chicago: American Library Association, 1996.

NOTES

[1] Charles H. Davis and James E. Rush, *Guide to Information Science* (Westport, CT: Greenwood Press, 1980): 101–39.

[2] Charles H. Davis, "Information Science and Libraries: A Note on the Contribution of Information Science to Librarianship," in *The Bookmark 51* (Chapel Hill: University Library and the Friends of the Library, University of North Carolina, 1982): 96.

[3] Judson D. Sheridan, "Perspectives from 202 Jesse Hall; The Research Continuum," *Graduate School and Research Note* 14 (February 1988): 1.

[4] Charles R. McClure, "Increasing the Usefulness of Research for Library Managers: Propositions, Issues, and Strategies," *Library Trends* 38 (Fall 1989): 282.

[5] Tom Wilson, "Electronic Resources for Research Methods; Research Methods; Action Research" [http://informationr.net/rm/RMeth6.html], Accessed December 12, 2002.

[6] Anna H. Perrault and Ron Blazek, "Transforming Library Services Through Action Research," *Florida Libraries* 40, no. 3 (1997): 60.

[7] Stephen Isaac and William B. Michael, *Handbook in Research and Evaluation*, 3d ed. (San Diego: EdITS Publishers, 1995): 59.

[8] Ibid., 59.

[9] John Carlo Bertot, Charles R. McClure and Joe Ryan, *Statistics and Performance Measures for Public Library Networked Services* (Chicago: American Library Association, 2001).

[10] Susan R. Jurow, "Tools for Measuring and Improving Performance," in *Integrating Total Quality Management in a Library Setting*, edited by S. Jurow and S. B. Bernard (New York: Haworth, 1993): 120.

[11] Thomas M. Peischl, "Benchmarking: A Process for Improvement," *Library Administration & Management* 9 (Spring 1995): 100.

[12] Nicolle O. Steffen, Keith Curry Lance, and Rochelle Logan, "Time to Tell the Who Story: Outcome-Based Evaluation and the Counting on Results Project," *Public Libraries* 41 (July-August 2002): 222–8.

[13] Keith Curry Lance, "What Research Tells Us About the Importance of School Libraries," *Knowledge Quest* 31 Supplement (September-October 2002): 17–22.

[14] Peter Hernon and Ellen Altman, *Assessing Service Quality: Satisfying the Expectations of Library Customers* (Chicago: American Library Association, 1998).

[15] Peter Hernon and John R. Whitman, *Delivering Satisfaction and Service Quality: A Customer-Based Approach for Librarians* (Chicago: American Library Association, 2001).

[16]Peter Hernon and Robert E. Dugan, *An Action Plan for Outcomes Assessment in Your Library* (Chicago: American Library Association, 2002).

[17]Peter Hernon and Ellen Altman, *Service Quality in Academic Libraries* (Norwood, NJ: Ablex Publishing Corporation, 1996): xv.

[18]Julia C. Bixrud, "The Association of Research Libraries Statistics and Measurement Program: From Descriptive Data to Performance Measures," (ED459726) 2001:1.

[19]David N. King, "Evaluation and Its Uses," in *Evaluating Bibliographic Instruction: A Handbook* (Chicago: ACRL, 1983): 16–7.

[20]Peter Liebscher, "Quantity with Quality? Teaching Quantitative and Qualitative Methods in an LIS Master's Program," *Library Trends* 46, no. 4 (1998): 669.

[21]Constance A. Mellon, "Library Anxiety: A Grounded Theory and Its Development," *College & Research Libraries* 47 (March 1986): 160.

[22]G. E. Gorman and Peter Clayton, *Qualitative Research for the Information Professional: A Practical Handbook*, with contributions from Mary Lynn Rice-Lively and Lyn Gorman (London: Library Association Publishing, 1997).

[23]Robert J. Grover and Jack Glazier, "Implications for Application of Qualitative Methods to Library and Information Science Research," *Library and Information Science Research* 7 (July 1985): 247–60.

[24]Louise H. Kidder and Charles M. Judd, *Research Methods in Social Relations*, 5th ed. (New York: Holt, Rinehart and Winston, 1986): 519.

[25]L. R. Gay, *Educational Research: Competencies for Analysis and Application*, 2d ed. (Columbus, OH: Charles E. Merrill, 1981): 431.

[26]Isaac and Michael, *Handbook in Research and Evaluation*, 48.

[27]Gay, *Educational Research*, 432.

[28]Edward T. O'Neill, "Operations Research," *Library Trends* 32 (Spring 1984): 512.

[29]Donald H. Kraft and Bert R. Boyce, *Operations Research for Libraries and Information Agencies: Techniques for the Evaluation of Management Decision Alternatives* (San Diego: Academic Press, 1991): 12.

[30]Raya Fidel, "The Case Study Method: A Case Study," *Library and Information Science Research* 6 (July 1984): 274.

[31]Ibid., 273.

[32]Robert K. Yin, *Case Study Research: Design and Methods* (Beverly Hills, CA: Sage, 1984).

[33]Robert K. Yin, *Case Study Research: Design and Methods*, rev. ed. (Newbury Park, CA: Sage, 1989): 23.

[34]Paul D. Leedy and Jeanne E. Ormrod, *Practical Research: Planning and Design*, 7th ed. (Upper Saddle River, NJ: Merrill Prentice Hall, 2001): 114.

[35]Michael I. Harrison, *Diagnosing Organizations* (Newbury Park, CA: Sage, 1987).

[36]Yin, *Case Study Research*, rev. ed.

[37]Paul D. Leedy, *Practical Research: Planning and Design*, 4th ed. (New York: Macmillan, 1989).

[38]Yin, *Case Study Research*, rev. ed., 53.

[39]Lynn Silipigni Connaway, "The Levels of Decisions and Involvement in Decision-Making: Effectiveness and Job Satisfaction in Academic Library Technical Services" (doctoral dissertation, University of Wisconsin-Madison, 1992).

[40]Marion Paris, "Thoughts on the Case Study," *Journal of Education for Library and Information Science* 29 (Fall 1988): 138.

[41]Ibid.

[42]R. M. Hayes, *Use of the Delphi Technique in Policy Formulation: A Case Study of the "Public Sector/Private Sector" Task Force* (Los Angeles: University of California, Graduate School of Library and Information Science, 1982): 1.

[43]Robert M. Losee, Jr., and Karen A. Worley, *Research and Evaluation for Information Professionals* (San Diego: Academic Press, 1993): 158.

[44]Delbert C. Miller and Neil J. Salkind, *Handbook of Research Design & Social Measurement*, 6th ed. (Thousand Oaks, CA: Sage, 2002).

[45]Heartsill Young, ed., *The ALA Glossary of Library and Information Science* (Chicago: American Library Association, 1983): 57.

[46]Jacqueline Kracker and Wang Peiling, "Research Anxiety and Student's Perceptions of Research: An Experiment. Part II. Content Analysis of Their Writings on Two Experiences Using Kuhlthau's Information Search Process at a Large Southeastern University," *Journal of the American Society for Information Science and Technology* 53 (February 2002): 295–307.

[47]Barbara Kopelock Ferrante, "Bibliometrics: Access in Library Literature," *Collection Management* 2 (Fall 1987): 201.

[48]Linus Ikpaahindi, "An Overview of Bibliometrics: Its Measurements, Laws, and Their Implications," *Libri* 35 (June 1985): 163.

[49]Emilie C. White, "Bibliometrics: From Curiosity to Convention," *Special Libraries* 76 (Winter 1985): 35.

[50]Danny P. Wallace, "Bibliometrics and Citation Analysis," in *Principles and Applications of Information Science for Library Professionals*, John N. Olsgaard, editor (Chicago: American Library Association, 1989): 10–26.

[51]Farideh Osareh, "Bibliometrics, Citation Analysis and Co-Citation Analysis: A Review of Literature I," *Libri* 46 (1996): 149–58.

[52]John Martyn and F. Wilfrid Lancaster, *Investigative Methods in Library and Information Science: An Introduction* (Arlington, VA: Information Resources Press, 1981): 52.

[53]White, "Bibliometrics," 35–42.

[54]Linda C. Smith, "Citation Analysis," *Library Trends* 30 (Summer 1981): 85.

[55]White, "Bibliometrics," 39.

[56]Ibid.

[57]Sara von Ungern-Sternberg, "Teaching Bibliometrics," *Journal of Education for Library and Information Science* 39, no. 1 (1989): 76–80.

[58]Wallace, "Bibliometrics and Citation Analysis."

[59]Osareh, "Bibliometrics," 149–58.

[60]Judit Bar-Ilan and Bluma C. Peritz, "Informetric Theories and Methods for Exploring the Internet: An Analytical Survey of Recent Research Literature," *Library Trends* 50 (Winter 2002): 371.

[61]John Carlo Bertot, Charles R. McClure, William E. Moen, and Jeffrey Rubin, "Web Usage Statistics: Measurement Issues and Analytical Techniques," *Government Information Quarterly* 14, no. 4 (1997): 373–95.

[62]Dorothy G. Collings, "Comparative Librarianship," in *Encyclopedia of Library and Information Science*, vol. 5 (New York: Marcel Dekker, 1971): 492.

[63]Chih Wang, "A Brief Introduction to Comparative Librarianship," *International Library Review* 17 (1985): 109.

[64]J. P. Danton, *The Dimensions of Comparative Librarianship* (Chicago: American Library Association, 1973).

[65]Ronald R. Powell, "Research Competence for Ph.D. Students in Library and Information Science," *Journal of Education for Library and Information Science* 36 (Fall 1995): 327.

[66]Allan B. Cox and Fred Gifford, "An Overview to Geographic Information Systems," *Journal of Academic Librarianship* 23, no. 6 (1997): 449.

[67]Ibid., 454.

[68]John R. Ottensmann, "Using Geographic Information Systems to Analyze Library Utilization," *Library Quarterly* 67 (1997): 373–95.

[69]Thomas A. Peters, *The Online Catalog: A Critical Examination of Public Use* (Jefferson, NC: McFarland, 1991): 151.

[70]Susan Wiedenbeck, Robin Lampert, and Jean Scholtz, "Using Protocol Analysis to Study the User Interface," *Bulletin of the American Society for Information Science* 15 (1989): 25–26.

[71]Denise Troll Covey, *Usage and Usability Assessment: Library Practices and Concerns* (Washington, D.C.: Digital Library Federation and Council on Library and Information Resources, 2002): 25.

[72]Ibid.

[73]Thomas Peters, "Using Transaction Log Analysis for Library Management Information," *Library Administration & Management* 10 (Winter, 1996): 20–25.

[74]Julie Banks, "Are Transaction Logs Useful? A Ten-Year Study," *Journal of Southern Academic and Special Librarianship* 1, no. 3 (February 2000). URL= http://www.icaap.org/iuicode?62.01.03.04

[75]Julie Banks, "Can Transaction Logs Be Used for Resource Scheduling? An Analysis," *Reference Librarian* 63 (Special Report, 1999): 95–108.

[76]Neal K. Kaske, "Studies of Online Catalogs," in *Online Catalogs/Online Reference*, edited by Brian Aveney and Brett Butler (Chicago: American Library Association, 1984).

[77]Joseph R. Matthews, Gary S. Lawrence, and Douglas K. Ferguson, *Using Online Catalogs: A Nationwide Survey, A Report of a Study Sponsored by the Council on Library Resources* (New York: Neal-Schuman, 1983).

[78]David J. Norden and Gail Herndon Lawrence, "Public Terminal Use in an Online Catalog: Some Preliminary Results," *College & Research Libraries* 42 (1981): 308–16.

[79]John E. Tolle, *Current Utilization of Online Catalogs: A Transaction Log Analysis*, vol. 1 (Dublin, OH: OCLC Office of Research, 1983).

[80]Jean Dickson, "An Analysis of User Errors in Searching an Online Catalog," *Cataloging & Classification Quarterly* 4, no. 3 (1984): 19–38.

[81]Brian Nielsen, "What They Say They Do and What They Do: Assessing Online Catalog Use Instruction Through Transaction Log Monitoring," *Information Technology and Libraries* 5 (1986): 28–33.

[82]Thomas Peters, "When Smart People Fail: An Analysis of the Transaction Logs of an Online Public Catalog," *Journal of Academic Librarianship* 15 (1989): 267–73.

[83]Rhonda N. Hunter, "Successes and Failures of Patrons Searching the Online Catalog at a Large Academic Library: A Transaction Log Analysis," *RQ* 30 (1991): 395–402.

[84]Steven D. Zink, "Monitoring User Search Success Through Transaction Log Analysis: The Wolf-PAC Example," *Reference Services Review* 19, no. 1 (1991): 49–56.

[85]Sally W. Kalin, "The Searching Behavior of Remote Users: A Study of One Online Public Access Catalog (OPAC)," in proceedings of the *54th Annual Meeting of the American Society for Information Science* (1991): 175–85.

[86]Janet L. Nelson, "An Analysis of Transaction Logs to Evaluate the Educational Needs of End Users," *Medical Reference Services Quarterly* 11, no. 4 (1992): 11–21.

[87]Joan M. Cherry, "Improving Subject Access in OPACs: An Exploratory Study of Conversion of Users' Queries," *Journal of Academic Librarianship* 18 (1992): 95–99.

[88]Patricia M. Wallace, "How Do Patrons Search the Online Catalog When No One's Looking? Transaction Log Analysis and Implications for Bibliographic Instruction and System Design," *RQ* 33 (1993): 239–352.

[89]Thomas A. Lucas, "Time Patterns in Remote OPAC Use," *College & Research Libraries* 54 (1993): 439–45.

[90]Larry Millsap and Terry Ellen Ferl, "Research Patterns of Remote Users: An Analysis of OPAC Transaction Logs," *Information Technology and Libraries* 12 (1993): 321–43.

[91]Kalin, "The Searching Behavior of Remote Users," 175–85.

[92]Lucas, "Time Patterns in Remote OPAC Use," 439–45.

[93]Millsap and Ferl, "Research Patterns of Remote Users," 321–43.

[94]Anne C. Ciliberti, Marie L. Radford, and Gary P. Radford, "Empty Handed? A Material Availability Study and Transaction Log Analysis Verification," *Journal of Academic Librarianship* 24 (July 1998): 282–99.

[95]Theresa Mudrock, "Revising Ready Reference Sites: Listening to Users Through Server Statistics and Query Logs," *Reference and User Services Quarterly* 42 (Winter 2002): 155–63.

[96]Charles W. Simpson, "OPAC Transaction Log Analysis: The First Decade," in *Advances in Library Automation and Networking*, edited by Joe Hewitt (Greenwich, CT: JAI Press, 1989): 35–67.

[97]Tolle, *Current Utilization of Online Catalogs.*

[98]Nielsen, "What They Say They Do and What They Do," 28–33.

[99]Millsap and Ferl, "Rearch Patterns of Remote Users," 321–43.

[100]Lynn Silipigni Connaway, John M. Budd, and Thomas R. Kochtanek, "An Investigation of the Use of an Online Catalog: User Characteristics and Transaction Log Analysis," *Library Resources and Technical Services* 39, no. 2 (April 1995): 142–52.

[101]Ibid.

[102]L. Keily, "Improving Resource Discovery on the Internet: The User Perspective," in *Proceedings of the 21st International Online Information Meeting* (Oxford: Learned Information, 1997): 205–12.

[103]Haidar Moukdad and Andrew Large, "Users' Perceptions of the Web as Revealed by Transaction Log Analysis," *Online Information Review* 25, no. 6 (2001): 349–59.

[104]C. Silverstein, M. Henzinger, H. Marais, and M. Moricz, "Analysis of a Very Large Web Search Engine Query Log," *SIGIR Forum* 33, no. 1 (1999): 6–12.

[105]T. Smith, A. Ruocco, and Bernard Jansen, "Digital Video in Education," in Proceedings of the *30th ACM SIGCSE Technical Symposium on Computer Science Education* (New Orleans, LA: 1998): 122–36.

[106]Jack L. Xu, "Internet Search Engines: Real World IR Issues and Challenges," Presentation to CIKM99 (Kansas City, MO: 1999).

[107]B. J. Jansen, Amanda Spink, and Tefko Saracevic, "Real life, Real Users, and Real Needs: A Study and Analysis of User Queries on the Web," *Information Processing and Management* 36 (2000): 207–77. URL=http://informationr.net/ir/6-11paper90.html

[108]Amanda Spink and Jack L. Xu, "Selected Results from a Large Study of Web Searching: The Excite Study," *Information Research* 6, no.1 (2000).

[109]Amanda Spink, Dietmar Wolfram, B. J. Jansen, and Tefko Saracevic, "Searching the Web: The Public and Their Queries," *Journal of the American Society for Information Science and Technology* 52, no. 3 (2001): 226–34.

[110]Bernard J. Jansen and Udo Pooch, "A Review of Web Searching Studies and a Framework for Future Research," *Journal of the American Society for Information Science* 52, no. 3 (2001): 235–46.

[111]Covey, *Usage and Usability Assessment*, v.

[112]Neal K. Kaske, "Research Methodologies and Transaction Log Analysis: Issues, Questions, and a Proposed Model," *Library Hi Tech* 11 (1993): 79–86.

[113]Joan Sieber, *Planning Ethically Responsible Research: A Guide for Students and Internal Review Boards* (Newbury Park, CA: Sage, 1992): 5.

[114]Charles M. Judd, Eliot R. Smith, and Louise H. Kidder, *Research Methods in Social Relations*, 6th ed. (Fort Worth, TX: Harcourt Brace Jovanovich, 1991).

[115]Sieber, *Planning Ethically Responsible Research*, 5.

[116]Miller and Salkind, *Handbook of Research Design*.

[117]Ibid., 100–17.

[118]Sieber, *Planning Ethically Responsible Research*.

[119]Judd, Smith, and Kidder, *Research Methods in Social Relations*.

[120]Graeme Johanson, "Ethics in Research," in *Research Methods for Students, Academics and Professionals: Information Management and System*, 2d ed., edited by Kirsty Williamson (Wagga Wagga, Australia: Charles Sturt University, Centre for Information Studies, 2002): 67.

[121]Russell K. Schutt, *Investigating the Social World: The Process and Practice of Research*, 2d ed. (Thousand Oaks, CA: Pine Forge Press, 1999): 218.

[122]Ibid., 269.

[123]Ibid., 270.

[124]Allan J. Kimmel, "Ethics and Values in Applied Social Research," in *Applied Social Research Methods*, vol. 12 (Newbury Park, CA.: Sage, 1988).

[125]Losee and Worley, *Research and Evaluation for Information Professionals*, 200.

[126]David R. Krathwohl, *Methods of Educational & Social Science Research: An Integrated Approach*, 2d ed. (New York: Longman, 1998): 217.

[127]Andrew P. Carlin, "Disciplinary Debates and Bases of Interdisciplinary Studies: The Place of Research Ethics in Library and Information Science," *Library & Information Science Research* 25 (2003): 3.

[128]Lynn Westbrook, *Identifying and Analyzing User Needs* (New York: Neal-Schuman Publishers, 2001): 47.

[129]Thomas J. Froehlich, "Ethical Considerations of Information Professionals," in *Annual Review of Information Science and Technology*, edited by Martha E. Williams, vol. 27 (Medford, NJ: American Society for Information Science, 1992): 309.

[130]Losee and Worley, *Research and Evaluation for Information Professionals*.

[131]Robert Hauptman, *Ethics and Librarianship* (Jefferson, NC: McFarland, 2002).

[132]Martha M. Smith, "Survival and Service: The Ethics of Research on the Uses of Information Provided by Librarians," *North Carolina Libraries* 65 (1994): 64–67.

[133]Carlin, "Disciplinary Debates and Bases of Interdisciplinary Studies," 14.

[134]Donald O. Case, *Looking for Information: A Survey of Research on Information Seeking, Needs, and Behavior* (London: Academic Press, 2002): 173–74.

[135]Robert A. Jones, "The Ethics of Research in Cyberspace," *Internet Research: Electronic Networking Applications and Policy* 4 (1994): 30–35.

[136]Krathwohl, *Methods of Educational & Social Science Research*, 204.

[137]*Wayne State University Policy and Procedures Regarding Scientific Misconduct*, Executive Order 89–4 (Detroit, MI: Wayne State University, 1989).

[138]Mary Burke, et al. "Editorial: Fraud and Misconduct in Library and Information Science Research," *Library & Information Science Research* 18 (1996): 199.

[139]Kenneth J. Ryan, "Scientific Misconduct in Perspective: The Need to Improve Accountability," *Chronicle of Higher Education* B1 (1996).

[140]John M. Braxton and Alan E. Bayer, "Perceptions of Research Misconduct and an Analysis of Their Correlates," *Journal of Higher Education* 65 (1994): 351.

[141]Burke, "Fraud and Misconduct," 200.

[142]Ibid.

[143]*Wayne State University Policy and Procedures*, 1.

[144]Ellen Altman and Peter Hernon, eds., *Research Misconduct: Issues, Implications, and Strategies* (Greenwich, CT: Ablex Publishing, 1997): 2.

[145]Ibid.

Chapter 4

Survey Research and Sampling

The survey is a group of research methods commonly used to determine the present status of a given phenomenon. The basic assumption of most survey research is that, by carefully following certain scientific procedures, one can make inferences about a large group of elements by studying a relatively small number selected from the larger group. For example, if one wanted to learn the opinions of all academic librarians in the United States regarding information literacy, one could study a sample of several hundred librarians and use their responses as the basis for estimating the opinion of all academic librarians in the United States. For a discussion of sampling in-library use, see the section written by Mundt after the Nonsampling Error section of this chapter.

SURVEY RESEARCH

The word *survey* literally means to look at or to see over or beyond or, in other words, to observe. *Observations* made during the course of a survey are not limited to those of the physical type, however, and techniques commonly used for collecting survey data will be considered later.

As was just indicated, a key strength of survey research is that, if properly done, it allows one to generalize from a smaller group to a larger group from which the subgroup has been selected. The subgroup is referred to as the *sample*, and techniques for drawing samples will be treated in considerable detail later. The larger group is known as the *population;* it must be clearly defined, specifically delimited, and carefully chosen.

The observations or measurements made during survey research, or any other kind of research, generate *data* or information. These data are particularly susceptible to *bias* introduced as a result of the research design (and at other stages in the research process), so that problem will be considered here and other places throughout this work.

MAJOR DIFFERENCES BETWEEN SURVEY RESEARCH AND OTHER METHODS

As has been noted, survey research has characteristics common to most other research methods, but at the same time, it exhibits certain important differences. For example, survey research is used to gather contemporary data, while historical research is, of course, primarily concerned with past data. Some argue that historical research, at least at present, is less bound to the scientific method of inquiry.

In contrast to experimental research, survey research does not enable the researcher to manipulate the independent variable, provides less control of the research environment, and therefore is not considered capable of definitely establishing causal relationships. In other words, survey research is considered to be less rigorous than experimental research.

On the other hand, survey research is better suited than experimental research to studying a large number of, and geographically dispersed, cases. Also, survey research is generally considered to be more appropriate for studying personal factors and for exploratory analysis of relationships.

TYPES OF SURVEY STUDIES

In selecting a research method, and a type of survey research in particular, the researcher must keep in mind the research problem, the sources of the desired information, the nature of the data to be collected, and the major purpose of the research. For example, if the purpose of the study is to formulate a problem for a more precise investigation or to develop more formal hypotheses, then a formative or exploratory type of survey may well be in order.

Exploratory Surveys

An exploratory survey, often conducted as qualitative research, can increase the researcher's familiarity with the phenomenon in question, it can help to clarify concepts, it can be used to establish priorities for future research, it can identify new problems, and last, but not least, exploratory survey research can be used to gather information with practical applications, although such results cannot always be anticipated. Specific kinds of exploratory research surveys include

1. *Literature surveys.* Literature surveys or reviews are in some respects exploratory in nature in that they often focus on developing hypotheses, based on previous research, that may suggest further research. Literature surveys may stand alone, but more often they are, of course, a part of a larger study. In the latter case, they are considered to be supportive of the research that follows rather than research studies themselves.
2. *Experience surveys.* Experience surveys, as the name suggests, are surveys that gather and synthesize the experiences of specialists and/or practitioners in a particular field. They too are exploratory in that their aim is to obtain "insight into the relationships between variables rather than to get an accurate picture of current practices or a simple consensus as to best practices."[1] The researcher's primary interest is in gaining provocative ideas and useful insights (i.e., suggestions for future research, rather than specific statistics). Experience surveys, as well as suggesting hypotheses, can provide information on the feasibility of doing other research. For example, they can provide information on where the facilities for research can be obtained, which factors can and cannot be controlled, how readily available the necessary data are, and so on. Experience surveys also may help to establish priorities for research in the area and to summarize the knowledge of practitioners regarding the effectiveness of various methods and procedures, or best practices in a particular field.
3. *Analysis of "insight-stimulating" examples.* Where there is little experience to serve as a guide, researchers have found the intensive study of selected examples to be a useful method of stimulating insights and suggesting hypotheses for future research. This method differs from the case study approach in that it tends to be more intensive and narrow in scope. The types of examples or cases likely to be of most value depend on the problem under study, but, in general, cases that provide sharp contrasts or have striking features tend to be the most useful.

Speaking of exploratory surveys in general, it is important to remember that exploratory studies merely suggest insights or hypotheses; they cannot test them. By selecting examples that have special characteristics, one no longer has cases that are typical, but has a biased sample instead. In addition, exploratory studies do not provide enough control of extraneous variables, nor should they, to permit the testing of a specific relationship. "An exploratory study must always be regarded as simply a first step; more carefully controlled studies are needed to test whether the hypotheses that emerge have general applicability."[2]

Analytical and Descriptive Surveys

A second general type of survey, but one that is seldom labeled as such in the literature, is the analytical survey. Leedy describes the analytical survey method as "appropriate for data that are quantitative in nature and that need statistical assistance to extract their meaning."[3] In practice, however, most researchers seem to consider an analytical survey essentially as a kind of descriptive survey, and they do not distinguish between the two. In fact, descriptive surveys are the most common type of survey, and many researchers use "survey research methods" and "descriptive surveys" synonymously.

Other Types of Surveys

In a workbook developed for an ACRL workshop, Golden listed nine different types of surveys, some of which could no doubt be subsumed under the broader types of surveys just discussed. These nine types are:

1. Cross-sectional study—a typical survey, such as a Gallup poll, designed to measure one or more phenomena across a sample representative of the population or whole.
2. Trend study—a survey conducted over a period of time so as to measure trends, patterns, or changes.
3. Cohort study—a survey conducted in order to collect data from the same population more than once. The same people are not surveyed, but the subjects are selected from the same population.
4. Panel study—a survey designed to collect data from the same sample of subjects often over time. In fact, the trend study and the panel study may be treated as *longitudinal* studies.
5. Approximation of a longitudinal study—an attempt to simulate a true longitudinal study by asking people to recall past behavior and activities.
6. Parallel samples study—a survey of separate samples regarding the same research problem. For example, a study of university library use might necessitate surveying both students and faculty.
7. Contextual study—a survey of a person's environment, conducted so as to learn more about the person. For example, a study of a person's information use might benefit from a consideration of the information resources available to that person.
8. Sociometric study—a comprehensive survey of more than one group, including the interrelationships among the groups. For example, a thorough study

of children's literature might well entail surveying authors, critics, publishers, librarians, parents, and children.

9. Critical incident study—an in-depth examination of a specific event or activity rather than a broad survey of many occurrences; similar to the "analysis of insight-stimulating examples" described above. [4]

Persons wishing to know more about these specific types of studies should consult some of the standard texts on survey research.

BASIC PURPOSES OF DESCRIPTIVE SURVEYS

The basic purposes of descriptive surveys usually are to describe characteristics of the population of interest, estimate proportions in the population, make specific predictions, and test associational relationships. (They can be used to *explore* causal relationships.) Looking first at describing the population, it should be kept in mind that a description of characteristics of the population is often based on a description of the characteristics of a (hopefully) representative sample—hence the importance of the sampling technique.

Having identified characteristics of the population, it then becomes important to estimate (if using a sample) their proportions in the population. Without such data, one can say little about the significance of the traits. For example, it may be interesting to learn that some academic librarians hold subject master's degrees, but little can be done to interpret the possible impact of this phenomenon without knowing what percentage of all academic librarians hold subject master's degrees.

Information regarding characteristics or proportions is also necessary in order to make predictions about specific relationships. In the course of the study just alluded to, one may find that a high percentage of libraries with an acquisitions budget of a certain size employs librarians with subject master's degrees. On the basis of such data, the researcher may be prepared to predict that, in most cases, libraries having an acquisitions budget over a certain amount will indeed have librarians with subject master's degrees.

In fact, the researcher may wish to go a step farther and "test" the relationship between budget size and librarians' credentials. The testing of a relationship between two or more variables will be described in greater detail later, but it should be noted that some tests are more rigorous than others. The consensus is that descriptive survey research can consider but not test causal relationships, and that it can test associational relationships. In other words, by using a survey, the researcher may find that libraries with large acquisitions budgets do tend to have more librarians with subject master's degrees, but such a study legitimately could conclude only that there seemed to be a correlation between budget size and librarians' credentials, not that budget size caused librarians with subject master's degrees to be hired. There are other factors or variables, such as degree of departmentalization, faculty role in book selection, and so on, that could have had as much or more influence than budget size on the criteria for hiring certain librarians. As the survey research study could not control these other variables, it could not test a causal relationship. (As was discussed earlier, the relationship must make sense conceptually as well, regardless of the methodology or technique used.)

Yet descriptive survey research, while usually less rigorous than experimental research, is stronger than exploratory research for testing relationships between variables. In gaining rigorousness, however, it tends to lose flexibility. In short, it tends to provide a compromise method for studying specific phenomena.

BASIC STEPS OF SURVEY RESEARCH: AN OVERVIEW

Formulating Objectives

As is true of any research, in selecting the method (and in designing the techniques to be employed) one must consider the objectives of the study, or how the data will be used. In turn, the objectives should be based on the problem to be investigated or the questions to be answered. The important concern here is that the method selected be precise enough to ensure that the data collected will be relevant to the question or problem under study.

Selecting Data Collection Techniques

Having selected the method (e.g., survey, historical, experimental), the next basic step is to select or design the specific technique or techniques to be used to collect the necessary data. Such techniques as observation, interviews, and questionnaires often are used, but if no suitable technique already exists, then a new one must be devised.

This stage is a critical point at which safeguards against bias and unreliability should be introduced. As Leedy notes, "data in descriptive survey research are particularly susceptible to distortion through the introduction of a bias into the research design. Particular attention should be given, therefore, to safeguard the data from the influence of bias."[5] Leedy and Ormrod define bias as "any influence, condition, or set of conditions that singly or together distort the data."[6] Bias can creep into a study at several points, including during sampling and data collection activities. Bias is difficult, if not impossible, to avoid completely, but at the very least it should be minimized. When bias does appear to exist, the researcher should acknowledge its presence and indicate how it affects the results of the study. Examples of such occurrences will be given later when these topics are discussed.

It is important to pretest the data collection tool at this time. This step will be covered in the section on questionnaires, but the desirability of pretesting applies to all data collection techniques.

Selecting the Sample

Another activity to be treated at some length later is the selection of the sample, a necessary step for all surveys based on portions of a population. It is worth reemphasizing at this time, however, that findings based on a sample should provide a reasonably accurate representation of the state of affairs in the total group, and consequently considerable attention must be given to the sampling technique.

Also, it is worth noting that, in deciding how representative of the total group the sample is, the researcher should consider both statistical and practical differences between the sample and total group. For example, in comparing libraries of a sample with their total group on collection size, one may find that a difference of a few thousand volumes in collection size indicates a significant statistical difference. If one were looking at small, or possibly even medium-sized libraries, this statistical difference might be noteworthy. But if one were studying large university library collections of two million volumes or more, a difference of a few thousand volumes would probably have no real significance, regardless of what the statistics indicated. In other words, the average size of the sample library collections might differ from the average collection size of the population being sampled, but one could still have a reasonably accurate or representative sample for most purposes.

Collecting the Data

Having selected an appropriate data collection tool and the sample to which it will be applied, the next basic step is to collect the data. If one is conducting a relatively large survey, there is a good chance that it will be necessary to employ one or more field workers—persons charged with actually gathering the data. It goes without saying that such field workers should be well trained in the techniques of data collection and should be familiar with the specific tool being used in the researcher's study.

Throughout the survey, the collectors should be supervised closely, and checks should be established to help ensure that they are accurate and that their data are unbiased. As soon as possible after collection, the data should be checked for completeness, comprehensibility, consistency, and reliability. This step is often referred to as "cleaning" the data, and a thorough cleaning of possibly "dirty" data can avoid numerous problems in subsequent statistical analysis. Cleaning the data can involve everything from simply reading the results, looking for surprising responses and unexpected patterns, to verifying or checking the coding of the data.

Analyzing and Interpreting the Results

The process of analyzing the data gathered basically involves coding the responses, or placing each item in the appropriate category (more on this later); tabulating the data; and performing appropriate statistical computations. It is advisable to improve the economy of the study by planning these steps well in advance and in considerable detail. As was indicated earlier, it is also important to provide safeguards against error. This can be accomplished, in part, by checking the reliability of the coders and by checking the accuracy of the tabulations and statistical analysis.

Looking ahead to the interpretation phase, it is useful to be systematic in describing the treatment of the data. The researcher should state clearly and specifically what data are needed to resolve the problem, where they are located, and how they were obtained. The researcher also should describe fully the different steps that will be taken to interpret the data. In addition, he or she should try to ensure that the statistics calculated have a rational base (i.e., explain why they were chosen; their limitations, if any; and how they will be used). Finally, the researcher should distinguish between the mere presentation of the data and the interpretation of the data. The former is basically descriptive in nature; the latter involves analysis and explanation.

Survey Research Designs

The most straightforward type of survey research is descriptive, and it is designed to ensure that the sample is reasonably representative of the population to which the researcher wishes to generalize, and that the relevant characteristics have been accurately measured.

Where more than mere description and simple tabulations are desired, for example in an analytical survey, it may be necessary to develop a more sophisticated design. A common design for survey research, and one that facilitates the analysis of relationships, is known as the "static-group comparison." It is quite similar to a so-called preexperimental design and can be diagrammed as follows:

$$\frac{X \quad O}{O}$$

With more than one level of X, the design becomes

$$\frac{X_1 \quad O_1}{X_2 \quad O_2}$$

This design depicts two groups, as indicated by the two lines or rows, with two levels of X. The "independent" variable, X, could represent age, and X_1 retired adults and X_2 middle-aged adults. The "dependent" variable, O, could represent library use, with O_1 representing library use for the retired adults and O_2 representing library use for the middle-aged adults. In other words, the Os represent observations or measurements of the dependent variable—library use.

The line between the two groups means that they are naturally occurring groups, or that X is a naturally occurring condition, in this case, age. This is in contrast to the manipulated independent variables to be discussed in the section on experimental research.

In analyzing the results of a survey employing the latter example of a static-group comparison design, the researcher would compare the O scores of the comparison groups to determine whether there is a relationship between X and O. In other words, does one age group seem to use the library more than the other?

The difficulty in interpreting the results of a static-group comparison is that there is a real possibility that other differences between the two groups may also be affecting library use. For example, retired adults may have more leisure time than middle-aged adults and therefore may be more inclined to use libraries. Or, had the middle-aged adults been found to be heavier library users, it might have been due to the fact that they tended to have higher incomes and that something about higher income encourages library use.

As has been stated, the best that survey research can demonstrate is correlational or associational relationships, and correlation does not demonstrate causation. On the other hand, correlation is necessary for causation, so evidence of a strong correlation between two variables would strengthen the case for causation.

A second relatively common example of a survey research design is known as the "panel design." The panel design is a slightly stronger design than the static-group comparison because it takes into account the time sequence and changes over time by collecting data on the Xs and Os at two or more times. The panel design is diagrammed as follows:

$$\frac{X_{1_1}\, X_{1_2}\, X_{1_3}\, O \dots X_{1_2}\, X_{1_3}\, O \dots X_{1_2}\, O}{X_{2_1}\, X_{2_2}\, X_{2_3}\, O \dots X_{2_2}\, X_{2_3}\, O \dots X_{2_2}\, O}$$

The first of the two subscripts on the Xs indicates the level of the "independent" variable, for example, for gender—male and female. The second subscript represents the variable identification. For example, X_{1_1} could represent males with a certain level of income, X_{1_2} males with a certain educational background. The Os represent the "dependent" variable or, in this example, frequency of library use. The line continues to indicate naturally occurring groups. The fact that the Xs and Os occur more than once in each group indicates that the data are collected and observations are made more than once for at least some of the variables.

In analyzing the results of survey research employing this design, the researcher may conclude that females, in conjunction with certain levels of income, education, and age, are more likely to use libraries than males with comparable values on those variables. But the researcher should draw such conclusions cautiously, as the time intervals may not be adequate to allow the Xs to effect changes in library use and, once again, there may be other important group differences affecting library use that have not been taken into account. Such designs do, however, help the researcher better to understand and analyze relationships between variables and to generalize from natural processes that have occurred. While they cannot establish causation, they can help to build a case for it.

Survey research has been applied in library-related research for a variety of purposes. It has been proven to be particularly useful for use and user studies, state-of-the-art surveys, and library performance evaluations. Busha and Harter review in some detail a selection of projects that were based on survey methods and that they consider to be successful.[7] Library surveys are indexed in *Library Literature*. A book by Fink and Kosecoff provides a useful step-by-step guide to conducting surveys in any discipline.[8]

Survey Research Costs

Survey research tends to be relatively inexpensive, at least if the sample or population being surveyed is not large, but it is still often desirable to reduce the costs. Recommended guidelines for reducing survey costs include the following:

1. Shorten the length of data collection
2. Reduce the number of follow-ups
3. Limit pilot or pretesting to a small number of participants
4. Shorten time spent developing data collection instruments by adapting already existing instruments
5. Make the instrument as short as possible
6. Use nonmonetary incentives to encourage respondents
7. Minimize staff costs
8. Shop around for least expensive supplies and equipment
9. Reduce the number of survey activities
10. Minimize the amount of time each activity takes.[9]

SAMPLING

As was indicated earlier, sampling is often one of the most crucial steps in survey research. In fact, rigorous sampling methods have been developed and used primarily within the context of survey research. However, "the basic logic and many of the specific techniques of sampling are equally applicable to other research methods such as content analysis, experimentation, and even field research."[10]

Basic Terms and Concepts

Before considering some standard techniques of sampling, it is important to have an understanding of the following basic terms and concepts related to sampling.

1. Universe—the theoretical aggregation of all units or elements that apply to a particular survey. For example, if one were surveying librarians, the study

universe would include all librarians, regardless of type, location, and so on. Universe is not frequently used today, is often used synonymously with "population," and is essentially a useless term.

2. Population—the total of all cases that conform to a prespecified criterion or set of criteria. It is more specific or better defined than a universe and is in effect a designated part of a universe. For example, American academic librarians would be part of the universe of librarians and could represent the population for a survey study. The population is the aggregation of units to which one wishes to generalize the results of a research study.

Selection of the population must precede the selection of the sample, assuming a sample is to be drawn, and is crucial to the success of the sampling stage. Selection of the population must be done carefully with regard to the selection criteria, desired size, and the parameters of the survey population. It is also important to consider costs, in terms of time and money, when selecting a population. If the population is too large or expensive to manage, then the study is handicapped from the start. Obviously, the members of the population must be readily accessible to the researcher; otherwise, it will be difficult, if not impossible, to collect the necessary data.

3. Population stratum—a subdivision of a population based on one or more specifications or characteristics. A stratum of the population of U.S. academic librarians could be U.S. academic librarians of libraries with a collection of at least one million volumes or with a budget of a certain size.

4. Element—an individual member or unit of a population. Each academic librarian would be an element of the population of academic librarians. The total number of elements of a population is usually designated by N.

5. Census—a count or survey of all the elements of a population, and the determination of the distribution of their characteristics. A complete census is usually not possible, or at least is impractical and unnecessary, so typically a sample of the population rather than the entire population is surveyed

6. Sample—a selection of units from the total population to be studied. It is usually drawn because it is less costly and time consuming to survey than is the population, or it may be impossible to survey the population. However, one can never be absolutely certain how representative a sample is of its population, unless a census is also made, which would obviate using the sample. The concept of representativeness is crucial to sampling and will be treated in greater depth later.

7. Case—an individual member of the sample. The total number of cases in a sample is usually designated by lower-case n.

8. Sampling frame—the actual list of units from which the sample, or some part of the sample, is selected. It is often used interchangeably with "population list." One problem with e-mail surveys is the acquiring of e-mail address lists, but the Web has made it possible to select samples without having to know respondents' e-mail addresses.[11]

TYPES OF SAMPLING METHODS

It is useful to distinguish between two basic types of sampling methods—probability sampling and nonprobability sampling. Probability sampling is the more scientific and useful of the two methods, and the bulk of this section will be devoted to that technique. Nonprobability sampling will be considered first.

Nonprobability Sampling

With a nonprobability sample, the researcher cannot state the probability of a specific element of the population being included in the sample. In fact, one cannot be assured that a specific element has any probability of being included in the sample. Therefore, nonprobability samples suffer from important weaknesses. When selection probabilities are unknown, one cannot make legitimate use of statistical inference. That is, a nonprobability sample does not permit generalizing from the sample to the population because the researcher has no assurance that the sample is representative of the population. Nor can the researcher, relying on a nonprobability sample, evaluate the risks of error involved in making inferences about the sample.

On the other hand, nonprobability samples are usually easier and cheaper to obtain than are probability samples, and for some purposes, such as where the focus is on the sample itself, may be quite adequate. "Samples of several" are commonly used for pretests. In some cases nonprobability samples may be the only feasible samples. There are measures one can take to try to improve the representativeness of nonprobability samples; these techniques will be referred to when discussing some of the different kinds of nonprobability samples that follow.

Accidental Sample. In utilizing an accidental sampling technique, the researcher simply selects the cases that are at hand until the sample reaches a desired, designated size. If one wished to conduct an academic library user study, one might elect to survey library patrons as they entered or exited the library, on a "first-come, first-served" basis. There would be little or no preferential selection of respondents.

Obviously, there would be relatively little if any assurance that the sample was reasonably representative of the library's users. One could not assume that the accidental sample was not atypical. The researcher might query users during some other time period and end up with quite different responses. Accidental sampling is seldom adequate for any kind of survey. Synonyms include convenience and availability samples.

Quota Sample. A type of nonprobability sample that improves somewhat on the simple accidental sample is the quota sample. Quota sampling is the same as accidental sampling except that it takes steps to ensure that the significant, diverse elements of the population are included. The quota sample method also attempts to ensure that the different elements are included in the sample in the proportions in which they occur in the population.

Returning to the researcher who wishes to survey the users of an academic library, he or she, in selecting a quota sample, would take measures to ensure that the sample includes the same percentages of faculty, graduate students, and so on as exist in the entire academic community. Or the researcher may choose to sample the same number of persons representing each element of the population, and then to assign them a weight according to their portion of the total population. The latter technique obviously requires knowledge of the proportions of the population according to each element.

Among the problems inherent in quota sampling is the difficulty in determining that the proportions for each element are accurate. Second, biases may exist in the selection of cases representing the various elements, even though their proportion of the population might have been accurately estimated. For example, the researcher sampling academic library users may survey the correct proportions of seniors, graduate students, and so on, but for whatever reason may tend to query those inclined to be more competent library users. If one were investigating library skills, such a bias would be damaging to the validity of the study.

Yet quota samples, while they should be used cautiously, are useful for exploratory studies, as are other nonprobability sampling techniques. Quota sampling is often used for public opinion surveys.

Snowball Sample.   Some refer to this type of sampling as accidental sampling. It is an appropriate method to use when members of the population are difficult to identify and locate, such as migrants and homeless individuals. The researcher contacts members of the population who can be identified and located and then asks these individuals to provide information to identify and locate other members of the population to participate in the research. This type of sampling is cumulative, hence the name, snowball sampling.[12] This type of nonprobability sampling is used in exploratory research since the technique can result in "samples with questionable representativeness."[13] It is commonly used in qualitative research and is described in Chapter 7 of this book.

Purposive Sample.   At times, it may seem preferable to select a sample based entirely on one's knowledge of the population and the objectives of the research. In designing a survey of the directors of large university libraries that are in the process of developing electronic reference services, one may decide that the easiest way of obtaining a sample of such libraries would be to select libraries known to the researcher to be engaged in such activities.

The researcher would be making the assumption that such a sample would be reasonably typical of all university libraries involved in developing electronic reference services. Unfortunately, such an assumption may not be justified. There is no assurance that a purposive sample is actually representative of the total population. Any sampling method not utilizing random selection is overly susceptible to bias.

Self-Selected Sample. As the label suggests, a self-selected sample is a group of cases, usually people, who have essentially selected themselves for inclusion in a study. A researcher might, for example, publish a notice in a professional journal asking individuals to volunteer to submit certain information or to participate in some other way. Again, there would be a strong possibility that these volunteers would not be representative of the entire population to which they belong.

Incomplete Sample. An incomplete sample, while not originally intended to be a nonprobability sample, in effect becomes one. For example, if a large percentage of the cases selected do not respond or participate in a study, then assurance that the sample is representative of the population is quite possibly lost, even though the sample may have been selected randomly. Another example of an incomplete sample is one drawn from an incomplete population list. Again, the sample may have been drawn randomly, but as the faulty list was in effect biased or not fully representative of the population, the sample must be considered unrepresentative and in effect a nonprobability sample.

Probability Sampling

As was indicated earlier, the primary purpose of sampling is to select elements that accurately represent the total population from which the elements were drawn. Probability sampling enhances the likelihood of accomplishing this objective and also provides methods for estimating the degree of probable success; that is, it incorporates probability theory, which provides the basis for estimating population parameters and error.[14] The crucial requirement of probability sampling is that every element in the population has a known probability of being included in the sample. A discussion of major types of probability sampling follows.

Simple Random Sample (SRS). Simple random sampling is the basic sampling method of survey research. The technique of simple random sampling gives each element in the population an equal chance of being included in the sample. It also makes the selection of every possible combination of elements equally likely. In other words, if one had a population or sampling frame of 500 elements, in drawing a simple random sample of that population one should be as likely to include elements 1 and 3 as 2 and 4, or 1 and 2, and so on.

In order for the probabilities of including each element and each combination of elements to be equal, it is necessary that there be independence from one draw to the next. This means that the selection of an element should have no effect on the chances of remaining elements' being selected. But this condition cannot be met fully unless the sampling is done with replacement. In sampling with replacement, the researcher would place every element back in the population list after being selected for the sample so that it is again available for selection. If replacement is not done, then the remaining elements would not have the same likelihood of being drawn as did the elements already selected. The remaining population would decrease in number as elements were selected, and the elements still in the population would have an increasingly greater chance of being selected. Similarly, the likelihood of every combination's being selected would not remain constant, because, as some elements were removed from the population and not replaced, certain combinations would no longer be possible.

However, if the elements selected for the sample are subsequently put back in the population list (after making note that they are now a part of the sample), then there is the possibility that some of them may be selected for the sample again. This obviously presents practical problems, so sampling with replacement is not often done. This normally does not invalidate the sample, however, as the sample usually represents a relatively small percentage of the population, and the chances of any element's being selected two or more times is slight. But if the sample is as much as one-fifth the size of the population, technically one should introduce correction factors if possible. However, samples drawn without re-placement do tend to be more representative.

There are mathematical formulas that can be used to correct for sampling without replacement, but if the sample represents a relatively small proportion of the population, use of a formula is unnecessary. In addition, exact correction fac-tors are seldom known. Yet, if correction does seem to be warranted, using such formulas is generally preferable to sampling with replacement and taking a chance of drawing some elements more than once. Those readers interested in correction formulas should refer to a standard text on sampling.

Selecting the Simple Random Sample.   There are several techniques available for selecting a simple random sample. Traditional methods include the roulette wheel or lottery type approach. Such methods have been criticized as being at least potentially biased, or not fully random, however, because of physical or lo-gistical imperfections. For example, if one were drawing ping pong balls from a large bowl or revolving drum, there is the possibility that the balls might not have been adequately mixed to begin with and that those placed in the container early, or late, have a greater chance of being selected. Consequently, it is advisable to consider other, more reliable techniques.

One recommended method commonly used for drawing a simple random sam-ple involves the use of a table of random numbers. A well-known example is the Rand Corporation's *A Million Random Digits* (see Table 4.1 for an illustrative page). A table of random numbers is simply that—a listing of randomly arranged numbers. The basic steps involved in using such a table are as follows:

1. The first step would be to number sequentially the elements of the popula-tion. Let us assume that we have a population of elements numbered from 1 to 500. (Obviously, each element now has a unique number.)

TABLE 4.1
Random Numbers[a]

---

10 09 73 25 33	76 52 01 35 86	34 67 35 48 76	80 95 90 91 17	39 29 27 49 45
37 54 20 48 05	64 89 47 42 96	24 80 52 40 37	20 63 61 04 02	00 82 29 16 65
08 42 26 89 53	19 64 50 93 03	23 20 90 25 60	15 95 33 47 64	35 08 03 36 06
99 01 90 25 29	09 37 67 07 15	38 31 13 11 65	88 67 67 43 97	04 43 62 76 59
12 80 79 99 70	80 15 73 61 47	64 03 23 66 53	98 95 11 68 77	12 17 17 68 33
66 06 57 47 17	34 07 27 68 50	36 69 73 61 70	65 81 33 98 85	11 19 92 91 70
31 06 01 08 05	45 57 18 24 06	35 30 34 26 14	86 79 90 74 39	23 40 30 97 32
85 26 97 76 02	02 05 16 56 92	68 66 57 48 18	73 05 38 52 47	18 62 38 85 79
63 57 33 21 35	05 32 54 70 48	90 55 35 75 48	28 46 82 87 09	83 49 15 56 24
73 79 64 57 53	03 52 96 47 78	35 80 83 42 82	60 93 52 03 44	35 27 38 84 35
98 52 01 77 67	14 90 56 86 07	22 10 94 05 58	60 97 09 34 33	50 50 07 39 98
11 80 50 54 31	39 80 82 77 32	50 72 56 82 49	29 40 52 41 01	52 77 56 78 51
83 45 29 96 34	06 28 89 80 83	13 74 67 00 78	18 47 54 06 10	68 71 17 78 17
88 68 54 02 00	86 50 75 84 01	36 76 66 79 51	90 36 47 64 93	29 60 91 10 62
99 59 46 73 48	87 51 76 49 69	91 82 60 89 28	93 78 56 13 68	23 47 83 41 13
65 48 11 76 74	17 46 85 09 50	58 04 77 69 74	73 03 95 71 86	40 21 81 65 44
80 12 43 56 35	17 72 70 80 15	43 31 82 23 74	21 11 57 82 53	14 38 55 37 63
74 35 09 98 17	77 40 27 72 14	43 23 60 02 10	45 52 16 42 37	96 28 60 26 55
69 91 62 68 03	66 25 22 91 48	36 93 68 72 03	76 62 11 39 90	94 40 05 64 18
09 89 32 05 05	14 22 56 85 14	46 42 72 67 88	96 29 77 88 22	54 38 21 45 98
91 49 91 45 23	68 47 92 76 86	46 16 28 35 54	94 75 08 99 23	37 08 92 00 48
80 33 69 45 98	26 94 03 68 58	70 29 73 41 35	53 14 03 33 40	42 05 08 23 41
44 10 48 19 49	85 15 74 79 54	32 97 92 65 75	57 60 04 08 81	22 22 20 64 13
12 55 07 37 42	11 10 00 20 40	12 86 07 46 97	96 64 48 94 39	28 70 72 58 15
63 60 64 93 29	16 50 53 44 84	40 21 95 25 63	43 65 17 70 82	07 20 73 17 90
61 19 69 04 46	26 45 74 77 74	51 92 43 37 29	65 39 45 95 93	42 58 26 05 27
15 47 44 52 66	95 27 07 99 53	59 36 78 38 48	82 39 61 01 18	33 21 15 94 66
94 55 72 85 73	67 89 75 43 87	54 62 24 44 31	91 19 04 25 92	92 92 74 59 73
42 48 11 62 13	97 34 40 87 21	16 86 84 87 67	03 07 11 20 59	25 70 14 66 70
23 52 37 83 17	73 20 88 98 37	68 93 59 14 16	26 25 22 96 63	05 52 28 25 62
04 49 35 24 94	75 24 63 38 24	45 86 25 10 25	61 96 27 93 35	65 33 71 24 72
00 54 99 76 54	64 05 18 81 59	96 11 96 38 96	54 69 28 23 91	23 28 72 95 29
35 96 31 53 07	26 89 80 93 54	33 35 13 54 62	77 97 45 00 24	90 10 33 93 33
59 80 80 83 91	45 42 72 68 42	83 60 94 97 00	13 02 12 48 92	78 56 52 01 06
46 05 88 52 36	01 39 09 22 86	77 28 14 40 77	93 91 08 36 47	70 61 74 29 41
32 17 90 05 97	87 37 92 52 41	05 56 70 70 07	86 74 31 71 57	85 39 41 18 38
69 23 46 14 06	20 11 74 52 04	15 95 66 00 00	18 74 39 24 23	97 11 89 63 38
19 56 54 14 30	01 75 87 53 79	40 41 92 15 85	66 67 43 68 06	84 96 28 52 07
45 15 51 49 38	19 47 60 72 46	43 66 79 45 43	59 04 79 00 33	20 82 66 95 41
94 86 43 19 94	36 16 81 08 51	34 88 88 15 53	01 54 03 54 56	05 01 45 11 76

---

[a]*Source*: The RAND Corporation. *A Million Random Digits* (Glencoe, Il.: Free Press, 1955).

2. The next step is to determine how many of the elements are to be selected for the sample. Techniques for determining a desirable sample size will be discussed later, so for now let us assume that we have decided on a sample of 50.
3. As there are three-digit numbers in the population, it will be necessary to select three-digit numbers from the table in order to give every element a chance of being selected.
4. The next step is to choose the starting point in the table and the pattern for moving through the table. Pure chance must determine the starting point. A simple way of selecting the starting point is to close one's eyes and place a pencil point on the table. The number under or nearest the pencil point then becomes the starting point.
5. For ease of illustration, let us assume that the pencil came down at the head of the fifth column of the table. As we must select three-digit numbers, we could then consider, along with the seven, the next two digits, and 732 becomes the first number to be considered for our sample. (It would be possible to move down the column from seven and consider 722 as the first three-digit number.) Regarding the pattern of movement, we could proceed from there across to the right, or left, down, or diagonally through the table. All that matters is that we be consistent.
6. As stated, we will first consider 732 for our sample. But as it is larger than any number in our population (the largest is 500), we will have to reject or ignore it and move to the next number. Assuming we have decided to move down the three-digit column to the bottom and then back up to the top of the next three-digit column, the next number to be considered would be 204. The number 204 does fall within the population, so the element represented by 204 would be included in the sample. This process would continue until 50 elements had been selected. If sampling without replacement, we would skip numbers that have already been included in the sample.

If the population list or sampling frame is in an electronic file, a random sample can be selected by a computer. In effect, the computer numbers the elements in the population, generates its own series of random numbers, and prints the list of elements selected. Computer generation of samples is particularly useful when drawing very large samples or working with large populations.

Systematic Sample. A method of selecting a random sample that is considered by most to be as reliable and accurate as simple random sampling is systematic sampling. This technique involves taking every n^{th} element from a list until the total list has been sampled. For example, the researcher may have a population list of 1,000 elements and decide to select every tenth element for the sample. This would be a sampling interval of 10, and would result in a sampling ratio of 1:10 and a sample of 100. The list should be considered to be circular in that the researcher would select every nth name, beginning with a randomly chosen starting point and ending with the first name of the interval immediately preceding the starting point.

Systematic sampling is easier and faster than simple random sampling for long lists. If one wished to draw a random sample from a telephone directory, for example, it would be considerably faster to take every n^{th} name than to use a table of random numbers.

However, with systematic sampling not every combination of elements has an equal chance of being drawn. So, if the list is not randomly arranged, such as is the case with an alphabetical listing, the sample would not be random. (For some variables or problems, however, an alphabetical arrangement would have no relevance and could be treated as a randomly arranged list.) For example, ranked lists such as lists of personnel, and hierarchically arranged, or cyclical lists, such as lists of houses, can easily produce biased samples. To elaborate on the first example, if one were selecting every 10th individual from an organization's personnel list arranged by department and rank within the department, and if the departments had approximately the same number of employees, then the sample might tend to include people of the same rank. If these individuals tended to have certain characteristics in common, then the sample would be biased. In short, systematic sampling is generally as satisfactory as simple random sampling, but only if the population list exhibits no trends or patterns.

Stratified Random Sample. In selecting a stratified random sample, one must first divide all of the population elements into groups or categories and then draw independent random samples from each group or stratum. This technique represents a modification of simple and systematic random sampling in that it reduces the number of cases needed to achieve a given degree of accuracy or representativeness. The strata should be defined in such a way that each element appears in only one stratum. Different sampling methods may be used for different strata. For example, a simple random sample may be drawn from one stratum and a systematic sample from another.

There are two basic types of stratified random samples—proportional and disproportional. In drawing a proportional stratified sample, one would draw the same percentage from each stratum. If there were 1,000 elements in a population, divided into ten strata of 100 each, and if one desired a total sample of 100, then ten elements, or 10%, would be drawn from each stratum. (It is more likely, however, that the strata would not all have the same number of elements. In that case, the same percentage would still be taken from each stratum, but the resulting numbers would vary.)

If a researcher were to stratify all public libraries in a state according to budget size, it is probable that there would be different numbers of libraries in each group. But if the groups were roughly equal in their number of libraries, and if the categories tended to be internally homogeneous, then it would be reasonable to select the same percentage of libraries from each stratum or to use a constant sampling rate. Doing so would produce a *proportional stratified sample* with libraries of certain budget sizes being included in the sample in the same proportions in which they occur in the population.

On the other hand, if there were considerable variations within individual strata, or if some strata were so small as to be in danger of barely being represented in the total sample, if at all, the researcher would be well advised to draw a *disproportional stratified sample*, sometimes referred to as optimum allocation. In doing so, one would draw approximately the same number of elements from each stratum regardless of its size. In order to do so, it would be necessary to use different sampling fractions or to select different percentages of cases from the strata. Consequently, some cases would represent a greater percentage of the sample than of the population. "Optimum precision is attained if sampling fractions in the different strata are made proportional to the standard deviations in the strata."[15]

This method would provide enough cases per category to allow meaningful comparisons among categories. As is true for proportional stratified sampling, it would help to assure a more representative total sample than might be expected with simple or systematic random sampling. Unlike proportional sampling, it could do so even when the groups are lacking in internal homogeneity. Disproportional stratified random sampling also can be used to take a relatively large sample from the stratum from which it is cheapest to gather data. In an interview survey of libraries, for example, this may be the group of libraries closest to the researcher. However, the increase in precision over proportional stratified sampling tends to be small, and optimizing the sample for group comparisons means the sample is no longer optimal for estimating the total population.

The choice of stratification variables typically depends on which ones are available and which ones are presumably related to the variables that one wants to represent accurately. Returning to the survey of public libraries within a state, it may well be that the researcher would decide to stratify public libraries by known budget size on the assumption that budget size would correlate with collection size—the actual variable to be studied, but yet to be determined. In other words, stratifying on budget size would help to ensure that there would be proper representation of collection sizes, and other variables, related to budget size. In general, the stratified sample would be more representative of a number of variables than would a simple random sample taken for the same purpose.

Table 4.2 presents stratification figures for a hypothetical population of 1,000 public libraries. As can be seen in the first row, 100 libraries have budgets of

TABLE 4.2
Proportional and Disproportional Stratified Sampling

Strata/Samples	Library Budget in Thousands of Dollars			
	0–100	101–250	251–500	501+
Strata	100	300	400	200 (N = 1000)
Proportional sample	10	30	40	20 (n = 100)
	10%	10%	10%	10%
Disproportional sample	25	24	24	24 (n = 97)
	25%	8%	6%	12%

$100,000 or less, 300 libraries have budgets of $101,000–$250,000, and so on. If one were to draw a proportional stratified sample using a uniform sampling ratio of 10%, then the sample would contain 10 libraries with budgets of $100,000 or less, and so on. The researcher might conclude, however, that a sample of 10 is too small to be very reliable and that comparisons of samples of such disparate size might be chancy. Therefore, he or she might decide to vary the sampling ratio across strata in order to end up with samples of about the same size (see the bottom line where sampling ratios vary from 6% to 25%). With either sampling technique, the total sample contains about 100 cases.

One statistical note—when computing estimates of means and estimating standard errors for disproportional stratified samples, one should compute values separately for each of the strata and then weight them according to the relative size of the stratum in the population. (This is not necessary for proportional stratification, as it is in effect "self-weighting.") In addition, it should be recognized that, in theory, one cannot make legitimate use of various nonparametric statistical tests, tests for the significance of correlation, analysis of covariance, and so on, without substantial modifications. Unfortunately, statistical textbooks seldom address this issue.

Cluster Sample.   In social science research, it is not unusual to encounter situations where the populations cannot be listed easily for sampling purposes. Examples include the populations of countries and states, all college students within the United States, and so on. When it is impossible or impractical to compile an exhaustive list of the elements of a total population, cluster sampling may be used effectively.

Essentially, the technique of cluster sampling involves dividing a population into clusters or groups and then drawing a sample of those clusters. In fact, the population might already be grouped into subpopulations, and cluster sampling becomes merely a matter of compiling a list of the subpopulations, or clusters, and selecting a random sample from them. For example, while a list of a city's residents may not exist, people do live on discrete blocks. Therefore, one could draw a sample of city blocks, compile lists of persons residing on those blocks, and then sample the people living on each block.

In using cluster sampling, it is desirable that each cluster's units be as heterogeneous as possible, but that characteristics of the clusters themselves be similar. This is particularly important if all members of each selected cluster are to be included in the final sample. Yet, typically, the elements constituting a given natural cluster within a population are more homogeneous than are all the elements of the total population. Therefore, relatively few elements may be needed to represent a natural cluster, while a relatively large number of clusters will be required to represent the diversity of the total population. The more heterogeneous the clusters, the fewer will be needed. "With a given total sample size, however, if the number of clusters is increased, the number of elements within a cluster must be decreased," unless the clusters are known to be especially heterogeneous.[16]

Cluster sampling may be either single-stage or multistage sampling. Single-stage cluster sampling occurs only once. In the earlier example involving the selection of city blocks, all elements or persons residing on each block would be included in a single-stage design. In a two-stage design, the simple random sampling of city blocks would be followed by a random sampling of the persons living on the blocks. Or, in a more complex design, a sampling of census tracts could be followed by a random sampling of smaller clusters of blocks, followed by a sampling of individual houses, and conclude with a sampling of persons living in those houses. A combination of probability and nonprobability sampling may be used in multistage sampling, but the researcher should keep in mind the likely loss of accuracy with nonrandom sampling.

The sampling procedure illustrated in Figure 4.1 is a combination of cluster, stratified, and simple random sampling that has been employed by the Institute for Social Research at the University of Michigan. The procedure involves the following steps:

1. The entire geographical area of the 48 contiguous states is divided into small areas called *primary sampling units* (PSU). The PSUs are usually counties, metropolitan areas, or telephone exchange areas. A stratified random sample of about 75 PSUs are selected from the total list.
2. Each PSU is stratified into large cities, smaller cities and towns, and/or rural areas. Each unit within a stratum is referred to as a *sample place*, and one or more sample places is selected from each stratum.
3. Each sample place is divided into *chunks*, which are distinct areas such as blocks. A number of chunks are randomly selected from each sample place.
4. The chunks are broken down into *segments*—areas containing from 4 to 12 dwelling units. Segments are then randomly drawn from each chunk.
5. *Dwelling units*, selected from each segment, constitute the final sample. A city directory can be used to obtain telephone numbers for the dwelling units so chosen.

As was noted earlier, cluster sampling may be the only feasible or practical design where no population list exists. It also tends to be a cheaper sampling method for large surveys. But multistage cluster sampling does sacrifice accuracy, because sampling error can occur at each stage. In a two-stage sampling design, the initial selection of clusters is subject to sampling error, and the sampling of elements within each cluster is subject to error. The researcher must decide if the greater efficiency gained from cluster sampling is worth the greater risk of sampling error, and must attempt to minimize the error by optimizing the number of clusters and elements selected. Theoretically, cluster sampling necessitates using special statistical formulas, especially when the clusters are of greatly differing sizes. Again, a text on sampling should be consulted if more information about this issue is desired.

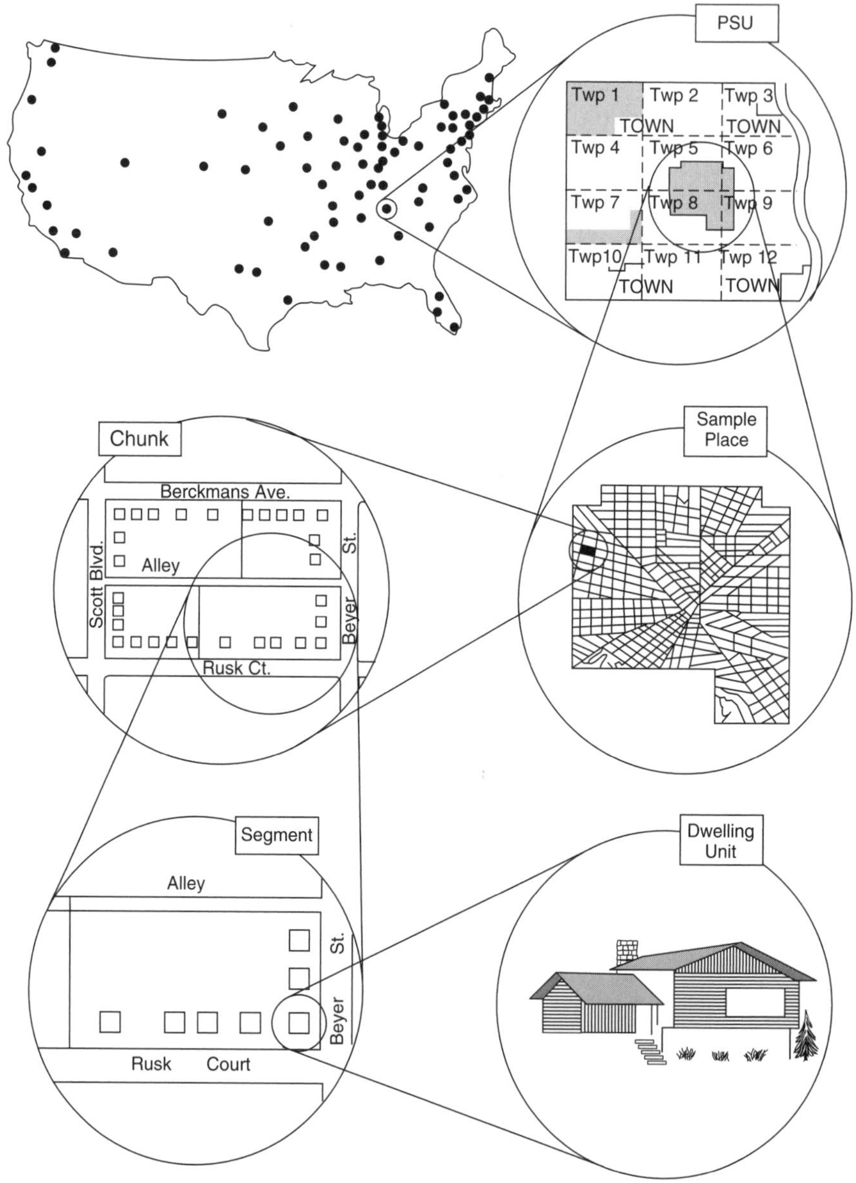

FIGURE 4.1.   Cluster Sampling Method

From Survey Research Center, *Interviewer's Manual*, rev. ed. Ann Arbor: Institute for Social Research, University of Michigan, 1976, p. 8–2.

TABLE 4.3
Population Characteristics and Appropriate Random Sampling Techniques

Population Characteristics	Example of Population Type	Appropriate Sampling Technique
A general homogeneous mass of individual units	First-year students of a private university	Simple random sampling (systematic sampling if the population list is long)
Definite strata, each as internally homogeneous as possible and of approximately the same size.	All undergraduate students of a private university; each level represents a stratum	Proportional stratified sampling
Definite strata, some of which are quite small and/or internally heterogeneous	All public libraries in a state, stratified by budget size, resulting in an upper budget category containing only a few libraries	Disproportional stratified sampling
Clusters whose group characteristics are similar, but whose elements or internal characteristics are quite heterogeneous	A population consisting of the users of the major urban public libraries in the nation; the libraries tend to be similar, but their users vary widely in characteristics	Cluster sampling

In summarizing the characteristics of some major random sampling techniques, the somewhat simplified outline presented in Table 4.3 may be helpful.

DETERMINING THE SAMPLE SIZE

The general rule of thumb for the size of the sample is, quite simply, the larger the better. Babbie states that probability samples of less than 100 are not likely to be very representative of the population.[17] Yet there is no point in utilizing a sample that is larger than necessary; doing so unnecessarily increases the time and money needed for a study. There are at least four general criteria that can help to determine the necessary sample size. The degree of precision required between the sample and the population is one. The less accuracy needed, the smaller the necessary sample. Two, the variability of the population influences the sample size needed to achieve a given level of accuracy or representativeness. In general, the greater the variability, the larger the sample needed. (Statistics commonly used to estimate the variability of a population will be noted in the chapter on data analysis.) Three, the method of sampling to be used can affect the size of the appropriate sample. As was noted in the discussion of random sampling, stratified sampling requires fewer cases to achieve a specified degree of accuracy than does simple or systematic random sampling. Four, the way in which the results are to be analyzed influences decisions on sample size. Samples that are quite small place significant limitations on the types of statistical analyses that can be employed.

Use of Formulas

Statistical formulas have been developed for calculating appropriate sample sizes. They typically take into account the confidence level, which relates to the probability of the findings, or differences between samples, being due to chance rather than representing a real difference. The confidence level is equal to 1 minus the level of significance, or 1 minus the probability of rejecting a true hypothesis. Formulas also consider the degree of accuracy with which one wishes to estimate a certain characteristic of the population and the variability of the population, usually as represented by its estimated standard deviation—a standard measure of dispersion. (The greater the spread of scores about the mean, the larger the standard deviation.)

One such formula is stated as follows:

$$n = \frac{S^2}{[S_1 E_1(\bar{x})]^2}$$

where

n = sample size
S = standard deviation of the variable or characteristic of the population (estimated)
$S_1 E_1(\bar{x})$ = standard error of the mean or sampling error.

The difficulty in using formulas is that S, the population's standard deviation, must be estimated. It is known only if the total population is analyzed, therein eliminating the need for taking a sample. In addition, if the sample represents a large proportion of the population, a finite population correction has to be included. Finally, "if more than one variable is to be studied, a sample that is adequate for one variable may be unsatisfactory for another."[18] One should consider the variability of all of the variables; the sample size tends to increase as the number of variables increases.

A proportional allocation formula, based on the assumption that a characteristic occurred 50% of the time, was used by Krejcie and Morgan to develop a table of sample sizes for given population sizes. This table is presented here (see Table 4.4) but, as was noted earlier, a variety of factors can influence desirable sample size. A table of sample sizes may represent a rather simplistic, and quite possibly conservative, method for ascertaining a sample size. Again, there is seldom much justification for using a sample that is larger than necessary.

Table 4.4 does not require any calculations. To obtain the required sample size, one need only enter the table at the given population size (e.g., 9,000) and note the adjacent sample size (368). Figure 4.2 illustrates the relationship between sample size and total population. It, as well as the table, indicates that, as the population size increases, the rate of requisite increase in sample size decreases.

TABLE 4.4
Table for Determining Sample Size from a Given Population

N	S	N	S	N	S
10	10	220	140	1200	291
15	14	230	144	1300	297
20	19	240	148	1400	302
25	24	250	152	1500	306
30	28	260	155	1600	310
35	32	270	159	1700	313
40	36	280	162	1800	317
45	40	290	165	1900	320
50	44	300	169	2000	322
55	48	320	175	2200	327
60	52	340	181	2400	331
65	56	360	186	2600	335
70	59	380	191	2800	338
75	63	400	196	3000	341
80	66	420	201	3500	346
85	70	440	205	4000	351
90	73	460	210	4500	354
95	76	480	214	5000	357
100	80	500	217	6000	361
110	86	550	228	7000	364
120	92	600	234	8000	367
130	97	650	242	9000	368
140	103	700	248	10000	370
150	108	750	254	15000	375
160	113	800	260	20000	377
170	118	850	265	30000	379
180	123	900	269	40000	380
190	127	950	274	50000	381
200	132	1000	278	75000	382
210	136	1100	285	1000000	384

Note: N is population size, S is sample size. The degree of accuracy = 0.05.

From Krejcie, Robert V., and Daryle W. Morgan, "Determining Sample Size for Research Activities," *Educational and Psychological Measurement* 30 (Autumn 1970): p. 608.

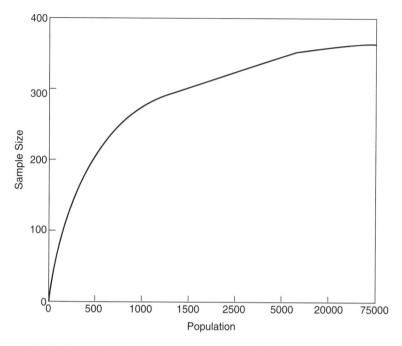

FIGURE 4.2.   Relationship Between Sample Size and Total Population

Adapted from Krejcie, Robert V., and Daryle W. Morgan, "Determining Sample Size for Research Activities," *Educational and Psychological Measurement* 30 (Autumn 1970): p. 609.

To calculate the optimal sample size when dealing with a continuous variable such as age, one could use the following formula:

$$n = \frac{z^2 s^2}{E^2}$$

where

n = sample size
z = z score for desired confidence level (see the chapter on analysis of data for a discussion of z scores)
s = standard deviation
E = allowable error.

Readers wanting to know more about determining sample size may wish to refer to works by Kraemer and Thiemann, Hernon, and Cohen.[19, 20, 21] The last work provides several tables of sample sizes as functions of the type and power (the probability that a statistical test will yield statistically significant results) of the statistical test being used.

SAMPLING ERROR

Formulas are also available for estimating the "sampling error" or, as it is often referred to, the "standard error of the mean." The standard error of the mean represents how much the average of the means of an infinite number of samples drawn from a population deviates from the actual mean of that same population. For example, if a population consisted of 50 libraries with collections averaging 500,000 volumes, one should be able to draw all possible sample combinations of 10 libraries, average the means of all the samples, and end up with 500,000 volumes as the mean of the sampling distribution. If the mean of the sampling distribution were based on a limited number of samples, it is possible that it would deviate somewhat from the actual population mean, thus indicating some sampling error.

If the population is large relative to the sample, the formula for calculating the standard error of the mean, or in fact the standard deviation of the sampling distribution of means, is as follows:

$$S_1 E_1(\bar{x}) = \frac{S}{\sqrt{n}}$$

where

S = the standard deviation of the population
n = the number of cases in the sample.

If the sample represents a relatively small proportion of the population, or if the population standard deviation is not known and must be estimated, as is usually the case, then modified versions of the formula must be used. The formula for the first situation is as follows:

$$S_1 E_1(\bar{x}) = \sqrt{\frac{S^2}{n} \cdot \frac{N-n}{N-1}}$$

where

S = the standard deviation of the population
N = the number of elements in the population
n = the number of cases in the sample.

The formula for the standard error of the mean, where the population standard deviation is not known, requires substituting an unbiased estimate (s), or the standard deviation of the sample, for the standard deviation of the population (S). "The term *unbiased estimate* refers to the fact that as one draws more and more samples from the same population and finds the mean of all these unbiased estimates, the mean of these unbiased estimates approaches the population value."[22]

The formula for the standard deviation of the sample is as follows:

$$s = \sqrt{\frac{\displaystyle\sum_{i-1}^{n(x_i - \bar{x})^2}}{n-1}}$$

where
  x_i = sample score
  $\bar{x}$ = sample mean
  n = the number of cases in the sample.

Dividing by n−1 instead of n is done in order to reduce bias or, according to some texts, to help compensate for a small sample. The value for s can then be substituted for S in the first formula given for calculating the standard error of the mean:

$$S_1 E_1 (\bar{x}) = \frac{s}{\sqrt{n}}$$

As was indicated earlier, there is a point of diminishing returns with regard to the sample size and sampling error. Starting with a sample of one person and then increasing the sample size, the accuracy of the sample will improve rapidly up to about 500 cases. Beyond 500, a relatively large increase in the number of cases is needed in order to increase significantly the accuracy of the sample. For example, if 600 cases are drawn for the sample, the amount of sampling error involved is about ±4%. To decrease this to ±3%, it would be necessary to increase the sample size to 1,067; to reduce error to ±2% requires an increase to 2,401 cases. In other words, after a certain point is reached, increasing the sample size will increase the researcher's workload without appreciably improving the accuracy of the sample. Thus, the researcher is well advised to base his or her decision regarding sample size on desired precision and confidence levels, and not to decide arbitrarily that some percentage of the population represents an optimal sample size. (See Figure 4.3 for an illustration of the relationship between sample size and error in this example.)

Again, one of the main purposes for selecting and analyzing samples is to obtain information about the population from which the sample has been drawn. "If an unbiased sample were taken from the population, it would be hoped that the sample mean would be a reasonable estimate of the population mean. Such an estimate is known as a *point estimate* but it is unlikely that the mean of a sample will be identical to the mean of the population."[23] Statisticians often content themselves with calculating *interval estimates* or the ranges within which the actual population means are likely to fall.

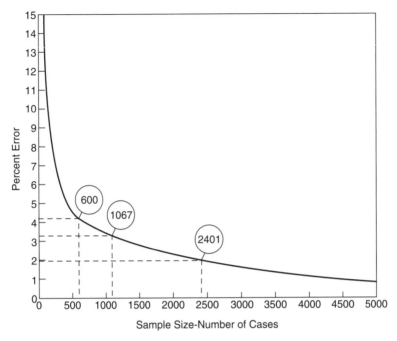

FIGURE 4.3.   Relationship Between Sample Size and Percent Error

From Benson, Dennis K., and Jonathan L. Benson, A *Benchmark Handbook: Guide to Survey Research Terms*, Columbus, OH: Academy for Contemporary Problems, 1975. p. 2.

Other Causes of Sampling Error

The size of a sample, or, more specifically, too few cases, is not the only cause of sampling error. A variety of factors can contribute to a sample's being less representative of its population than is satisfactory. If not guarded against, bias of one sort or another can easily contaminate a research study. Bias is particularly a problem with nonrandom samples, as there is less of a safeguard against personal attitudes, preferences, and so on affecting the researcher's selection of cases. For example, if a researcher were selecting library users for an interview on library services, he or she might be inclined, if even unconsciously, to slight persons who appeared to be unskilled library users or were slovenly dressed.

Even utilizing probability or random sampling techniques, the unwary researcher can end up with a biased or inaccurate sample. Bookstein, in a *Library Quarterly* article, discussed several faulty selection procedures that can result in inadequate samples.[24] The first of these he referred to as "faulty use of random-number tables." This problem includes any techniques used by the researcher resulting in each element in the list not having an equal chance of being included.

The second general category of faulty selection procedures is labeled by Bookstein as "frame problems." In this case, he is referring to problems related to faulty listing of the population. For instance, if one desired to draw a random sample of a library's holdings, and did so by selecting a random sample of catalog records, a certain amount of bias would be unavoidable. This is so because there is not a one-to-one correspondence between books and catalog records, and the more records representing a title in the catalog, the greater the probability that that book will be selected. Books tending to be represented by a large number of catalog records probably tend to have certain characteristics in common, hence a biased sample.

The third general category of "bad" sampling discussed by Bookstein is referred to as "unintentional modification of population." This category represents more subtle problems than does "frame problems," and it is even more difficult to deal with. Bookstein includes an illustration of this type of problem in which he considers how one might attempt to randomly sample a library's holdings without using a list or catalog. In one simple example, he points out that if one sampled the collection by randomly sampling locations on the shelves, fat books would have a greater chance of being selected than would thin books. In another example, if a researcher were attempting to survey catalog use by randomly selecting times and then randomly selecting users during those times, this technique would be biased toward users tending to spend more time using the catalog. Users of subject headings, for example, might be more likely than some others to be included in the sample.

As Bookstein notes in his conclusions, some of these problems can be corrected by such methods as using weighted averages to compensate for biased sampling techniques. Regardless, it is important for the researcher to be careful to avoid faulty selection techniques. It is critical that random samples be drawn correctly if one is to have "some insurance against the impact of extraneous factors that can distort our results, but whose existence we may not be aware of at the time the sample is taken."[25]

NONSAMPLING ERROR

The information gathered from a sample can be inaccurate not only as a result of the inaccuracy or the lack of representativeness of the sample but also errors of measurement. For example, in responding to a questionnaire or interview, persons may lie about their age or report figures inaccurately for a variety of reasons. Nonsampling error is difficult to estimate but, generally, as sample size goes up, so does nonsampling error. Another way of stating this relationship is that as sampling error decreases, nonsampling error tends to increase. Since sampling error generally decreases as sample size increases, one is faced with some conflict between sampling and nonsampling error. Some sort of balance is usually desirable, and the largest sample size possible is not necessarily the best.

SAMPLING IN-LIBRARY USE
by Sebastian Mundt

Whenever a full count or census is practically impossible, too time-consuming or costly and/or too monotonous, libraries traditionally applied sampling procedures to study specifics of the collection and to revise their card catalogues.[1] More recent applications focus on sampling for user surveys and on collecting data for performance indicators.[2]

In general, sampling has been used to reduce complexity by selecting and analysing a subset of the population in question. It can be "selective" as regards

- time (e.g. reporting period)
- location (e.g. branches or service points)
- objects of library use (e.g. collection)
- subjects of library use (e.g. users).

Literature on sampling in libraries regularly provides thorough information and guidance on estimating *percentages;* examples mostly focus on user surveys. Statistics of library use, however, usually aim at *total numbers.* Selecting over time is the most widely applied form of sampling totals and will be the focus of this section. Other perspectives of "selecting" a sample have been described in the literature: Cullen and Gray have sampled branches and service points of a public library system;[3] Fussler and Simon,[4] Line and Sandison[5] and Baker and Lancaster[6] have gone into detail about the methodology and issues of sampling collections. For the basics of sampling, especially for random and non-random sampling methods, sampling and measurement error and the calculation of sample sizes, the reader should refer to the previous sections of this chapter.

Non-Random Sampling

To achieve the highest possible accuracy, "official" library statistics have usually required that all statistical reporting be based on a full count: *"Data referring to a period should cover the specified period in question, not the interval between two successive surveys."*[7] In most countries, important activities of use were therefore not reported on a national level.

The revised International Standard ISO 2789:2003 "Information and documentation—International library statistics" now allows for the use of

This section is a slightly revised version of Sebastian Mundt, "Sampling In-Library Use," in *Statistics in Practice—Measuring & Managing; Proceedings of IFLA Satellite Conference*, Loughborough, August 2002, edited by Claire Creaser. Loughborough, England: Loughborough University, Library & Information Statistics Unit, 2003, pp. 61–66. It is presented by permission of the publisher.

(Continued)

sampling procedures to estimate annual totals of library visits, in-house use and information requests. It denotes that "*the annual total is to be established from a sample count*" and "*the sample should be taken in one or more normal weeks and grossed up.*"[8] This principle was regarded as the "highest common factor" for statistical reporting on the international level. It takes into consideration that this kind of purposive (judgement) sampling only requires basic statistical knowledge. Expanding upon this definition, the NISO Z39.7-2002 Draft Standard for Trial Use details in its Data Dictionary Version 2002a a *typical week* as "*time that is neither unusually busy nor unusually slow*" and "*in which the library is open its regular hours.*"[9] Holidays, vacation periods, days when unusual events are taking place in the community or in the library should be avoided.

In the following example gate count data from Münster University Library are used to discuss the potentials and pitfalls of (1) weekly sampling and (2) sampling by judgement. Figure 1 displays the average number of gate counts per weekday between 1998 and 2000. Although the number of visits per weekday was not found to be normally distributed, visits to the library seem to follow a weekly pattern with relatively low standard deviation: Note that the average number of visits (gate counts) starts to decline on Tuesday, and due to the academic week Fridays and Saturdays (and Sundays if applicable) are generally less busy. Weeks can therefore be regarded as *clusters* which represent various activity levels in recurrent order. Depending on the level of detail required, other (e.g. daily) sampling units may be preferable: Cullen and Gray[10]

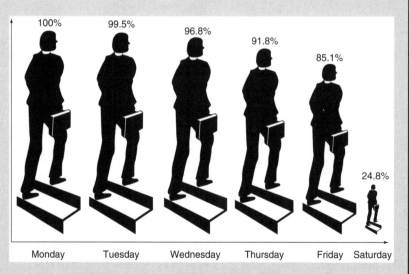

FIGURE 1.   Average Gate Counts Per Weekday
(Münster UL, 1998–2000)

and Maxstadt,[11] for example, chose to sample service hours as they had to consider different opening hours across several service points in a public library system. Clearly, one week of sampling requires less organizational input than an equivalent number of separate days or hours, and many libraries therefore prefer to count in weekly intervals.

In contrast to a random selection of the sample, the deliberate pre-selection of *normal* or *typical* weeks implies detailed knowledge about the variable in question. It is well-known that, for example, daily use of academic libraries' services is influenced by general factors like the "academic year", events inside the library and the availability of "competitive" library services on the campus. It can be argued furthermore that a number of randomized factors like technical readiness of buildings and systems, local daily weather conditions or important cultural or other events in the vicinity will blur any set of in-library use data.

Even if it is difficult, if not impossible, to take these fuzzy elements into consideration, the selection of "normal" weeks implies that data of previous years provide sufficiently reliable information on weeks representing an average level of activity, and that library staff are aware of these patterns. Figure 2 underlines this problem by displaying adjusted data of weekly gate counts at Münster University Library for the years 1998 to 2000:

Hardly any week or even longer time frame can be identified as a reliable basis for purposive sampling over several years, as many weeks show varying gate counts over the years in question, and periods of high use blend into

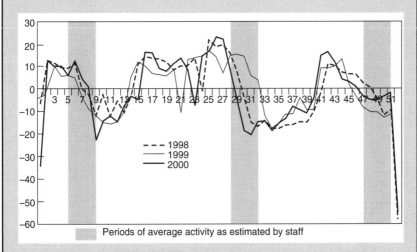

FIGURE 2.   Weekly Gate Counts in Percent of Deviation from
Yearly Mean (Münster UL, 1998–2000)

(Continued)

periods of lower use. Furthermore, experienced members of staff in user services were asked to determine periods of average in-library use intensity. As seen in Figure 2, gate counts in the periods chosen by staff still vary between +15.8 and −20.5 percent from the mean. Staff in other libraries may even come to different results. Thus, the significantly smaller variation of values indicates that staff judgement can in fact improve the sample, but it is not a very solid foundation for statistical reporting and comparisons.

Random Sampling Over Time

While non-random sampling cannot be counted on for precision, the "accuracy" of random samples can be measured in terms of error and confidence level. The following examples apply different methods of random sampling to reference and other use statistics. As the methods were applied to different library settings, the results and boundaries were generally not compared except where indicated.

A description of the "purest" sampling method, a simple random sample of opening hours throughout the year, can be found in Maxstadt.[12] For the fiscal year 1986/87, staff at Louisiana State University Libraries calculated a sample size of 52 hours (of 4,103 hours of service a year) setting a confidence level of 90% and error boundaries of ±10%. With an increased sample size of 60 hours, the actual overall error range was later determined as ±11.23%. The yearly total of reference questions was estimated by linear extrapolation of the sample count.

To avoid any bias or service delays, additional library staff were assigned to collect the sample data. If no extra staff are available, this method may be criticized because the hourly count as practiced here requires a great deal of coordination, especially in large libraries with several service points. A similar (daily) approach is applied by Bauer.[13]

Kesselman and Watstein[14] describe the use of additional information to stratify the sample and thereby—compared to a simple random sample—reduce its variation. Based on fully counted reference statistics at New York University's Bobst Library from the year 1982/83, weekly reference counts were stratified in high, medium and low activity. Given a 95% confidence limit and an error of ±400 (≈10%) a sample size of 15 weeks was calculated, which represented the number of weeks in each of the classes or "strata." The yearly total was estimated by linear extrapolation of the weighted class means.

It was recognized, however, that the stratification of reference weeks may vary from year to year due to a number of reasons, academic or school holidays being the most obvious. Consequently, library staff may find it difficult to determine in advance whether information from previous years is still reliable. In the Bobst Library case, the sample mean of medium weeks was higher than the one of high weeks. The problem was solved by merging both into one stratum, thereby losing some of the expected improvement.

Starting from the procedure chosen at Bobst Library, Lochstet and Lehman[15] developed a correlation method that makes use of a highly significant, almost linear direct correlation (+.957) between weekly reference statistics values and door counts as found by staff at Thomas Cooper Library, University of South Carolina in 1996. In this case, the door count was used as a boundary distribution to extrapolate the reference sample values and estimate the yearly total.

The correlated total and the total sampled from the same weeks differed by only .05 percent. The standard error with the correlation method, however, was considerably high. The authors recommend collecting and correlating data of two variables for one or even two years to provide a substantial set of comparable data before the correlation method could be regarded as a functional alternative. After an accurate correlation coefficient is obtained, however, it is expected that the amount of time spent on recording reference statistics can be significantly reduced. Only a small random sample of a few weeks will be needed to verify that the correlation has not changed.

Staff at Münster University and Regional Library in Germany examined whether the correlation method used at Thomas Cooper Library could be extended to certain datasets from the library system. At first all in-library usage data were regarded as possible high correlates to the gate count because all these activities could only be initiated by persons who had previously entered the library. Second, the data to be analysed should be collected automatically by the library system, i.e. available with only minimal staff input. Weekly gate counts (and reference questions) were then correlated with the selection of automated data shown in Table 1. The highest correlation values (>+.75) with gate counts and reference were found in (a) user-initiated reservations and (b) accesses to user accounts from PC workstations inside the library.

In contrast, loans and reservations from workstations outside the library premises are obvious examples of unsuitable correlates. While loans differ in their seasonal patterns from library visits over a year, users frequenting the automated system from outside the library are unlikely to be included in the gate count on the same day; yet it seems likely that remote use can also show high correlation values, e.g. online reference with virtual visits of the library website.

Seemingly corresponding data may in fact be pure coincidence as the correlation coefficient only measures the nature and extent, but not the causal connection ("direction") of a relationship between two variables. Before high correlation values can be used, it is therefore important to pre-select possible correlates carefully and analyse them for logical consistency, and to monitor

(Continued)

TABLE 1
Correlation Between Weekly Gate Count and Data from
Automated System (Münster UL, 1999/2000)

	Visits	Reference	Reservations (In Library)	Reservations (Remote)	Account Information	Renewals	Textbook Loans	Normal Loans
visits	1.000							
reference	.876**	1.000						
reservations (in library)	.802**	.751**	1.000					
reservations (remote)	.437**	.347	.269**	1.000				
account information	.800**	.765**	.796**	.220**	1.000			
renewals	.523**	.512*	.568**	.256**	.759**	1.000		
textbook loans	.473**	.383	.558**	.117	.312**	.140*	1.000	
normal loans	.506**	.057	.656**	−.019	.508**	.283**	.483**	1.000

**The correlation is significant at the 0.01 level (2-sided). *The correlation is significant at the 0.05 level (2-sided).

the correlation values over a longer period of time to ensure that the correspondence is not purely accidental.

Conclusions

Sampling procedures have always been widely applied in libraries because the full count of some data was impossible or too costly. The introduction of sampling in international statistical reporting reflects a general shift of focus from input to output measures, many of which can only be counted in sample form.

- From the point of data collection management, it seems useful to choose a week as the sampling unit. "Normal" weeks, when selected by judgement, may be difficult to anticipate even from data collected over several years, and the precision of judgement sampling cannot be calculated in terms of error and confidence level.
- It is likely that certain usage data show significant correlation and can provide useful information for estimating totals. Its significance, however, should be revised at regular intervals as correlation only indicates the extent, not any causal connection, of a relationship between variables.

Due to the lack of comparable data, it seems unreasonable to recommend an overall "best" or "most appropriate" sampling method for international statistical reporting. Libraries are therefore asked to carefully apply sampling methods with respect to all possible sources of error, and their regional and national institutions will have to monitor and actively supervise the quality of data delivered to them.

NOTES

[1]Ben-Ami Lipetz, "Catalog Use in a Large Research Library," *Library Quarterly* 42, no. 1 (1972); Abraham Bookstein, "Sampling from Card Files," *Library Quarterly* 53, no. 3 (1983).

[2]F. Wilfrid Lancaster, *If You Want to Evaluate Your Library* . . . 2nd ed. (Champaign, IL: Univ. of Illinois, Graduate School of Library and Information Science, 1993) 145–151.

[3]Rowena Cullen, and Alistair Gray, "A Method for Taking a Reliable Statistical Sample of Reference Inquiries in a New Zealand Public Library System," *Journal of Library Administration* 22, no. 1 (1995).

[4]Herman H. Fussler, and Julian L. Simon, *Patterns in the Use of Books in Large Research Libraries* (Chicago: University of Chicago Press, 1969).

[5]Maurice B. Line, and Alexander Sandison, " 'Obsolescence' and Changes in the Use of Literature with Time," *Journal of Documentation* 30 (September 1974).

[6]Sharon L. Baker, and F. Wilfrid Lancaster, *The Measurement and Evaluation of Library Services*, 2nd ed. (Arlington, VA: Information Resources Press, 1991) 51–75.

[7]ISO 2789:1991 *Information and Documentation—International Library Statistics*, 2nd ed. (Geneva: International Standards Organisation, 1991) 3.

[8]ISO 2789:2003 *Information and Documentation—International Library Statistics*, 3rd ed. (Geneva: International Standards Organisation, 2003) 15.

[9]NISO Z39.7-2002 Draft Standard for Trial Use *"Information Services and Use: Metrics Statistics for Libraries and Information Providers—Data Dictionary"* (Version 2002a), *http://www.niso.org/emetrics/current/complete.html.*

[10]Cullen and Gray, "Method for Taking a Reliable Statistical Sample," 116.

[11]John M. Maxstadt, "A New Approach to Reference Statistics," *College & Research Libraries* 49 (February 1988).

[12]Ibid.

[13]Kathleen Bauer, *Gathering ARL Reference Data*, 2000. *http://info.med.yale.edu/library/assessment/ methods.html.*

[14]Martin Kesselman, and Sarah B. Watstein, "The Measurement of Reference and Information Services," *Journal of Academic Librarianship* 13, no. 1 (1987).

[15]Gwenn Lochstet, and Donna H. Lehman, "A Correlation Method for Collecting Reference Statistics," *College & Research Libraries* 60, no. 1 (1999).

SUMMARY

"The strength of survey research is in answering questions of fact and in assessing the distributions of the characteristics of populations."[26] It does not permit causal inferences, although it can facilitate the analysis of relationships between variables, particularly correlational relationships. Survey research is typically weak on internal control or validity, but, if based on random sampling, it is strong in external validity. This is due to the fact that survey research generally concerns itself with naturally occurring variables in natural settings.

However, the only reliable way to ensure that the results of survey research can be generalized from a sample to a population or beyond a single study is to draw a representative sample. The most common, and one of the best, techniques for selecting a representative sample is simple random sampling. Depending on certain characteristics of the population, or on the purpose of the research, other probability techniques may be preferable in a given situation.

Other closely related concerns include the size of the sample and sampling error. There are formulas for estimating these properties, but, again, the nature of the population and the purpose of the research should be considered. There are no absolute criteria for sample size and sampling error. What is satisfactory for one study may not be for another. There may even be occasions where nonprobability sampling is preferable to probability sampling, but the researcher should keep in mind that the generalizability of studies using nonprobability samples is open to serious question.

NOTES

[1]Claire Selltiz, Lawrence S. Wrightsman, and Stuart W. Cook, *Research Methods in Social Relations*, rev. ed. (New York: Rinehart and Winston, 1959): 55.

[2]Ibid., 65.

[3]Paul D. Leedy, *Practical Research: Planning and Design*, 2d ed. (New York: Macmillan, 1980): 76.

[4]Gary Golden, *Survey Research Methods* (Chicago: ACRL, 1982): 5.

[5]Paul D. Leedy, *Practical Research*, 124.

[6]Paul D. Leedy and Jeanne E. Ormrod, *Practical Research; Planning and Design*, 7th ed. (Upper Saddle River, NJ: Merrill Prentice Hall, 2001): 221.

[7]Charles A. Busha and Stephen P. Harter, *Research Methods in Librarianship: Techniques and Interpretations* (New York: Academic Press, 1980): 79–87.

[8]Arlene Fink and Jacqueline Kosecoff, *How to Conduct Surveys: A Step-by-Step Guide*, 2d ed. (Thousand Oaks, CA: Sage Publications, 1998).

[9]Arlene Fink, *The Survey Handbook* (Thousand Oaks, CA: Sage Publications, 1995): 114.

[10]Earl R. Babbie, *The Practice of Social Research*, 2d ed. (Belmont, CA: Wadsworth, 1979): 197.

[11]Matthias Schonlau, Ronald D. Fricker, and Marc N. Elliott. *Conducting Research Surveys via E-mail and the Web* (Santa Monica, CA: Rand, 2002): 19–20.

[12]Earl R. Babbie, *The Practice of Social Research*, 9th ed. (Belmont, CA: Wadsworth, 2001).

[13]Ibid., 180.

[14]Ibid., 186.

[15]Edward Lakner, "Optimizing Samples for Surveys of Public Libraries: Alternatives and Compromises," *Library & Information Science Research* 20, no. 4 (1998): 329.

[16]Babbie, *The Practice of Social Research*, 9th ed., 205.

[17]Babbie, *The Practice of Social Research*, 2d ed., 197.

[18]Chava Frankfort-Nachmias and David Nachmias, *Research Methods in the Social Sciences*, 4th ed. (New York: St. Martin's Press, 1992): 190.

[19]Helena C. Kraemer and Sue Thiemann, *How Many Subjects? Statistical Power Analysis in Research* (Newbury Park, CA: Sage Publications, 1987).

[20]Peter Hernon, "Determination of Sample Size and Selection of the Sample: Concepts, General Sources, and Software," *College & Research Libraries* 55 (March 1994): 171–79.

[21]Jacob Cohen, *Statistical Power Analysis for the Behavioral Sciences*, 2d ed. (Hillsdale, NJ: Lawrence Erlbaum Associates, 1988).

[22]David Nachmias and Chava Nachmias, *Research Methods in the Social Sciences*, 2d ed. (New York: St. Martin's Press, 1981).

[23]I. S. Simpson, *Basic Statistics for Librarians*, 3d ed. (London: Library Association, 1988): 44.

[24]Abraham Bookstein, "How to Sample Badly," *Library Quarterly* 44 (April 1974): 124–32.

[25]Ibid., 132.

[26]Louise H. Kidder, *Research Methods in Social Relations*, 4th ed. (New York: Holt, Rinehart and Winston, 1981): 80.

Chapter 5

Data Collection Techniques

This chapter will deal with three frequently used data collection techniques—the questionnaire, the interview, and observation. (See Chapter 7, Qualitative Research Methods, for more information about interviews, observation, and content analysis.) These methods for gathering data are most commonly, but not exclusively, used in survey research. They are data collection techniques or instruments, not research methodologies, and they can be used with more than one methodology. Observation is the possible exception, in that some texts do treat observational research as both a technique and a methodology. Regardless, their purpose is to collect data. Achievement tests, aptitude tests, and so on are, of course, often used to collect data for educational research and to assess or evaluate performance, ability, knowledge, and behavior. Readers wishing to learn more about that type of data collection tool should refer to texts by Gay and Airasian and others.[1]

THE QUESTIONNAIRE

Pre-Questionnaire Planning

The planning that should precede the design of a questionnaire is not that dif-ferent from the planning that should go into the early development of a research study. The process will be given here in brief outline form as a way of reviewing the major steps and of emphasizing decisions that should be made before the data collection instrument is selected or designed.

1. Define the problem (and purpose).
2. Consider previous, related research, the advice of experts, and so on.
3. Hypothesize a solution to the problem (or at least identify research questions, the answers to which will shed some light on the problem).
4. Identify the information needed to test the hypothesis. This step should in-clude deciding which aspects of the problem will be considered, and plan-ning ahead to the presentation and analysis of the data. Deciding how the data will be organized, presented, and analyzed can significantly influence what types of data will have to be collected. It may be useful at this point to construct so-called dummy-tables, or tables presenting the important vari-ables with hypothetical values, to help anticipate possible problems regard-ing presentation and analysis.
5. Identify the potential respondents or subjects. As noted earlier, practical questions should be asked at this time, such as, Are the potential respondents accessible? Are they likely to respond?
6. Select the best or most appropriate technique for collecting the necessary data. It is here that the researcher should consider the relevant advantages and disadvantages of the questionnaire, interview, observation, and other techniques in relation to the more general methodology to be used.

To some extent, research findings are affected by the nature of the data collec-tion technique used. In fact, findings strongly affected by the technique can lose their validity. Consequently, a researcher may elect to use two or more techniques and methods to test hypotheses and/or measure variables; this process is referred to as *triangulation*. For example, information about library use could be col-lected with questionnaires, interviews, documentary analysis, and observation. Consistent findings among the different data collection techniques would suggest that the findings are reasonably valid. Discrepancies among the results would indicate a need for further research.

Advantages of the Questionnaire

The questionnaire, which *Webster's New Collegiate Dictionary* defines as "a set of questions for submission to a number of persons to get data," offers several important advantages over other techniques or instruments for collecting survey data. Among them are the following:

1. The questionnaire, especially the mail questionnaire, tends to encourage frank answers. This is in large part due to the fact that it is easier for the researcher to guarantee anonymity for the respondent when using a mail questionnaire. In addition, the respondent can complete the questionnaire without the researcher's being present. Thus the questionnaire can be quite effective at measuring attitudes (see number 4 below for another consideration).
2. The characteristics of the questionnaire that help to produce frank answers also eliminate interviewer bias. This is not to say that the questions could not be worded in a biased manner, but that the style of verbal presentation cannot influence the response. (The problem of biased questions is a serious one and will be treated in greater detail later.)
3. Another way of stating the second advantage is that the fixed format of the questionnaire tends to eliminate variation in the questioning process. Once the questions have been written in their final version and included in the questionnaire, their contents and organization will not change. This does not rule out the possibility of respondents interpreting the same questions in different ways, however.
4. The manner in which a mail questionnaire is distributed and responded to also allows it to be completed, within limits, at the leisure of the participants. This encourages well thought out, accurate answers. On the other hand, if the researcher is more interested in obtaining spontaneous or immediate reactions, as in an attitudinal survey, then the relatively large amount of time allotted for completion of the questionnaire could be a disadvantage.
5. Questionnaires can be constructed so that quantitative data are relatively easy to collect and analyze.
6. Questionnaires can facilitate the collection of large amounts of data in a relatively short period of time. Questionnaire-based surveys of several thousand people are not unusual, and responses typically are expected within one to two weeks.
7. Last, but not least, questionnaires are usually relatively inexpensive to administer.

Disadvantages of the Questionnaire

While the advantages of the questionnaire seem to outweigh the disadvantages, there are several of the latter that should be noted:

1. Use of the mail questionnaire eliminates personal contact between the researcher and the respondent. However, this also can be seen as an advantage, for, as stated earlier, the absence of direct contact eliminates interviewer bias from the questioning process.
2. The mail questionnaire does not permit the respondent to qualify answers to ambiguous questions or, at least, makes it more difficult. On the other hand,

the more difficult it is for respondents to qualify answers, the more likely the researcher is to obtain consistent responses.

3. Studies have shown that persons who are highly opinionated regarding the subject of a questionnaire are more likely than others to be motivated enough to complete and return it. This phenomenon tends to result in a biased sample or return, as the less opinionated members of the sample will be underrepresented and may well have certain characteristics in common.

4. Questionnaires may be more difficult for uneducated participants to complete, again possibly resulting in a biased return. The researcher can minimize this problem by keeping his or her audience in mind when developing the questionnaire and writing the questions.

5. In general, there simply seems to be a resistance to mail questionnaires. In the extreme case, this can result in some participants attempting to "sabotage" a survey by purposefully responding incorrectly to some questionnaire items. This problem can be alleviated through appropriate research design, specific techniques of which will be mentioned later.

6. Nonresponse rates are relatively high for mail, e-mail, and Web-based questionnaires, although Web-based surveys often first use another survey method to identify participants. Since survey respondents are usually female, more educated, and older than those who do not respond to surveys, nonresponses reduce the sample size and may introduce sampling error by eliminating a subset of the population. The researcher should correct for sampling bias incurred from nonresponse or minimize nonresponse rates by combining several data collection techniques.[2]

7. If the questionnaire is distributed electronically, it will reach only those who have access to and are comfortable using e-mail and Web technology.

CONSTRUCTING THE QUESTIONNAIRE

Proper construction of the questionnaire is essential to its success. In general, the researcher must consider his or her information needs and the characteristics of the participants. The former concern will be dealt with first.

Type of Question According to Information Needed

In selecting or writing specific types of questions, the researcher must first consider what kind of data he or she needs. The major types of questions, according to the kind of information needed, include the following:

1. Factual questions: questions used to ascertain such things as the respondent's age, gender, and so on. They are probably the most straightforward type of questionnaire item.

2. Opinion and attitude questions: questions intended to determine a person's ideas, inclinations, prejudices, convictions, and so on. (Questionnaires used for an attitudinal survey are usually known as "attitude scales" or "indexes."). They tend to be considerably more subjective than factual questions and are more difficult to validate externally.

3. Information questions: questions designed to measure the respondent's knowledge about some topic. They typically require the greatest response time.

4. Self-perception questions: questions quite similar to attitude questions, but restricted to one's opinions about himself or herself.

5. Standards of action questions: questions used to determine how respondents would act in certain circumstances. For example, one may ask library patrons how they would react to a new library service or a change in hours.

6. Questions about actual past or present behavior: questions that potentially fall within some of the categories of questions already identified but tend to be more narrow in that they focus on behavior. For example, the kind of information gathered to describe past or present behavior could be factual, attitudinal, or informational in nature. Behavioral questions also tend to be rather subjective but usually become more valid as they become more specific. Data on past and present behavior can serve to some extent as a predictor of future behavior.

7. Projective questions: questions that allow respondents to answer questions indirectly by imposing their personal beliefs, attitudes, and so on onto others. In other words, they permit the respondent to indicate how he or she would react to some question or situation by reporting how peers, colleagues, and so on would react in the same situation. This technique can be particularly useful for eliciting responses on a topic about which participants may be reluctant to express their own, true feelings openly or directly. For example, certain public librarians could be asked how their colleagues feel about censorship, with the researcher assuming that the attitudes of the respondents are similar to the attitudes of the colleagues. The researcher must be aware, however, that such measures may be weak in validity as indicators of the characteristics they are designed to measure.

Projective questions are considered to be a type of indirect method of questioning people and as such require only minimal cooperation on the part of the individuals being studied. Judd, Smith, and Kidder discuss a variety of specific projective methods, as well as several more structured indirect tests.[3] The reader interested in learning more about indirect assessment should consult Judd, Smith, and Kidder, keeping in mind that the validity and reliability of indirect methods are open to question. Such techniques are probably most appropriate for exploratory research.

All or most of the items in a questionnaire may be focused on one specific topic and, in aggregate, considered to constitute a *scale* for the topic of interest.

In the typical survey in LIS, however, the questionnaire is likely to consist of a variety of questions addressing a number of components of a broader topic.

Type of Question According to Form

In selecting or designing questionnaire items, the researcher must consider the question format that will best obtain the information desired. The form of the question in turn determines the method of response. The researcher must decide which response format will be the easiest for the respondent while still producing adequate, definite, and uniform answers. Whenever possible, it is recommended that consistent response formats be employed. This results in less confusion for the respondent and makes speedier replies possible.

There are two basic types of questions—open-ended questions and fixed-response questions. *Open-ended*, or *unstructured questions*, as the name indicates, are designed to permit free responses from participants rather than ones limited to specific alternatives. They are especially useful for exploratory studies; they "are called for when the issue is complex, when the relevant dimensions are not known, or when the interest of the researcher lies in exploration of a process or of the individual's formulation of an issue."[4]

On the negative side, as there is almost no limit to the possible responses to an open-ended question, their answers are usually more difficult to categorize and analyze than responses to structured questions. Open-ended questions may also discourage responses because they typically take longer to answer.

Examples of open-ended questions are

1. What do you think about the library?
2. Which library services do you value the most?
3. I typically use the library in order to _____

Fixed-response or *structured questions*, also known as closed questions, limit the responses of the participant to stated alternatives. The possible responses may range from a simple "yes" or "no," to a checklist of possible replies, to a scale indicating various degrees of a particular response.

Structured questions have several advantages and disadvantages in comparison with unstructured questions. Structured questions more easily accommodate precoding in that the possible responses are generally known and stated. The precoding, in turn, facilitates the analysis of the data gathered by the questions. Precoding essentially involves anticipating responses, establishing numerical codes or symbols for the various responses, and including the codes on the questionnaire. An example of a precoded questionnaire item follows:

	Yes	No
Do you have a current library card?	1	2

In this example, the respondent would be asked to circle the number representing his or her answer. A 1 or a 2, whichever the response happens to be, would be entered into the data set for future analysis. (This technique will be discussed in greater detail in Chapter 9, Analysis of Data.) The use of precoded forms is sometimes referred to as direct data entry or DDE. The respondent, in this example, could have been asked to circle "yes" or "no" rather than circle a code. After receiving the questionnaire, the researcher would then have to assign a numerical code to that response and enter it, thus adding an extra step to the analysis process. Golden identified seven different coding schemes: listing, simple factual, bracket, scales, combination, frame of reference, and series.[5]

Other advantages of the structured question format include the fact that responses to structured questions tend to have more reliability than responses to unstructured questions. This occurs because there is a limited set of responses, and thus less potential for variation from test to test. Fixed-alternative questions also have the advantages of being "standardizable," simple to administer, and more easily understood by the respondent in terms of the dimensions along which the answers are sought. Having fixed responses also helps to ensure that the answers are given in a frame of reference that is relevant to the purpose of the inquiry.

Among the disadvantages of the structured question is a real possibility that a limited set of possible replies can force respondents to select inaccurate answers. None of the choices may correspond exactly with the participant's position, or may not allow for qualification. Having an "other" category can alleviate this problem somewhat, but respondents tend to limit their answers to those provided rather than utilizing the "other" option.

Similarly, a closed question may force a statement of opinion on an issue about which the respondent does not have one. The inclusion of a "don't know" or "no opinion" type response can help to provide an indication of no opinion, but again the respondent is inclined to give a more definite response. The omission of possible responses can also introduce bias. For example, in a question asking a library user to check the services he or she uses regularly, the list may be biased toward print rather than electronic resources, or traditional rather than more innovative services, in that more options are provided for one or the other orientation. Again, an "other" category does not completely eliminate this problem.

Providing possible answers can also help the respondent to cover up a certain amount of ignorance. The respondent will be able to provide a reasonable answer even when he or she knows nothing about the subject. Whether this is a problem depends on the nature of the study.

In conclusion, "closed questions are more efficient where the possible alternative replies are known, limited in number, and clear-cut. Thus they are appropriate for securing factual information . . . and for eliciting expressions of opinion about issues on which people hold clear opinions."[6] In practice, a combination of structured and unstructured questions can be most efficient. In addition, two surveys, or a survey followed by a survey of a subsample, can effectively utilize both types of questions and thereby complement one another. For example, following a survey based on structured questions, a subsample could be studied in greater depth with unstructured questions.

Structured questions come in a variety of specific formats, including the following:

1. A checklist, each item of which requires a response. (An example is provided for this and each of the other types of structured questions to follow.)

   Have you ever done any of the following while using a library? (Circle one number on each line.)

	Yes	No
a. Asked a reference question?	1	2
b. Checked out a book?	1	2
c. Read a magazine?	1	2
d. Read a newspaper?	1	2
e. Listened to a recording?	1	2

2. A checklist of items, one or more of which represents the "best" answer.

   Which of the following types of library services do you use at least five times a year? (Circle all numbers that apply.)

a. Reference	1
b. Circulation	2
c. Audiovisual	3
d. Periodicals	4
e. Photocopying	5
f. Children's department	6

3. A checklist of items with subdivisions or categories.

   What is the highest grade of school you have completed? (Circle one number.)

Grade school	01	02	03	04	05	06	07 08
High school			09	10	11	12	
College or technical school			13	14	15	16	
Beyond college				17			

4. A checklist of bracketed or grouped responses.

   How many times did you use a public library during the past 12 months? (Circle one number.)

None	1
1–5	2
6–10	3
11–15	4
16–20	5
21 or more	6

5. Fill-in the blank.
   The reference desk is on the _____ floor of the library.

Scaled Responses

A variety of questions utilize scales of one type or another in order to obtain responses. One kind of scale is the *rating scale*. Specific rating scales, with examples, include the following:

1. An itemized rating or specific category scale.
   How important would each of the following items be to you in deciding to use a library? (Circle one number on each line.)

	Of great importance	Of some importance	Of little importance	Of no importance
a. Adequate hours of service	1	2	3	4
b. Multiple copies of best-sellers	1	2	3	4
c. Adequate parking	1	2	3	4
d. Helpful staff	1	2	3	4

   An itemized rating scale often has a category representing "no opinion" or "undecided."
2. A graphic rating scale. (This too is a scale designed to collect ordinal-level data, but, unlike the specific category scale, the graphic scale allows the respondent to check anywhere along a continuum.)
   For each of the following statements, indicate your degree of agreement by placing a checkmark on the continuum.
   a. The library does an adequate job of teaching students how to use its collections.

   Strongly agree   Strongly disagree

   b. The library's collection is usually adequate to meet my needs.

   Strongly agree   Strongly disagree

   The second and third points along the continuum could have been labeled as "Agree" and "Disagree," but doing so might have encouraged respondents to limit their responses to four labeled check points.
   Such scales typically have from four to seven categories or checkpoints and are often used for measuring attitudes. It may be desirable to include a

response for "undecided" or "no opinion." Careful consideration must be given to the placement of such a category, however, in that its location on the continuum determines its point value. (If it were placed in the middle of the graphic scale given above, its value would be three. If placed at the end, its value might be one or five.) If the code for the value is treated as a real number, then the value of statistics such as those representing the average can be misleading and the results of the data analysis difficult to interpret.

3. A rank-order or comparative rating scale.

Please rank, in order of importance, the following types of library services. (Record "1," for the most important, through "5," for the least important.)

Library instruction programs _____
Reference services _____
Circulation services _____
Audio-visual services _____
Study facilities _____

Ranking type questions are not uniformly recommended and should be used carefully. They become especially difficult for the respondent to deal with when many items are listed.

Other scaling methods use multiple responses or measurements and combine the responses into a single scale score. According to Judd, Smith, and Kidder, *multiple-item scales*, even more so than rating scales, can help to reduce the complexity of data.[7] They also hold more potential for testing hypotheses and are considered to have better validity and reliability. Multiple-item scales can be categorized as differential, summated, and cumulative.

A *differential scale*, often referred to as a Thurstone type scale, utilizes a series of statements or items with equidistances between them. Each item, therefore, receives a value point equidistant from those immediately preceding and following it. The respondent is asked to check each statement with which he or she agrees or the two or three statements that best represent his or her position. Statements about a public library might include the following examples:

Statement	Scale value
I believe the public library is an important agency for educating citizens.	1.0
I believe the public library plays a major role as a cultural agency.	1.5
I believe the public library duplicates educational services provided elsewhere.	7.4
I believe the public library is of value only for recreational reading.	8.2

The statements would represent favorable and unfavorable attitudes toward the public library and would be arranged in a random order. The respondent's overall attitude would be the mean of the scale values of the items with which he or she agreed.

Differential scales do have certain disadvantages. They are time-consuming to develop, in that it is difficult to design questions that truly represent values equidistant from one another. In addition, it is difficult to avoid rater or compiler bias in developing questions utilizing differential scales.

Summated scales also consist of series of statements or items, but no effort is made to distribute them evenly along a continuum. In fact, only items that are favorable or unfavorable to the attitude of interest are used (unless a "no opinion" type of response is included.) The Likert scale is one of the most commonly used summated scales. An example follows.

Item	Strongly agree	Agree	Disagree	Strongly disagree
A college reference librarian should refer students to sources of information.	SA	A	D	SD
A college reference librarian should teach students how to obtain their own information.	SA	A	D	SD
A college reference librarian should provide students with needed information.	SA	A	D	SD

In this case, the sum of responses to the items favoring the provision of library instruction, minus the sum of responses to the items opposing library instruction, would constitute the scale score. (The response values would be those values assigned to "strongly agree," "agree," etc.) Likert-type scales are often used with individual, nonsummated scales as well. (See the examples of itemized rating and graphic scales given above.)

The major disadvantage of summated or Likert-type scales is that, since they represent an ordinal scale of measurement, they do not permit one to say anything about the exact amount of differences in attitudes. For example, one could not say that a respondent who checked "strongly disagree" was twice as unfavorable toward some library service as a respondent who checked "disagree." Some do argue that the data collected by a Likert-type scale are, for all practical purposes, interval level, and proceed to analyze the data accordingly. A more conservative, rigorous approach would not permit this assumption.

The third basic category of multiple-item scales utilized in questionnaires is the *cumulative scale*. It consists of a series of statements with which the respondent indicates agreement or disagreement; however, the items are related to each other, so one "should" respond to subsequent items in a manner similar to preceding ones. It is generally assumed that cumulative scales represent the ordinal level of measurement. Examples of cumulative scales include the Bogardus-type scale, used for measuring social attitudes, and the Guttman scale, also known as "scale analysis" or "the scalogram method." As was the case with the Likert scale, all items or statements must be either clearly favorable or unfavorable to the topic. A unique feature of the cumulative scale is that none of the respondents should give a negative response before a positive response or a positive response after a negative response.

A specialized scale which shares some of the characteristics of the summated scales is the *semantic differential scale*. This scale provides pairs of antonyms and synonyms, along with five- to seven-step rating scales. An example follows:

For each pair of items below, what number comes closest to describing the conditions of your public library? (Circle one number on each line.)

	Extremely	Moderately	Neither	Moderately	Extremely	
a. Pleasant	1	2	3	4	5	Unpleasant
b. Clean	1	2	3	4	5	Dirty
c. Organized	1	2	3	4	5	Disorganized
d. Helpful	1	2	3	4	5	Unhelpful
e. Available when needed	1	2	3	4	5	Unavailable when needed

To obtain the respondent's overall rating of the library, the researcher would sum the total value of each column and divide by the number (five) of rows.

All of these scales possess one or more weaknesses. As was noted earlier, one common problem relates to the determination of the neutral position when provided. Another concerns the conceptual validity of assigning one value or point that represents a person's attitude along a continuum when, in fact, a wide range of values may be more accurate.

Self-ratings are subject to a variety of limitations resulting from personal bias and the subjectivity of the questions. Ratings by others can suffer from certain *systematic errors* which decrease the validity and reliability of the results. One of these, the *halo effect*, occurs when the respondent generalizes the rating from one item to another in an unconscious attempt to make his or her ratings consistent. This phenomenon is especially likely to occur when a general, all-encompassing question is asked before more specific questions on the same topic. For example, if a participant responds positively to a general question about a library, he or she is more likely to give positive responses to subsequent questions about specific services of the same library. Another constancy error, the *generosity error*, involves the rater's overestimating the desirable qualities of subjects. A third systematic error, the *contrast error*, results when respondents tend to view persons as different than themselves on the trait being rated. A variety of other factors relating to the construction and administering of questions can decrease the reliability of their scales. These problems will be considered later in the text as appropriate.

Having selected a specific form of response, the researcher must make other decisions regarding that particular format. If a researcher had decided to utilize the check answer, he or she must then decide if it would be best to provide dichotomous, multiple-choice, or scaled responses. He or she should be satisfied that a checklist provides enough alternatives, and that the categories are mutually exclusive. In other words, there should be (within limits) a category for every possible response, and no response should require more than one category to contain it. For many fixed-response questions, the researcher must decide whether to provide a "don't know" response option. There is a difference of opinion on the desirability of doing so, but a good case can be made for providing that option when it is reasonable to expect that some respondents will not have an opinion or any knowledge on which to base an answer.

Question Content and Selection

Having decided on the type(s) of questions to be employed in terms of the information needed and the form of response desired, the researcher must next decide what specific questions to ask, and consider their content and wording. The questioner should first ask himself or herself whether a specific question is actually necessary or will be useful. If the answer is "yes," how many questions are needed on that particular topic in order to obtain the necessary information? One should never ask any more questions than are absolutely necessary.

One technique that can help the researcher avoid unnecessary and redundant questions, while asking those that are necessary, is to construct a variable-question matrix. This matrix is simply a table with the questions numbered across one edge and the variables across an adjoining edge. Corresponding boxes or cells are then checked when there is a question about a variable. If several cells are checked for any one variable, it may suggest that more questions are being asked about that topic than is necessary. Too few or no checks for a variable would raise the opposite concern.

Another question that the researcher should ask himself or herself is whether the respondents can be expected to have the information needed to provide an answer. Perhaps a question needs to be more concrete, specific, or related to the respondents' personal experiences. (On the other hand, the question should be general enough that it is free from spurious concreteness or specificity, i.e., it should not be more specific than it sounds.)

In general, a question should not be biased, or at least it should be accompanied by a question designed to balance any emphasis or perspective. The researcher also should avoid questions that are misleading because of unstated assumptions or unanticipated implications.

Last but not least, the researcher should be satisfied that each question asks only one question. This is a common occurrence in questionnaires, and yet it does not receive the attention that it deserves. Consider the following real questionnaire item as an illustration: "Ability to describe the various theories of learning and assess their relevance to particular adult learning situations." In this case, the respondents were asked to rate the degree to which they agreed with this statement. But what if one agreed with "describing the various theories" but disagreed with "assessing their relevance?" Obviously a single response could not represent both of the participants' attitudes. In addition, a question containing more than one concept presents difficulties for subsequent analysis and interpretation.

Question Wording

The way in which the contents of questionnaire items are worded also can affect their validity and reliability. Consider the following two questions:

"Do you think the U.S. should forbid public speeches against democracy?"
"Do you think the U.S. should not allow public speeches against democracy?"

In 1940, the two forms of this attitude question were asked in a "split-ballot" experiment using two comparable national samples. Although there seems to be no real difference between forbidding and not allowing something, in one sample, 54% of the respondents said the U.S. should forbid speeches against democracy, but in the other, 75% said the government should not allow such speeches. It appears that the variation in wording significantly affected the responses to essentially the same question. This test was replicated in the mid-1970s, and again there was a difference between samples of about 20%.[8]

During the Watergate scandal, Gallup polls never found a majority of Americans to be in favor of "impeaching" President Nixon; however, a majority never failed to favor impeachment when defined as an "indictment" or a decision to bring the president to trial before the Senate. In a *Reader's Digest* poll, when the pollsters asked if "government spending to aid foreign nations should be increased, decreased or kept where it is now," 67% said that they wanted spending cut. When asked the same question worded differently—this time in the context of cutting programs to reduce the federal deficit—83% favored reducing foreign aid. For discussions of how words can be interpreted differently in library settings, the reader may wish to consult articles written by Bookstein and Kidston.[9, 10]

It is, therefore, a good idea to avoid questions that tend to be misunderstood because of difficult and unclear wording. Such questions can result from the use of biased and emotionally laden terms. In general, it is also a good idea not to use slang, jargon, and technical terms. It is even possible for some words to be objectionable to certain respondents, thereby biasing their answers or resulting in their not completing the questionnaire.

In most cases, questionnaire items should be impersonal, but whether they should request information directly or indirectly depends on the type of information needed. When the researcher doubts that subjects will be willing or able to give accurate information about themselves, indirect methods of collecting data may be necessary. However, the validity of indirect methods tends to be more suspect, and they sacrifice precision and reliability in the interest of breadth and depth of information.

In constructing questionnaire items, one should be careful that the wording used in certain questions does not bias responses to later questions. To help alleviate this problem, as well as others mentioned earlier, it is important to provide clear definitions of key terms where needed. The researcher must avoid making too many assumptions about the respondent's knowledge or the likelihood that all respondents will interpret important terms in the same way.[11]

Sequencing of Questionnaire Items

Even the sequencing of questions can influence how they are answered. Changes in question order can produce "context errors" resulting in substantial differences in responses to the same question. In a 1979 study, a question was asked about whether a pregnant woman should be allowed "to obtain a legal abortion if she is married and does not want any more children."[12] When this question was asked alone, responses were considerably more favorable than when it followed a question about allowing abortion if "there is a strong chance of serious defect in the baby." During the U.S. presidential campaign in 1992, voters were asked to name their favorite candidate in a two-way race between George Bush and Bill Clinton and in a three-way race among Bush, Clinton, and Ross Perot. Perot always fared better if the three-way question was asked last rather than first.

Due to the effects of "context," it is important to maintain the same order of questions if a survey is being repeated in order to investigate trends. Within a single study, the researcher should consider whether a question is likely to be influenced by the context of the preceding questions. Also, is the question led up to in a natural way? Does it occur too early or too late with regard to arousing sufficient interest and avoiding undue resistance?

It is generally recommended that questions with a similar context be placed together. Another rule of thumb is to sequence the questions from the general to the specific. Particular topics may dictate other sequences, however. The first question is generally considered to be the most crucial one, and it has a relatively large influence on the response rate. Therefore, it should be clearly related to the topic, interesting, neutral, and easy to answer. The first question should be well constructed, and it is usually desirable for it to be one that all subjects can answer.

Sources of Error

Before continuing with the outline of the procedures for developing a questionnaire, it may be worthwhile to consider some of the types of questionnaire error not already discussed. Some of the more common types of error or bias, not all of which are limited to questionnaires, are

1. Researcher bias—In essence, this bias results from the researcher's unconsciously developing the questionnaire in a manner that will increase the likelihood of obtaining the desired results.
2. Sponsorship bias—This bias results from the researcher's, hopefully unconscious, attempt to produce research results that will please the outside agency funding the research. A researcher may well be suspected of such bias if his or her research is sponsored by an agency with vested interests in certain outcomes.
3. Imperfections of design—Weaknesses in the design of the questionnaire can result in biased or inaccurate responses. Such imperfections include haphazard sequencing, inadequate instructions, and a failure to explain the purpose and scope of the study.
4. Respondent interpretations—As implied earlier, varying interpretations of the "facts" and key terms by the respondents also can result in inaccurate answers.
5. Time lapse—It has been found that answers to the same question tend to vary over time even when not directly affected by the passage of time. It must be realized that perceptions, attitudes, and so on are not static in most cases.
6. Circumstances—A variety of factors, such as carelessness and mood of the respondent, ambiguous questions, "unthinking" answers, and general resistance to questionnaires, can produce inaccurate responses.
7. Response bias—Error can result from the response rate being low and thus the final sample ending up less representative than originally conceived. Some of the steps that can be taken to minimize response bias include using questionnaires only when one is reasonably certain that the subjects are interested in the topic, making responses confidential or anonymous, sending reminders to complete mailed questionnaires, providing gift or cash incentives to encourage responses (some incentives can be included with an e-mail or Web-based questionnaire by initiating a trigger for the gift when the questionnaire is completed and submitted), and being realistic about eligibility criteria for subjects.
8. Reactive insight—There is a growing concern that, as subjects participate in surveys over time, especially in surveys dealing with sensitive topics, they may begin to rethink their lives, attitudes, and so on. This activity could then result in the participants' being biased in certain areas and less representative of their larger populations.

Preparing the First Draft

Much of the preceding section relates, of course, to the preparation of the first draft of the questionnaire. As was suggested above, the researcher must decide on the sequence of questions that best serves his or her purpose. In some cases, this may result in the questions being sequenced in the most logical arrangement. This may mean ordering the items from the general to the particular, or the best arrangement may be by the subject. For example, a questionnaire about the administration of a library could be categorized by staff, services, collections, budget, and so on. Questions within these sections could then be ordered from the most general to the most particular. When the topic changes noticeably, it is a good idea to provide a lead-in statement as a transition.

On the other hand, the researcher may wish to achieve the optimal psychological sequence, which may not be the same as the most logical arrangement. This can be an important consideration when a questionnaire contains sensitive questions, or questions that ask for rather confidential information, or questions that take a lot of time to answer. Such questions can prompt a person to quit answering a questionnaire and return it partially finished or, worse yet, discard it. But if these questions occur near the end of the questionnaire, the respondent is more likely to go ahead and complete the questionnaire because of the time and effort already invested in it.

In light of the types of errors discussed above, the best psychological sequence may also mean that questions that are likely to bias questions that follow should be located at or near the end of the questionnaire. This will at least reduce the error or bias that they introduce into the study.

In preparing the first draft of the questionnaire, the researcher may decide that some questions are of such a nature that respondents are unlikely to answer them accurately or honestly. In this case, he or she may be well advised to incorporate some "cross-check" questions to check the reliability of certain questions. Cross-check questions are those that ask for the same information as one or more others, but each is worded differently. If the respondents answer essentially the same question differently, then one must question their reliability. Keep in mind, however, as was discussed earlier, the wording of a question can affect its responses. In addition, respondents may be irritated, or even insulted, if they detect the use of cross-check questions. Such a reaction can affect their responses to the questionnaire as a whole and bias the results.

Evaluating the Questionnaire

Once the first draft of the questionnaire has been completed, and before it is actually pretested, it is a good idea to get one (or more) expert's opinion of the questionnaire. A person who is expert in research methodology can help to catch methodological weaknesses in the instrument, such as faulty scales, inadequate instructions, and so on. A person who is familiar with the topic of the questionnaire can help in assessing the face validity of the questions. Do they make sense, are they easy to understand, do they ask what they are supposed to be asking?

The Pretest

After obtaining an informal evaluation of the questionnaire, it should be pretested fully. This pretest is sometimes referred to as a "pilot study," although pilot study is actually more synonymous with "exploratory study." A pretest gives the researcher an opportunity to identify questionnaire items that tend to be misunderstood by the participants, do not obtain the information that is needed, and so on. But, in addition to testing the actual questionnaire items, the pretest should include interviews with some or all of the pretest participants or at least incorporate one or more open-ended questions. Interviews and/or open-ended questions are necessary in order for the respondents to have ample opportunity to point out problem questions, poor instructions, and unnecessary or missing questions, and to give their general reactions to the instrument. Pretest participants are sometimes encouraged to call the researcher if they wish to make additional comments about the questionnaire.

The pretest also offers certain advantages beyond helping to refine the data collection instrument. It can permit a preliminary testing of the hypothesis, point out a variety of problems not anticipated relating to design and methodology, facilitate a practice run of the statistical procedures to be used, and perhaps even indicate that the final study may not produce any meaningful results and therefore should be rethought or abandoned.

Ideally, the pretest sample should be as scientifically selected as the sample for the final study. That is, it should be randomly selected and of an adequate size to permit generalizations to the population. In actual practice, pretest samples are seldom so rigorously selected. Sometimes known as "samples of several," they often are in effect nonprobability, convenience samples, selected because of their members' proximity and willingness to participate. But the pretest sample should be reasonably representative of the final study group, or there is little value in conducting the pretest.

Researchers also should be careful that they do not view the pretest as a mere formality. This means that, if the pretest does turn up any problems, the questionnaire should be revised accordingly. If substantial problems are found, resulting in significant revisions, another pretest should be conducted. This process should continue until the researcher is prepared to move to the final study with a questionnaire that does not represent an instrument that is significantly different from the last one pretested.

As the researcher evaluates the results of the pretest, there are some good questions to ask: Did each of the items measure what it was intended to measure? Were all of the words understood? Did all respondents similarly interpret all questions? Did each fixed-response question have an answer that applied to each respondent? Were some questions regularly skipped or answered unintelligibly?

Final Editing

Having been pretested, the questionnaire is ready for final editing before distribution. It is recommended that the title of the study or survey be placed at the top of the questionnaire. The organization will benefit from the employment of an outline format in lettering and numbering sections and questions. The questions on each page should be arranged so that there is adequate white space among them and in the margins. Adequate lines or spaces should be left for responding to open-ended questions. Nothing frustrates the respondent more than being asked to provide answers for which there is inadequate room. One less than ideal solution to this is asking the respondent to use the back side of the page when necessary.

The general rule is that the questionnaire should be as short as possible in order to encourage complete responses. (Other factors, such as the respondent's motivation, which is affected by his or her interest in the topic, probability of benefiting from the study, etc., may make a longer questionnaire feasible, however.)

Keeping in mind that a reasonable amount of white space is desirable, there are a variety of steps one can take to keep the questionnaire length to a minimum. One, while instructions must be clear, they also should be kept as brief as possible. Two, if the questionnaire is to be mailed, the original questionnaire can be typed in a small font. Three, relatively long questionnaires can be printed on both sides of the sheets, in order to at least minimize the thickness of the instrument. Finally, and for other reasons as well, the questionnaire should ask only for information not already held by the researcher. Unnecessary and redundant questions should be avoided. It is a waste of the respondent's time to supply information already held by the researcher or available from other sources, and if the respondent becomes aware of being asked to do so, there is a greater chance that the questionnaire will not be completed and returned.

In order to facilitate accurate, easy responses, the researcher should strive for simplicity in word use and question construction. As much as possible, the questionnaire's response format should be consistent. For example, the respondent should be asked to "circle the number" or "check the appropriate box" throughout as much of the questionnaire as is appropriate. Changing formats can create some confusion as well as increase the response time. (It typically requires more than one format to obtain all needed information, such as age, job, etc., however, and some researchers argue that switching formats helps to keep the respondent alert and to avoid response patterns.) It will generally increase the respondent's accuracy if factual questions are tied to a definite time period. For example, rather than asking a person how often he or she uses a library during a typical year, it may be better to ask how often he or she used the library between January and December of the preceding year.

Other measures that will help both the researcher and the respondent include holding open-ended questions to a minimum in *self-administered* questionnaires. While they may be necessary in certain types of studies, they are more susceptible to inconsistencies in interpretation and unreliable responses. As was indicated earlier, the analysis will be expedited by utilizing as much precoding as possible, and this is not practical with open-ended questions. Some questionnaires are designed to be optically scanned after they are completed.

It may be useful to screen out respondents who should not answer certain questions. This will save response time for the participant and analysis time for the researcher. One technique for doing so involves the use of filter questions or skip patterns. A filter question may, for example, ask the respondent if he or she has used the library's reference service during the preceding 12 months. If the answer is no, then the respondent may be asked to skip the next few questions pertaining to reference services and go on to those asking about the collection. (Skip patterns can easily be automated in an electronic questionnaire by deleting questions if a specific answer is checked or by not allowing an answer to be inserted if the question does not correspond to the previous answer.) A graphic format may be utilized by drawing a line to the next pertinent question so as to avoid any confusion. An illustration of this method follows:

1. Are you a member of the American Library Association?

    □ 1) Yes↓   □ 2) No→Go to Question 2.

    | If yes: 1.a. Please indicate the year you first joined. ___ Year |
    | 1.b. Has your membership been continuous? __ Yes __ No |

And finally, the questionnaire should have a thank you note at the end and repeat the instructions for how and by when the questionnaire should be returned. An accompanying letter might have contained this information but could have been misplaced.

Cover Letter

In most cases, a cover letter should accompany the questionnaire. The basic purpose of the cover letter is to explain briefly the purpose of the study and to stress the importance of each person's responding. In some situations, such as with instruments designed to measure certain values indirectly, it may be necessary to be somewhat vague, if not actually misleading, about the scope of the study. This does present ethical concerns, however, and in general it is best to be open regarding the purpose of the study. It is not easy to conceal the true nature of a study, and if respondents become aware that they have been misled, they are not likely to view the questionnaire favorably. Persons receiving the letter and questionnaire generally appreciate being told how they were selected to participate in the study. Miller and Salkind also suggest including in the cover letter a statement that informs the respondents that by returning the questionnaire they are consenting to participate in the study.[13]

If one can be used legitimately, it is a good idea to employ a letterhead, whether it is a mail or electronic survey, to lend some authority to the study. In addition to, or in lieu of, a letterhead, a second cover letter signed by a person influential within the field of study can help increase the response rate. Cover letters should be written in a friendly, but professional, style.

Persons are more likely to complete the questionnaire if the cover letter stresses the potential usefulness of the study for the respondent. Along those lines, it may help to offer each respondent the results, or at least a summary of the results, of the study. In order to avoid having to distribute any more results than necessary, it is a good idea to ask respondents to indicate whether they wish to receive some report of the study results. Instead of promising to send results of the study to respondents, the researcher may simply emphasize that results will be disseminated via the professional literature or via a Web site and include the URL for the site, or state that the URL will be distributed when the results are available.

Another useful technique for increasing the response rate, as well as helping to ensure frank answers, is to guarantee confidentiality and/or anonymity for all respondents. The researcher should keep in mind, however, that confidentiality and anonymity do not mean the same thing. Confidentiality merely assures the respondent that his or her replies and name will not be associated publicly. Anonymity requires the use of techniques that make it impossible for anyone, including the researcher, to link a respondent with his or her answers. The latter is more difficult to achieve, especially in an electronic environment, and it should not be promised to the respondents unless it is actually going to be provided.

DISTRIBUTION OF THE QUESTIONNAIRE

There are three main methods of administering the survey questionnaire. The questionnaire can be self-administered, which means that the respondents are asked to complete the questionnaire themselves; administered face-to-face to respondents by researchers; or administered to respondents via the telephone by interviewers. The self-administered questionnaire can be mailed or electronically transmitted via e-mail or the Web. On the Web site, "Research Methods on the WWW," Stephenson includes bibliographies, with many links to full-text papers, on utilizing the Web for data gathering and analysis.[14]

Mail Questionnaire

Unless the questionnaire is designed as a self-mailer, or is to be faxed or e-mailed back to the researcher, it should be accompanied by a self-addressed, stamped, return envelope. Again, almost anything that will help to encourage responses is worth doing. In deciding when to mail the questionnaire, the researcher should take into account common vacation periods and other such factors that may affect how quickly persons are likely to respond. If one were mailing questionnaires to university faculty members and asking that they be completed and returned within 10 days, it obviously would not be wise to mail them just before semester break. Apparently most librarians prefer to receive work-related questionnaires at the office rather than at home.[15] A timetable can be quite useful for keeping track of when certain activities relating to the distribution of the questionnaire should take place.

Most researchers utilizing a mail (or e-mail or Web-based) questionnaire should expect to have to conduct one or more follow-up mailings in order to reach an adequate response rate. In so doing, the researcher must first decide how long to wait before distributing a follow-up mailing. This decision will depend upon how long the participants were given to respond to the first mailing. The response period should be long enough to avoid rushing the participants but short enough that they do not forget about the questionnaire. One to two weeks is usually considered to be a reasonable period of time.

A second decision relating to the follow-up is whether another copy of the questionnaire should be included with the reminder letter. Once again, any device that will help to increase the number of responses should be considered. Obviously, the more duplicate questionnaires mailed, the greater the costs for the researcher. (The cost of postage is not an issue with the e-mail or Web-based questionnaire; however, there are still costs associated with the researcher's time.) Persons receiving a follow-up with no questionnaire are not likely to take the time to write for another copy if they have lost the first one. Some experts recommend designing the follow-up to be as eye-catching as possible, through the use of clever letters, humorous pictures, and so on. Items such as free pencils, books, and so on are sometimes offered with the follow-up to encourage responses.

Another important decision regarding follow-up mailings concerns whether to send them to all participants in the study or only to those who have not yet responded. In order to avoid sending follow-up questionnaires to all participants, obviously one must maintain some sort of record of returns. The most common method of keeping track of who has returned his or her questionnaire, unless respondents are asked to write their names, is to code each questionnaire. This is usually done by placing somewhere on each questionnaire a number that represents each participant in the survey. When a questionnaire is returned, the code number is noted, and the corresponding name is checked as having returned the questionnaire.

This method, however, has a serious drawback when utilized in a study guaranteeing *anonymity*. People are becoming more aware of this technique and realize that a number or code on their questionnaire probably means the researcher will be able to associate their answers with their names. Consequently, they may well doubt the researcher's promise to maintain anonymity, if given. As a result, they may refuse to answer the questionnaire, or at least the validity of their responses may be weakened.

One method for dealing with the need to maintain a record of who has returned his or her questionnaire, in order to avoid sending follow-up questionnaires to all participants, while still assuring anonymity, involves the use of postcards. A postcard can be sent with each questionnaire with a code number for, or the name of, each participant. No identifier is put on the questionnaire itself. The participant is asked to mail the postcard separately but at about the same time that the questionnaire is returned. The researcher will thus receive something indicating who has returned his or her questionnaire but will not be able to associate a particular response with an individual, or at least not on the basis of code numbers.

Another technique involves removing the respondent's name from a master list upon receipt of his or her questionnaire. Having done so, if any identifier is

removed from the questionnaire, there is no longer any way to associate responses with names of respondents. When a follow-up questionnaire is mailed, it
is sent only to those names remaining on the master list. (If either of these two
techniques is to be used for follow-up mailings, it probably is a good idea to explain it briefly in the cover letter.) Readers particularly interested in follow-up
mailings may wish to refer to a work by Erdos.[16]

No matter how many steps one takes to maximize the response to a questionnaire, there is still a good chance that the response rate will be lower than what
was desired, especially with a mail questionnaire. One rule of thumb has been
that a response rate of at least 75% is needed if one to be able to assume that
what was learned about the respondents is reasonably equivalent to what would
have been learned about all the individuals included in the survey had everyone
responded. Seventy-five percent is a rather high threshold, however, and many
surveys have gathered reliable data with lower response rates. The critical issue is
how much the non-respondents differ from those who did respond. An acceptable
response rate can be lower for a homogeneous population than for a heterogeneous one. If one is concerned about the response rate, then it is advisable to
learn as much as possible about the non-respondents, at least on the key variables, to determine how much they differ from the respondents. Information can
be obtained about non-respondents by, for example, examining other sources of
data such as census reports, checking the findings of studies of the same population, and conducting telephone interviews with non-respondents

Electronic Questionnaire

In the relatively recent past, a few surveys have been designed for participants
to enter their responses directly into a personal computer; however, in the late
1980s and early 1990s e-mail questionnaires were more often used because of
the ease of transmission, the immediacy of the delivery, and the low cost of distribution. These early survey instruments were text-based and allowed for no in-
teractivity. They were basically paper questionnaires delivered electronically. The
World Wide Web became more available and more popular in the mid-1990s and
made multimedia and interactive surveys possible. One can even use dynamic
forms that store the responses, permit downloading the data, and often compile
the results. Some facilities for conducting online surveys are provided free on the
Web. One problem with e-mail surveys is acquiring e-mail address lists, but
the Web has made it possible to acquire convenience samples without having to
know respondents' e-mail addresses.[17]

A literature review conducted by Schonlau, Fricker, and Elliot indicates "that
surveys using a mail response mode and surveys using both a mail and Web response mode tend to have higher response rates than those using just an e-mail or
Web response mode."[18] In the studies reported, "response rates range from 7 to 44
percent for Web surveys and from 6 to 68 percent for e-mail surveys."[19] Roselle
and Neufeld, in a survey reported in 1998, found "that e-mail as a follow-up

method is as effective as postal mail in terms of both the speed and size of the survey response."[20]

Although there is a belief that e-mail questionnaires are less expensive than mail questionnaires, this may pertain only to postage and printing costs. Schonlau, Fricker, and Elliot state that Web surveys are more economical than mail surveys when several hundred to a thousand surveys are distributed.[21] They caution that technical problems and programming costs associated with Web surveys can rapidly increase costs.

Electronic questionnaires should be designed using most of the criteria that are discussed in the preceding text. Schonlau, Fricker, and Elliot provide a list of guidelines specifically for developing an electronic questionnaire.[22] They suggest listing only a few questions per screen, using graphics sparingly, and providing an indication of the respondents' progress in answering the survey.[23]

E-mail and Web-based surveys can be designed to automate skip patterns and automatically validate answers. Electronic surveys can be designed to skip questions, based on the respondents' answers to previous questions, and to validate the respondents' answers to identify missed questions or unusable answers. These automated functions help to reduce measurement errors. There are numerous commercial and open source electronic survey tools available. These tools enable researchers to create and administer surveys using a Web interface. The survey responses are stored in databases that can be accessed online or downloaded into software programs.

The sources of error for e-mail and Web-based questionnaires include those discussed above for the mail survey. The lack of coverage for Internet surveys is the most readily identified source of error. As more of the population has access to the Web, this error will become less of an issue in the sampling design for Web-based surveys. As noted by Schonlau, Fricker, and Elliot, when developing e-mail and Web-based surveys, the researchers should develop a method for stripping the e-mail addresses of the respondents to maintain confidentiality and anonymity of the respondents' names. Schonlau, Fricker, and Elliot also recommend that the respondents be assured that all survey data are encrypted and saved to a private server in order to retain the respondents' privacy.[24] Miller and Salkind state that it is possible that someone other than the intended recipient may see the subjects' responses; therefore, the subjects should be informed that while every effort will be made to retain the subject's privacy and confidentiality, it cannot be guaranteed.[25] But the most serious weaknesses of electronic surveys are that e-mail addresses often cannot be randomly dialed and that such surveys underrepresent people who do not have computers—people who tend to have lower income and less education.

Nicholls, Baker, and Martin report that computer-assisted survey research techniques may be more efficient than conventional techniques, without reducing the quality of the data. This is dependent upon the design of survey instruments that adhere to criteria such as the following:

1. Easy to read online.
2. Don't often require respondents to leave their computers to find information.
3. Don't take up excessive space in electronic mailboxes.

4. Are preceded by a separate introductory message.
5. Provide adequate instructions, and on the screen where needed.
6. Anticipate how different systems will format the questionnaire.
7. Minimize cursor movement.
8. Don't assume more than basic computer skills.[26]

Schonlau, Fricker, and Elliott provide guidelines for e-mail and Web-based survey design and implementation for those who are interested in more detailed information on this subject.[27] Covey outlines the different methods of developing and administering survey questionnaires in library research.[28] Hsu describes "a software program designed exclusively for the creation of survey questionnaires. Its main goal is to enable a user to create, edit, modify and run online surveys using the markup language system."[29]

THE INTERVIEW

Developing the Interview

The basic steps in developing a *standardized* or *structured* interview are not that different from those for developing most other kinds of survey studies. One of the first steps must be development of the list of questions to be asked, or the *interview schedule*. The techniques for constructing questionnaires and structured interview schedules are quite similar and consequently will not be repeated here. As is true for questionnaires, it is highly recommended that interview schedules be pretested. Again, the pretest should provide the respondents with ample opportunity to comment on the questions.

An additional step in the development of the interview involves the training of interviewers. Even if one is working with experienced interviewers, they need to become familiar with the researcher's particular questions. The same interviewers should be involved in the pretest as in the final interview.

Conducting the Personal Interview

In conducting an interview, the interviewer should attempt to create a friendly, nonthreatening atmosphere. Much as one does with a cover letter, the interviewer should give a brief, casual introduction to the study; stress the importance of the person's participation; and assure anonymity, or at least confidentiality, when possible. The interviewer should answer all legitimate questions about the nature of the study and produce appropriate credentials upon request. He or she should be prepared to respond to such questions as: How did you happen to pick me? Who gave you my name? Why don't you go next door?

When possible and appropriate, the researcher should set up the interview well in advance, and of course the interviewer should appear for the interview punctually. Some researchers recommend sending the list of questions to the participant before the scheduled interview. This may be inadvisable, however, if the interviewer is particularly concerned about obtaining frank, spontaneous responses.

Giving respondents a lot of time to consider answers is likely to reduce their candidness. If the interview has been scheduled ahead of time, it is a good idea to confirm the date in writing and to send a reminder several days before the interview. Audiovisual aids may be used to facilitate the questioning or improve the recording of responses. If the interviewee's responses are to be taped, his or her permission to do so should be obtained in advance.

Following the interview, the researcher may wish to submit a typescript of the questions and responses to the interviewee for confirmation of the accuracy of the answers. It should be made clear, however, that the respondent is not to use this opportunity to revise the meaning or the substance of his or her answers. At this point, if not before the interview, it may be desirable to obtain the interviewee's permission to use the information in the resulting research report.

When asking the questions, the interviewer should avoid rephrasing questions for the interviewee. One of the advantages of interviews is the inherent personal contact, but one must be careful that this does not become a liability. Expansions or revisions of questions, or unnecessary explanations, in effect result in different questions being asked of different participants. Consequently, comparisons of responses become invalid. For similar reasons, the interviewer should not alter the sequence of the questions from respondent to respondent, nor should he or she omit questions. As was discussed earlier, the context of the question can affect or bias its response. And, as was true for questionnaires, the interviewer should avoid asking more than one question at a time. In contrast to mail, e-mail, or Web-based questionnaires, the reactions of the researcher can affect the respondent's answers. The interviewer must be careful not to show surprise or other emotions as a result of any of the interviewee's responses. Such reactions can bias future responses of the participant.

In obtaining or encouraging responses, the interviewer may find it necessary to repeat certain questions. This should not present a problem so long as the interviewer does not significantly change the wording of such questions. In order to obtain an adequate response from the interviewee, it may on occasion be necessary for the interviewer to ask the respondent to elaborate on his or her reply. If done carefully, this should be legitimate, but one should always avoid putting words into the respondent's mouth. The interviewee's responses should represent his or her thoughts alone, not a combination of his or hers and the interviewer's. To obtain as many responses as possible, the interviewer must also learn how to deal with "don't knows." Often, people need a certain amount of encouragement before they will respond fully to a particular question. There is a fine line, however, between encouraging a response and helping to word it or forcing an answer where there should not be one. Consequently, one should be conservative or cautious in encouraging a response when the interviewee seems reluctant to provide one. Probing for complete answers can take the form of repeating the question (with the caveats given above), making an expectant pause, repeating the respondent's answer, making reassuring remarks, asking for further clarification, and asking neutral questions such as: Anything else? Any other reason? Could you tell me more about that?

As is the case with questionnaires, it is desirable to precode the answer sheets when possible. This is feasible only with fixed or structured responses, of course. Free-answer responses should be recorded verbatim, if at all possible, to facilitate subsequent analysis and to prevent the loss of data. Tape recorders provide one relatively easy method of recording answers word for word. It is a good idea to record responses during the interview and to use the respondent's own words (rather than summaries or paraphrases). If any probes for more complete answers are used, they should be noted.

Disadvantages of the Interview

As with other research methods and techniques, bias presents a real threat to the validity of interviews. Particularly critical is the bias that may be introduced by the interviewer. As was indicated earlier, some interviewer bias can be avoided by ensuring that the interviewer does not overreact to responses of the interviewee. Other steps that can be taken to help avoid or reduce interviewer bias include having the interviewer dress inconspicuously and appropriately for the environment, holding the interview in a private setting, and keeping the interview as informal as possible.

The Internet interview diminishes the chances of introducing some of these biases. The Internet interview utilizes computer-mediated communication (CMC) which allows humans to interact directly with each other in synchronous or real time using monitors, text, and keyboards. Researchers have used Internet interviewing to investigate Internet use and culture, the demographics and characteristics of Internet users, experiences with distance learning, and general human behavior.[30] One of the main biases of Internet interviewing is the unrepresentativeness of the sample since a small percentage of the world's population is on-line ("only approximately .01 of the world's population was on-line at the start of 2002"[31]).

Rapport and interpersonal relationships are more difficult to develop in an on-line interview than in person. It is possible to establish a relationship on-line, but it requires a specific skill and can be more challenging than in a face-to-face or telephone interview. The interview can be quite expensive in terms of travel and long distance telephone costs. An Internet interview is a more cost-efficient and practical method for conducting in-depth interviews if there is an economical telecommunications system and if the interviewers and researchers are comfortable with and knowledgeable of the technology used for the Internet interviews.

As with the electronic questionnaire discussed above, the Internet interview raises legal and ethical issues. Mann and Stewart state, "There is little agreement about how to proceed ethically in a virtual arena, and few research practice conventions are available."[32] It is difficult to authenticate the responses in an Internet interview, which necessitates taking steps to ensure that the appropriate person is participating in the interview.

Advantages of the Interview

In contrast to the mail or electronic questionnaire, the interview does have certain important advantages. Perhaps most important, it almost always produces a better response rate. Thus the sample of persons actually participating in the study tends to represent a large percentage of the original sample and is, therefore, more representative of the population than would be a sample representing a relatively low response rate. Apparently the personal contact of the interview helps to encourage, or put more pressure on, persons to respond fully. Consequently, it is also possible to employ interview schedules of greater length than comparable questionnaires, without jeopardizing a satisfactory response rate.

As was suggested earlier, the personal contact also provides a greater capacity than the mail or electronic questionnaire for the correction of misunderstandings by participants. Again, one must be careful that this capability is not abused and becomes a disadvantage as a result.

It is generally believed that the interview is better at revealing information that is complex or emotionally laden. The use of visual aids can sometimes facilitate presenting and recording complicated information. The data gathered from Internet interviews can be easily uploaded to data analysis software packages.

FOCUS GROUP INTERVIEWS

In contrast to what has been covered thus far, there are less-structured interview techniques available to the researcher. The unstructured interview is more flexible than the structured one and most appropriate in the early stages of an investigation and in qualitative studies. It is generally better for studying perceptions, attitudes, and motivation, but it tends to be more difficult to administer and analyze. Examples of less-structured interviews include the focus(ed) group, the clinical interview or personal history, and the nondirective interview.

The *focus group* is a group interview designed "to explore in depth the feelings and beliefs people hold and to learn how these feelings shape overt behavior."[33] "They are called focus groups because the discussions start out broadly and gradually narrow down to the focus of the research."[34] The focus group interview technique can be used as a self-contained research method or in combination with other quantitative and qualitative research methods. Focus groups are useful for orienting oneself to a new field; developing ideas and concepts or even generating hypotheses based on informants' insights; evaluating different research sites or study populations; developing and refining research instruments, such as interview schedules and questionnaires; and getting participants' interpretations of results from earlier studies. As a self-contained method, focus groups can be used to explore new research areas or to examine known research questions from the participants' perspective, facilitate complex decision making, and identify and address important issues. The focus group interview may be used to replace the questionnaire or individual interviews, if the research questions warrant use of the method.

Library and information agencies can utilize the focus group interview method to develop needs assessment, community analysis, and promotional strategies for new services. Focus group interviews can be utilized in library and information science research to answer research questions concerned with the evaluation of library resources and services, including on-line public access catalogs and on-line resources. The method can be used in all types of libraries and indeed has been used in public, academic, special, and state libraries.

The method can also be used to identify the information gathering patterns of scholars and other specific user groups. The participants could be asked to discuss the sources they use to find information, what types of information they find most useful, how they evaluate the information they retrieve, and what resources or tools would facilitate information retrieval for their specific purposes. The literature does not reflect this use of the method.

Focus group interviews have been used in academic, newspaper, hospital, public, and state libraries to gather information on users' perceptions of services and collections.[35] A public library system utilized the method to gather information on the lifestyles of senior citizens in order to identify barriers and methods to increase library use by the elderly.[36] The New York State Education Department used the focus group interview method in conjunction with other methods to evaluate advisory and information referral services.[37] Mellon incorporated focus group interviews in the evaluation of bibliographic instruction by undergraduate students.[38] An LIS program conducted focus groups to identify the need for professional library and information science education within a state and the role of the program in providing such education.[39] The method can and has been used to gather information about the work and beliefs of practicing librarians.

Reference and technical service librarians participated in focus group interviews to identify their perceptions of a need for on-line authority control systems.[40] In Wisconsin, academic and public library technical services managers and catalogers participated in focus group interviews to assist the researchers in developing hypotheses for an extensive study of the decisions made and the tasks performed by technical services managers and catalogers.[41] The technical services managers and catalogers were asked to describe their typical day on the job, the decisions made during a workday, and how the job had changed over the past two years. The focus group interview method was used as an exploratory approach in this instance to develop a list of tasks performed by technical services managers and catalogers and to assign these tasks to decision levels.

The focus group interview technique has also been used in libraries to evaluate on-line searching by end users, as well as in the research and development of on-line public access catalogs.[42] Faculty and undergraduate and graduate students were asked to describe the on-line library catalogs they had used and their reasons for using the catalogs, to identify the difficulties encountered in the use of the university online catalog, and to discuss the characteristics of an on-line cata-log that they would find useful. The data were used by the library administration to identify necessary improvements to the existing on-line catalog.[43] Connaway includes readings and a bibliography of the uses of focus group interviews in li-brary and information agencies.[44] Covey outlines how focus group interviews are used in library research.[45]

In designing a focus group interview, the researcher, keeping in mind the ob-jectives of the study, must first decide who will be interviewed. Focus groups typically consist of from 5 to 12 people. Volunteers are often recruited for focus groups (though they may be reimbursed), but it is desirable to select participants who are as representative as possible of their population. Selection of the moder-ator is equally important. Preferably, the moderator will be an outside person, trained in focus group techniques, with good communication skills.

Focus groups are usually scheduled for one session of one or two hours, but it may be necessary to hold more than one session in some cases. It also may be desirable to break or stratify groups into smaller, more homogeneous groups. For example, college students could be divided into subgroups of undergraduate, graduate, and professional students. The interview should be held in a conve-nient, comfortable, informal location that is conducive to discussion. It may be necessary to use a room that accommodates audio taping and/or observation be-hind a one-way mirror. Refreshments may be a good idea.

The focus group session should open with appropriate introductions and "ice-breakers" and then shift to the interview itself. The moderator, of course, has the primary responsibility for conducting the interview. He or she should utilize an interview schedule or discussion guide. This guide should not be a list of struc-tured questions, all of which must be posed. Rather, it "should be designed as a projective technique, designed to deliberately stimulate a relaxed free-flow of as-sociations and bypass people's built-in censoring mechanisms."[46]

The moderator asks questions intended to initiate discussion of pertinent issues, but beyond that should "keep guidance and direction to a minimum".[47] He or she should listen to, not edit or judge, participants' comments. The moderator should employ standard techniques for conducting unstructured interviews, such as prob-ing for more complete responses, encouraging everyone to participate, establish-ing a nonthreatening environment, and not asking leading questions. It is a good idea to assign another person the primary responsibility for recording the content of the interview and to utilize someone else as an assistant and neutral observer.

Notes of the focus group sessions are often taken with the aid of audio recorders, but at some point tape recordings must be transcribed and reduced to a more manageable size. Recorders often use forms to facilitate initial note taking or the summarizing of mechanically recorded data. When taking notes, the recorder should attempt to

1. Trace the threads of an idea throughout the discussion;
2. Identify the subgroup or individual to whom an idea is important;

3. Distinguish between ideas held in common from those held by individuals;
4. Capture the vocabulary and style of the group; and
5. Distinguish, if possible, among perceptions, feelings, and insights.[48]

Analysis and Reporting of the Focus Group Data

The information acquired from focus group interviews is generally used to help researchers understand perceptions and attitudes of the target population. The results of focus group interviews cannot be used to generalize to an entire population, as the groups may not be representative of their total populations. Instead, the results give one the opportunity to consider a range of responses to questions.

The focus group interview permits assessment of nonverbal responses and reveals group interaction patterns. The researcher analyzes the data acquired from the moderator's reports and taped interview sessions. The analysis begins with getting an overview or global picture of the entire process and involves consideration of words, tone, context, nonverbal communications, responses, and ideas of the interviewees.

There are then two basic approaches to analyzing focus group data—ethnographic summary and content analysis. The content analysis approach produces numerical descriptions of the data. Content analysis is the tallying of mentions of very specific factors. Mentions can be brief or very extensive and can be weighted.

Ethnography involves establishing rapport, selecting research participants, transcribing observations and conversations, and keeping diaries, although Geertz believes that none of these techniques or procedures adequately defines the venture. He believes ethnography is defined by the kind of intellectual effort it is, "an elaborate venture in 'thick description.'"[49] Reality, as perceived by the observer, is described in such detail that the reader can experience the total event as if he or she had actually been involved in it. The data must be interpreted in a manner that retains this richness. This thick description, including group interactions, is one of the advantages of the focus group interview method. The ethnographic summary and the content analysis approach are not conflicting means of analysis. The combination of the two approaches brings an additional strength to the analysis.[50]

One of the recurring questions that arise with the discussion of the focus group interview technique is that of its validity and reliability as a research method. "Focus groups are valid if they are used carefully for a problem that is suitable for focus group inquiry."[51] If the researcher deviates from the established procedures outlined above and if the research questions do not lend themselves to focus group interview methods, the focus group interviews are invalid. The focus group interview method is similar to other social science methods where validity depends not only on the procedures used but also on the context within which the procedures are used.[52]

The validity of the analysis of the data collected during the focus group interviews is another concern. If content analysis is used as a method of data analysis, "the validity between the classification schemes, or variables derived from it, and the validity of the interpretation relating content variables to their causes or consequences" is crucial.[53] This means that in the dissemination and interpretation of the results, the researcher must ascertain that the findings are not generalizable beyond, nor dependent upon, specific methods, data, or measurements outside the specified study.[54]

Reproducibility, or intercoder reliability, can be determined when the same data are coded with the same results by more than one coder. Intercoder reliability is important in content analysis because it measures the consistency of understandings or meaning held by two or more coders.[55] Intercoder reliability should be determined when analyzing focus group interview data. If one person examines one set of transcripts, while another concentrates on a different set of transcripts, two perceptions and perspectives of discovery can also be included in the reporting of the results.[56]

Other Advantages and Disadvantages of the Focus Group Interview

The main advantage of focus group interviews is the opportunity to observe a large amount of interactions on a topic in a limited period of time.[57] In contrast to most other techniques, focus group interviews are able to benefit from the interactions of more than one respondent. "In focus groups, people tend to be less inhibited than in individual interviews."[58]

The methodology can also be used with hard-to-reach groups, such as library nonusers, minorities, and children. It is a data gathering technique that can be useful to both practitioners and researchers when they want to find out not only what a specific group thinks, but why the group thinks what it does. The format gives the moderator a chance to probe and to develop questions and discussions not anticipated by the researcher. The results can be analyzed and reported shortly after the data have been collected.[59]

Focus group interviews are quite susceptible to bias caused by the interview setting, the moderator, faulty questions, and an unrepresentative sample. The cost of the sessions can be another disadvantage of the focus group methodology. Each session can cost as much as $2,500.[60] The cost of the session may include gifts and gratuities for the participants, as well as moderator fees, refreshments, and travel expenses. Libraries and other nonprofit organizations can utilize this research technique at a lesser cost by training staff to be moderators, paying mileage only for the participants, using library facilities for the sessions, and offering refreshments to the participants instead of gifts or gratuities.

The success of the focus group interview is dependent upon the skills of the moderator. The moderator must be carefully trained in the technique. If the moderator is not capable of directing the participants' discussions to the research questions, the participants can redirect the focus of the interview. The group experience may intimidate and suppress individual differences, causing some participants to withdraw and not participate in the discussions. Focus group interviews can also foster conformity among group members. The group participants can display a collective pattern of defensive avoidance and practice self-censorship by pressuring any member who expresses strong arguments counter to the group's stereotypes or rationalizations. This can intensify group loyalties and rigidly polarize individual opinions. The focus group interview methodology is vulnerable to manipulation by an influential and skillful member of the group. A skillful and trained moderator can control these disadvantages.

"Focus groups should be followed up with statistically sound quantitative research"[61]; they should not be used as the sole basis for making policy decisions. They can provide another type of data for decision making when used in combination with other methods and data analyses.

TELEPHONE INTERVIEWS

Another important type of interview is the telephone interview. Because more and more interviews are being conducted over the telephone, this technique deserves special attention. Like the researcher-administered questionnaire, the telephone interview tends to combine the advantages and disadvantages of the mail questionnaire and the personal interview.

Among the advantages of the telephone interview are the following: one, it tends to provide significant savings in actual time and cost in contrast to the personal interview; two, it can be conducted more quickly after an event has occurred; three, it is generally easier to supervise, train, and monitor the staff for a telephone interview than for a personal interview (telephone interviewing does require some special skills, however, that should be incorporated in the training); and four, telephone interviews lend themselves to a certain amount of computer assistance. CATI, or computer-assisted telephone interviewing, can build in skip patterns to expedite the interview process and thereby increase the savings in time and money.

CATI is quite popular with survey researchers. There are various CATI practices, but it basically involves the automatic dialing of computer-generated random digit telephone numbers and an interviewer equipped with a headset and the script and questions displayed on a computer monitor. When the respondent answers the telephone, the interviewer begins asking the questions and inputs the respondent's answers into the computer. The data are automatically prepared for analysis.[62] CATI was first introduced in 1971, but it did not gain in popularity until the early 1990s with the introduction of computer-assisted personal interviewing (CAPI), which is similar to CATI, but involves face-to-face interviews.[63]

One major disadvantage of the telephone interview is that the process obviously favors those people who have telephones. The Institute for Social Research at the University of Michigan has estimated that from 9% to 10% of American adults do not have telephones, and that a high percentage of those who do not are poor and live in rural areas. Consequently, a sample of telephone subscribers would tend to underrepresent poor and rural households, thus producing a bias that may weaken a particular study.

Further aggravating this problem is the fact that unlisted telephone numbers are becoming more common. Computerized, random digit dialing helps to alleviate this problem, however, in that this technique can generate unlisted, as well as listed, telephone numbers. In addition, it can help to ensure the respondent's

TABLE 5.1
Advantages & Disadvantages of Four Survey Designs

Characteristics of Design	Mail Survey	Phone Survey	In-Person Survey	Electronic Survey
Representative sample				
Opportunity for inclusion is known				
For completely listed populations	High	High	High	Medium
For incompletely listed populations	Medium	Medium	High	Low
Selection within sampling units is controlled	Medium	High	High	Low
(e.g., specific family members must respond)				
Respondents are likely to be located	High	High	Medium	
If samples are heterogeneous	Medium	High	High	Low
If samples are homogeneous & specialized	High	High	High	High
Questionnaire construction & question design				
Allowable length of questionnaire	Medium	Medium	High	Medium
Ability to include				
Complex questions	Medium	Low	High	High
Open-ended questions	Low	High	High	Medium
Screening questions	Low	High	High	High
Tedious, boring questions	Low	High	High	Low
Ability to control question sequence	Low	High	High	High
Ability to ensure questionnaire completion	Medium	High	High	Low
Distortion of answers				
Odds of avoiding social desirability bias	High	Medium	Low	High
Odds of avoiding interviewer bias	High	Medium	Low	High
Odds of avoiding contamination by others	Medium	High	Medium	Medium
Administrative goals				
Odds of meeting personnel requirements	High	High	Low	Medium
Odds of implementing quickly	Low	High	Low	High
Odds of keeping costs low	High	Medium	Low	High

Source: Russell K. Schutt, *Investigating the Social World: The Process and Practice of Research, Third Edition*, copyright © 2001. Reprinted with permission of the Pine Forge Press/Sage Publications, Inc.

anonymity. A manual technique known as "added digit dialing" or "add-a-digit sampling" can also help to ease the problem of unlisted numbers.

Finally, in comparison with the personal interview, the person being interviewed over the telephone tends to find it easier to terminate the interview before it is finished. Therefore, the response rate tends to be a bit lower for telephone than for personal interviews. Babbie provides a list of survey research techniques that have developed because of advances in technology.[64] Frey has authored a book specifically on survey research by telephone.[65]

In order to summarize some of the advantages and disadvantages of the mail survey, phone survey, in-person survey, and electronic survey, a chart comparing the three techniques on major criteria is given in Table 5.1

OBSERVATION

Observe means to watch attentively in a scientific or systematic manner. In an observational study, the current status of a phenomenon is determined not by asking but by observing. Observation is sometimes treated as a research method, sometimes as a data collection technique to be utilized with a research method. As a data collection technique, it is used in both basic and applied research and in quantitative and qualitative studies. In applied research, it probably is most frequently used in evaluation. In basic research, it is used with both experimental and survey research designs. Observational methods are central to much qualitative research.

Observation is one of the oldest forms of data collection, but, in order to qualify as scientific observation, it should meet certain criteria. Scientific observation should be systematic, objective, and free from bias; quantitative whenever possible; and strong in usability, reliability, and validity.[66]

Advantages of Observational Research

As a data collection technique, observation has several important advantages, including the following:

1. The use of observation makes it possible to record behavior as it occurs.
2. Observation allows one to compare what people actually did with what they said they did. Participants in a study may consciously or unconsciously report their behavior as different than it in fact occurred; the observed behavior may well be more valid.
3. Observational techniques can identify behavior, actions, and so on that people may not think to report because they seem unimportant or irrelevant. It can enable the researcher to examine the relative influence of many factors.[67]
4. With observational techniques, a researcher can study subjects who are unable to give verbal reports.

5. The use of observation is generally independent of the subjects' willingness to participate. For example, one could observe how library patrons are using the catalog without asking each patron beforehand if he or she were willing to be observed. There are ethical and sometimes legal implications that should be explored before deciding to observe persons without their permission, or at least their awareness, however.

Limitations of Observational Research

Observational techniques do suffer from a few limitations; some of the more important ones are as follows:

1. It is not always possible to anticipate a spontaneous event and thus be prepared to observe it. Some of the most critical activity at the library's on-line catalog, for example, may take place when no one is there to observe.
2. The duration of an event affects the feasibility of observing it. The activities at an on-line catalog are generally short enough to be easily observed; such would not be the case in trying to observe how a faculty member conducts his or her research.
3. Some types of behavior are obviously too private or personal in nature to be observed. This is less of a disadvantage in library-related research, however, than it is in the behavioral sciences.
4. It is generally somewhat more difficult to quantify observational data than other kinds. Behavior simply cannot always be broken down into neat categories.

Unstructured Observation

There are essentially two basic types of observation—structured and unstructured; the latter will be considered first. Unstructured observation is sometimes equated with participant observation, but its most important characteristic reflects the fact that the researcher does not have predetermined sets of categories of behavior to use. Therefore, it is a relatively flexible technique and is particularly useful in exploratory research.

In planning unstructured, observational research, one must take into account the participants or subjects, the setting, the purpose for the subjects' being where they are, the type of behavior to be observed, and the frequency and duration of the behavior. In other words, the researcher must be as well prepared as possible to record accurately the upcoming behavior without going so far as to predesignate specific categories of behavior or to limit the observations to those types of behavior.

The researcher must also decide beforehand what kind of relationship he or she plans to have with the subjects. The observer may be obtrusive—that is, obviously observing certain behavior and known to the subjects—or unobtrusive.

If he or she is going to participate in the activities of the subject, is it going to be in an active or passive role? Finally, the researcher must decide whether the observation will take place with or without the permission of the subjects. Again, ethical considerations come into play here, especially if the observation is to be unobtrusive. (See Chapter 7 for more consideration of these issues.)

In recording unstructured observation, it is best if records are made on the spot and during the event in order to maximize their accuracy. As to techniques, it is best to record observations as unobtrusively as possible, even if the researcher is a participant. Record keeping should not be distracting for the subjects, or it may affect their behavior. Common techniques include taking notes (anecdotal records) and remembering behavior to be recorded later. The latter technique obviously tends to be less reliable and less accurate.

There are steps that can be taken to increase the accuracy of unstructured observations. They include the following:

1. Using two or more observational techniques, such as sound and visual recordings, and then comparing results.
2. Having two or more people observe the same behavior, with the same technique, and then comparing the results.
3. Being careful to distinguish between actual behavior and perceptions or interpretations of the behavior when taking notes. Researcher bias can easily creep in during this stage.
4. Avoiding becoming involved in the activity being observed.
5. Being careful not to take behavior for granted.
6. Obtaining reactions from the participants regarding the accuracy of the observations can be useful in situations where the subjects are fully aware of the role of the researcher. But one would have to be careful that doing so did not affect or bias future behavior of the subjects.

Structured Observation

Structured observation is a more formal technique, often used in quantitative studies in order to provide systematic description or to test causal hypotheses. It may be used in field studies or in laboratory type settings, but it should focus on designated aspects of behavior.

As was the case with unstructured observation, the observer must decide in advance what type of relationship should exist between him or her and the subjects to be observed. Beyond that, the steps involved in planning structured observation are somewhat different from those for unstructured observation.

The most basic step involves developing the observational categories to be employed. (These are set up in advance but may be adjusted later if necessary.) Developing such categories involves defining appropriate, measurable acts, establishing time units or the time length of observations, and anticipating patterns of the phenomena likely to occur. The observer also must decide on his or her

TABLE 5.2
Flander's Category System for Classroom Behavior

Response	1. Accepts Feeling
	2. Praises or Encourages
	3. Accepts or Uses Ideas of Pupils
Teacher Talk	4. Asks Questions
Imitation	5. Lecturing
	6. Giving Directions
	7. Criticizing or Justifying Authority
Pupil Talk	8. Pupil-Talk Response
	9. Pupil-Talk Imitation
Silence	10.

frame of reference; for example, will certain behavior be categorized according to a subject's actions or intentions, or by the reactions of others?

Specific techniques used for recording structured observations include the use of rating scales, with which characteristics or behaviors are rated according to the degree to which they are present. Similarly, one may use "all-or-none" or dichotomous categories where the behavior is simply present or absent.

If the researcher can be quite specific about the types of behavior likely to occur, he or she may elect to utilize sheets with checklists of categories to be coded and cells to be checked as their respective categories of behavior occur. Checklists also may employ symbols to represent certain types of behavior in order to speed up the process of recording observations. An example of a checklist of categories is presented in Table 5.2. This is Flander's system, in which classroom behavior is classified according to ten categories.[68]

The researcher may choose to use mechanical recording instruments or audiovisual equipment to record observations as accurately as possible. Using audiovisual equipment is useful for providing an overall view of some behavior, and it permits the researcher to analyze the behavior more closely and at his or her leisure. It does not systematically record or categorize the data; the researcher must still do this. Having the opportunity to observe again behavior at a more controlled, slower pace can help to avoid overloading the observer, which is one of the most serious threats to observational accuracy. Otherwise, one must be careful not to assign too much activity to be observed to one observer.

Other steps that can be taken to increase the reliability of structured observation, as well as unstructured observation in some cases, include the following:

1. Developing adequate definitions of the kinds of behavior that are to be recorded, and being certain that they correspond to the specific concepts to be studied.

2. Carefully training the observers to ensure that they are adequately prepared and that they have confidence in their ability or judgment to check the appropriate categories.
3. Avoiding observer bias. Generally the observer should take behaviors at their face value and not attempt to interpret their "real" meaning, at least not at the time the observations are made.

The researcher also should be concerned with the validity of the observation, or the extent to which the recorded differences in subjects represent actual differences rather than the observer's perceptions of differences. Some of the measures that can be taken to improve the accuracy of unstructured observations apply to structured observations as well.

SUMMARY

In conducting survey research, the researcher has several data collection techniques at his or her disposal. This chapter has considered three of the most commonly used techniques—the questionnaire, the interview, and observation.

Questionnaires and interviews are frequently used for obtaining information about a person's perceptions, beliefs, attitudes, and so on. As the Internet has become more widely available and popular, it is being utilized to distribute questionnaires and to conduct interviews. With the Web survey, more "attention has been focused on the role of the survey interviewer in an automated data collection environment."[69]

With these techniques, heavy reliance is placed on the respondent's report; normally, the investigator has not observed the events in question. This raises the issue of the validity of verbal reports in particular, but the question of validity (and reliability) is important in deciding upon any technique of data collection. Observational methods are best suited for describing and understanding behavior as it occurs. They are less effective for gathering information about a person's perceptions, beliefs, attitudes, and so on.

In developing any of the three data collection techniques, the researcher must make decisions regarding the specific types of questions to be used or the types of behavior to be observed. These decisions are greatly affected by the kinds of information needed and whether the study is exploratory in nature. Throughout the design process, the researcher must be particularly careful not to introduce bias into the study. Even the sequencing of questions can affect their accuracy.

Finally, in selecting a specific technique or instrument, the researcher should weigh the various pros and cons of each method. For example, if one were particularly anxious to achieve a high response rate, he or she might choose the interview over the questionnaire. If cost were the major concern, then the questionnaire would be the obvious choice, other considerations being roughly equal. No one method is likely to be perfect for a given situation, but it should be possible to select one technique as the best alternative, given the objectives, subject, priorities, and limitations of the investigation. Survey data collection techniques may be combined in order to provide richer data.

NOTES

[1] L. R. Gay and Peter W. Airasian, *Educational Research: Competencies for Analysis and Application*, 7th ed. (Upper Saddle River, NJ: Merrill/Prentice Hall, 2003).

[2] Jacquelyn Burkell, "The Dilemma of Survey Non-response," *Library & Information Science Research* 25 (Autumn 2003): 239–63.

[3] Charles M. Judd, Eliot R. Smith, and Louise H. Kidder, *Research Methods in Social Relations*, 6th ed. (Fort Worth: Holt, Rinehart, and Winston, 1991).

[4] Claire Selltiz, Lawrence S. Wrightsman, and Stuart W. Cook, *Research Methods in Social Relations*, rev. ed. (New York: Holt, Rinehart & Winston, 1959): 262.

[5] Gary Golden, *Survey Research Methods* (Chicago: ACRL, 1982): 43–46.

[6] Selltiz, Wrightsman, and Cook, *Research Methods in Social Relations*, 262.

[7] Judd, Smith, and Kidder, *Research Methods in Social Relations*, 147.

[8] "Questions and Answers," *ISR Newsletter* (Spring–Summer 1982): 6–7.

[9] Abraham Bookstein, "Questionnaire Research in a Library Setting," *Journal of Academic Librarianship* 11 (March 1985): 24–28.

[10] James S. Kidston, "The Validity of Questionnaire Responses," *Library Quarterly* 55 (April 1985): 133–50.

[11] Abraham Bookstein, "Sources of Error in Library Questionnaires," *Library Research* 4 (1982): 85–94.

[12] "Questions and Answers," 7.

[13] Delbert C. Miller and Neil J. Salkind, *Handbook of Research Design & Social Measurement*, 6th ed. (Thousand Oaks, CA: Sage Publications, 2002): 123.

[14] Mary Sue Stephenson, September 1, 2003. Available, *http://www.slais.ubc.ca/resources/research_methods/quantita.htm*.

[15] Marilyn Wurzburger, "Conducting a Mail Survey: Some of the Things You Probably Didn't Learn in Any Research Methods Course," *College & Research Libraries News* 48 (December 1987): 698.

[16] Paul L. Erdos, *Professional Mail Surveys*, rev. ed. (Malabar, FL: Robert E. Krieger Publishing, 1983).

[17] Matthias Schonlau, Ronald D. Fricker, and Marc N. Elliott, *Conducting Research Surveys via E-mail and the Web* (Santa Monica, CA: Rand, 2002).

[18] Ibid., 20.

[19] Ibid., 20.

[20] Ann Roselle and Steven Neufeld, "The Utility of Electronic Mail Follow-ups for Library Research," *Library & Information Science Research* 20; no. 2 (1998): 153–61.

[21] Schonlau, Fricker, and Elliott, *Conducting Research Surveys*, 26.

[22] Ibid., 42.

[23] Ibid., 46.

[24] Ibid., 46.

[25] Miller and Salkind, *Handbook of Research Design & Social Measurement*, 123.

[26] William L. Nicholls II, Reginald P. Baker, and Jean Martin, "The Effect of New Data Collection Technology on Survey Data Quality," in *Survey Measurement and Process Quality*, edited by L. Lyberg, P. Biemer, M. Collins, C. Dippo, N. Schwarz, and D. Trewin (New York: Wiley, 1996): 221–48.

[27] Schonlau, Fricker, and Elliott, *Conducting Research Surveys*.

[28] Denise Troll Covey, *Usage and Usability Assessment: Library Practices and Concerns* (Washington, D.C.: Digital Library Federation and Council on Library and Information Resources, 2002): 6–14.

[29]Jeffrey Hsu, "The Development of Electronic Surveys: A Computer Language-Based Method," *Electronic Library* 13, no. 3 (June 1995): 197.

[30]Chris Mann and Fiona Stewart, "Internet Interviewing," in *Handbook of Interview Research: Context & Method*, edited by Jaber F. Gubrium and James A. Holstein (Thousand Oaks, CA: Sage Publications, 2002): 604.

[31]Ibid., 605.

[32]Ibid., 609.

[33]Alfred E. Goldman and Susan S. McDonald, *The Group Depth Interview* (Englewood Cliffs, NJ: Prentice-Hall, 1987): 7.

[34]Victoria L. Young, "Focus on Focus Groups," *College & Research Libraries News* 7 (July–August 1993): 391.

[35]Barbara M. Robinson, *A Study of Reference Referral and Super Reference in California* (Sacramento, CA: California State Library, 1986); Charles T. Townley, "Developing Relationships Between Academic Libraries and the State Library of Pennsylvania: A Report of the Research Recommendations," unpublished consultant's report, report no. ED250542, August 1984; Debra Wilcox Johnson and Lynn Silipigni Connaway, "Arrowhead Library System, the Older Adult in Rock County: Implications for Library Service," unpublished consultants' report, March 1991; Jean Ward, Kathlen A. Hansen, and Douglas M. McLeod, "The News Library's Contribution to Newsmaking," *Special Libraries* 79, no. 2 (Spring 1988): 143–47; Kathryn Robbins and Ruth Holst, "Hospital Library Evaluation Using Focus Group Interviews," *Bulletin of the Medical Library Association* 78, no. 3 (July 1990): 311–13; M. K. Scharf and Jean Ward, "A Library Research Application of Focus Group Interviews," in *Association of College and Research Libraries National Conference, Energies for Transition* (Chicago: ACRL, 1986): 191–93; Richard Widdows, Tia A. Hensler, and Marlaya H. Wyncott, "The Focus-Group Interview: A Method for Assessing Users' Evaluation of Library Service," *College & Research Libraries* 52 (July 1991): 352–59; Suzanne Walters, *Focus Groups: Linkages to the Community, Denver Public Library* (Denver: US West Communications, 1988).

[36]Johnson and Connaway, "Arrowhead Library System."

[37]Marilyn D. Jacobson, *New York State Education Information Centers Program: Summative Evaluation Report*, ED 250542 (Albany: New York State Education Department, 1984).

[38]Constance A. Mellon, *Naturalistic Inquiry for Library Science: Methods and Applications for Research, Evaluation, and Teaching* (New York: Greenwood Press, 1990).

[39]Roger Verny and Connie Van Fleet, "Conducting Focus Groups," in *Library Evaluation: A Casebook and Can-Do Guide*, edited by Danny P. Wallace and Connie Van Fleet (Englewood, CO: Libraries Unlimited, 2001): 43–51.

[40]Liz Bishoff, "Public Access to the Library of Congress Subject Headings," paper presented at the Annual Conference of the American Library Association (San Francisco, 1987).

[41]Debra Wilcox Johnson and Lynn Silipigni Connaway, "Cataloger as Decision Maker," paper presented at the annual meeting of the Wisconsin Library Association (Appleton, 1990).

[42]Debra Wilcox Johnson and Lynn Silipigni Connaway, "Use of Online Catalogs: A Report of Results of Focus Group Interviews" unpublished consultants' report, report no. 19, 1992; Karen Markey, *Subject Searching in Library Catalogs: Before and After the Introduction of Online Catalogs* (Dublin, OH: OCLC, 1984); Kenneth W. Berger and Richard W. Hines, "What Does the User Really Want? The Library User Survey Project at Duke University," *Journal of Academic Librarianship* 20 (November 1994): 306–9; Sharon W. Schwerzel, Susan V. Emerson, and David L. Johnson, "Self-Evaluation of Competencies in Online Searching by End-Users After Basic Training," in proceedings of the Forty-fifth ASIS Annual Meeting, edited by Anthony E. Petrarca, Celianna I. Taylor, and Robert S. Kohn (White Plains, NY: Knowledge Industry, 1982): 272–75.

[43]Neal K. Kaske, "Studies of Online Catalogs," in *Online Catalogs/Online Reference*, edited by Brian Aveney and Brett Butler (Chicago: American Library Association, 1984): 20–30; Neal K. Kaske and N. P. Sanders, "Online Subject Access: The Human Side of the Problem," *RQ* 19 (Fall 1980): 52–58.

[44]Lynn Silipigni Connaway, "Focus Group Interviews: A Data Collection Methodology for Decision Making," *Library Administration & Management* 10 (Fall 1996): 231–39.

[45]Denise Troll Covey, *Usage and Usability Assessment,* 15–23.

[46]Young, "Focus on Focus Groups," 392.

[47]Karen Markey Drabenstott, "Focused Group Interviews," in *Qualitative Research in Information Management*, edited by Jack D. Glazier and Ronald R. Powell (Englewood, CO: Libraries Unlimited, 1992): 85–104.

[48]Mary M. Wagner and Suzanne H. Mahmoodi, *A Focus Group Interview Manual* (Chicago: American Library Association, 1994): 10.

[49]Clifford Geertz, *The Interpretation of Cultures: Selected Essays* (New York: Basic Books, 1973): 6.

[50]David L. Morgan, *Focus Groups as Qualitative Research* (Newbury Park, CA: Sage Publications, 1988): 64–69.

[51]Richard A. Krueger, *Focus Groups: A Practical Guide for Applied Research* (Beverly Hills, CA: Sage Publications, 1988): 41.

[52]Ibid.

[53]Robert Philip Weber, *Basic Content Analysis*, 2d ed. (Newbury Park, CA: Sage Publications, 1990): 18.

[54]Ibid.

[55]Ibid.

[56]Morgan, *Focus Groups as Qualitative Research*, 64.

[57]Ibid., 15.

[58]Young, "Focus on Focus Groups," 391.

[59]Krueger, *Focus Groups*, 44–46.

[60]Morgan, *Focus Groups as Qualitative Research*, 40.

[61]Young, "Focus on Focus Groups," 393.

[62]Earl R. Babbie, *The Practice of Social Research*, 10th ed. (Belmont, CA: Wadsworth/Thomson Learning, 2004): 269.

[63]Mick P. Couper and Sue Ellen Hansen, "Computer-Assisted Interviewing," in *Handbook of Interview Research: Context & Method*, edited by Jaber F. Gubrium and James A. Holstein (Thousand Oaks, CA: Sage Publications, 2002): 557.

[64]Babbie, *Practice of Social Research*, 271.

[65]James H. Frey, *Survey Research by Telephone* (Beverly Hills, CA: Sage Publications, 1983).

[66]George J. Mouly, *Educational Research: The Art and Science of Investigation* (Boston: Allyn & Bacon, 1978): 216–17.

[67]Robert Grover and Jack Glazier, "A Conceptual Framework for Theory Building in Library and Information Science," *Library and Information Science Research* 8 (July–September 1985): 257.

[68]Louise H. Kidder, *Research Methods in Social Relations*, 4th ed. (New York: Holt, Rinehart & Winston, 1981): 278.

[69]Couper and Hansen, "Computer-Assisted Interviewing," 557.

Chapter 6

Experimental Research

In some ways, experimental research is the most rigorous of all research methods and is arguably the best method for testing cause and effect relationships. Yet a review of the literature reveals that it is used in only 8% to 10% of LIS research studies. Some of the probable reasons why that is the situation will be explored during the course of this chapter; however, before discussing experimental research methods per se, causality, a concept which is crucial to experimental research, will be considered.

CAUSALITY

Simply stated, causality suggests that a single event (the "cause") always leads to another single event (the "effect").[1] Anderson states, "causes and consequences concentrate on the relationships between phenomena—how one phenomenon affects another."[2] In the social sciences, at least, the focus is normally on a variety of determining factors, which increase the probability of a certain event occurring, rather than on a single factor. Goldhor even argues that the "demonstration of causality in any rigorous sense is philosophically impossible," and he suggests that causality and "explanation" can be used interchangeably.[3] Yet at least an

165

understanding of causality is essential to the proper testing of causal hypotheses or relationships and is useful in designing research studies to be as rigorous as possible.

The Conditions for Causality

In attempting to confirm causality in a relationship, one must consider the so-called conditions or factors that may exist. A *necessary condition* is one that must occur if the phenomenon of which it is a cause is to occur. That is to say, if *X*, the independent variable, is a necessary condition of *Y*, the dependent variable, *Y* will never occur unless *X* occurs. For example, if library instruction were a necessary condition of effective library use, then the latter would never occur unless library instruction had been provided.

A *sufficient condition* is one that is always followed by the phenomenon which it "causes." In other words, if *X* is a sufficient condition of *Y*, then whenever *X* occurs, *Y* will always occur. If library instruction were a sufficient condition of effective library use, then after an individual received appropriate library instruction, he or she would begin using the library effectively.

A condition may or may not be both necessary and sufficient for the occurrence of a phenomenon. (If both, *Y* would never occur unless *X* had occurred, and whenever *X* occurred, *Y* would occur also.) In fact, in the example provided, one can see that it is quite possible for neither condition to exist. Library instruction is probably not a necessary condition for effective library use, as a patron may teach himself or herself to use the library; and it certainly is not a sufficient condition, as effective library use does not always follow library instruction, regardless of how well it is presented.

As was noted earlier, in the social sciences especially, a variety of factors tend to cause or influence any one dependent variable. The example of effective library use is a good case in point. In addition to library instruction, effective library use might be affected by motivation, intelligence, previous experiences, role models, peer pressure, and so on. In short, the researcher rarely finds a single factor or condition that is both necessary and sufficient to cause an event, so he or she is well advised to consider other types of conditions.

One type of condition that can be considered, in addition to necessary and sufficient conditions, is the *contributory condition*. Contributory conditions increase the probability that a certain phenomenon will occur, but they do not make it certain. So, if library instruction were considered to be the factor likely to have the strongest effect on library use, then the other factors named, such as peer pressure, might be considered to be contributory conditions. And in fact, the combination and interaction of all of the relevant factors or independent variables would probably best explain effective library use.

The picture is further complicated by the fact that certain variables will represent contributory conditions in some situations, but not in others. Again, social science concepts tend to be complex and the interaction of variables, or how they affect one another and combine influences, must be taken into account. The conditions under which a given variable is a contributory cause are referred to as *contingent conditions*. In the previous example, the various factors suggested as likely causes of effective library instruction might do so only if the library's services and collections were strong. In other words, the environment may increase or decrease the influence of certain variables.

The researcher should also be aware of the possibility of *alternative conditions* that might make the occurrence of a certain phenomenon more likely. Alternative conditions, in essence, refer to the different forms that a given factor or variable may take and how the factor's influence is affected by its form. Library instruction can be provided in different formats, and it may be that one type of library instruction would promote effective library use and another would not. For example, library orientation may be inappropriate for graduate students and have no real effect on how they use the library, while instruction in the use of the literature of a certain discipline may greatly improve library use effectiveness. In turn, the alternative conditions would continue to be affected by other contributory conditions, such as how well the library is able to support research in the specific area of graduate study.

A less commonly discussed factor, *mechanism*, refers to the conditions that create the causal connection, or the intervening variables. Consideration of the mechanism helps us to understand how variation in the independent variable(s) results in variation in the dependent variable(s). This condition seems to be conceptually similar to the contingent condition discussed earlier in that it is concerned with the context in which the cause has its effects.

Bases for Inferring Causal Relationships

Unfortunately, as Goldhor implied, it is usually impossible to demonstrate directly that one variable causes another variable, either by itself or in combination with other variables. As a result, the social science researcher normally has to infer a causal relationship between two or more variables based on the data gathered.[4]

One type of evidence for inferring a causal relationship is known as *concomitant variation*. Evidence of concomitant variation, or covariation with two variables, indicates that the independent variable (X) and the dependent variable, or assumed effect (Y), are associated in the way predicted by the causal hypothesis. For example, one might have hypothesized that, as the amount of library instruction is increased, the level of library skills will increase.

The relationship just specified is an example of a positive one. A relationship in which both variables decrease simultaneously is in effect a positive relationship as well. Other possible relationships include a negative or inverse relationship, in which, as one variable decreases, the other increases; and a curvilinear relationship, where the degree to which one variable affects the other tends to diminish beyond a certain point.

In the case of a hypothesis that predicts that the independent variable is a contributory condition of the dependent variable, the "logical consequence" would be that Y would appear in more cases where X is present than in cases where it is not present. So, if it were hypothesized that library instruction is a contributory condition of effective library use, then persons who had received library instruction would be more likely to be effective library users than those who had not received library instruction. But one would not be able to assume that every person who had received library instruction would be an effective library user. Other types of causal hypotheses (e.g., X is a necessary cause of Y) would call for other patterns of associations between the independent and the dependent variables.

A second basis for inferring a causal relationship between two variables relates to the *time order* of occurrence of the variables. To establish the necessary time order requires evidence that the dependent variable did not occur before the independent variable. One could not support a hypothesis predicting a necessary causal relationship between library instruction and effective library use if it were found that the effective library use was occurring before the patrons received any library instruction.

The third basis for inferring a causal relationship is nonspuriousness or evidence *ruling out other factors* as possible causes of the dependent variable. However, such evidence merely helps to provide a reasonable foundation for inferring that X is or is not a cause of Y. It cannot absolutely confirm a relationship because the researcher may have overlooked one or more other factors that are actually the determining conditions. The process of ruling out other factors, or controlling for the effects of extraneous variables, will be considered further in upcoming sections of this chapter.

In conclusion, there are certain conditions that should exist, and certain kinds of inferences that must be made, in order to support causal relationships. The most effective method for collecting the necessary evidence, or testing a causal hypothesis, is the experiment.

CONTROLLING THE VARIABLES

Certain characteristics or capabilities are essential to the experimental research method. Virtually all quantitative research requires the measurement of variables, but experimental research necessitates the control and manipulation of certain variables as well. In addition, the variables must vary under different conditions, or have at least two values; otherwise, they are not variables. The independent variable is the experimental variable. It also is referred to as the cause or causal variable and the predictor variable. It is the variable that the researcher manipulates. (Organismic variables are variables such as age and income, which are often treated as independent variables but over which the researcher has no real control.) The dependent variable is often known as the effect, the subject variable, or the criterion variable. It is "caused," or at least affected, by the independent variable.

True experimental manipulation also requires the use of at least one experimental group and one comparison or control group, each consisting of an appropriate number of subjects. The experimental group receives the experimental treatment, and the comparison group receives no treatment, thereby creating an independent variable with at least two values. The dependent variable is represented by the measurement of the effect of the experimental treatment, and several dependent variables or measures of effect may be used.

If one were conducting an experiment to measure the effect of library instruction on library use, library instruction would be the independent variable and library use would be the dependent variable. The two values for library instruction could be the provision of instruction to the experimental group and no instruction for the comparison group. The dependent variable could be measured by a tally of the frequency of library use for the members of both groups. Another dependent variable could be represented by types of reference questions asked by members of the two groups.

One of the difficulties in exerting adequate control in an experiment relates to the fact that there typically are a variety of extraneous independent variables that conceivably are influencing or causing the dependent variable(s), in addition to the one or ones being investigated. (Extraneous variables can also influence both the independent and the dependent variables and thus create a spurious association between them.) In order to isolate the effects that the experimental variable or variables are having, the researcher must control the extraneous independent variables, which could include, in the most recent example, assignments made by instructors, increased "marketing" by the library, and so on.

There are three major techniques for controlling the influence of extraneous variables, two of which are intended to equate the experimental and comparison groups prior to the experiment. One technique involves holding the other variables constant by matching or selecting subjects with the same traits for the experimental and comparison groups. That is, as a subject is selected for the experimental group, another one which is quite similar on all characteristics or variables that are relevant or capable of affecting the dependent variable, is selected for the comparison group. For example, after a subject had been selected for the experimental group in a study on the effects of library instruction, then a subject with a comparable IQ, previous library experience, GPA, age, and so on would need to be assigned to the comparison group. It is difficult to identify all relevant variables when matching subjects, but the researcher may derive some consolation from the fact that key variables tend to correlate highly with other, unidentified variables.

If the subjects are not completely equivalent going into the experiment, the extraneous variables may be controlled statistically during the analysis stage. However, this approach is less reliable than others, as it is done ex post facto, or after the experiment. No amount of statistical control can completely undo the preceding effects of other factors. And it is effective at all only if the relevant extraneous variables are identified and properly measured.

Random Assignment

The third and best technique for equating two or more groups before the experimental treatment begins is referred to as random assignment or randomization (not to be confused with random sampling or selection). It is a procedure used after the sample is selected but before the experimental treatment is applied. It involves randomly assigning the subjects in the total sample to the experimental and comparison groups. Specific techniques used for random assignment are often essentially the same as those used for selecting random samples. The researcher may elect, for example, to draw names from a hat, use a table of random numbers, or employ a computer to generate a list of random numbers.

One can assume, however, that the groups are equivalent only within certain probability levels. But "equating" the experimental and comparison groups is essential for making causal inferences about the effects of the experimental treatment. It improves the external validity, or generalizability, of the experiment, as well as its internal validity, or the dependability of the results. Random assignment does not necessarily control for the effects of the experimental setting. The researcher must take other steps to eliminate or minimize the influence of such factors as the mode of instruction, quality of tests, and interaction of subjects.

INTERNAL VALIDITY

Briefly defined, internal validity "refers to the possibility that the conclusions drawn from experimental results may not accurately reflect what went on in the experiment itself."[5] Stated more positively, it is "the conclusiveness with which the effects of the independent variable are established in a scientific investigation, as opposed to the possibility that some confounding variables may have caused the observed results."[6]

Generally speaking, the greater the control the experimenter has over the experiment, including the extraneous variables, the greater the internal validity. The greater the control, however, the more artificial or unnatural is the setting and the lower the external validity. (This relationship will be referred to again when discussing experimental designs.)

Threats to Internal Validity

Internal validity is crucial to the dependability of the results of an experiment, and it is closely related to replicability. It indicates the extent to which the experiment adequately tested the treatment under study by helping to rule out rival explanations and ensuring freedom from bias. In short, internal validity provides confidence that the observed effect on the dependent variable is actually due to the independent variable.

Unfortunately, a number of factors can jeopardize the internal validity of experimental research. Those factors most frequently cited in standard texts are as follows:

1. History, or specific events, in addition to the experimental treatment or variable, which occurs between measurements of the dependent variable. During an experimental study of the effects of library instruction on the frequency of library use, subjects might be exposed to some event or influence such as a midterm exam that would encourage them to use the library more than usual. The researcher might then be uncertain about how much of the increase in library use was caused by the midterm exam and how much by the library instruction provided.

2. Maturation, or processes *within* the subjects operating as a function of time such as growing older, or more mature. During the course of the experiment just referred to, the subjects might naturally develop into more frequent library users regardless of any library instruction received.

3. Testing, or the effects of taking a test, upon the scores of a subsequent testing. In a library instruction experiment, students would tend to do better on a second test of library skills simply because they had already taken the test.

4. Instrumentation, or the process wherein changes in the techniques used for the measurements, or changes in the persons making the measurements, affect a second set of measurements or observations. For example, if a pretest on library use measured use as the number of *volumes* borrowed, and a second test measured it as the number of *titles* borrowed, then the second measurement would probably be different simply because the method of measurement had been changed.

5. Statistical regression, or the statistical phenomenon wherein extreme scores obtained on a first test tend to gravitate toward the mean on subsequent tests. This is especially significant where groups have been selected on the basis of their extreme scores. If subjects in one group made extremely high scores on a test of library skills, and subjects in a second group earned exceptionally low scores, the odds are that many of the subjects in both groups would tend to be closer to the mean score on a retest. Again, this event would confound the effects of any library instruction provided between tests.

6. Biases in differential selection of subjects for the comparison groups. If a researcher selected for the comparison group (the group not receiving any library instruction) students not likely to evidence much use of the library, then he or she would be guilty of biasing the experiment in favor of the experimental treatment. The students in the experimental group, or those receiving library instruction, would probably use the library more than those in the comparison group, with or without library instruction, but it might appear that library instruction was having a positive effect.

7. Experimental mortality, or the differential loss of subjects from the comparison group. If during the course of an experiment, students who tended to be

infrequent library users, perhaps because of their area of study, dropped out of the comparison group, then the remaining members might produce scores higher than would be normal. Such an occurrence would suggest that library instruction was having less effect than it actually was because the difference in scores between the experimental and comparison groups would be less than expected.

8. Interaction of selection and other sources of invalidity. The results of interaction can be mistaken for the effects of the experimental variable. For example, the students selected for the experimental group might have been exceptionally receptive to library instruction because they had matured intellectually during the experiment. Therefore, their retest scores would be higher than their pretest scores, and the gain probably would be attributed to the library instruction received. At least some, if not all, of the increase in test scores could have resulted, however, solely from the intellectual maturation that had taken place.

To repeat, these threats to internal validity, if not controlled, may well produce effects confounded with the effect of the experimental stimulus.[7] Types of experimental designs that can help to control these extraneous variables will be discussed later.

EXTERNAL VALIDITY

Before taking up specific types of experimental designs, external validity, the second type of validity important to successful experimental research, will be considered. External validity is important because it relates to "the possibility that conclusions drawn from experimental results may not be generalizable to the 'real' world."[8] Kidder defines external validity as "the generalizability of a research finding, for example, to other populations, settings, treatment arrangements, and measurement arrangements."[9]

Threats to External Validity

Unfortunately, as Campbell and Stanley note, the question of external validity is never completely answerable.[10] (As is the case with internal validity, certain experimental designs can help to maximize external validity.) The major factors jeopardizing external validity, or representativeness, are as follows:

1. The reactive or interactive effect of testing. This occurs when a *pretest* increases or decreases the subject's sensitivity or responsiveness to the experimental variable, and thus makes the results unrepresentative of the general, or unpretested, population from which the subjects were selected. If a student were pretested on his or her library skills, given library instruction for one semester, and then tested again on his or her library skills, there is probably a

good chance that the skills would be higher on the retest. However, the researcher would have to question how much of the increase in skills was due to the pretest's making the student more aware of library services and resources and therefore more likely to improve his or her library use with or without the library instruction.

2. The interaction effects of selection biases and the experimental variable. This threat is similar to the sixth listed threat to internal validity. It simply means that one must be careful not to select experimental subjects who are likely to be more receptive to the experimental variable than is the general population. For example, if one selected English honors students for an experiment on the effects of library instruction, there is a chance that they would be more motivated to utilize library instruction than more average students. Consequently, the ability to generalize the results of the study to other, more typical, students would be diminished.

3. The reactive effects of the experimental arrangements can prevent the researcher from being able to generalize about the effect of the experimental variable on persons exposed to it in nonexperimental settings. In other words, the experimental environment, or elements thereof, might have been influencing the subject along with, or instead of, the experimental treatment. Behavior in the laboratory has a tendency not to represent accurately what would happen in similar circumstances in real life. A well-known example of this phenomenon is the classic Hawthorne study, in which workers became more productive whenever they were studied, regardless of whether their working conditions improved or worsened, simply because they were aware that they were being observed.

4. Multiple treatment interference may occur whenever more than one treatment is applied to the same subjects basically because the effects of prior treatments do not entirely disappear. For example, if a student were given different types of library instruction, one after another, they would tend to have a cumulative effect on the student's library skills. Consequently, it would be difficult for the researcher to distinguish between the effects of any one mode of library instruction and those of the others.

In summary, the threats to external validity are basically interaction effects, involving the experimental treatment and some other variable. On the other hand, the factors jeopardizing internal validity are those that directly affect the dependent variables or scores. They are factors which by themselves can produce changes which might be mistaken for the results of the experimental treatment.[11]

EXPERIMENTAL DESIGNS

In spite of the challenges associated with creating equivalent groups, controlling for the threats to internal and external validity, and establishing adequate control over the experimental setting, experimental research holds significant potential for the resolution of library-related problems. As has been noted, the testing of causal hypotheses increases our ability to explain why certain phenomena occur, and experimental research may be the best equipped method for such testing. Survey research methods, for example, are not able to provide the researcher with enough control over extraneous variables to be able to say with any certainty that one variable is the direct cause of another. In a survey of students' library usage, we could ask them why they used the library, but data gathered in that manner would at best allow us to establish associational relationships. For a number of reasons, even including a desire to please the researcher, the subject might attribute more influence to the library instruction than was warranted.

As was indicated earlier, a variety of designs can be employed for experimental research, and the stronger they are the better they can minimize or control the various threats to internal and external validity. Some of the designs appropriate for true experiments, or those experiments designed to investigate causal relationships, exercising considerable control and utilizing random assignment, will be considered first.

True Experimental Designs

1. The Pretest-Posttest Control Group Design. One of the classic, true experimental designs is usually referred to as the pretest-posttest control group design. As will be seen after a few examples, the standard names of basic designs tend to describe them rather well, but diagrams point out their major features even better. The diagram for this design appears as follows:

$$R \ O_1 \ X \ O_2$$
$$R \ O_3 \quad O_4$$

In this illustration, and in the others to follow, the X symbolizes the experimental treatment or independent variable or cause. The O represents the process of observation or measurement of the dependent variable or effect. These observations can take the form of questionnaires, tests, interviews, etc. Each row represents one group of subjects; the left-to-right direction indicates the temporal order, and Xs and Os vertical to one another occur simultaneously. The R indicates that the subjects in the group so designated have been randomly assigned to their treatment, or lack of treatment.

Therefore, this first diagram indicates that there are two groups, both randomly assigned. Both groups have been pretested and retested, but only the first group received the experimental treatment. The random assignment means that the two groups should be equivalent, or nearly so. This experimental design is considered strong because it controls for all eight of the threats to internal validity. For example, history is controlled because historical events that might have produced a change from O_1 to O_2 would also produce a comparable change from O_3 to O_4. In other words, due to random assignment, the groups are equivalent and should be equally affected by historical events, especially if the experiment is controlled as carefully as possible. For example, a study conducted as a double-blind experiment, in which the person(s) administering the experimental treatment does not know who the subjects are and the subjects do not realize they are part of an experiment, will be proportionately stronger in internal validity. In our library instruction study, assignments given to students outside the experimental setting should have similar effects on both groups. The other threats to internal validity would be controlled in essentially the same manner.

The pretest-posttest control group design is not as effective at controlling the threats to external validity. The interaction of testing and X remains a concern, because attitudes and behavior may be affected by the pretest. The design's ability to control the interaction of selection biases and X is questionable. It should account for differences between the experimental and control groups, but the results may still be atypical due to the nature of the subjects selected. This design's control of reactive arrangements is probably less than satisfactory also. There remains a good possibility that phenomena such as the Hawthorne effect may influence the effect of X. Multiple treatment interference is not an issue here because only one experimental treatment is involved.

In summary, this particular design is stronger in internal validity than in external validity. This suggests that the researcher could be confident that the experimental treatment, not extraneous variables, caused the measured effects; however, he or she would have to be cautious in generalizing the results to other groups as they might have been unique for those particular subjects.

2. The Solomon Four-Group Design. A second standard, true experimental design is referred to as the Solomon four-group design. It is diagrammed as follows:

$$R\ O_1\ X_1\ O_2$$
$$R\ O_3\ \quad O_4$$
$$R\ \quad X_2\ O_5$$
$$R\ \quad\quad O_6$$

As can be seen, this design involves four randomly assigned, or equivalent, groups, two of which receive the experimental treatment, and two of which are given posttests only.

This design "scores" the same on internal validity as does the pretest-posttest control group design because it controls all eight threats. It is better than the pretest-posttest control group design in controlling the factors that jeopardize external validity in that it is able to control the interaction of pretesting and X. It can do this because one experimental group and one control group are not pretested, thus allowing the researcher to measure the effects of the experimental treatment without the "contamination" of a pretest. It also benefits from the fact that the effect of X can be determined in four ways: the differences between O_2 and O_1, O_2 and O_4, O_5 and O_6, and O_1 and O_3. In short, this design is somewhat stronger than the pretest-posttest control group design and should be used in preference to it when possible.

3. The Posttest-Only Control Group Design. The posttest-only control group design diagrams the same as the last two groups of the Solomon four-group design and looks as follows:

$$R \quad X\ O_1$$
$$R \qquad O_2$$

This design is not used as frequently as it deserves to be, perhaps because of its lack of a pretest. Yet one can assume that the two groups are equivalent at the start of a study because of the random assignment, and a pretest should not be necessary to confirm that assumption. In fact, this design achieves the same control of internal and external validity as does the Solomon four-group design, but without the necessity of establishing four groups. Therefore, it is in some ways preferable to the Solomon four-group design, as well as to the pretest-posttest control group design. Not having pretests, however, precludes the researcher's being able to calculate differences in the dependent variable before and after the experiment, or gain scores.

4. Factorial Designs. The three preceding designs are examples of designs capable of accommodating only one independent and one dependent variable. Factorial designs can deal with two or more independent variables and one dependent variable. They tend to be higher in external validity than other true experimental designs because they can consider more independent variables and can measure interaction. As can be seen in the following example, a factorial design contains every possible combination of the independent variables.

$$R\ X_1\ X_2\ O_1$$
$$R\ X_1 \qquad O_2$$
$$R \qquad X_2\ O_3$$
$$R \qquad\quad O_4$$

Not only would this design allow the researcher to measure the specific effects of the two independent variables on the dependent variable, but it should give some indication of the interaction of X_1 and X_2. In other words, it controls for multiple treatment interference.

A simpler factorial design is as follows:

$$R \quad X_1\ O_1$$
$$R \quad X_2\ O_2$$
$$R \qquad O_3$$

This is a multivariate equivalent of the pretest-posttest control group design. It does not measure the interaction of treatments, but that should be unnecessary, as no one group receives more than one treatment. (There may be some situations, such as in library instruction experiments, however, where one would be interested in knowing if the different modes of instruction had any cumulative effects on library skills or use.)

True Experiments and Correlational Studies

Having discussed the essential criteria for true experimental research and having looked at a few examples of true experimental designs, it should be kept in mind that it is not always possible to assign people to experimental treatments in a laboratory-like setting. For example, if one were designing a study to test the effects of library instruction provided to English literature students on their use of the library, in most cases it would not be possible to assign particular students to the sections designated to receive and not to receive library instruction. Probably, the researcher would have to accept the two groups as they were already constituted. Thus, there would be no assurance that the two groups were equivalent.

Consequently, much social research is correlational, or associational, in nature. This type of research may well permit one to predict change in one variable based on knowledge about another variable, but it would not allow the establishment of a causal relationship between the variables. Correlational studies tend to be relatively high in external validity but relatively low in internal validity and, therefore, less able to account for rival explanations of a relationship.

Essentially true experiments can be conducted in real-life settings, assuming the controls are adequate. Such experiments are often referred to as field experiments. They tend to be less artificial than laboratory type experiments but may still lose validity if the subjects are aware that they are being studied.

Reiterating a point made earlier, properly conducted true experiments should be high in internal validity. This means that the researcher should be able to be quite confident that the experimental treatment was the cause of the observed effect. True experiments have less external validity, however. That is, true experiments are poor representations of natural situations. More specifically, they provide a relatively artificial test of the hypothesis, tend to be low in generalizability, and often produce relatively little descriptive data about the population, unless the subjects are unusually representative.

Difficulties to Be Avoided

In order to design an experiment that will be as reliable and valid as possible, the researcher should attempt to avoid the following:

1. Relying too heavily on a single experiment.
2. Using poorly designed or faulty data collection instruments.
3. Not identifying all of the variables that may affect the results.
4. Not choosing subjects that are as representative of the population as possible.

5. Introducing experimenter bias.
6. Introducing subject bias.
7. Making the subjects aware of the hypothesis being tested through unconscious signaling or behavior.
8. Using an insufficient number of subjects.

Evaluating the Experiment

In evaluating the design and results of an experiment, there are several points that the researcher should consider. One, the experiment should have the ability to test a null hypothesis, which suggests that there is no relationship between the variables being studied. Two, the experiment should be sensitive. That is, it should be able to detect relatively small effects or differences. Increasing the number of subjects, which decreases the chance of random or experimental error, and exerting additional control, such as by matching subjects, helps to increase the experiment's sensitivity. The selection of subjects can be facilitated with the use of power tables, which provide the number of subjects for each group, given the effects of power or sensitivity of the experiment, the effect size, and the significance level.[12] "Experiments should be planned so that the size of each treatment group provides the greatest sensitivity that the effect on the outcome is actually due to the experimental manipulation in the study."[13] The formulas used for determining optimal sample sizes for surveys are of limited use for experiments.

In evaluating the results of the experiment, the researcher should assess the reliability of the data and its external validity, or generalizability. Last, but not least, the significance or scientific importance of the results should be considered.

Preexperimental Designs

If random assignment of subjects and laboratory-like control are not possible, it will be necessary for the researcher to use a pre-experimental or quasi-experimental design. Preexperimental designs, which will be considered first, are those designs which not only lack random assignment but which have few observation points as well. A few examples of preexperimental designs follow.

1. The One-Shot Case Study. The one-shot case study, which can be diagrammed simply as $X O$, is an extremely weak design. As there is only one group, there is no basis for comparison of subjects who have received and have not received the experimental treatment.

With neither random assignment nor pretests, this design is susceptible to numerous alternative influences or threats to its internal validity. It is threatened particularly by history, maturation, selection biases, and experimental mortality. Regarding external validity, this design is unable to control for interaction between selection biases and the experimental variable. For practical reasons, however, the one-shot case study is used fairly frequently.

2. The One-Group Pretest-Posttest Design. The one-group pretest-posttest design represents a slight improvement over the one-shot case study, because it incorporates a pretest, or one more observation point. It appears as follows:

$$O_1 \ X \ O_2$$

If posttest scores are higher than the pretest scores, this design should rule out selection biases as a rival explanation. It does not, however, control for the effects of history, maturation, testing, instrumentation, interaction of selection and other factors, and quite possibly statistical regression. It also is about as weak as the one-shot case study at controlling threats to external validity.

3. The Static-Group Comparison. Another preexperimental design, which improves a bit more on the preceding designs, known as the static-group comparison, diagrams as follows:

$$\begin{array}{ll} \text{Group 1} & X \ O_1 \\ \hline \text{Group 2} & O_2 \end{array}$$

As can be seen, this design utilizes two groups rather than one, each of which is observed once. The line, however, as well as the absence of R's, indicates that the groups occurred naturally and were not based on random assignment. In other words, "this is a design in which a group which has experienced X is compared with one which has not, for the purposes of establishing the effect of X."[14] An example of naturally occurring groups might be two English literature classes, to which the researcher was unable to assign particular students and which had already experienced some level of an experimental variable such as library instruction. Since the researcher was unable to create two equivalent groups, there is no assurance that the two groups had experienced the same amount of the experimental variable or that the experimental treatment actually produced the differences, if any, in the final group scores. Differences in group scores might have resulted entirely because one or the other group was atypical.

Consequently, as the researcher using this design cannot be certain whether X actually caused O, or natural selection did, the static-group comparison is at best a correlational design. The X represents what the subjects naturally brought to the study, and the researcher can only ascertain that there is some sort of association between the variables in question. In fact, the static-group comparison is often considered to be a survey design.

To its credit, the static-group comparison does control relatively well for several threats to internal validity. Those controlled are history, testing, instrumentation, regression, and possibly maturation. It is not considered to be capable of controlling the threats to external validity.

Quasi-Experimental Designs

A type of experimental design which represents an improvement over pre-experimental designs, including those just considered, is the quasi-experimental design. Quasi-experimental designs usually include naturally occurring groups, but they often involve more than one group and typically have more observation points than do preexperimental designs. The employment of naturally occurring groups means there is no random assignment of subjects to the control and experimental groups.

Quasi-experimental designs are not as strong as those for true experiments. As they do not have randomly assigned treatment and comparison groups, comparisons must be made with nonequivalent groups or with the same subjects in one group prior to and after treatment. In most cases the independent variable(s) cannot be fully manipulated by the researcher. Quasi-experimental designs also have less control than do true experiments but are able to rule out more threats to internal validity than preexperiments. In fact, if the quasi-experimental design is strong enough to rule out many of the threats to internal validity, it may be used to infer cause and effect.[15] A few examples of quasi-experimental designs follow.

1. The Time-Series Design. The time-series design is an example of a single-group quasi-experimental design. It takes this form:

$$O_1 \; O_2 \; O_3 \; O_4 \; X \; O_5 \; O_6 \; O_7 \; O_8$$

As a comparison will reveal, this design represents an extension of the one-group pretest-posttest design $(O_1 \; X \; O_2)$. The longer sequence of observation points helps to control additional factors jeopardizing internal validity, such as maturation and testing, because it allows one to examine trends in the data before, at the time of, and after the experimental treatment. (Graphing the Xs and Os can help to reveal any patterns that might exist.) For example, if one were testing the library skills of students and learned that their skills were regularly rising even before X, or library instruction, was applied, one would have to question the apparent effects of library instruction.

The time-series is still relatively weak in external validity. It does possibly control for interaction of selection biases and reactive arrangements.

2. The Equivalent Time-Samples Design. A second single-group quasi-experimental design, the equivalent time-samples design, employs two equivalent measurements, one when the experimental variable is present and another when it is not, and then repeats the sequence. This design diagrams as follows:

$$X_1 \; O \; X_0 \; O \; X_1 \; O \; X_0 \; O$$

This type of design is particularly useful where the effect of the experimental treatment is expected to be of transient or reversible character (e.g., library instruction, environmental conditions within the library, etc.). This arrangement is relatively high on internal validity but low on external validity because of the effects of multiple treatment interference.

3. The Pretest-Posttest Nonequivalent Control Group Design. This multiple-group design has some of the features of the static-group comparison and the one-group pretest-posttest design. As can be seen from the following diagram, it provides

$$\begin{array}{ccc} \text{Group 1} & O_1 \ X \ O_3 \\ \hline \text{Group 2} & O_2 \quad O_4 \end{array}$$

pretest information and a comparison group, but the groups are not fully matched or randomly assigned and thus cannot be assumed to be equivalent. (The comparison group would be selected for its similarity to the experimental group, however.) Its major advantage over the static group comparison is that one can measure preexisting differences between the groups. It is widely used in educational research.

4. The Multiple Time-Series Design. A second multiple-group quasi-experimental design is the multiple time-series design. It is the multiple-group counterpart of the time-series design and could be diagrammed thus:

$$\begin{array}{c} \text{Group 1} \quad O_1 \ O_2 \ O_3 \ O_4 \ X \ O_5 \ O_6 \ O_7 \ O_8 \\ \hline \text{Group 2} \quad O_1 \ O_2 \ O_3 \ O_4 \quad O_5 \ O_6 \ O_7 \ O_8 \end{array}$$

Assuming that the groups were exposed to the same historical conditions, this design should control for the effects of history. It is considered to be a useful design for conducting research in schools.

Ex Post Facto Designs

Ex post facto designs represent a weaker type of quasi-experimental design. They are designed to simulate real experimentation by using a static-group type comparison such as

$$\frac{X \ O}{O}$$

to accomplish a pre-X equation of groups by matching on pre-X characteristics *after* the members of the groups have experienced the experimental variable. Perhaps, for example, one has assumed the directorship of a library soon after the library gave some sort of library instruction to all first-year English students. It might be tempting to try to determine whether the library skills of those students were better than those of other first-year students not given library instruction. The experimental group, those students who received library instruction, is in effect already established. In order to simulate a real experiment, the librarian must attempt to establish a comparison group of students equivalent to those in the "experimental group." It would be necessary, therefore, to identify students comparable to those students who had received library instruction. The librarian must try to match the two groups of students on every relevant trait, such as previous training in library skills. As Mouly states, "this is experimentation in reverse, and it is very difficult to match subjects on enough variables to rule out other influences."[16] The researcher has no control over events that have already occurred and can never be certain how many factors might have been involved.

In spite of the fact that quite a few significant studies have employed ex post facto analysis, such designs are considered to be quite weak. Yet they sometimes represent the only feasible approach for investigating a particular question. Specific types of ex post facto analysis include case studies and the so-called causal-comparative studies.

SUMMARY

Experimental research is generally considered to be the most rigorous of the basic research methods. Unlike historical and survey methods, experimental research is considered capable of supporting causal relationships. It is able to do so primarily because, at least in the case of true experiments, it employs equivalent comparison groups, permits manipulation of the experimental variable, and controls alternative influences on the dependent variable. Experimental methods can be used to examine questions such as the effect of certain types of resources on the success of reference transactions, the effect of changes in facilities on user behavior, and users' reactions to certain characteristics of reference staff.

Experimental studies have been criticized for being artificial and for not reflecting real life situations. However, designs, other than true experimental designs, can be used to allay this problem. One of these alternatives, the preexperimental design, is the weakest type of experimental design, but it is higher in external validity. The second alternative, the quasi-experimental design, represents a compromise between preexperiments, which are low in internal validity, and true experiments, which are high in internal validity. Stated somewhat differently, it is a compromise between maximizing internal validity and external validity. It is a good choice of design when a natural setting must be used, when random assignment of subjects is not feasible, and when the independent or experimental variable cannot be manipulated fully (e.g., when the independent variable represents a demographic variable or a process of natural selection).

There are an almost unlimited number of quasi-experimental designs; the researcher is not restricted to those already developed by others but may create his or her own. The amount of control built into a quasi-experimental design can vary, but it is almost always less than that of true experimental designs. Consequently, the results of quasi-experimental designs tend to be more subject to incorrect interpretation.

NOTES

[1]Claire Selltiz, Lawrence S. Wrightsman, and Stuart W. Cook, *Research Methods in Social Relations*, rev. ed. (New York: Holt, Rinehart & Winston, 1959): 80.

[2]James A. Anderson, *Communication Research: Issues and Methods* (New York: McGraw-Hill, 1987): 9.

[3]Herbert Goldhor, *An Introduction to Scientific Research in Librarianship* (Urbana: University of Illinois, Graduate School of Library Science, 1972): 87.

[4]Ibid.

[5]Earl R. Babbie, *The Practice of Social Research*, 10th ed. (Belmont, CA: Wadsworth/Thomson Learning, 2004): 230.

[6]Louise H. Kidder, *Research Methods in Social Relations*, 4th ed. (New York: Holt, Rinehart & Winston, 1981): 447.

[7]Donald T. Campbell and Julian C. Stanley, *Experimental and Quasi-Experimental Designs for Research* (Chicago: Rand McNally, 1963): 5.

[8]Babbie, *The Practice of Social Research*, 233.

[9]Kidder, *Research Methods in Social Relations*, 446.

[10]Campbell and Stanley, *Experimental and Quasi-Experimental Designs*, 5.

[11]Ibid., 16.

[12]G. Keppel, *Design and Analysis: A Researcher's Handbook*, 3d ed. (Englewood Cliffs, NJ: Prentice-Hall, 1991).

[13]John W.Creswell, *Research Design: Qualitative and Quantitative Approaches* (Thousand Oaks, CA: Sage Publications, 1994): 128.

[14]Campbell and Stanley, *Experimental and Quasi-Experimental Designs*, 12.

[15]Kidder, *Research Methods in Social Relations*, 57.

[16]George J. Mouly, *Educational Research: The Art and Science of Investigation* (Boston: Allyn & Bacon, 1978): 257.

Chapter 7

Qualitative Research Methods

The theories and techniques associated with the naturalistic paradigm and qualitative research methods pervade modern sociological research production. Library and information science (LIS) research makes substantial use of this approach to address complex questions of human-information interaction. Fidel's excellent "guided tour through the world of such research"[1] provides an invaluable context for librarians considering the use of these methods. In this chapter the following elements will be discussed: the underlying principles of naturalistic work, ethical concerns, data gathering techniques, data analysis tools and methods, developing grounded theory, ensuring integrity, and the presentation of findings. Exemplary studies are cited throughout, but they are representative rather than exhaustive. (For a taxonomic, annotated bibliography of qualitative studies in LIS as well as detailed discussions of observation, interviewing, and coding in information settings, see the book by Gorman and Clayton.[2])

This chapter is a revised and expanded version of Lynn Westbrook, "Qualitative Research Methods: A Review of Major Stages, Data Analysis Techniques, and Quality Controls," *Library & Information Science Research* 16, no. 3 (1994): 241–54. It is presented by permission of Elsevier Publishing.

UNDERLYING PRINCIPLES OF NATURALISTIC WORK

In virtually every area of LIS research, from system design to user education evaluation, the concatenation of factors that finally lead a user to an interaction with some part of an information system is increasingly complex. Naturalistic work seeks out all aspects of that complexity on the grounds that they are essential to understanding the behavior of which they are a part. "It is difficult to imagine a human activity that is context-free."[3] The flexibility and sensitivity of the human instrument are critical to understanding this complexity.

Naturalism as a Research Paradigm

When defined as a research paradigm, rather than as a research method, naturalism is an approach that posits reality as holistic and continually changing. Therefore, theory formation becomes an organic, continuous process designed to understand phenomena. As such, the naturalistic approach provides much needed insights into information-seeking experiences. The research goal centers on understanding rather than on predicting.

Naturalism in LIS Research

Primarily developed within living memory, the naturalistic paradigm has gradually gained acceptance in much of academia. As Bogdan notes, it is only recently, however, that it has been accepted in the applied or "professional" schools.

> The professional schools of social work . . . and information studies have always lagged behind the academic disciplines in accepting new theoretical and methodological trends. . . . Because of their marginal position, people in these fields tend to be conservative—the imitators rather than the innovators.[4]

Nevertheless, resultant theories (such as Mellon's "library anxiety"[5]) and major funded research (such as that of Chatman[6] and Kuhlthau[7]) have opened the doors for new projects in LIS. There "is no question that naturalistic inquiry, involving techniques well established in such fields as cultural anthropology, has its place in librarianship."[8] Works such as Gorman and Clayton's handbook on qualitative research in information settings[9] and Maylone's special issue of *Library Trends* on the place of this approach in the field[10] exemplify its acceptance.

The wellspring of literally hundreds of qualitatively based studies in information seeking is the extensive work of Dervin. Her sense-making approach to understanding communication, decision-making, and information-seeking behaviors provides a sound theoretical basis for a great deal of LIS research. (For more information on this approach, see her collection of germinal essays: *Sense-Making Methodology Reader.*[11])

Most Useful Approach

The research problem must determine the research approach and the methods employed. No single approach fits every problem; a reasoned choice must be made. Some areas of LIS research are so new, so complex, or so unexplored that librarians are looking for additional or different approaches.

If enough is known of an area to sustain a priori patterning, hypothesis formation, or even theory explication, then the positivist approach with its more quantitative methods might be used. If so little is known of an area that the simple identification of what is not known becomes problematic, then the naturalistic approach with its more qualitative methods might be used.

Of course, in many research situations some combination of the positivist and naturalist approaches provides the most complete or insightful understanding. Using the former for the segments of a research problem that support hypothesis testing and the latter for areas that are yet to be so well understood, for example, can maximize the benefits gained in large-scale research studies. Given the rapidly changing environment of LIS work, it is of critical importance that this positivist/naturalist choice be made in terms of what best answers the research problem. A mixed-methods approach, in some cases, provides the necessary array of data. (See, for example, Lincoln[12] and Stevens and McElhill.[13])

ETHICAL CONCERNS

As in any research involving human beings, a number of ethical concerns demand careful attention. The usual issues of subject confidentiality and harmless involvement are compounded in naturalistic settings. University and grant funding sources usually have human subject review committees (institutional review boards) which are used to considering both of these issues, but researchers must take particular responsibility for them when no outside review is required.[14]

Subject confidentiality is more the norm than subject anonymity in much of this research. The face-to-face involvement of interviews, general observation, focus groups, and participant observation preclude any pretense of subject anonymity. Even written documents, such as questionnaires and journals, can contain such revealing information that identification of some subjects is relatively easy. Therefore, the goal of confidentiality becomes crucial. By using pseudonyms, removing identifying details, and employing careful record keeping, the researcher does everything possible to ensure that the subjects will never be identified to anyone outside of the study team.

This confidentiality is just as important for information seekers as it is for any other population. They have an absolute right to their privacy within the context of the study. People may reveal illegal or immoral behaviors, such as plagiarism, copyright infringement, or theft of library materials. They may reveal gaps or weaknesses in their knowledge, understanding, or appreciation of the fundamentals of information seeking; that revelation may imperil their status in the workplace or at home. For example, junior faculty could find their tenure status jeopardized by public revelation of their inability to manage the information of their discipline. Therefore, confidentiality demands rigorous protection. The consent form which many subjects must sign should spell out the mechanisms by which that confidentiality will be protected and the extent to which it will be breached. For example, if a transcription service is hired to handle taped interviews, then an unknown person will be hearing the tapes. The schedule for the destruction of notes, tapes, computer files, and other records should be included.

Harmless involvement is the second ethical issue to consider. While confidentiality is meant to ensure that subjects are not harmed by the revelation of their studied words or actions, this issue refers to any harm which might ensue as a result of simply participating in the study. For example, in a study of the differing levels of reference accuracy of support staff and librarians, it would be necessary to consider patron involvement. It would not be unreasonable to assume that patrons whose complex reference questions are answered only by support staff would be "harmed" to the extent that their questions would be less accurately answered than they might have been.

Even those who do not participate in the study may be affected by it. They might hesitate to approach an online public access catalog (OPAC) which prominently displays a sign indicating that those who use the system will have their searches logged and studied. As Mellon's work indicates, at least some users are afraid of displaying poor judgment in public.[15] They may choose to do without help or information rather than risk becoming involved in a study.

The issue here is one of balancing the possible benefits of the study against the possible harm to the subjects. Minimizing the latter and maximizing the former strengthen the balance. Since very few information-seeking situations involve actual physical or significant psychological harm to individuals, most studies are able to manage research ethics with the application of careful analysis. (For more on ethics, see Chapter 3 of this book; Babbie, Chapter 3, for general discussion and pages 306–7 for issues pertaining to qualitative research[16]; Buchanan for applications in studies of cyber space interactions[17]; Darlington and Scott for exemplars[18]; Citro, Ilgen, and Marrett for explication of institutional review board regulations.[19])

DATA GATHERING TECHNIQUES

The act of gathering data for a qualitative study is an evolving process rooted in ongoing analysis. It involves more than obtaining discrete units of information. Simply holding a set number of interviews, for example, does not constitute meaningful data gathering. Instead, the researcher engages in reiterative, cyclical movement between data gathering and data analysis. Initial interviews might well, for example, spark a tentative point of analysis, which would then be fed back into the interview protocol. The next interviews, by virtue of that tentative data analysis effort, would be somewhat richer than their predecessors. Thus data gathering is envisioned as a process rather than a procedure; it requires analytic judgment rather than a preplanned routine. "Design remains flexible throughout the study because you have to work out questions to examine new ideas and themes that emerge during [data gathering]."[20]

That is not to imply that qualitative data gathering lacks planning and preparation. In addition to the exercise of thoughtful judgment during the process, the researcher must exercise care in planning two crucial elements: sampling and techniques, both of which are discussed below.

Finally, although this forum does not allow extensive discussion of the point, it must be noted that almost all data gathering is, to some extent, socially constructed. The interaction between two or more people is created within the social contexts of the individuals involved. Their contact involves factors which are beyond the control of the researcher and the participants, such as their race, age, gender, class, and more. Those factors influence the rapport, trust, and honesty of both parties. The hierarchical nature of the research relationship means that the participant is often in a subordinate position.[21] The impact of those factors on a constructed, hierarchical relationship must not be underestimated. Decisions regarding both ethics and data integrity are impacted.

Sampling

No single formula provides the "correct" sample size for a qualitative study. The depth, complexity, and "richness" of the data are critical, but identifying a representative sample is not even a consideration since the purpose of the research is to understand, not to generalize. For many LIS studies, an effective solution is to continue gathering data until critical elements of the study have become "saturated," or until further exemplars fail to add new nuance or to contradict what is understood. For example, in a study of the reasons behind library anxiety among first-semester doctoral history students at a major research university, a researcher might interview 10 of the 40-member population, choosing those 10 carefully to include as many known variables among subjects as possible such as race, gender, area of study, and length of time in the program. If subjects 8 through 10 yielded no information that had not already been uncovered in working with subjects 1 through 7, then there would be little point in insisting on a larger sample.

The standard of saturation will not, however, answer all questions regarding sample size. A second key factor must be involved, namely the nature of the research question being asked. Consider again the question of library anxiety among doctoral history students.

- A phenomenological study would seek to understand the nature of the anxiety as felt by those students. In that case, the researcher needs only a small sample (5 to 8), but each person must be studied in great depth.

- An ethnographic study would seek to describe the in-library behavior of those students. The researcher would, therefore, need a larger sample of the student population (15 to 20) plus some data from those who interact with the students, such as reference librarians and circulation staff.
- A grounded theory study would seek to describe the social and psychological processes which those with library anxiety go through in their use of the library. The researcher would again need a larger sample (15 to 20), although it would consist only of the students themselves. (For more of this perspective on sampling, see Morse.[22])

In each case, the nature of the research question affects the sample size requirements.

In addition to saturation and the nature of the research question, a third element is required in each sampling decision, namely the purpose of the first sample. "In purposeful sampling, members of the sample are deliberately chosen based on criteria that have relevance to the research question rather than criteria of randomness of selection."[23] Rather than "a sample," the researcher might think of "the first sample." Since the sample is used to gather data which immediately undergoes initial analysis, there is always the possibility that something will be learned which changes the study parameters. In that case, the first sample may be adjusted, augmented, enlarged, or otherwise modified to meet the new parameters. This multistage approach to sampling requires that a decision be made about the purpose of the first sample.

The most common sampling techniques in qualitative studies follow the thread of "purpose." Rather than the probabilistic sampling of a positivist approach, the naturalist approach starts with a purpose for working with one participant rather than with another. In LIS work, the following methods may be most useful:

- Maximum variety sampling. The purpose of maximum variety sampling is to find as heterogeneous a sample as possible. This method is useful when seeking to identify the patterns and commonalities that exist across otherwise divergent individuals.[24] This is analogous to the classic, experimental sampling technique known as "stratified random sampling" in that population variables are identified, as much as possible, in advance so that a deliberate effort can be made to maximize heterogeneity.
- Extreme case sampling. The purpose of extreme case sampling is to select participants who "exemplify characteristics of interest."[25] Choosing these individuals helps to clarify the critical issues in an area. For example, those who experience severe cases of library anxiety might be interviewed and observed in depth to help identify key factors in the phenomenon.
- Intensity sampling. The purpose of intensity sampling is to identify participants who have a great deal of experience (rather than extreme experience) with a phenomenon.[26] For example, in a study of reference librarians' use of visual memory regarding reference book placement, those who have

worked for a number of years in one library might be selected as an intensity sample.
- Snowball sampling. As its name implies, the purpose of snowball sampling is to identify participants who are linked in some way. Through shared experiences, perspectives, or other factors, these individuals lead the researcher to others in the same population. People who use library computer labs to play forbidden, group-based computer games might be identified through snowball sampling.

Several other purposive sampling techniques are available to the researcher. Patton, for example, discusses opportunistic, convenience, criterion, operational construct, and combination techniques.[27] When combined with the concept of saturation and a clear idea of the nature of the research question, the techniques provide several viable options.

Observation

LeCompte, Preissle, and Tesch described observation as "a method relying on watching, listening, asking questions, and collecting things."[28] Jorgensen concurred, noting in addition that it is critical for researchers to "remain open to the unexpected."[29] The observer must choose a point of balance between observing and participating then supplement it with judicious interviewing. "Participant observation in its various forms is not new to library or information research."[30] For one of the earliest discussions of this method in LIS research, see Bruyn's study, reprinted in 1970, which was originally published in 1963.[31]

Understanding observation requires a focus on two points. First, as Gold discussed, there are four different positions on a continuum of roles that researchers play when using the observation technique: complete participant, participant-as-observer, observer-as-participant, and complete observer[32] (also discussed in Babbie,[33] Chatman,[34] and Schwartz and Schwartz[35]). This variety allows use of whatever perspective will best answer the research question thereby providing a "here-and-now experience in depth."[36] Second, as Whyte noted, it is really a "set of methods including interviewing, since any able field worker will supplement what is learned from observing and participating with some interviewing."[37] Chatman, for example, used the combination of "participant observation and an interview guide consisting of 28 items"[38] in her two-year study of the information needs of janitorial workers.

The obvious advantage of this method has been noted by LeCompte, Preissle, and Tesch:

> One problem researchers encounter is that participant reports of activities and beliefs may not match their observed behavior. Participant observation is a check, enabling the researcher to verify that individuals are doing what they (and the researcher) believe they are doing.[39]

Denzin rated observation as "excellent"[40] in its ability to counter the ill effects of time, order, history, and maturation.

Although only unobtrusive observation in the natural setting, with all its attendant ethical and logistical difficulties, can negate the impact of the observer on the observed, much can be accomplished through properly conducted general observation. Of course it must always be kept in mind that, so much as possible, the point of observation is to understand what actually occurs without deliberately introducing new stimuli or manipulating the participants.[41] Of necessity, in some settings, the observation must be highly structured, as in Wilson and Streatfield's 1981 study of information needs in an organizational setting.[42] In every case, however, the "intent is to fit into the setting in such a way that the usual behavior of the people being studied is changed as little as possible."[43] As Schwartz and Schwartz note, the researcher must attempt to "strike that balance between active participation in the lives of the subjects and observation of their behavior which will be most productive of valid data."[44]

Focusing the observational field should "begin with the widest possible range of phenomena, gradually limiting our attention to particular phenomena."[45] The observer must "take account of practices, supporting ideologies, and ranges of deviation, and relate these to each other."[46] As Diesing noted in his chapter on this method, one "learns concepts and distinctions not just by asking people or reading an article but by participating in innumerable activities."[47]

The setting and purpose are always crucial in determining the techniques used in an observation no matter what participants are being studied. Anything from stationing a video camera in front of the reference desk to blending in as a parent at a storytelling session could constitute observation. (In every case, the ethical concerns mentioned earlier must be carefully addressed.) For much LIS research, the setting varies along several lines:

- Number of participants—for example, settings can be crowded (as in a busy branch library) or sparsely populated (as in a quiet map library)
- Public vs. private—for example, settings can be as public as a reference desk or as private as a professor's office
- Size of the observable actions—for example, settings can be limited to small actions, such as keyboard motions, or they can focus on large actions, such as routes taken through the library building
- Staff or public—for example, settings can involve library staff, the public, or some combination thereof.

Just as the settings will vary, so too will the purpose of the study, as mentioned earlier.

Observation techniques vary widely depending on the setting and purpose of the research. An ethnographic approach requires moving into the setting as fully as possible so as to disturb the participants as little as possible. Participant observation of the use of self-revelation by reference staff, for example, would require the researcher to appear as a patron to the librarians under study. Unobtrusive observation in a public setting requires the researcher to fade quietly and naturally into the surroundings. Observing the instances of peer instruction at OPACs in a school library would require the researcher to sustain a believable, probable, unobtrusive activity near the terminals. Obtrusive observation requires the researcher to build enough rapport with the participant(s) to overcome the natural reactions which anyone might have to the activity. Observing the search strategies employed on Dialog searches among a group of corporate librarians, for example, would require the researcher to develop a relationship with each individual—one that is informal enough to promote easy conversation yet formal enough to reinforce the nonjudgmental nature of the interaction. (For more on the use of dress to promote this balance, see McCracken.[48])

Interviews

In all their variety, interviews are a valuable qualitative method. Researchers must choose their own points along the continuum between structured and unstructured interviews. The

> structured interview is the mode of choice when the interviewer *knows what he or she does not know* and can therefore frame appropriate questions to find it out, while the unstructured interview is the mode of choice when the interviewer *does not know what he or she doesn't know* and must therefore rely on the respondent to tell him or her.[49]

Another choice can be made along the continuum between exit interviews (taking place at the end of an event, such as an on-line search) to in-depth interviews (often taking place over the course of several hours) to focus group interviews.[50] Finally, a choice must be made as to the number of people involved in the interview: one, a small group, or a larger group.

There are several strengths to interviewing such as the fact "that it permits the respondent to move back and forth in time."[51] The flexibility of the technique allows the investigator to probe, to clarify, and to create new questions based on what has already been heard. Whyte recommended that the interviewer "let the conversation flow naturally but note what aspects of events the informant describes or leaves out so that later the interviewer can phrase questions to fill in omissions or to check his or her understanding of what has been said."[52] This "flexibly structured" interview style allows the researcher to "recognize statements which suggest new questions or even new lines of investigation."[53] Kvale recommends the thoughtful sequencing of different mechanisms for eliciting information. He notes that direct questions are useful in following up on topics which a participant has identified as critical; silence allows people the time needed to reflect on a topic; structuring questions pulls an interview back on track.[54]

Although there is obvious benefit to the researcher, the appeal of interviewing to the informants may be less evident. Whereas actual payment is employed as a motivator in certain projects, informants "generally find it a rewarding experience to be interviewed by a skilled and sympathetic person. . . . [It can be] useful in helping them to gain perspectives on and understanding of their ideas and experiences."[55] As Argyris put it, the informants "must feel that they are contributing to something whose completion will be quite satisfying to them."[56]

As with participant observation, specific skills and methods have long been used to strengthen the depth of the resultant data. The use of certain questioning techniques is one example. While carefully adjusting the "rules" of good interviewing to meet the needs of whatever situation is at hand, the researcher can employ proven techniques. For example, the type of question can vary. "Comparison questions ask people to tell how things are like one another while contrast questions ask people to tell how things differ from one another."[57] Dewdney and Harris urged the use of probing and clarifying questions.[58] The former explores the unknown background on a statement, and the latter seeks to elucidate what has already been stated. Clark and Schrober wrote at length regarding the most productive techniques for framing questions.[59] For example, effective questions are framed so as to build upon the shared understanding between researcher and participant. That common ground can be personal or cultural.[60] Gorden discussed various difficulties in the interview process including the participants' concerns regarding ego-threatening questions, ability to remember certain types of information, tendency to generalize, and more (passim).[61] Jorgensen discusses various means of establishing rapport and the restating of informants' observations as two useful techniques.[62] (For an example of interview work, see Shenton and Dixon[63]; for practical insights on conducting interviews, see Chapters 6 and 7 of Bernard.[64])

Documents: Questionnaires, Diaries, Journals, Papers, and More

Finally, the written word can be a source of data. Materials written by participants vary greatly in their format, content, and impetus. With few exceptions, the methodologies involved are well documented elsewhere so only a general overview will be given here.

Questionnaires vary in two primary areas: (1) means of delivery (in person, telephone, mail, e-mail, Web, and point of contact) and (2) format (open-ended questions, Likert scales, multiple-choice questions, and rankings). This is perhaps the most thoroughly studied form of data gathering. For more detail than is appropriate here, see the following: Kalton,[65] Fowler,[66] Fink[67] and relevant sections of this book.

The various means of delivery have their advantages and disadvantages. An in-person questionnaire allows the researcher to clear up any obvious misunderstandings on the spot but it is time consuming. A telephone questionnaire allows contact with distant participants, but it is difficult to convince people to complete one without advance, written preparation. Mailed questionnaires are relatively simple to conduct but require significant follow-up to produce sufficient response rates. (See Fowler for methods of writing such questionnaires and increasing the response rate.[68]) Although they are the bane of discussion lists, e-mail question-naires are cheap to conduct; of course, they reach a very limited portion of many populations. Some Web sites have embedded questionnaires for their users, and those are often productive, assuming all users have equal facility in responding and that individuals do not submit multiple forms. Finally, point-of-contact question-naires (commonly found in libraries at the reference or circulation desk) are simple and affordable but do limit responses to those who choose to, or who can be persuaded to, complete the forms on-site. Obviously, the more interaction possible between the researcher and the participant, the more naturalistic is the inquiry.

The format variations of questionnaires also have their strengths and weak-nesses. The use of open-ended questions provides participants with a greater forum for expressing their responses, but it can intimidate those who do not feel comfortable or confident in their answers, do not have the time to devote to the complexities of answering, or do not have a great facility with written or spoken communication in the language used. The use of Likert scales and rankings have been extensively discussed in the literature. Producing ordinal level data, they are not really qualitative techniques at all. Finally, multiple-choice questions can be designed to help participants identify their own answers out of a full range of possible answers. The trick here, of course, is either to provide a "full" range or to sufficiently encourage respondents to write in any additional items.

In addition to questionnaires, participants can sometimes be persuaded to keep written records of their activities, thoughts, motivations, emotions, and decisions throughout the life of an information-seeking activity or project. Kuhlthau's early work, for example, involved the use of self-reported, written records from high school students.[69] These documents can provide great depth and detail when par-ticipants fully engage in the project. Among their obvious disadvantages are the tendency to reveal only what the participants choose to share with the researcher and the tendency to be incomplete (due to factors such as time, stress, or shame) on those points of extreme difficulty that are often most crucial to the researcher. To minimize these weaknesses, self-reported documents are often used in careful conjunction with other data gathering techniques. Kuhlthau, for example, in-cluded interviews and observations in her research design.[70]

Event sampling provides a variation on this approach by focusing participant attention on the specific areas of most interest to the researcher. In this situation, "participants are asked to monitor and describe ongoing activity according to schedules and formats defined and regulated by the investigator."[71] By getting people to explicate what just happened to them, investigators minimize distor-tions of memory and retrospection. Obviously, the question under review must center on discrete, defined events or moments so that such recording becomes reasonable and relatively straightforward.

Finally, the natural end-products of various information-seeking activities can be obtained for research purposes. For example, the I-Search paper is a fairly common format among high school and college populations in which students report the problems and solutions encountered during the information search, as well as the more traditional information on the topic at hand. Those papers lack the artificial nature of a research-induced diary but do include all the problems of an assigned, course-related document. Nevertheless, they can be revealing, particularly when combined with interviews.

DATA ANALYSIS TOOLS AND METHODS

One of the most commonly used data analysis techniques of qualitative research, content analysis can be defined as "a research technique for making replicable and valid inferences from data to their context."[72] Weber characterized it as "a research method that uses a set of procedures to make valid inferences from text. These inferences are about the sender(s) of the message, the message itself, or the audience of the message."[73] It is based on the premise that the many words from interviews, observations, and documents can be reduced to categories in which words share the same meaning or connotation.

The classification procedure that is used to accomplish this reduction must be consistent so that anyone (with training) would get the same results.[74] Data analysis involves "working with data, organizing it, breaking it into manageable units, synthesizing it, searching for patterns, discovering what is important and what is to be learned, and deciding what you will tell others."[75]

Data Analysis Principles

Two principles of qualitative data analysis are quite consistent in virtually all descriptions of it. First, it is an ongoing process that feeds back into the research design right up to the last moment of data gathering. Second, whatever theory or working hypothesis eventually develops must grow naturally from the data analysis rather than standing to the side as an a priori statement that the data will find to be accurate or wanting.

Because the purpose is to understand rather than to predict, qualitative research requires a cyclical approach in which the collection of data affects the analysis of the data which, in turn, affects the gradual formation of theory which, in turn, affects the further collection of data. "Data collection and analysis form an integrated activity."[76]

> On site, the investigator must engage in *continuous* data analysis, so that every new act of investigation takes into account everything that has been learned so far. Inductive data analyses can be performed on a daily basis, so that insights, elements of theory, hypotheses, questions, gaps, can be identified and pursued beginning with the next day's work.[77]

The coding of observed behavior exemplifies most immediately the interplay of data gathering and data analysis as the very act of choosing rudimentary coding terms refocuses the mental lens with which people are viewed. (For an in-depth analysis of this relationship, see Bakeman.[78])

Currently, the majority of work in LIS grows from research questions which center on understanding users in their information-seeking contexts. A few scholars, however, are beginning to examine data from a more sociological perspective by using discourse analysis instead of a constant comparison analysis. Discourse analysis "concentrates on the analysis of knowledge formations, which organize institutional practices and societal reality on a large scale.[79] This approach is still in development within LIS.

Content Analysis Terms

Before exploring the actual techniques of content analysis, it is necessary to review a few of the basic terms. A *datum* "is a unit of information that is recorded in a durable medium, distinguishable from other data, analyzable by explicit techniques, and relevant to a particular problem."[80] These units may be any of the following: physical (pages), syntactical (words), referential (objects, events, persons, acts), propositional (words which are required to conform to a certain structure), and thematic (requiring a deep understanding of the language).[81]

Essential to coding units of data is the term *category* which refers to "groups of words with similar meanings and/or connotations."[82] The term *theme* then refers to clusters of categories that share some commonality such as reference to a single issue.

Field notes, another data collection tool, contains everything the investigator says, experiences, and remembers, as well as notes on emotions and initial analytic comments.[83] These field or observation notes come in various formats including the following: running notes, field experience logs or diaries, and notes on thematic units.[84]

Memos are brief, informal essays written by the investigator to capture some part of the content analysis process that has been inductively recognized. "Memoing should begin as soon as the first field data start coming in, and will usually continue right up to the production of final report text. . . . Memoing contributes strongly to the development/revision of the coding system."[85] It is critical to recognize that "memos are always conceptual in intent. They do not just report data, but they tie different pieces of data together in a cluster, or they show that a particular piece of data is an instance of a general concept."[86]

Finally, a *coding manual* contains the codification of the decisions made on the process. The units of analysis, the elements of classification, and the rules for applying the codes constitute the manual. Carefully written to serve as a record, as well as an application tool, the manual will be revised until its application is consistent and meaningful. (For more on the entire process, see Smith.[87])

The Constant Comparative Method

The constant comparative method, codified by Glaser and Strauss,[88] is generally recognized as one of the most effective means of content analysis (Lincoln and Guba,[89] Mellon[90]). It involves joint coding and analysis during the continual review of data to form categories gradually. The constant comparative method can be described in four stages: (1) comparing incidents applicable to each category, (2) integrating categories and their properties, (3) delimiting the theory, and (4) writing the theory.[91] These categories are carefully defined and made mutually exclusive so that relationships can be identified between those elements that fall into the categories.

The investigator must go through several cycles until the coding criteria are accurate and consistent.[92] "By constant comparison of all current incidents in a category, the researcher begins to develop ideas about the category, its dimensions and limitations, and its relationship to other categories."[93] This cyclical approach to analysis helps ensure that the theory develops out of the data. The

> constant comparative method is designed . . . to guarantee that two analysts working independently with the same data will achieve the same results; it is designed to allow, with discipline, for some of the vagueness and flexibility that aid the creative generation of theory.[94]

As Glaser explains, the "purpose of the constant comparative method of joint coding and analysis is to generate theory . . . systematically . . . by using explicit coding and analytic procedures."[95]

Like other methods, comparative analysis can be used to generate both substantive and formal theory.[96] Substantive theory refers to specific areas, such as OPAC use and Internet search strategies. Formal theory refers to conceptual areas, such as information-seeking patterns and relevance criteria.

Coding Data

Coding lies at the heart of the constant comparative method in that units of data are compared to each other in terms of their fit into the developing coding scheme. Coding does not descriptively paraphrase the interview or observation notes; instead, it identifies the main categories as well as associated subcategories so that, eventually, all units of data can be categorized according to these codes.[97] Stempel pointed out that these categories must be pertinent and functional.[98] "By comparing where the facts are similar or different, we can generate properties of categories that increase the categories' generality and explanatory power."[99]

Field notes, in their many formats, serve as the documents upon which are written both initial codes and memos.[100] Immediately following an interview or observation period, the investigator must organize and complete the notes so that initial analysis can begin.[101] Periods of preliminary data analysis are interpolated between periods of data gathering. This analysis consists, in part, of fleshing out skeletal field notes and reviewing the results to locate any preliminary patterns that might begin to emerge.[102]

Strauss listed several advantages of coding data. He noted that

> coding (1) both follows upon and leads to generative questions; (2) fractures the data, thus freeing the researcher from description and forcing interpretation to

higher levels of abstraction; (3) is the pivotal operation for moving toward the discovery of a core category or categories; and so (4) moves toward ultimate integration of the entire analysis; and (5) yields the desired conceptual density (i.e., relationships among the codes and the development of each.[103]

Three different types of coding generally follow the progression of a content analysis. *Open coding* is the initial, provisional work done on an unrestricted basis to produce concepts that fit the data.[104] *Axial coding* takes place during the latter portions of open coding as major categories emerge from the data. By focusing on one category in terms of its conditions, consequences, and other features, the researcher develops cumulative knowledge about the category as well as its subcategories and related categories.[105] *Selective coding* takes place as soon as open and axial coding have begun to establish core categories. At this point, even if the other two methods are still in use, everything gradually becomes subservient to the core categories.

The principle of saturation is critical in data analysis. A category can be considered saturated when no new information about it develops out of the data. Once a category is as fully understood as possible in all of its ramifications and detail then the continuous assignment of new data to that category becomes unnecessary for the generation of theory.

Coding Techniques

Only practice and experience can translate the mechanics of coding guidelines into efficient, effective methods. Nevertheless, certain helpful techniques can facilitate that process. Strauss recommended, for example, that during the initial, open coding the researcher look for terms used by the subjects and use those terms as major coding terms.[106] Once the categories are firmly in mind, the focus moves to understanding each day's observations and interviews so that recoding the data as necessary becomes critical.[107]

After leaving the field but prior to conducting final data analysis, various guidelines are useful. For example, if a memo becomes central to the theory, then saturate the redeveloped category or property that is the point of the memo.[108] Memos, from theoretical to methodological, have their own special guidelines. Two of the most common are to "give priority to memoing"[109] and to indicate in memos when saturation has been reached.[110]

No single mechanism exists for determining the categories in which the data are sorted. In general, "it is presumptuous to assume that one begins to know the relevant categories and hypotheses until the 'first days in the field,' at least, are over."[111]

Although categories must evolve from the data, several types of categories are quite common in coding. Bogdan and Biklen, for example, noted 10 such category types,[112] whereas Lofland and Lofland formulated 11 "thinking units"[113] which could be used as coding categories.

To manage all of these codes, memos, and data, researchers used to keep separate items on note cards which could then be organized and reorganized as needed. Today, of course, there are several software packages that do all of this. They allow researchers to apply, remove, and modify codes in relationship to discrete pieces of text. In addition, reports can be generated which list every instance of a code's application, every participant whose input received a particular code or combination of codes. NVivo or N6 (formerly Nud*ist) and Hyper-Research are two of the most common packages. For further information on each, see the following URLs:

- HyperResearch: http://www.researchware.com/
- NVivo or N6: http://www.qsr.com.au/index.htm

(For more on computer-assisted data analysis, see Chapter 7 of Coffey and Atkinson,[114] Lee and Esterhuizen,[115] Gilbert,[116] and Hesse-Biber.[117])

Once the categories have formed, certain guidelines assist in their application. Entries can be continuous rather than dichotomous in their intensity, and some units may be used in two categories where one is the main category and the other is a subcategory.[118] "Ordinarily, use a single code for a segment. Dual or even multiple coding is warranted if a segment is both descriptively and inferentially meaningful."[119]

There are six major ways of grouping categories, of which clustering has the most potential for LIS research. Clustering seeks to group together categories that share some observed qualities or, alternatively, to partition them into mutually exclusive classes whose boundaries reflect differences in the observed qualities of their members.[120] For example, in a study of information-seeking behavior among faculty, it might be quite natural to cluster those interview statements that have to do with technology; similarly, a researcher might partition those statements that have to do with people from those that deal with objects.

Throughout the entire process, it is worth remembering that the purpose of this work is to "help us imagine new and fruitful 'categories' of thinking about lived, human experience. Although we often say, in shorthand fashion, that categories 'emerge' from the data, in fact, categories do not often 'reside' in data, as that turn of phrase would have us believe. Categories arise in the interaction between data studying and researcher ordering; they are a product of the interaction effect between deep study of data and the researcher's own cultural predilections, definition of the problem, and previous experience."[121]

Moving from Codes to Theory

The process of moving from coding to theory or pattern generation is ongoing but at some point it is necessary to leave the field and begin the final analysis.[122] "Once coding is achieved, the data have to be . . . systematically explored to generate meaning."[123] After all the data are finally coded, analysis gradually reveals a framework of patterns and contrasts from which, in some cases, theory can be developed. "The truly emergent integrating framework, which encompasses the fullest possible diversity of categories and properties, becomes an open-ended scheme, hardly subject to being redesigned."[124] Reducing terminology and generalizing gains a parsimony of variables as well as a scope in the applicability of the theory to a wide range of situations.

Eventually the investigator is ready for what Glaser and Strauss referred to as "delimiting the theory."[125] This curbs what could become an overwhelming task and occurs at two levels: the theory and the categories. First, the theory solidifies in the sense that major modifications become fewer and fewer as the analyst compares the next incidents of a category to its properties. Second, categories become theoretically saturated. Lincoln and Guba described a mechanism for delimiting theory that involves sorting data within categories, reviewing categories for overlap, and looking at relationships among categories.[126]

Ensuring Coding Integrity

During coding, certain techniques should be used to ensure the integrity of the work. The acceptable reliability level must be established prior to test coding and met regularly before final coding.[127] Reproducibility (i.e., intercoder reliability) is a minimum standard. "Double-coding the same transcripts is essential. . . . get code-recode consistencies over 90 percent before going on."[128] "Stability is the degree to which a process is invariant or unchanging over time. Stability becomes manifest under test-retest conditions."[129] Face validity refers to the correspondence between investigators' definitions of concepts and their definitions of the categories that measured them. This is necessary but far from sufficient. A category should appear to measure the construct it is intended to measure.[130]

During the analysis of data, certain techniques can strengthen the resultant claims. Sometimes other sources can be used to confirm inferences from data. These may include past successes, contextual experiences, established theories, and representative interpreters. "A content analysis is valid to the extent its inferences are upheld in the face of independently obtained evidence."[131] Of course that independent evidence is not always available. (For more on various aspects of validity, see Maxwell[132] and Johnson.[133])

DEVELOPING GROUNDED THEORY

Although not the only means of generating a final theoretical analysis of data, the grounded theory approach stands out as central to the naturalistic paradigm. "The grounded theory approach is a method for discovering theories, concepts, hypotheses, and propositions directly from data, rather than from a priori assumptions, other research, or existing theoretical frameworks."[134] When data collection and analysis cease, the resultant theory provides a depth of understanding pertinent to the entities studied. This work has "a high emphasis on theory as process; that is, theory as an ever-developing entity, not as a perfected product."[135] Generalizability is not a factor because the "aim is understanding the phenomenon rather than controlling it. . . . The intent is to understand the situation as it exists in one particular setting rather than to predict what might happen in similar settings."[136] This inquiry "attempts . . . to understand why people . . . behave as they do."[137]

Although not predictive in nature, the resultant theory does have concrete value.[138] Applications are tentative and can be applied only in other settings if multisite studies have been extensive or if a fit is made between two similar settings. Because "in-depth understanding of human actions is the primary focus,"[139] results of naturalistic work will vary but will not be the flat statements of what hypothesis has been proved or disproved commonly found in positivist approaches. "In generating grounded theory researchers do not seek to prove their theories, but merely to demonstrate plausible support for them."[140] The explanations of these theories are "grounded" in the "details, evidence, and examples"[141] of the data.

A working hypothesis is most likely to be presented as it describes the patterns encountered and their broad relationships to each other. The working hypothesis is best seen as a general guide in that it has neither the artificiality of the scientist's hypothesis nor the narrowness of the single case study's description but, instead, offers the "broad range of the related."[142] However, it must be remembered that "working hypotheses are not that powerful; their transferability depends upon the degree of fittingness."[143] Some of these hypotheses may later be tested in a quantitative approach, but many will describe an ongoing process of mutual shaping so complex that verifying any subset thereof is meaningless.

Turner delineated several advantages of the grounded theory approach. "It promotes the development of theoretical accounts and explanations which conform closely to the situations being observed, so that the theory is likely to be intelligible to, and usable by, those in the situations studied."[144] Grounded theories are likely to reflect the complexity of that which is studied rather than oversimplifying it. (For a lucid, illustrated explanation of grounded theory, see Charmaz.[145])

ENSURING INTEGRITY

Ensuring integrity is no more difficult for naturalistic work than it is for positivist work but, again, the means differ. As Dewdney remarked, field studies "need not lack rigor and the field setting in itself does not necessarily imply deficiencies in control if the researcher develops systematic procedures for documenting the observed behavior."[146] Whereas positivists use techniques such as random sampling to support aspects such as generalizability, naturalists use techniques such as prolonged contact to support aspects such as transferability. Given the necessity of research within whatever setting is most natural for the subjects, the investigator cannot escape bias and so must recognize its impact upon the study in much the same way that a positivist recognizes the impact of an artificial laboratory setting upon a subject's response.[147] Central to that axiom is the belief that "the human instrument is as capable of refinements as any other variety."[148] The judgment required during the research process points to the accuracy of Maxwell's statement that the "validity of your results is not guaranteed by following some prescribed procedure."[149]

The techniques and approaches discussed below focus on ensuring the integrity, trustworthiness, and value of naturalistic data gathering and analysis as well as the theory or working hypothesis that results from them. As with the positivist paradigm, there are no absolute guarantees of results that are both meaningful and unbiased.

Major Techniques

Several scholars have delineated their methods of ensuring integrity but those of Lincoln and Guba include most of those mentioned elsewhere.[150] They listed five major techniques to establish the credibility of naturalistic work.

1. Certain activities increase "the probability that credible findings will be produced."[151]These include prolonged engagement, persistent observation, and triangulation (which includes "different modes of data collection, using any that come logically to hand but depending most on qualitative methods.")[152] Fortner and Christians offered further insights.[153]
2. Peer debriefing "is a process of exposing oneself to a disinterested peer in a manner paralleling an analytic session and for the purpose of exploring aspects of the inquiry that might otherwise remain only implicit within the inquirer's mind."[154] It must be noted that some disagree with the value of critical peer reactions, thinking it better to have supportive peers who give constructive feedback than oppositional peers who play the devil's advocate.[155]
3. The use of negative case analysis is done to "refine a hypothesis until it accounts for all known cases without exception."[156] Although that ideal may not really be possible, "if a hypothesis could be formulated that fit some reasonable number of cases—even as low, say, as 60 percent—there would seem to be substantial evidence of its acceptability. After all, has anyone ever produced a perfect statistical finding, significant at the .000 level?"[157]
4. Although difficult for the resource-poor investigator, referential adequacy can be valuable. This technique requires the investigator to "earmark a portion of the data to be archived—not included in whatever data analysis may be planned."[158] Once the analysis is completed then the archived data are retrieved and examined in light of the results with an eye to inconsistencies and gaps.
5. "The member check, whereby data, analytic categories, interpretations, and conclusions are tested with members of those stakeholding groups from

whom the data were originally collected, is the most crucial technique for establishing credibility."[159] It can be both formal and informal. Member checking is particularly vital as meaningful feedback from subjects can rapidly expose gaps or flaws in any data gathering technique, working hypothesis, or emerging theory.[160]

Additional Techniques

"Both implicitly and explicitly, the analyst continually checks out [the] theory as the data pour in."[161] Standard techniques, in addition to those listed earlier, include category saturation, collection of referential adequacy materials, establishing structural corroboration or coherence, reflexive journals, audits,[162] self-transcription,[163] explicit recording instructions,[164] a personal log, and a methodological log.[165]

In addition, Miles and Huberman listed 12 tactics for "confirming meanings, avoiding bias, and assuring the quality of conclusions,"[166] namely, counting, noting patterns or themes, seeing plausibility, clustering, making metaphors, splitting variables, subsuming particulars into the general, factoring, noting relations between variables, finding intervening variables, building a logical chain of evidence, and making conceptual or theoretical coherence.

Chatman's techniques for seeking reliability, which she defined as pertaining "to the degree to which observations are reported as consistent with some phenomenon during the life span of the inquiry,"[167] were varied. She did each of the following: consistently took notes, immersed herself in the setting, exposed herself to multiple situations, and built on what she learned from other research studies. She also stated that "*validity* pertains to truth or the degree to which the researcher is given a true picture of the phenomenon being studied."[168] Her research sought to build on all three "components of validity: face, criterion, and construct."[169]

PRESENTATION OF FINDINGS

The material in Chapter 11 of this volume explains all of the critical points regarding the presentation of general research findings. Two points specific to the presentation of qualitative research findings, however, bear mention.

First, in almost any forum, it may be necessary to explain the concepts behind a naturalistic approach. Although more and more reviewers are familiar with the naturalistic paradigm, there are still those who require authors to provide a basic primer for readers. In writing a journal article, for example, an author may be required by reviewers to explain fully the paradigmatic approach underlying all of the research design decisions. Researchers who work from a positivist perspective and use experimental techniques can take all of that background for granted.

In giving conference presentations, it may be possible to assume a greater knowledge of the issues depending on the nature of the group being addressed. (For more on writing up a qualitative study, see Wolcott[170] and Holliday.[171])

Second, one ethic unique to qualitative research requires the researcher to make some return to the community. For example, offering to share findings in a public forum with those who participate or might have participated in the study is common. Sometimes a copy of the findings is presented to individual participants who request the information. In almost every case, some decision regarding "giving voice" to the participants must be made. Mellon's use of direct quotes from her frightened students, for example, gave voice to their needs in a community meant to support them.[172] Within the context of the research problem, an effort to reciprocate should be made. (For more on these points, see the following: Mellon, Chapter 5[173]; Coffey and Atkinson, Chapter 5.[174])

SUMMARY

The value of much of qualitative research methods lies in the possibility that others may find some aspects of it that transfer to their own settings. It becomes important for the investigator to supply full information regarding anything that might affect that transfer. "It is . . . not the naturalist's task to provide an index of transferability; it is his or her responsibility to provide the data base that makes transferability judgments possible on the part of potential appliers."[175]

As LIS scholars lead the information community's development of information systems and services for users, they must maintain a solid grounding in the purpose behind their work. Understanding what users encounter as they move through the complex, multidimensional, and dynamic experience of information seeking provides that solid grounding. Qualitative research methods enrich and augment the toolbox of LIS research approaches.

NOTES

[1]Raya Fidel, "Qualitative Methods in Information Retrieval Research," *Library and Information Science Research* 15 (1993): 219

[2]G. E. Gorman and Peter Clayton, *Qualitative Research for the Information Professional: A Practical Handbook* (London: Library Association Publishing, 1997).

[3]Yvonna S. Lincoln and Egon G. Guba, *Naturalistic Inquiry* (Newbury Park, CA: Sage Publications, 1985): 114.

[4]Robert Bogdan, "Foreword," in *Naturalistic Inquiry for Library Science: Methods and Applications for Research, Evaluation, and Teaching*, by Constance Ann Mellon (New York: Greenwood Press, 1990): xiii.

[5]Constance Mellon, "Library Anxiety: A Grounded Theory and Its Development," *College and Research Libraries* 47 (March 1986): 160–5.

[6]Elfreda Chatman, *The Information World of Retired Women* (Westport, CT: Greenwood Press, 1992).

[7] Carol Collier Kuhlthau, *Seeking Meaning: A Process Approach to Library and Information Services*, 2d ed. (Norwood, NJ: Ablex, 2003).

[8] Charles Davis, "On Qualitative Research," *Library and Information Science Research* 12 (1990): 327–8.

[9] Gorman and Clayton, *Qualitative Research for the Information Professional*.

[10] Theresa Maylone, ed. "Qualitative Research," *Library Trends* 46, no. 4 (1998): 597–768.

[11] Brenda Dervin, Lois Foreman-Wernet, and Eric Lauterbach, eds. *Sense-Making Methodology Reader: Selected Writings of Brenda Dervin* (New York: Hampton Press, 2003).

[12] Yvonna Lincoln, "Insights into Library Services and Users from Qualitative Research," *Library and Information Science Research* 24 (2002): 3–16.

[13] G. Ruggeri Stevens and J. McElhill, "A Qualitative Study and Model of the Use of E-Mail in Organizations," *Internet Research* 10, no. 4 (2000): 271–83.

[14] Joan Sieber, *Planning Ethically Responsible Research: A Guide for Students and Internal Review Boards* (Newbury Park, CA: Sage Publications, 1992).

[15] Mellon, "Library Anxiety," 160–5.

[16] Earl Babbie, *Practice of Social Research*, 10th ed. (Belmont, CA: Wadsworth, 2004).

[17] Elizabeth Buchanan, "Ethics, Qualitative Research, and Ethnography in Virtual Space," *Journal of Information Ethics* 9, no. 2 (2000): 82–87.

[18] Yvonne Darlington and Dorothy Scott, *Qualitative Research in Practice: Stories from the Field* (Philadelphia: Open University Press, 2002).

[19] Constance Citro, Daniel Ilgen, and Cora Marrett, eds. "Panel on Institutional Review Boards, Surveys, and Social Science Research; Committee on National Statistics and Board on Behavioral, Cognitive, and Sensory Sciences, Division on Behavioral and Social Sciences and Education, National Research Council of the National Academies," *Protecting Participants and Facilitating Social and Behavioral Sciences Research* (Washington, D.C.: National Academies Press, 2003).

[20] Herbert Rubin and Irene Rubin, *Qualitative Interviewing: The Art of Hearing Data* (Thousand Oaks, CA: Sage Publications, 1995): 45.

[21] Andrea Fontana and James Frey, "Interviewing: the Art of Science," in *Handbook of Qualitative Research*, edited by Norman Denzin and Yvonna Lincoln (Thousand Oaks, CA: Sage Publications, 1994): 369.

[22] Janice Morse, "Designing Funded Qualitative Research," in *Handbook of Qualitative Research*, edited by Norman Denzin and Yvonna Lincoln (Thousand Oaks, CA: Sage Publications, 1994): 220–35.

[23] Jana Bradley, "Methodological Issues and Practices in Qualitative Research," *Library Quarterly* 63, no. 4 (1993): 440.

[24] Morse, "Designing Funded Qualitative Research," 220–35.

[25] Ibid., 229.

[26] Ibid., 220–35.

[27] Michael Quinn Patton, *Qualitative Evaluation and Research Methods*, 2d ed. (Newbury Park, CA: Sage Publications, 1990): 169–83.

[28] Margaret LeCompte, Judith Preissle, and Renata Tesch, *Ethnography and Qualitative Design in Educational Research*, 2d ed. (New York: Academic Press, 1993): 196.

[29] Danny Jorgensen, *Participant Observation: A Methodology for Human Studies* (London: Sage Publications, 1989): 82.

[30] Raya Fidel, "The Case Study Method: A Case Study," *Library and Information Science Research* 6 (July 1984): 275.

[31] Severyn Bruyn, "The Methodology of Participant Observation," in *Reader in Research Methods for Librarianship*, edited by Mary Lee Bundy, Paul Wasserman, and Gayle Raghi (Washington, D.C.: Microcard Editions, 1970).

[32] Raymond Gold, "Roles in Sociological Field Observation," in *Issues in Participant Observation*, edited by George McCall and J. L. Simmons (Reading, MA: Addison-Wesley, 1969): 33.

[33] Earl Babbie, *Practice of Social Research*, 8th ed. (Belmont, CA: Wadsworth, 1998).

[34]Chatman, *Information World of Retired Women.*

[35]Morris Schwartz and Charlotte Schwartz, "Problems in Participant Observation," *American Journal of Sociology* 60 (1955): 343–56.

[36]Lincoln and Guba, *Naturalistic Inquiry*, 273.

[37]William Whyte, "On Making the Most of Participant Observation," *American Sociologist* 14, no. 1 (1979): 56.

[38]Chatman, *Information World of Retired Women*, 442.

[39]LeCompte, Preissle, and Tesch, *Ethnography and Qualitative Design in Educational Research*, 197.

[40]Norman Denzin, *The Research Act: A Theoretical Introduction to Sociological Methods*, 3d ed. (Englewood Cliffs, NJ: Prentice Hall, 1989): 30.

[41]Patricia Adler and Peter Adler, "Observation Techniques," in *Handbook of Qualitative Research*, edited by Norman Denzin and Yvonna Lincoln (Thousand Oaks, CA: Sage Publications, 1994): 378.

[42]T. D. Wilson, and D. R. Streatfield, "Structured Observation in the Investigation of Information Needs," *Social Science Information Studies* 1 (1981): 173–84.

[43]Constance Mellon, *Naturalistic Inquiry for Library Science: Methods and Applications for Research, Evaluation, and Teaching* (New York: Greenwood Press, 1990): 40.

[44]Schwartz and Schwartz, "Problems in Participant Observation," 349.

[45]Jorgensen, *Participant Observation*, 84.

[46]Paul Diesing, *Patterns of Discovery in the Social Sciences* (London: Routledge & Kegan Paul, 1972): 19.

[47]Ibid., 291.

[48]Grant McCracken, *The Long Interview* (Newbury Park, CA: Sage Publications, 1988).

[49]Lincoln and Guba, *Naturalistic Inquiry*, 269.

[50]Jorgensen, *Participant Observation*.

[51]Barney G. Glaser and Anselm L. Strauss, *The Discovery of Grounded Theory: Strategies for Qualitative Research* (New York: Aldine de Gruyter, 1967): 273.

[52]Whyte, "On Making the Most of Participant Observation," 57.

[53]Ibid.

[54]Steinar Kvale, *InterViews: An Introduction to Qualitative Research Interviewing* (Thousand Oaks, CA: Sage Publications, 1996): 133–35.

[55]Whyte, "On Making the Most of Participant Observation," 60.

[56]Chris Argyris, "Creating Effective Relationships in Organizations," *Human Organization* 17, no. 1 (1958): 39.

[57]Jorgensen, *Participant Observation*, 88.

[58]Patricia Dewdney and Roma Harris, "Community Information Needs: The Case of Wife Assault," *Library and Information Science Research* 14 (1992): 5.

[59]Herbert Clark and Michael Schober, "Asking Questions and Influencing Answers," in *Questions about Questions: Inquiries into the Cognitive Bases of Surveys*, edited by Judith Taylor (New York: Russell Sage Foundation, 1992): 17–18.

[60]Ibid., 18.

[61]Raymond Gorden, "Dimensions of the Depth Interview," in *Reader in Research Methods for Librarianship*, edited by Mary Lee Bundy, Paul Wasserman, and Gayle Araghi (Washington, D.C.: NCR, 1970).

[62]Jorgensen, *Participant Observation*.

[63]Andrew Shenton and Pat Dixon, "Youngsters' Use of Public Libraries for Information: Results of a Qualitative Research Project," *New Review of Children's Literature and Librarianship* 8 (2002): 33–54.

[64]Russell H. Bernard, *Social Research Methods: Qualitative and Quantitative Approaches* (Thousand Oaks, CA: Sage Publications, 2000).

[65]Graham Kalton, *Introduction to Survey Sampling* (London: Sage Publications, 1990).

[66]Floyd J. Fowler, Jr., *Survey Research Methods*, 3d ed. (Newbury Park, CA: Sage Publications, 2001).

[67]Arlene Fink, *How to Ask Survey Questions* (Thousand Oaks, CA: Sage Publications, 1995).

[68]Floyd J. Fowler, Jr., *Survey Research Methods*, 2d ed. (Newbury Park, CA: Sage Publications, 1993).

[69]Kuhlthau, *Seeking Meaning.*

[70]Ibid.

[71]Harry Reis and Shelly Gable, "Event-Sampling and Other Methods for Studying Everyday Experience," in *Handbook of Research Methods in Social and Personality Psychology*, edited by Harry Reis and Charles Judd (New York: Cambridge University Press, 2000): 190.

[72]Abraham Kaplan, *The Conduct of Inquiry: Methodology for Behavioral Science* (San Francisco: Chandler Publishing, 1964): 21.

[73]Robert Phillip Weber, *Basic Content Analysis*, 2d ed. (London: Sage Publications, 1990): 9.

[74]Ibid.

[75]Robert Bogdan and Sari Knopp Biklen, *Qualitative Research for Education: An Introduction to Theory and Methods*, 4th ed. (Boston: Allyn and Bacon, 2003): 147.

[76]Mellon, *Naturalistic Inquiry for Library Science*, 24.

[77]Lincoln and Guba, *Naturalistic Inquiry,* 209.

[78]Roger Bakeman, "Behavioral Observation and Coding," in *Handbook of Research Methods in Social and Personality Psychology*, edited by Harry Reis and Charles Judd (Cambridge: Cambridge University Press, 2000).

[79]Sanna Talja, "Analyzing Qualitative Interview Data: The Discourse Analytic Method," *Library and Information Science Research* 21, no. 4 (1999): 474.

[80]Klaus Krippendorff, *Content Analysis: An Introduction to Its Methodology* (London: Sage Publications, 1980): 53.

[81]Ibid., 61–63.

[82]Weber, *Basic Content Analysis*, 37.

[83]Mellon, *Naturalistic Inquiry for Library Science.*

[84]Lincoln and Guba, *Naturalistic Inquiry.*

[85]Matthew Miles and Michael Huberman, *Qualitative Data Analysis: A Sourcebook of New Methods* (Beverly Hills, CA: Sage Publications, 1984): 71.

[86]Ibid., 69.

[87]Charles Smith, "Content Analysis and Narrative Analysis," in *Handbook of Research Methods in Social and Personality Psychology*, edited by Harry Reis and Charles Judd (Cambridge: Cambridge University Press, 2000).

[88]Glaser and Strauss, *The Discovery of Grounded Theory.*

[89]Lincoln and Guba, *Naturalistic Inquiry.*

[90]Mellon, *Naturalistic Inquiry for Library Science.*

[91]Barney Glaser, "The Constant Comparison Method of Qualitative Analysis," *Social Problems* 12 (Spring 1965): 439.

[92]Krippendorff, *Content Analysis.*

[93]Mellon, *Naturalistic Inquiry for Library Science*, 72–73.

[94]Glaser and Strauss, *The Discovery of Grounded Theory*, 103.

[95]Glaser, "The Constant Comparison Method," 437.

[96]Glaser and Strauss, *The Discovery of Grounded Theory.*

[97]Anselm Strauss, *Qualitative Analysis for Social Scientists* (Cambridge England: Cambridge University Press, 1987).

[98]Guido Stempel, "Content Analysis," in *Research Methods in Mass Communication*, 2d ed., edited by Guido Stempel and Bruce Westley (Englewood Cliffs, NJ: Prentice Hall, 1989).

[99]Glaser and Strauss, *The Discovery of Grounded Theory*, 24.

[100]Ibid.

[101]Lincoln and Guba, *Naturalistic Inquiry.*

[102]Ibid.

[103]Strauss, *Qualitative Research for Social Scientists*, 55–56.

[104]Ibid.

[105]Ibid.

[106]Ibid.

[107]Glaser and Strauss, *The Discovery of Grounded Theory*.

[108]Ibid.

[109]Miles and Huberman, *Qualitative Data Analysis*, 71.

[110]Babbie, *Practice of Social Research*, 8th ed.

[111]Glaser and Strauss, *The Discovery of Grounded Theory*, 34.

[112]Bogdan and Biklen, *Qualitative Research for Education*.

[113]John Lofland and Lyn Lofland, *Analyzing Social Settings: A Guide to Qualitative Observation and Analysis*, 2d ed. (Belmont, CA: Wadsworth, 1984).

[114]Amanda Coffey and Paul Atkinson, *Making Sense of Qualitative Data: Complementary Research Strategies* (Thousand Oaks, CA: Sage Publications, 1996).

[115]Raymond Lee and Lea Esterhuizen, "Computer Software and Qualitative Analysis: Trends, Issues, and Resources," *International Journal of Social Research Methodology* 3, no. 3 (2000): 231–43.

[116]Linda Gilbert, "Going the Distance: 'Closeness' in Qualitative Data Analysis Software," *International Journal of Social Research Methodology* 5, no. 3 (2002): 215–28.

[117]Sharlene Nagy Hesse-Biber, "Unleashing Frankenstein's Monster? The Use of Computers in Qualitative Research," in *Approaches to Qualitative Research: A Reader on Theory and Practice*, edited by Sharlene Nagy Hesse-Biber and Patricia Leavy (New York: Oxford University Press, 2004).

[118]Weber, *Basic Content Analysis*.

[119]Miles and Huberman, *Qualitative Data Analysis*, 64.

[120]Krippendorff, *Content Analysis*.

[121]Lincoln, "Insights into Library Services and Users," 13.

[122]Margot Ely et al. *Doing Qualitative Research: Circles Within Circles* (London: Falmer Press, 1991).

[123]Coffey and Atkinson, *Making Sense of Qualitative Data*, 46.

[124]Glaser and Strauss, *The Discovery of Grounded Theory*, 41.

[125]Ibid.

[126]Lincoln and Guba, *Naturalistic Inquiry*.

[127]Weber, *Basic Content Analysis*.

[128]Miles and Huberman, *Qualitative Data Analysis*, 64.

[129]Krippendorff, *Content Analysis*, 130.

[130]Weber, *Basic Content Analysis*.

[131]Krippendorff, *Content Analysis*, 155.

[132]Joseph Maxwell, "Understanding and Validity in Qualitative Research," in *Qualitative Researcher's Companion*, edited by Michael Huberman and Matthew Miles (Thousand Oaks, CA: Sage Publications, 2002): 37–64.

[133]R. Burke Johnson, "Examining the Validity Structure of Qualitative Research," *Education* 18, no. 2 (1997): 282–92.

[134]Steven Taylor and Robert Bogdan, *Introduction to Qualitative Research Methods*, 2d ed. (New York: John Wiley and Sons, 1984): 126.

[135]Glaser and Strauss, *The Discovery of Grounded Theory*, 32.

[136]Mellon, *Naturalistic Inquiry for Library Science*, 5.

[137]Ibid., 2–3.

[138]Glaser and Strauss, *The Discovery of Grounded Theory*.

[139]Mellon, *Naturalistic Inquiry for Library Science*, 20.

[140]Taylor and Bogdan, *Introduction to Qualitative Research Methods*, 126.

[141]Rubin and Rubin, *Qualitative Interviewing*, 4.

[142]Lincoln and Guba, *Naturalistic Inquiry*, 122.

[143]Ibid., 124.

[144]Barry Turner, "Some Practical Aspects of Qualitative Data Analysis: One Way of Organizing the Cognitive Processes Associated with the Generation of Grounded Theory," *Quality and Quantity* 15, no. 3 (1981): 226–27.

[145]Kathy Charmaz, "Grounded Theory," in *Approaches to Qualitative Research: A Reader on Theory and Practice*, edited by Sharlene Nagy Hesse-Biber and Patricia Leavy (New York: Oxford University Press, 2004).

[146]Patricia Dewdney, "Recording the Reference Interview: A Field Experiment," in *Qualitative Research in Information Management*, edited by Jack Glazier and Ronald Powell (Englewood, CO: Libraries Unlimited, 1992): 122.

[147]Mellon, *Naturalistic Inquiry for Library Science*.

[148]Lincoln and Guba, *Naturalistic Inquiry*,194.

[149]Maxwell, "Understanding and Validity in Qualitative Research," 86.

[150]Lincoln and Guba, *Naturalistic Inquiry*.

[151]Ibid., 301.

[152]Ibid., 306–7.

[153]Robert Fortner and Clifford Christians, "Separating Wheat from Chaff in Qualitative Studies," in *Research Methods in Mass Communications*, edited by Guido Stempel and Bruce Westley (Englewood Cliffs, NJ: Prentice Hall, 1989): 375–87.

[154]Lincoln and Guba, *Naturalistic Inquiry*, 308.

[155]Ely et al., *Doing Qualitative Research*.

[156]Lincoln and Guba, *Naturalistic Inquiry*, 309.

[157]Ibid., 312–13.

[158]Ibid., 313.

[159]Ibid., 314.

[160]Ely et al., *Doing Qualitative Research*.

[161]Glaser and Strauss, *The Discovery of Grounded Theory*, 26.

[162]Lincoln and Guba, *Naturalistic Inquiry*.

[163]Mellon, *Naturalistic Inquiry for Library Science*.

[164]Krippendorff, *Content Analysis*.

[165]Lincoln and Guba, *Naturalistic Inquiry*.

[166]Miles and Huberman, *Qualitative Data Analysis*, 215.

[167]Chatman, *Information World of Retired Women*, 8.

[168]Ibid., 12.

[169]Ibid.

[170]Harry Wolcott, *Writing Up Qualitative Research* (Thousand Oaks, CA: Sage Publications, 2001).

[171]Adrian Holliday, *Doing and Writing Qualitative Research* (London: Sage Publications, 2002).

[172]Mellon, *Naturalistic Inquiry for Library Science*.

[173]Ibid.

[174]Coffey and Atkinson, *Making Sense of Qualitative Data*.

[175]Lincoln and Guba, *Naturalistic Inquiry*, 316.

Chapter 8

Historical Research

A number of researchers, including some historians, have argued that historical research cannot be considered true scientific research because it does not permit enough precision and objectivity. In other words, it does not have the rigor of such research methods as experimental and survey methods. Others argue that historical research can meet the standards of inquiry of other methods.[1] Regardless, there is a consensus that historical research has much to contribute to library and information science.

NATURE AND VALUE OF HISTORICAL RESEARCH

"As used by the Greeks, history meant an inquiry designed to reconstruct past events, and, in a sense, historical research can still be defined as a scholarly attempt to discover what has happened."[2] Currently, historical research, or "documentary research" as it is sometimes labeled (although historical research is not limited to documents), typically goes beyond mere description and attempts to interpret the facts as reconstructed. In other words, the historian attempts to give meaning to the facts in light of a relevant theory. The basic purposes of historical research are to "provide a clear perspective of the present" and to facilitate planning for the future by identifying general principles applicable to recurring situations.[3] Or, as stated by Tosh, readers turn "to history for two kinds of guidance: for lessons on how to act in situations which have occurred before, and for a broader intimation of where they stand in the flow of time and thus of what may lie in the future."[4]

Chronology

It may be useful, at this point, to distinguish true historical research from chronology. *Chronology* can be defined as simply the describing of events in the order of their occurrence, a process similar to the older concept of historical research. Chronology is important, however, as it represents the first step in the process of historical research and provides material or data for the steps to follow.

In contrast, true historical research, or *historiography* or intellectual history, is concerned with analyzing and interpreting the meaning of historical events within their contexts. It is the process by which a researcher is able to reach a conclusion as to the probable truth of an event in the past by studying objects available for observation in the present.[5]

History has two dimensions, both of which are important to the interpretation of historical data. One dimension is *historical time*, or the chronology which takes into account the spacing of events and patterns. A good example of such a chronology, which is sometimes referred to as a time line, is *Libraries in the U.S. Timeline*, compiled by Wiegand for the American Library Association in 1999.[6] The second dimension is *historical space*, or where events occurred (i.e., geographical location).

Importance of Historical Research to Librarianship

In addition to fulfilling the basic purposes noted above, historical research can make specific contributions to the advancement of library and information science. As Busha and Harter indicate, historical research can contribute to the body of knowledge about librarianship; it can increase our understanding of how, when, and why past events occurred; and it can expand our appreciation of the significance of these events.[7] Busha and Harter also quote Harris, who stated that "a clear understanding of the historical definition of the functions of libraries may well contribute to increased communication between libraries."[8] Harris notes that Shera has argued that library history allows librarians better to understand the present and to fulfill their social responsibility more effectively.[9] More specifically, as Gorman and Clayton note, historical research can, for example, help to gain historical understanding of the long-term development of library collections, inform budgetary decision making, provide a basis for decisions concerning services, and inform an investigation of changing information culture.[10]

According to the Library History Round Table of the American Library Association,

> A knowledge of history and an understanding of historical methodology are indispensable elements in the education of library and information professionals. A knowledge of history provides a necessary perspective for understanding the principles and practices of library and information science. Many of the most important issues of our day—including, for example, intellectual freedom, fees for service, service to minorities, access to government information, the role of new technologies, and the place of women in the profession—can only be understood in the light of their historical contexts. And the research process, an essential component of contemporary professional education and practice, can be significantly informed by awareness of both historical precedents and historical methodology.[11]

Both Davis and Shiflett call for the inclusion of library and information science history in LIS program curricula.[12,13] They believe that LIS professionals must know and understand the history of the profession in a historical context of society and culture in order to become leaders instead of merely practitioners. By studying history, LIS professionals will look beyond practice and will "strive continuously to raise the standards of the profession and improve the system in which it functions."[14]

Shiflett suggests utilizing sense-making methodology to teach and learn history.[15] This approach would enable both teachers and students to "make retrospective sense of the situations in which they find themselves and their creations."[16] In short, a knowledge and understanding of good historical research can help librarians build on the past in an efficient, effective manner to avoid reinventing the wheel and to develop new theories and systems to advance the profession.

Types of Historical Research

Hillway identifies six different types of historical research or documentary study: (1) biographical research, (2) histories of institutions and organizations, (3) the investigation of sources and influences, (4) editing and translating historical documents, (5) studying the history of ideas, and (6) compiling bibliographies. The extent to which these different types are employed depends on the nature of the inquiry and the subject field. Whether they represent true historical research, or the mere compilation of facts, depends on the manner in which they are conducted.[17]

This also may be an appropriate place to note that the manner in which a historian collects and interprets his or her data may be somewhat influenced by the historical school of thought to which he or she adheres. Students of historical research have identified a number of trends in U.S. historiography, for example, ranging from the "providential" perspective of the 17th and 18th centuries to the more recent "new social history." As Winkler suggests, historians are moving away from new social history and back to an earlier school of thought known as the narrative mode. At the same time, she concludes that narrative history, with its emphasis on how the account is written, is not replacing new social history, with its use of social science–type analysis. What is happening, according to Winkler, is that scholars are becoming more willing to accommodate a diversity of approaches to conducting and reporting historical research.[18]

SOURCES OF HISTORICAL INFORMATION

The data gathered in historical research can come from a wide variety of sources. Among the more commonly used are the following:

1. Official records, such as laws, deeds, annual reports of organizations, charters, and so on.
2. Newspapers and other periodicals
3. Eye-witness accounts of events
4. Archives
5. Manuscripts
6. Letters and personal diaries
7. Biographies, autobiographies, and memoirs
8. Historical studies
9. Literary writings
10. Oral evidence
11. Memorials
12. Catalogs
13. Schedules, agendas, and so on
14. Archaeological and geological remains (nondocuments).

Virtually all written sources of historical information can be categorized as either primary or secondary documents. *Primary* sources represent the data which lie closest to the historical event. They are considered to include the testimony of eyewitnesses, or observations made with one of the other senses or by some mechanical device. In most cases, primary sources are the written record of what the writer actually observed, or the firsthand expression of his or her thoughts. *Secondary*, or secondhand, sources may be considered virtually everything not viewed as primary. Everything that historians and others have written about the past are secondary sources and include most textbooks, journal articles, histories, and encyclopedias. The use of primary sources tends to ensure the integrity of a study and to strengthen its reliability. Their use provides the only solid base for conclusions reached in documentary research.[19] As Bates has written, primary sources "are the raw materials of historical interpretation."[20] They are critical for the consideration of complex historical issues.

Library-related primary sources may include official records, government documents, manuscripts, newspaper articles, letters, and statistics, but whether these sources are truly primary depends on whether they represent firsthand accounts. (Readers particularly interested in sources for library-related research should see

Shiflett's article in the Spring 1984 issue of *Library Trends*.[21]) Statistics, for example, could be based on other, primary sources and thus become secondary sources themselves. In other words, the distinction between primary and secondary sources is not as clear-cut as it might first appear, and it can vary with the authority. Primary sources are defined as being contemporary with the event or thought to which they refer, but different people can define "contemporary" differently. Some prefer a broader definition which recognizes different levels of "primary." For example, a report of a conversation that occurred a week ago would no doubt be primary. A report of the conversation written 20 years later for an autobiography might be considered primary as well, but somewhat less so than the more immediate account. And what about the increasing number of electronic facsimiles? According to Duff and Cherry, some users have expressed concern about the authenticity of Web-based digital copies of original documents.[22] Others, however, view facsimiles, whether electronic or photographic, as primary resources for all practical purposes.

It is seldom possible, or even desirable, for a historical researcher to base his or her work entirely on primary sources. In fact, secondary sources may provide important insights and conceptual development not available elsewhere. By synthesizing the existing research literature, secondary sources help to round out the setting or fill in the gaps between primary sources of information and can suggest topics for future research. Because secondary sources do not represent eyewitness accounts, the researcher should keep in mind their limitations and avoid an overreliance on such materials, however. In evaluating secondary data sources, for example, the researcher should ask questions about the qualifications of the person responsible for the data collection, what data were collected and what they were intended to measure, when the information was collected, the methods that were used to collect the data, and the consistency of the data with data from other sources.

EVALUATION OF HISTORICAL SOURCES

In selecting specific sources of data for a historical study, it is critical that they be evaluated properly. The researcher should want to know if the sources are relevant to the study, substantial enough to be worthwhile, and competent (i.e., genuine, accurate, and reasonable). The assessment of the last criterion—competency—should involve two basic processes: external criticism and internal criticism.

External Criticism

External criticism, or the gathering of external evidence, is done to determine if a source in fact provides authentic, primary data. Are the author, the place, and the date of writing what they purport to be? The process of external criticism is crucial to the credibility of historical research. External criticism may be used interchangeably with textual criticism and usually takes into account the provenance, or origin, of a document. In other words, can the document be traced back to the office or person who supposedly produced it?

External criticism often cannot prove the authenticity of a source, but it can provide reasonable confidence that a particular source is authentic. To assess the authenticity of a work, the investigator may use bibliographical techniques (see the section on bibliographical research later in this chapter) or draw upon expertise in a number of auxiliary disciplines such as linguistics, epigraphy (the study of inscriptions), genealogy, paleography, and heraldry. He or she may need to utilize certain techniques of the physical sciences such as chemical analysis of paper and ink. The contents of the document should be examined for consistency with known facts and with information available to the author at the time the document was written. In short, external criticism can involve physical, textual, and bibliographical analysis.

Internal Criticism

Having decided that a document or source is genuine, the researcher should then confirm the validity and reliability of its contents. He or she is concerned, at this point, with what the source says (i.e., its meaning, accuracy, and general trustworthiness). Internal criticism is generally more challenging than external criticism, and it too is often difficult, if not impossible, to achieve with absolute certainty. Many old documents no longer exist in their original forms, and there is no guarantee that their contents have not changed somewhat as they have been copied, translated, and republished over the years.

Babbie states that the more sources that "point to the same set of 'facts'," the more accurate the research findings. He cautions historical researchers to "always be wary of bias" in the data sources and, if possible, encourages obtaining "data from a variety of sources representing different points of view[23]" concerning a topic or event. These measures will increase the validity and reliability of the research.

Some evidence of internal validity and reliability can be gained by considering the reputation and integrity of the author, allowing for the circumstances under which a document was written, and comparing "facts" within a document with the writings of other authors considered to be authoritative. Shafer recommends asking the following questions, among others, when evaluating the internal evidence of a document:

1. Do the real meanings of words differ from their literal meanings?
2. How well could the author have observed the things he or she is reporting?
3. Are there internal contradictions?
4. Are any statements inherently improbable?
5. Are factual data in agreement with standard reference works?
6. Does the document seem to call for further corroboration?[24]

Additional questions could include the following: Did the historian have full access to all of the relevant documents, or were some withheld from him or her? Was the author of the document biased? Finally, what significance does the document have as a source of information? Aminzade and Laslett have also identified a list of questions for historians to use when reading and evaluating documents.[25]

BASIC STEPS OF HISTORICAL RESEARCH

Different historians may espouse somewhat different procedures of historical research. For example, one school of thought may emphasize the collection and description of facts, while another may emphasize the interpretation stage. Some believe that a historical study should be guided by a formal hypothesis; others argue for a more flexible methodology such as the source-oriented approach. In the latter case, the historian examines a source or group of sources relevant to his or her interests and extracts whatever is of value, allowing the content of the source to determine the nature of the inquiry.[26] But there seems to be a consensus that historical research generally should meet the same criteria and follow the same procedures as the other basic methods of scientific research.[27] In other words, historical research tends to involve the following steps:

1. Identification of a problem of historical significance
2. Collection of background information (i.e., literature review of the secondary sources)
3. Formulation of a hypothesis when possible (more on this later)
4. Gathering of evidence or data (including verification of the authenticity of the primary sources and the validity and reliability of their contents)
5. Organization and analysis of the pertinent data (more often qualitative than quantitative)
6. Interpretation of the findings or the drawing of conclusions.

In short, true historical research tends to resemble a scientific method of inquiry or a problem-oriented approach.

The Hypothesis in Historical Research

Generally speaking, the most significant and useful results of any basic research lie in the generalizations or principles which are derived from the factual data. Consequently, historical research, as well as other types of research, tends to benefit from the incorporation of a hypothesis. Indeed, "the hypothesis is a natural and useful device" in the historical method.[28]

More specifically, the use of a hypothesis in historical research helps to increase the objectivity of the study and minimize researcher bias. It also guides the researcher in the collection, analysis, and interpretation of data by indicating what is relevant to the study. The hypothesis provides a basis for considering various factors in relation to one another and for synthesizing them into a generalization or conclusion that puts their overall significance in focus.[29] In effect, the use of the hypothesis in historical research amounts to an application of theory.

For example, one could hypothesize that academic libraries have been used to a greater extent when they have had substantive library instruction programs than when they have not. Based on this hypothesis, the researcher will know that, at the very least, he or she will need to collect historical data on use and library instruction programs for one or more academic libraries in order to "test" the relationship expressed.

In essence, the hypothesis would be tested by ascertaining the factual truth of specific, relevant events and organizing them to determine whether the presence of the independent variable seemed to have any effect on, or contributed to, the dependent variable. In the example just given, the researcher would attempt to determine whether libraries were more heavily used during periods when they had active library instruction programs than when they did not. The measurement of these two variables would be based on how they were operationally defined. (As is the case with other research methods, however, one test cannot really prove a hypothesis, but it can lend support to or increase confidence in it.)

It tends to be more difficult to test historical hypotheses than those developed in other types of research. This is largely due to the fact that historical research is ex post facto in nature, and the researcher obviously has no control over the relevant variables, as they have already occurred. One "cannot re-enact the past but only interpret it."[30] Nor can the historian always anticipate the facts that he or she will uncover as the examination of sources proceeds. Consequently, the historical hypothesis may have to be employed in a more flexible manner than is the case for more structured research.

Causal hypotheses are particularly complex and difficult to establish in historical research, but in spite of being inherently difficult to deal with, causality is often thought to be important to consider in a historical study. Beard stated that "no historical account that goes beyond the form of a chronicle can be written without the assumption of causal connection. And no historical chronicle exists in which assumptions of this character are not important."[31]

More specifically, considering causality tends to improve the formulation of the hypothesis and the strategies for collecting data. It also promotes the development of generalizations and basic principles. In short, the consideration of causality forces the researcher to move beyond mere description and to reflect on why certain relationships seem to exist. On the other hand, not all historians are in agreement that consideration of causality (and hypotheses) is essential to good historical research.

Collecting the Data

"While historical research is similar to the reviews of literature which precede other forms of research, the historical approach is more exhaustive, seeking out information from a larger array of sources. It also tracks down information that is much older than required by most reviews and hunts for unpublished material not cited in the standard references."[32] In fact, one of the greatest challenges facing the historian is the extent to which his or her research relies on unpublished materials. Many such documents are housed in archives which have developed arrangement and description techniques that differ from those of libraries, and the historian should be well versed in how to identify and access archival collections.

The data collection technique for historical research, or at least for documentary research, basically involves putting together in a logical fashion the evidence derived from documents or records. This process also often involves the comparing and reconciling of information gathered from two or more sources. Indeed, the use of a variety of sources is considered to be one of the hallmarks of historical research. It is important to note, however, that, owing to the great volume of data typically collected, it is essential to organize the data as systematically as possible. Before beginning a historical study, the researcher should have a specific plan for the acquisition, organization, storage, and retrieval of the data. *Tertiary* sources, such as library catalogs and periodical indexes, are routinely used to identify and access resources. The use of note cards, bibliography cards, multiple files, and so on can be quite helpful when gathering data from the resources. Storing notes in database files provides automatic search capabilities and enables the researcher to code the data for content analysis. Electronic files can also facilitate the use of computer software and programs for data analysis.

Shafer, in his chapter on collecting historical evidence, begins with a discussion of recording bibliographic information.[33] He describes the process of preparing bibliography cards and notes how critical they are to the overall process. In the third and final section of his chapter, Shafer discusses the mechanics of making and analyzing research notes. He stresses the importance of using standard methods and provides some examples of research notes. Next, Shafer reviews some of the standard bibliographic aids used by historians, including library catalogs, bibliographies, government publication guides and indexes, newspaper and journal indexes, national bibliographies, manuscript and archival guides, dissertation indexes, guides to reference books, booksellers' catalogs, and guides to locations such as union lists. According to Tibbo, other guides to primary resources commonly used by historians include repository Web sites, bibliographical utilities, and Web search engines.[34]

The Presentation of Findings

In writing the historical report, the researcher should take care to be objective and to preserve intellectual honesty. This is not to suggest that historical researchers are more prone to partiality than others, but to serve as a reminder that historical research is often rather subjective in nature and thus relatively susceptible to researcher bias. The report is normally directed to the knowledgeable scholar, and the facts and interpretations should be presented so that the reader can evaluate conclusions in light of documented evidence. It goes without saying that the data should be related to the purpose of the study, and that clear and unambiguous expression is important.

"The dual aspect of the historical enterprise—the effort to establish what happened and the attempt to explain why things happened in the way they did— explains the twofold task in historical writing: 1) to convey a sense of time or to show chronological development, 2) to analyse and explain the interrelationships of the events studied, to detect underlying patterns, and to unify the various elements in a satisfactory whole which provides a response to the initial research problem."[35] Thus historical writings are represented by a variety of literary forms which combine description, narrative, and analysis in different ways and proportions. Description and narrative tend to suffice when the historian merely desires to recreate the past, while analysis is necessary for interpretation of the past. The nature of the subject matter also may influence the literary form of the report.

LIBRARY HISTORY

Historical research conducted in library and information science has often been referred to as "library history." Shiflett defines library history as "a rubric that covers a myriad of topics associated with libraries and other information systems. Its major form consists of the traditional library, but it also includes the history of any activity or event that might be part of the domain of library and information science."[36] Busha and Harter note that library history is "commonly applied to an account of events that have affected any library or group of libraries, as well as to the social and economic impacts of libraries on their communities."[37] (A related, but more narrow, area of inquiry is the history of the book.) According to Irwin, since libraries function within a larger context, library historians should be concerned with "the history not only of scholarship in its narrower sense, but of human civilization and culture and literacy."[38]

Unfortunately, the fact that the history of library and information science has been given a special label seems to suggest that it is a special type of history. Some would even argue that it has been an inferior type of history or historical research. In 1952, Shera pointed out that library history had evidenced "an excessive preoccupation with antiquarian detail and a provincial point of view."[39] In 1965, Bartlett argued that "there is never a dearth of library history, but . . . its existence has been consistently marred by a tragic shortage of quality."[40]

A review of the more recent literature of library history, however, suggests that the quality of historical research in library and information science has improved. (See Davis and Tucker for a comprehensive guide to the literature of American library history[41].) As far back as 1978, Kaser pointed out that "we are vastly better equipped today with sound, rigorous, scholarly understanding than we were a few years ago."[42] Shiflett stated, "The condemnation of library history as mere antiquarianism is only valid if the short view of history is held."[43]

As to the future of library history, there continues to be a need for more historical research that considers libraries and other information systems in broad contexts. Hagler pointed out, more than 30 years ago, there is a need for more unified interpretations of library history based on comprehensive visions.[44]

BIBLIOGRAPHICAL RESEARCH

Another area of scholarly work that some consider to be a special type of historical research is bibliographical research. Others would argue that bibliographical research does not represent true research, at least as prescribed by the scientific method of inquiry. Most would concede, however, that bibliographical research that takes the form of descriptive bibliography certainly comes closer to being true research than does systematic or enumerative bibliography. The latter is not even considered to be true bibliographical research. There is no question, however, that both types of bibliographical work are important scholarly endeavors which, at the very least, support the work of "true" researchers or historians.

Systematic Bibliography

Persons involved in the compilation of systematic or enumerative bibliographies are concerned with the book (and other materials) as an intellectual entity. Their purpose is to assemble information about individual works into a logical and useful arrangement. The results are one of the following compilations or lists:

1. Universal bibliography—a bibliography that includes everything published or issued in a subject field regardless of date of publication
2. National bibliography—a bibliography that lists everything published (and possibly distributed) in a given country
3. Trade bibliography—a bibliography compiled primarily to aid the book trade by supplying information as to what books are in print or for sale; when, where, and by whom they were published; and their price
4. Subject bibliography—a bibliography that lists materials relating to a specific topic.

Descriptive Bibliography

In contrast to systematic bibliography, descriptive bibliography is concerned with the book as a physical entity or material object. As was noted above, it resembles true research more than does systematic bibliography. Sir Walter Greg, quoted in Eaton, once defined descriptive bibliography as follows:

> Bibliography is the study of books as tangible objects. It examines the materials of which they are made and the manner in which these materials are put together. It

traces their place and mode of origin, and the subsequent adventures which have befallen them. It is not concerned with their contents in a literary sense, but it is certainly concerned with the signs and symbols they contain (apart from their significance) for the manner in which these marks are written or impressed is a very relevant bibliographical fact. And, starting from this fact, it is concerned with the relation of one book to another; the question of which manuscript was copied from which, which individual copies of printed books are to be grouped together as forming an edition, and what is the relation of edition to edition.[45]

A more succinct definition found in the *Oxford English Dictionary* defines bibliography as "the systematic description and history of books . . . "[46]

An important function of descriptive bibliography is to describe the "ideal copy," or primary document, and its variants. This process can be broken down into more specific bibliographical research, including the following:

1. Analytical bibliography, which is concerned with the physical description of the book in order to determine the details of the physical process of its manufacturing.
2. Textual bibliography, which focuses on certain textual variations between a manuscript and the printed book or among various editions. It is more concerned with the author's words than the physical aspects of the book.
3. Historical bibliography, which deals with the identification of original editions and the placing and dating of individual books.

Other terms that are sometimes used to represent specific types of descriptive bibliography, or are used as synonyms, include comparative, technical, and critical bibliography.

As was pointed out earlier, descriptive bibliographical research is a scholarly activity which may be thought of as historical research in and of itself, but it is also of critical importance to all historians needing assurance of the authenticity and accuracy of their documentary resources. As Ronald McKerrow stated,

> bibliographical evidence will help us to settle such questions as that of the order and relative value of different editions of a book; whether certain sections of a book were originally intended to form part of it or were added afterwards; whether a later edition was printed from an earlier one, and from which; whether it was printed from a copy that had been corrected in manuscript, or whether such corrections as it contained were made in proof, and a number of other problems of a similar kind, which may often have a highly important literary bearing. It will indeed sometimes enable us to solve questions which to one entirely without bibliographical knowledge would appear quite incapable of solution.[47]

Readers interested in learning more about the process of bibliographical research should consult the literature on historical research, reference, and bibliography, including works by Wynar,[48] Robinson,[49] Bowers,[50] and Harmon.[51] Those interested in examples of bibliographical research may wish to read Eaton's article in the July 1964 issue of *Library Trends*.[52]

PROBLEMS IN HISTORICAL RESEARCH

A variety of problems are common to most types of research but tend to be particularly important in historical research, including the following:

1. Deciding how much data are enough. This tends to be a relatively subjective decision. At one time, historians generally attempted to collect virtually all relevant data; they now tend toward a more selective approach. Yet the historian must continue to avoid an overreliance on an insufficient amount of data or evidence. Using too little information can lead to the "argument from silence."[53] In other words, the researcher must be careful not to assume that some event did not occur simply because he or she is not aware of some record of the event.
2. Improperly selecting data. Briefly stated, the historian must avoid improper or faulty selection of data, including such tactics as ignoring some data, exaggerating others, and so on. Such action will significantly increase the bias in a study.
3. Relying too heavily on secondary sources of information. This is particularly likely in studies not dealing with relatively recent events.
4. Investigating an overly broad problem. This is difficult to avoid because historical issues tend to be complex.
5. Failing to evaluate adequately the historical data and their sources. (These techniques were covered briefly in an earlier section.)
6. Failing to interpret the data. As was noted earlier, historical research is most productive when the researcher attempts to synthesize or integrate the facts into meaningful generalizations.
7. Reading the present into the past even though the historical data may not support such an interpretation.

Other problems in historical research and criteria for evaluating historical research can be drawn from the general research guidelines discussed earlier in this work. In addition, Mouly has pointed out several criteria for evaluating historical studies, most of which have already been presented.[54] He, and others, emphasizes the desirability of a writing style that will attract as well as inform. He calls for a report that will make a significant contribution on the basis of new knowledge and not simply represent "uninspired hackwork." Finally, Mouly asks that the historical study reflect scholarliness. Again, such criteria are not unique to historical research, but they do seem to receive more attention in this area.

SUMMARY

"Though the methods of historical investigation can be shown to be the appropriate counterparts of the methods used in other sciences to investigate the phenomena that specially concern them, there appears to be a general reluctance to accord to historical conclusions the kind of logical validity that the conclusions of other sciences are deemed to possess."[55] This may be the case because historical research is ex post facto in nature. The historical researcher must work from evidence back to the event. In addition, the historian is usually in the situation of having to investigate exceptionally complex phenomena. Consequently, it is especially difficult for the historian to support causality within a relationship, or even to draw conclusions with a very high level of confidence. For these reasons, it is generally considered advisable for the historical researcher to follow some sort of scientific method of inquiry, including the formulation and testing of a hypothesis and the analysis and interpretation of data. Such processes help to distinguish true historical research from mere chronology.

Regarding the collection of data, it is important for the researcher to draw upon primary, rather than secondary, sources as much as possible. It is also crucial that the researcher establish the internal and external validity of his or her sources. Bibliographical research methods are often used for evaluating the latter.

The criteria for evaluating historical research are much the same as those for other methods of research. It is particularly important that historical research be well presented in a readable but scholarly style. There is a continuing need for genuine historical research in library and information science, and the better its presentation, the more impact it is likely to have. To paraphrase Arthur Bestor, there is no logical reason why historical knowledge cannot, in principle, be as exact as knowledge in other sciences and, therefore, make a real contribution to the advancement of the field.[56] Those interested in more information about historical research in LIS should refer to Gorman and Clayton, who provide a detailed discussion and examples of historical investigation in information organizations.[57]

NOTES

[1]George J. Mouly, *Educational Research: The Art and Science of Investigation* (Boston, MA: Allyn & Bacon, 1978): 157.

[2]Ibid., 157.

[3]Ibid., 158.

[4]John Tosh, *The Pursuit of History: Aims, Methods and New Directions in the Study of Modern History*, 2d ed. (London: Longman, 1991): 10.

[5]Herbert Goldhor, *An Introduction to Scientific Research in Librarianship* (Urbana: University of Illinois, Graduate School of Library Science, 1972): 98.

[6]Wayne Wiegand, comp., *Libraries in the U.S. Timeline* (Published by the American Library Association and the ALA Public Information Office, December 1999; inserted in *American Libraries* 30, no. 11, December 1999).

[7]Charles A. Busha and Stephen P. Harter, *Research Methods in Librarianship: Techniques and Interpretations* (New York: Academic Press, 1980): 92.

[8]Michael H. Harris, ed., *Reader in American Library History* (Washington, DC: NCR Microcard Editions, 1971): 1.

[9]Jesse H. Shera, "On the Value of Library History," *Library Quarterly* 22 (July 1952): 240–51.

[10]G. E. Gorman and Peter Clayton, with contributions from Mary Lynn Rice-Lively and Lyn Gorman, *Qualitative Research for the Information Professional: A Practical Handbook* (London: Library Association Publishing, 1997): 171.

[11]Library History Round Table, "Statement on History in Education for Library and Information Science" (Chicago: American Library Association: 1989).

[12]Donald G. Davis, Jr., "Ebla to the Electronic Dream: The Role of Historical Perspectives in Professional Education," *Journal of Education for Library and Information Science* (Summer 1998): 229–35.

[13]Lee Shiflett, "Sense-Making and Library History," *Journal of Education for Library and Information Science* (Summer 2000): 254–59.

[14]Derek Bok, *Higher Learning* (Cambridge, MA: Harvard University Press, 1986): 168–69.

[15]Shiflett, "Sense-Making and Library History," 254–59.

[16]Karl Weick, *Sensemaking in Organizations* (Thousand Oaks, CA: Sage Publications, 1995): 14.

[17]Tyrus Hillway, *Introduction to Research*, 2d ed. (Boston, MA: Houghton Mifflin, 1964): 159.

[18]Karen J. Winkler, "Disillusioned with Numbers and Counting, Historians Are Telling Stories Again," *Chronicle of Higher Education* 28 (June 1984): 5–6.

[19]Hillway, *Introduction to Research*, 147.

[20]Rolland E. Stevens, ed., *Research Methods in Librarianship: Historical and Bibliographical Methods in Library Research* (Urbana: University of Illinois, Graduate School of Library Science, 1971): 11.

[21]Orvin L. Shiflett, "Clio's Claim: The Role of Historical Research in Library and Information Science," *Library Trends*, 32 (Spring 1984): 385–406.

[22]Wendy M. Duff and Joan M. Cherry, "Use of Historical Documents in a Digital World: Comparisons with Original Materials and Microfiche," *Information Research* (October 2000). Available, http://informationr.net/ir/6-1/paper86.html

[23]Earl R. Babbie, *The Practice of Social Research*, 10th ed. (Belmont, CA: Wadsworth/Thomson Learning, 2004): 335.

[24]Robert J. Shafer, ed., *A Guide to Historical Method*, 3d ed. (Homewood, IL: Dorsey Press, 1980): 166–67.

[25]Aminzade, Ron, and Barabara Laslett. In *The Practice of Social Research*. 10th ed., by Earl Babbie, 336, Belmont, CA: Wadsworth/Thomson Learning, 2004: 336.

[26]Tosh, *The Pursuit of History*, 54.

[27]Mouly, *Educational Research*, 159.

[28]Shafer, *A Guide to Historical Method*, 176.

[29]Mouly, *Educational Research*, 160.

[30]Goldhor, *An Introduction to Scientific Research*, 111.

[31]Ibid., 109–10.

[32]Stephen Isaac and William Burton Michael, *Handbook in Research and Evaluation: A Collection of Principles, Methods and Strategies Useful in the Planning, Design, and Evaluation of Studies in Education and the Behavioral Sciences*, 3d ed. (San Diego, CA: EdITS, 1995): 49.

[33]Shafer, *A Guide to Historical Method*.

[34]Helen R. Tibbo, "How Do Historians Find Primary Resources?," Paper presented at the Second National Library Research Seminar, College Park, University of Maryland, November 3, 2001.

[35]Gorman and Clayton, *Qualitative Research for the Information Professional,* 171.

[36] Shiflett, "Clio's Claim," 402.

[37]Busha and Harter, *Research Methods in Librarianship*, 93.

[38]Raymond Irwin, *The Golden Chain: A Study in the History of Libraries* (London: H. K. Lewis, 1958): 3–4.

[39]Shera, "On the Value of Library History," 249.

[40]Richard A. Bartlett, "The State of the Library History Art," in *Approaches to Library History*, edited by John D. Marshall (Tallahassee: Florida State University Library School, 1965): 19.

[41]Donald G. Davis, Jr. and John M. Jucker, American Library History: A Comprehensive Guide to the Literature (Santa Barbara, CA: ABC-Clio, 1989).

[42]David Kaser, "Advances in American Library History," in *Advances in Librarianship*, vol. 8, edited by Michael H. Harris (New York: Academic Press, 1978): 192.

[43]Shiflett, "Clio's Claim," 388.

[44]Ronald Hagler, "Needed Research in Library History," in *Research Methods in Librarianship: Historical and Bibliographical Methods in Library Research*, edited by Rolland E. Stevens (Urbana: University of Illinois, Graduate School of Library Science, 1971): 132.

[45]Thelma Eaton, "Bibliographical Research," *Library Trends* 13 (July 1964): 44.

[46]*The Oxford English Dictionary*, 2d ed., vol. 2, prepared by J. A. Simpson and E.S.C. Weiner (Oxford: Clarendon Press, 1989): 169.

[47]Eaton, "Bibliographical Research," 44–45.

[48]Bohdan S. Wynar, *Introduction to Bibliography and Reference Work*, 4th ed. (Rochester, NY: Libraries Unlimited, 1967).

[49]A. M. Robinson, *Systematic Bibliography* (London: Clive Bingley, 1979).

[50]Fredson Bowers, *Principles of Bibliographical Description* (New Castle, DE: Oak Knoll Books, 1994).

[51]Robert B. Harmon, *Elements of Bibliography: A Guide to Information Sources and Practical Applications*, 3d ed. (Lanham, MD: Scarecrow Press, 1998).

[52]Eaton, "Bibliographical Research," 44–45.

[53]Goldhor, *An Introduction to Scientific Research*,107.

[54]Mouly, *Educational Research*, 170.

[55]Stevens, *Research Methods in Librarianship*, 111.

[56]Ibid.

[57]Gorman and Clayton, *Qualitative Research for the Information Professional*, 158–76.

Chapter 9

Analysis of Data

A knowledge of basic statistics is imperative both to the research producer and re-search consumer in library science, just as it is imperative to the research producer and consumer in any social science or in any field which relies on empirical evidence for the development of principles.[1]

Statistical analysis, or "statistics," is concerned with the development and application of methods and techniques for organizing and analyzing data (usually quantitative) so that the reliability of conclusions based on the data may be evaluated objectively in terms of probability. There are two major areas or types of statistics—theoretical and applied. The former is concerned with the mathematical aspects of statistics; the latter involves the practical applications of statistics and is the focus of this chapter.

This text will not attempt to teach readers how to conduct a statistical analysis; it will indicate the kinds of things that statistical analysis can and cannot do and emphasize the care that should be exercised in using statistics. Specific examples will be given for the major types of analysis; in no way do they represent a comprehensive listing of all of the statistical tests that may be employed. Readers looking for other relatively nonmathematical, nonthreatening introductions to statistics may wish to refer to Norman and Streiner[2]; Spirer, Spirer, and Jaffe[3];

Rowntree[4]; and Jaeger.[5] Texts written primarily for library and information professionals include ones by Simpson[6]; Hafner[7]; Hernon et al.[8]; Hernon[9]; Boyce, Meadow, and Kraft[10]; and Stephen and Hornby.[11] The *Dictionary of Statistics and Methodology* is an excellent resource for "nontechnical definitions of statistical and methodological terms used in the social and behavioral sciences."[12]

THE ROLE OF STATISTICS

Generally speaking, statistical analysis may be used to accomplish four basic purposes. One, statistics may indicate the central point around which a mass of data revolves. Two, they may show how broad or diverse the spread can be for a mass of data. Three, statistics may reveal how closely or distantly certain features within the mass of data are related, as well as whether a relationship even exists. Four, they may indicate the degree to which the facts might have occurred by mere chance, or whether there is a probability of their having been influenced by some factor other than pure chance.[13] (The last function is accomplished with statistical tests of the hypothesis.)

In short, the basic purpose of statistical analysis is to summarize observations or data in such a manner that they provide answers to the hypothesis or research questions. Statistics facilitate drawing general conclusions based on specific data. Stated somewhat differently, "the field of statistics involves methods for describing and analyzing data and for making decisions or inferences about phenomena represented by the data."[14] Both methods, even the second one, are essentially methods of analysis and should be distinguished from interpretation. Interpretation of the results follows the analysis stage, and its purpose is to search for the broader meaning of the results by linking them to other available knowledge.

CAUTIONS IN USING STATISTICS

In addition to keeping in mind that the statistical analysis cannot do the interpretation, the researcher should be aware of other concerns in using statistics. For example, the nature of the data determines to a large extent the statistical techniques that can be used legitimately. That is to say, certain techniques are appropriate for use with categorical data, others with ordinal data, and so on. Specific examples illustrating this principle will be given later. Second, the more controlled the research setting, the less is the need, in general, for certain statistical techniques. Most, if not all, of the important relevant variables are already controlled, and replication of the study is less likely to produce different results. Fennick describes the problems associated with statistics that are not used properly and provides interesting and understandable examples.[15]

Statistics are necessary for most research studies involving quantitative data and are particularly crucial at the sampling and analysis stages. The analysis process should be planned well in advance in order to anticipate problems that may be encountered. In fact, the analysis of a study is shaped, to a considerable extent, before the data are collected.

The anticipation of the analysis process determines what kinds of data will be needed. For example, a researcher may wish to determine if there is a significant difference between the average frequency of library use of students who have and have not received library instruction. In order to do so, he or she will need to employ an appropriate statistical test, such as the difference of means test. As the difference of means test requires interval level data, the researcher will need to be certain to measure the frequency of library use on an interval scale. Simply ranking users as high, moderate, low, and so on would not be adequate in this case. Once the data have been collected, there is little potential for changing them, and the researcher is at that point limited to certain statistical techniques.

The conceptual development of a research study should not, however, be dictated by the statistical techniques to follow. In the example given above, the researcher should decide what is the most valid measure of library use, and then utilize the best statistical methods available. He or she should not decide to use factor analysis, for example, and then proceed to force the data into that technique, regardless of its appropriateness. Sophisticated statistical analysis cannot substitute for early, sound conceptual development.

STEPS INVOLVED IN STATISTICAL ANALYSIS

Regardless of the specific techniques or tests employed, there are certain basic steps common to virtually all statistical analyses. Those steps will be discussed briefly before taking a more detailed look at the major types of analysis.

The Establishment of Categories

In order to organize and analyze the data collected for a study, it is necessary to place them in categories. The identification or establishment of categories should take place before the data are gathered. The actual categorization of the data takes place during or after the collection process. In establishing categories, four basic rules or guidelines should be followed:

1. The set of categories or values (i.e., the classification scheme) for any one variable should be derived from a single classificatory principle, which is determined by the research question or hypothesis being investigated. For example, if one were studying the relationship between size of the reference collection and reference performance, two sets of categories would be needed. Reference collection size might well be categorized according to the

number of volumes, and would represent a ratio level scale. Reference performance could be categorized according to the percentage of reference questions answered correctly, another ratio scale. Another variable might be the type of reference question. Questions could be assigned to a set of nominal categories, such as directional and research questions.

2. Each set of categories should be exhaustive. That is, it should be possible to place every observation in one of the categories of the set. This does not preclude the use of a miscellaneous or catchall category, such as "other." However, if one is finding it necessary to place a substantial number of observations in an "other" category, or if a large percentage of such observations seem to have certain characteristics in common, the establishment of one or more additional categories should be considered. It is generally preferable to establish as many categories as possible and, if necessary, reduce or combine them later.

3. The categories within each set should be mutually exclusive. This means that it should not be possible to place a specific observation correctly in more than one category. Returning to the categorization of reference questions, every reference question received should logically fit into one, but no more than one, of the categories. It should not, for example, be possible for a question to be placed accurately in both the directional category and the research category. If it is conceivable to do so, then the categories are not adequately defined or the observations are not accurate.

4. Last, but not least, the development of categories should be based on a sound knowledge of the subject matter and an anticipation of likely responses. A person establishing categories for reference questions should have had enough reference experience, and have done enough reading about the topic, to be able to predict the types of questions that will appear in a study and establish categories accordingly.

Coding the Data

Once the categories have been established and data "assigned" to them, it is necessary to convert the new data or responses to numerical codes, so that they can be tabulated or tallied. These codes are, in turn, assigned to specified locations in data files, particularly if computer data analysis is planned. (A codebook is useful for describing the locations of variables and for indicating the codes assigned to the categories or values of each variable.) If, however, original responses are already numerical, such as are test scores, volume counts in libraries, and so on, then they do not need to be assigned new codes, unless they are being recoded or assigned to groupings.

One of the most important considerations in coding is reliability. Problems of reliability in coding can result from inadequacies in the data. For example, a poorly worded questionnaire item may not produce enough relevant information for the purpose of the study. Answers to questions that actually ask more than one question are, of course, difficult, if not impossible, to code accurately. Problems with the categories may also lead to a lack of reliability, particularly if they do not meet the basic guidelines outlined above. Inaccuracies can emerge during the coding process itself as a result of observations being assigned to the wrong category. For that reason, it is important to see that coders are adequately trained and to verify or check the accuracy of their work. As was noted in the section in Chapter 5 on questionnaire construction, precoding can help to minimize the amount of coding errors and thus increase reliability.

In actually coding the data, researchers traditionally have transcribed the observations or scores for each individual or case from the data collection instrument to coding or transfer sheets. Once the coding sheets were complete, the researcher, if he or she were analyzing the data manually, could then work directly from them. But if the mass of data was large, or the statistical techniques to be employed were relatively complex and time consuming to conduct, the researcher would probably elect to use a computer to analyze the data. Today, most researchers input their data into computer programs, many of which still utilize a computer card image of 80 columns per record for organizing the data to be analyzed. Those individuals wanting to read more about the coding process may wish to refer to Golden,[16] Barnes,[17] Hernon,[18] and Vaughan.[19]

Increasingly, techniques that eliminate the need for coding sheets are being used to create computer data files. Some researchers are able to take advantage of optical scanning for producing data files; however, direct data entry may now be the most common technique for creating data files. It is based on a computer program that displays each question on the screen and prompts the researcher to input the response directly on the screen (and into the computer file). Most survey research organizations use a database management program to control data entry. The program prompts the data entry clerk for each response, checks the response to ensure that it is a valid response for that variable, and then saves the response in the proper data file. As discussed in Chapter 5, many researchers are optimizing the opportunities made available to researchers via the Web. Web-based and e-mail surveys enable the responses to be input into the software program for analysis when respondents submit their questionnaires.

After the data have been prepared and saved as an electronic file, they can then be analyzed using a software program such as those identified later in this chapter. The manuals that accompany these programs explain how to create data files that can be manipulated by the particular software and how to calculate certain statistics by executing appropriate commands. Some of the manuals even explain how to reformat data files originally created for analysis by another software program.

ANALYZING THE DATA—DESCRIPTIVE STATISTICS

Once the data are ready to be analyzed, the researcher can choose to utilize descriptive statistics, inferential statistics, or both. Looking first at descriptive statistics, which have represented the predominant type of data analysis employed by researchers in library and information science, there are at least six basic functions that they can perform.[20]

One, at the most basic level, the statistical analysis can indicate how many persons, objects, scores, or whatever achieved each value (or fell into each category) for every variable that was measured. These calculations, known as frequency distributions, are usually reported in tables. Common types of frequency distributions include simple or absolute, cumulative, percentage, and grouped distributions.

Two, when it may be difficult to grasp the overall meaning of frequency distribution tables, pictorial representations can be used to portray a variety of characteristics of the cases or individuals with respect to the variable or variables measured. This process typically involves the use of one or more data displays such as bar graphs or charts, pie charts, histograms, and frequency polygons (see Figures 9.1, 9.2, 9.3, and 9.4). Graphic representations generally sacrifice some detail in an effort to improve communication of data, but the loss of detail may well be desirable and justifiable. Graphs are especially useful for displaying the

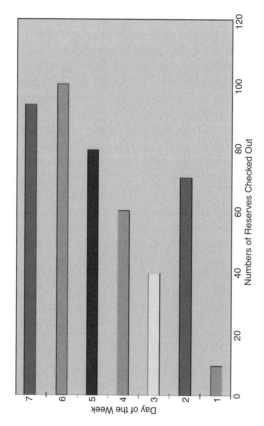

FIGURE 9.1.   A Bar Graph/Chart

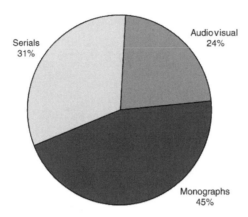

FIGURE 9.2.   A Pie Chart

findings of a research study that has a large number of cases. The design of such devices has become easier with the widespread availability of word processing and spreadsheet programs. Tufte has authored two interesting and useful books about the visual display of quantitative information.[21]

Three, descriptive statistics are capable of characterizing what is typical in a group of cases. Such statistics, referred to as measures of *central tendency*, commonly include the mean, the median, and the mode. The mean is what is commonly called the average. It is the sum of the scores divided by the total number of cases involved. The median is the value of the middle item when the scores are arranged according to size. The mode refers to the category that occurs most frequently.

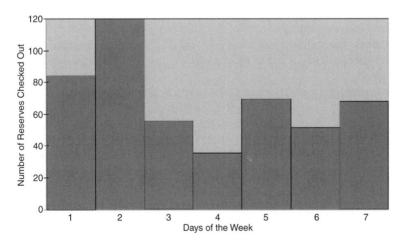

FIGURE 9.3.   A Histogram

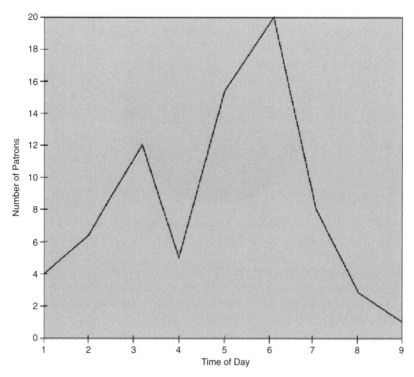

FIGURE 9.4.   A Frequency Polygon

Four, descriptive statistics can indicate how widely cases in a group vary. These statistics are known as measures of *dispersion* or *variability*; examples include the range of scores (the highest score minus the lowest score), their mean deviation (the arithmetic mean of the absolute differences of each score from the mean), the standard deviation (the square root of the arithmetic mean of the squared deviations from the mean), and the variance (the mean squared deviation).

The standard deviation is one of the most frequently used measures of dispersion, but it is also one of the more difficult to comprehend. As noted, it reflects the amount of deviation from the mean for the observed scores. Stated differently, it is the positive square root of the variance. Its size increases whenever the size of the deviation scores increases. It is a useful measure of dispersion because, in many distributions of scores, we know what percentage of the scores lie within plus or minus one, two, and three standard deviations. Its usefulness is enhanced because its units of measure are the same as those of the original data. The standard deviation is useful for comparing groups.

Assume, for example, that a survey of a public library's users found that their ages ranged from 3 to 60 years, their mean age was 45, and the standard deviation was three. We would thus know that 67% of the users fell between ± one standard deviation, or three years, or between the ages of 42 to 48, and so on for ± two and three standard deviations.

The formula for the standard deviation is as follows:

$$S = \sqrt{\frac{\Sigma X_i^2}{N}}$$

where ΣX_i^2 equals the total of the squared deviation scores, and N equals the number of cases.

Five, descriptive statistics can measure the relationship between or among the different variables in the data. These are generally referred to as correlational or associational statistics. They have the ability to allow prediction of one variable based on another, but they cannot be used to establish causal relationships. Correlation coefficients are, of course, correlational or descriptive statistics, but they also are often treated as inferential statistics and will be discussed in the section treating that type of statistical test.

Another common type of correlational statistic is the cross-tabulation or bivariate frequency. Bivariate frequencies are the products of tables in which two variables have been cross-classified. The tables consist of rows and columns, where the categories or values of one variable are labels for the rows, and the categories of the second variable are labels for the columns. Usually the independent variable is the column variable, and the dependent variable is the row variable.

The calculation and analysis of bivariate frequencies is an essential step in discovering or testing relationships between variables, so an example of a bivariate table will be presented and discussed next. In reading Table 9.1, one should first

TABLE 9.1
Frequency of Library Use by Age (hypothetical data)

Library Use Per Year	1–12	13–25	Age 26–50	51+	Total
0–5	6	12	15	40	73
	9%	15%	25%	43%	25%
6–12	10	13	12	35	70
	16%	16%	20%	38%	24%
13–24	25	30	12	10	77
	39%	38%	20%	11%	26%
25+	23	25	20	7	75
	36%	31%	34%	8%	25%
Total	64	80	59	92	295
	100%	100%	100%	100%	100%

note the title and headings in order to learn what information is contained in the table. In this example, the title and headings indicate that the table summarizes data on annual frequency of library use and age. It also is apparent that the data have been grouped or categorized in ranges. Each range represents a value for the respective variable. As was indicated earlier, the reader probably can assume that the column variable, age, is the independent variable, and the row variable, library use, is the dependent variable.

The reader next should check at the bottom of the table to see if the source for the data is identified. Knowing the source helps the reader to assess the reliability of the data. If the source is not given at the foot of the table, it should be indicated at the appropriate place in the text. (Remember that every table should be referred to within the text and summarized or highlighted in some fashion.)

Then the reader should determine in which direction the percentages have been calculated. It is important to know whether the percentages have been calculated down the columns or across the rows. This can be learned by noting where the 100%s have been placed. In Table 9.1, the percentages have been calculated down the columns. It is possible to calculate percentages in both directions.

Finally, the reader should compare the percentage differences in the table in order to determine the extent to which relationships, if any, between the variables exist. Comparisons are always made in the direction opposite to the one in which the percentages were calculated. In Table 9.1, the reader would examine percentages across rows in order to determine whether given levels of library use significantly varied according to age. In looking at the first row, one can see that 9% of the persons who were between the ages of 1 and 12 used the library 0 to 5 times, 15% of those aged 13 to 25 used the library 0 to 5 times, and so on. An examination of the entire row indicates that the older age groups tended to exhibit less library use in that higher percentages of them fell into the lowest library use category. The relative percentages in the other rows tend to support this conclusion. The only noteworthy anomaly is represented by the percentage of persons aged 26 to 50 who used the library 25 or more times (34%). (An occasional anomaly does not necessarily weaken a pattern or resulting conclusion, but it generally is worth further consideration for the insights it may provide.)

The figures in the "total" column indicate what percentages of the total number of cases fell into the different ranges of library use. The figures across the "total" row indicate the numbers and percentages of persons who occurred in each age category. The numbers in the final column and row are referred to as marginals, or univariate, frequencies. They are purely descriptive in nature. The numbers within the individual cells are the cross-tabulations or bivariate frequencies. They are the figures that can help to point out relationships, as they represent the cases that have certain values for both variables. For example, the six cases in the first cell represent persons who were aged 1–12 and who used the library 0–5 times during the preceding year. By examining such figures, the reader may detect a pattern of covariation, or a relationship between two variables. In this case, use tended to decrease as age increased. Barnes has a useful chapter on preparing and analyzing tables for those wanting to read more about this topic.[22] Most statistical software and spreadsheet programs provide easy methods for displaying statistical analyses in tables and charts.

The sixth basic function that descriptive statistics can perform is to describe the difference between two or more groups of individuals. This is really no more than a special case of showing the relationship between two variables. Such uses of descriptive statistics often involve measures of central tendency. For example, if one had measured the library skills of two groups of students, it could be revealing to compare the mean scores of the two groups. If the two groups had received different types of instruction, such a comparison could help to indicate the superior instructional method.

ANALYZING THE DATA—INFERENTIAL STATISTICS

In contrast to descriptive statistics, which simply summarize and describe the data (though, as indicated above, they can at least suggest relationships), inferential statistics can perform certain more sophisticated functions. They are most commonly used to predict or estimate population *parameters* or characteristics based on random sample *statistics*, and to test hypotheses using tests of statistical significance to determine if observed differences between groups or variables are "real" or merely due to chance. In short, inferential statistics help one to make inferences and judgments about what exists on the basis of only partial evidence.

Using inferential statistics as first described, one could measure the loss rate for a sample of books and then predict the loss rate for the entire population or collection based on the sample statistic. Applying inferential statistics in the second manner, one could test the relationship between loss rate and circulation loan periods by analyzing the difference in loss rates for two groups of books—one housed in a library with a long loan period, and one in a library with a short loan period. In evaluating the difference, if any, it would be necessary to determine if the difference were too large to be due merely to chance, rather than to the effects of different loan periods.

It should be remembered that statistics are used to test the null hypothesis, or the hypothesis of no relationship, as opposed to the research hypothesis, which does predict a relationship (usually a positive one). Null hypotheses are necessary in order to avoid the "fallacy of affirming the consequent" (i.e., we must eliminate false hypotheses rather than accept true ones). In other words, demonstrating that B occurred does not mean that theory A is necessarily true, or caused B. We must eliminate other theories before concluding A is true. Stated yet another way, to support a hypothesis that two or more variables are related, one must first demonstrate that they are not unrelated. Or, one must demonstrate that it is safe to conclude that the null hypothesis is wrong so as to conclude that the variables really are related. Demonstrating that the null hypothesis is unlikely to be true before concluding that there is a real relationship also helps to rule out chance as the cause of the relationship.

Accepting the null hypothesis as true means that any observed difference or relationship is not statistically significant and is probably due to chance or sampling error, and that the research hypothesis is not supported. Rejecting the null hypothesis means that the research hypothesis is supported.

Both of these applications of inferential statistics are based on an assumption of random sampling and on probability theory, and the researcher should have a good understanding of their basic concepts. Random sampling was discussed in the chapter on survey research. Probability theory relates to the mathematical likelihood of an event occurring. Central to probability theory is the assumption that, while repeated events will exhibit a certain pattern over time, individual, or short-time, events tend to differ from overall long-term patterns of events. For example, if we flip a coin enough times, the law of averages should take effect, and we should end up with 50% of the flips resulting in heads and 50% in tails. On the other hand, ten flips of the coin might well produce as few as three or four or as many as seven or eight heads.

If the difference between the outcome (say six heads) and 50% was small, then we might attribute the difference to chance. If nine of ten flips resulted in heads, then we might suspect that something was amiss and that some variable, such as a defective coin, was affecting or biasing the outcomes of the coin flips. Fortunately, "the mathematical theory of probability provides a basis for evaluating the reliability of the conclusions we reach and the inferences we make when we apply statistical techniques to the collection, analysis, and interpretation of quantitative data."[23] As probability theory does play such a crucial role in statistical analysis, the reader is encouraged to consult one or more standard texts on statistics regarding this subject.

Inferential statistics themselves are of two basic types—parametric statistics or tests, and nonparametric statistics or tests. Either type should be used only when certain conditions exist. Parametric statistics will be discussed first.

Parametric Statistics

Most important, parametric statistics require the assumption of a normal population or distribution. When the data of a normal distribution are plotted on a graph, they should produce a curve that is symmetrical and unimodal (see Figure 9.5); its mean, median, and mode should all coincide; and there should be a constant area, or proportion of cases, between the mean and an ordinate which is a given distance from the mean in terms of standard deviations. In fact, slightly more than two-thirds of the cases should fall within plus or minus ($\pm$) one standard deviation of the mean, slightly more than 95% within plus or minus two standard deviations, and almost all cases within plus or minus three standard deviations.

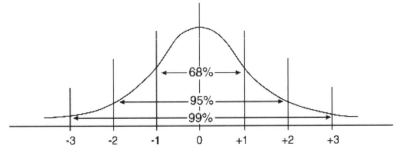

FIGURE 9.5.   A Normal Curve

However, if the sample drawn from the population has 100 or more cases, the normality assumption can almost always be relaxed. That is, a normal population is not required, as the sampling distribution of sample means is likely to be normal. In fact, "no matter how unusual a distribution we start with, provided N [the sample size] is sufficiently large, we can count on a sampling distribution that is approximately normal."[24] It is sampling distributions, not populations, that form the basis for tests of significance. (See the section on sampling error in Chapter 4 for a definition of the "mean of the sampling distribution.")

If the sample size falls somewhere between 50 and 100, and if there is evidence to the effect that departure from normality is not great, then statistical tests of this type can be used with some confidence. If the sample is less than 30, the researcher should use such tests cautiously unless the approximation to normality is known to be good.[25]

Parametric tests also assume that the variance of each group in question is similar, and that the samples are randomly drawn. In addition, they require that the data being analyzed be primarily interval or ratio level.

Parametric tests are relatively powerful, or likely to detect a difference between groups if a difference really exists. In other words, the power of a test is directly related to its ability to eliminate false null hypotheses. Power may be defined as 1 minus the probability of a type II error. (A type II or "beta error" is the error of failing to reject a null hypothesis when it is actually false; a type I or "alpha error" is the error of rejecting a true null hypothesis. When the probability of one type increases, the other decreases.)

Some examples of frequently used parametric tests include the following:

1. Z test—this test, using standard scores, tests the difference between a group's results and the results that would be expected due to chance alone. Or, stated somewhat differently, it is used to determine whether the mean of a sample is significantly different from the mean of the population from which it is taken. (A standard, or Z, score is a score that is relative to the mean and measured in standard deviation units. It equals the deviation from the mean

divided by the standard deviation.) A Z test could be used, for example, to decide whether the physical condition of a sample of books selected from a library's collection is representative of the physical condition of the entire collection in general.

2. Student's t-test—a test that can be used in place of the Z test where there is still only one group but where, in contrast to the Z test, the standard deviation of the population is not known.

3. Difference of means—a commonly used statistical test which utilizes the t statistic, and which determines if the statistical difference between the mean scores of two groups is significant. It does not require that the population standard deviations be known. (For an example of how the difference of means t-test might be used, see the section later in this chapter on selecting appropriate statistical tests.)

4. Analysis of variance—a statistical test which represents an extension of the difference of means test. It utilizes the F statistic, and it tests for differences among the means of more than two samples or groups. Analysis of variance (ANOVA) can be used with only two groups but would produce the same results as a t-test in that case. Multiple analysis of variance (MANOVA) is designed for situations where one needs to test relationships that involve more than one dependent variable.

5. Tukey's HSD (Honestly Significant Difference) test—this test is used to examine the pattern of mean difference and can be used with more than two groups. The HSD score is the within group variability and is part of the ANOVA result. It is compared with all of the possible pairs of means to determine if there is a significant difference between the HSD score and each mean difference.

6. Pearson's product-moment correlation coefficient—this test generally is referred to as simply the correlation coefficient; it measures the degree of linear association between two variables or the extent to which changes in one value correspond with changes in another value. It can take a value of -1 to $+1$. A negative coefficient indicates a negative relationship, or, as one variable increases, the other decreases. A positive value indicates a positive relationship, or, as one variable increases, the other increases, or they both decrease. A coefficient of 0, or near 0, means that there is little or no linear relationship between the variables. Use of this statistic requires interval level data. Referring back to our concern about the physical condition of books, we could measure the correlational relationship between the number of times certain books are borrowed and the number of times they must be repaired.

Relationships between two variables can be plotted on a graph, which is usually called a scattergram. A straight line can then be plotted that relates specific values of one variable to values of the other. In the graph below (Figure 9.6), the scores of one of the variables are represented on the abscissa (horizontal line), and the scores of the second variable are represented on the ordinate (vertical line). For example, the X value on the horizontal axis could be the number of items checked out; the Y value on the vertical axis could be length of visit. When two variables are highly correlated, the plotted points tend to be very close to the straight line, and as was noted above, the correlation coefficient would be close to 1. This line is called a line of regression, and the equation of this line is called a regression equation.

A major aim of quantitative research is prediction. When two variables are correlated, regression equations can be used to predict what value of variable Y would most likely be associated with a given value of X. Regression analysis itself is considered next.

7. Regression—a type of analysis that, as is the case for correlation, can be used for descriptive and inferential purposes. In the former case, Pearson's correlation coefficient is used as the basis for developing a simple linear regression equation to predict the value of one variable when the value of the

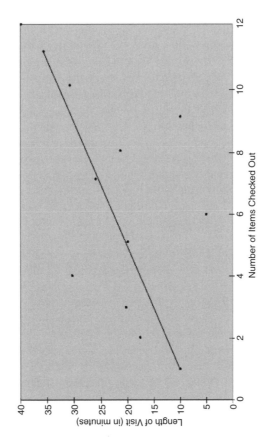

**FIGURE 9.6.   A Scatter Diagram with
a Regression Line**

other variable is known. As an inferential technique, linear regression can be used to generalize findings from a sample to the population from which the sample was randomly selected. For example, using data collected from a sample, one could predict that a certain percentage increase in the median age of a library's population would result in a certain percentage increase in the use of the library.

Regression, and correlation, analysis can be used with two variables or "can readily be extended to include any number of interval scales [variables], one of which can be taken as dependent and the remainder independent".[26] Utilizing multiple regression analysis, one could measure a number of characteristics of reference librarians and use those as a basis for predicting how successful a reference librarian would be in answering reference questions.

Nonparametric Statistics

In contrast to parametric statistics, nonparametric statistics are considered to be distribution-free. That is, they do not require the assumption of a normal population and, therefore, are often used with smaller samples. As they involve weaker assumptions, they are less powerful than the parametric tests and require larger samples in order to yield the same *level of significance*. (The level of significance is the probability of rejecting a true hypothesis. It usually is set at .05 or .01, which means that the null hypothesis, or the prediction of no relationship, is to be rejected if the sample results are among the results that would have occurred no more than 5%, or 1%, of the time. Stated somewhat differently, a significance level of .05 means that there is a 5% probability that the researcher will reject a hypothesis that is actually true.)

Nonparametric tests are usually, but not always, used with ordinal level data. Five common examples are as follows:

1. Chi-square test—this test is useful for determining if a statistically significant relationship exists between two categorical variables. If the population is known to be normally distributed, chi-square can be treated as a parametric statistic and frequently is used for causal, comparative studies. The process for calculating a chi-square is essentially the same as described in the section on bivariate frequencies, and it produces the same kind of cross classification. It can indicate only if there is a significant relationship; statistics such as Cramer's V must be used to determine the strength of any relationships. Returning again to our concern about the physical condition of a library's book collection, we might use a chi-square test to determine whether there is a significant relationship between the location of books and their condition (as assigned to categories).
2. Mann-Whitney U-test—this is one nonparametric equivalent of the difference of means test, and is used to test for a significant difference between

two groups. It cannot be used unless the population is symmetric about its median.

3. Wilcoxon Sign test—this test can be used instead of the Mann-Whitney when the data are not symmetrical. It also is useful in determining the significance of the difference between two correlated groups.

4. Spearman rank-order correlation, or Spearman's ρ—this is a nonparametric correlation coefficient that can be calculated for ranked or ordinal level data. It is interpreted in the same manner as Pearson's correlation coefficient.

5. Kruskall-Wallis test—a nonparametric alternative to analysis of variance; it is appropriate when one has a number of independent random samples and an ordinal scale level of measurement.

Selecting the Appropriate Statistical Test

As has been indicated for most of the examples given above, the various statistical tests must meet certain conditions before being appropriate for use. For example, certain tests call for a normal population, others for a particular level of measurement (see Chapter 2 for a consideration of the basic measurement scales). Most of the examples presented here were intended for the analysis of either one group or two groups. There are also statistical tests intended for more than two variables; such techniques are referred to as multivariate analyses and include multiple regression and factor analysis. One also should consider the primary purpose of the research in choosing statistics; that is, whether it is descriptive or analytical in nature. Other questions relate to the need to distinguish between independent and dependent variables and to the sampling method used.

These and other kinds of questions should be answered before selecting a statistical test. Otherwise, an inappropriate test may be used and thereby invalidate the results of the analysis. The selection of a proper statistic can be facilitated by using some sort of decision tree to systematize the process. An example of the use of decision trees in selecting appropriate statistical tests can be found in a booklet published by the Institute for Social Research of the University of Michigan. In using this guide, one starts by noting how many variables are involved, and then continues along the "branches" of the decision tree, answering questions at each decision point. Eventually one arrives at a box which will contain a statistical technique, measure, or test appropriate to the situation.[27] The same information is available in most standard statistical texts but in a less compact, sequential format. Computer programs which will help the researcher select the appropriate statistical test are available as well.

Let us now work through an example of how a statistical test might be selected, and used, to test a hypothesis. Suppose an experiment had been conducted to test the effect of bibliographic instruction (BI) on the library skills of certain university students. The researcher established two groups of randomly selected students. One group of students was given BI during the course of the study; one group received no instruction. At the end of the experiment, the library skills of the students in both groups were measured with a test. The mean test score of the experimental group (instruction) was 85; the mean score of the control group (no instruction) was 65. Thus the difference between mean test scores was 20. The research hypothesis for the study predicted that there would be a significant difference between the mean scores. The implicit null hypothesis was that there would not be a statistically significant difference.

In this scenario, two groups have been observed (i.e., we have calculated the mean library skills scores for two groups of subjects). We are assuming that the two groups were drawn independently from a normally distributed population (all of the students enrolled at the university) in terms of their library skills, but we do not know what the standard deviation for the population is. The test scores represent ratio-level data. We determine prior to the study that BI would be considered the independent variable and library skills (scores) the dependent variable. Thus the difference of means t-test is identified as an appropriate and legitimate statistic for testing our hypothesis.

As indicated, there is a difference of 20 points between the mean test scores of the two groups. The question is whether 20 points represent a statistically significant difference. In order to answer this question, we first must select the significance level and critical region to be used with the test. Assume we selected the .01 level of significance, which means that the test would have a 1% chance of rejecting the null hypothesis when it is actually true. Or, as stated earlier, it is the probability of making a type I error.

In selecting the *critical region*, the researcher is deciding whether one or both tails of the sampling distribution will be used to determine whether the hypothesis will be accepted or rejected. (If normal, the sampling distribution would resemble the curve in Figure 9.5.) If the researcher is able to predict the direction of the relationship, he or she is well advised to use a one-tailed test so all of the critical region can be concentrated in one end of the curve. If the direction of the relationship cannot be predicted, a two-tailed test is preferable. In this case, we expect BI to increase library skills, so we elect to use a one-tailed test. Since our significance level is .01, the critical region would be the extreme right 1% of the curve or distribution. If our outcome falls into that area, then we would reject the null hypothesis, with a 1% chance of having made an error.

Next, we must calculate the value of "t" for our difference of means test. This can be done using the appropriate formula or computer program. Once computed, the t value must be checked in a table of t values to determine whether it is statistically significant (or a computer program can do this for us). If the value is equal to or greater than the value in the table for the appropriate level of significance and "degrees of freedom,"* then it is deemed statistically significant or not likely to have occurred by chance. Therefore, the researcher is justified in rejecting the

---

*For many statistical tests, the number of degrees of freedom (df) is defined as one less than the size of the sample, or $n-1$.

null hypothesis of no relationship and at least tentatively accepting the research hypothesis. We conclude, therefore, that BI does appear to have a positive impact on the library skills of certain university students. A t value lower than the corresponding one in the table would, of course, dictate the opposite conclusion. Gerhan has written an article to help reference librarians understand how statistical significance is employed by the researchers they assist.[28]

CAUTIONS IN TESTING THE HYPOTHESIS

In using statistics to test hypotheses, one must always keep in mind that statistical inferences are based on probability, and one can never rely on statistical evidence alone for a judgment of whether a hypothesis is true. Such a decision must be based on the presuppositions or conceptual basis of the research as well.

It is also important to remember that a single statistical "acceptance" of a hypothesis does not prove it to be true with absolute certainty. It is seldom if ever possible to accept a hypothesis outright as the single correct one, since there are a large number of additional hypotheses which also could be accepted. One simply decides, based on the statistical results, that a hypothesis should not be rejected. This does provide, of course, some support for the hypothesis. In fact, there is a growing interest in *meta-analysis*, which generally refers to a set of statistical procedures used to summarize and integrate many studies that focused on the same issue. It represents a numerical rather than narrative method of relating findings and is considered to be more objective, reliable, and rigorous.

According to Trahan, the term meta-analysis is used to refer to a variety of methods that have the following points in common:

> A research question of interest, on which a large quantity of experimental data has accumulated, is identified. An exhaustive literature search is performed to locate experimental studies on the topic. These studies are then analyzed and coded for their various methodological features. Effect sizes are computed from the reported numerical results of the studies. These effect sizes are combined to produce an overall result. The results are then analyzed on the basis of the coded study features to determine if any of these features had a consistent effect on the study outcomes.[29]

Trahan also describes a pilot study that indicated that it is feasible to integrate data from library and information science research using meta-analytic methods. Lopez-Lee analyzes meta-analytic articles written by policy makers and social scientists.[30] He concludes that meta-analysis can either blur the distinctions between the studies or provide misleading conclusions. A 1987 article by Chow provides a critique of meta-analysis.[31] An older, but still useful, Sage publication presents an overview of meta-analysis in social research.[32]

Even when statistical tests, the results of other studies, and so on suggest that there is a consistent difference or relationship between groups or variables, this finding still does not explain the reason for the relationship. In order to make causal inferences, one must meet assumptions over and above those required for establishing the existence of a statistical relationship.

As an example of this point, one must always be aware of possible spurious relationships. "An apparent relationship between two variables, X and Y, is said to be spurious if their concomitant variation stems, not from a connection between them, but from the fact that each of them is related to some third variable or combination of variables that does not serve as a link in the process by which X leads to Y."[33] In other words, X is not a determining condition of Y. For example, if some variable (Z) occurred before both X and Y, and was in fact causing both of them, then the relationship between X and Y would be spurious. (If Z serves as a link between X and Y, then an indirect relationship exists.) This phenomenon is also referred to as *confounding* the dependent and independent variables. Again, only a sound understanding of the conceptual basis for an apparent relationship can explain its nature; statistics alone cannot.

Other caveats regarding the use of statistics include the fact that a statistically significant result is not necessarily socially or practically significant. Differences of a few thousand volumes between two university library collections could produce significant statistical differences, but in the context of multimillion volume collections, such a difference holds little if any practical significance.

Finally, "weighted data, missing data, small sample sizes, complex sample designs, and capitalization on chance in fitting a statistical model are sources of potential problems in data analysis."[34] When one of these situations exists, statistics should be used with extra caution.

COMPUTER-AIDED STATISTICAL ANALYSIS

"Today, quantitative analysis is almost always done by computer programs such as SPSS and MicroCase."[35] Depending upon the methodology, the data are often inherently numerical and easily uploaded into statistical software packages. With the use of on-line questionnaires, the data can be transported into statistical software programs as soon as the respondents submit the completed survey. Numerical data can be submitted into statistical software programs on personal computers (PCs) and on mainframe computers.

Using a statistical software package on a mainframe computer is an efficient technique for analyzing large amounts of data. An example of such a statistical package is BMDP (Biomedical Computer Programs). It can be used for a variety of statistical analyses and is not limited to medical research.

Another comprehensive computer system for data analysis is known as SAS, or Statistical Analysis System. It tends to be used most frequently by researchers in technical fields, but the system can in fact be used for virtually all kinds of data. MINITAB is a relatively easy-to-use, statistical and graphical analysis software package which provides for extensive use of alphabetic data. MicroCase, another statistical analysis and data management system, was developed for social science researchers.

Probably the most widely available mainframe statistical package is SPSS (Statistical Package for the Social Sciences). The SPSS system is a comprehensive, relatively easy to use computer program for statistical analysis, report writing, tabulation, and general purpose data management. It provides numerous statistical procedures, from simple tables to multivariate analyses. Other SPSS features include a color graphics package and a conversational software system which allows interaction between the data and user.

These and other statistical analysis programs are even more widely available for PCs. The SPSS/PC + System includes a basic program for calculating a number of standard statistics as well as programs for more advanced statistics and tables. The *SPSS 11.0 Syntax Reference Guide* is one of the best and easiest manuals to use, and it provides a lot of information normally found in statistics texts.[36] A briefer introduction to SPSS can be found in the base system user's guides published by SPSS. There are numerous versions of the guide, based upon operating systems and on whether the program will be used on a PC or a mainframe. Persons wishing to use an abbreviated guide to SPSS should consult the *SPSS 11.5 Brief Guide*.[37] Numerous editions and versions of the SPSS publications are available.

The SAS system for PCs supports statistical analysis as well as report writing and data management and retrieval. SYSTAT is a comprehensive statistics, graphics, and data management software package. SYSTAT, as is true of some of the other packages developed for the PC, provides statistical and graphics capabilities comparable to those available with mainframe programs. *StatPac for Windows*, v9.0, released in 2004, a software package that was developed for marketing and survey research, provides many of the statistical methods used in library and information science research. Hernon provides an overview of the files that can be created and produced with *StatPac IV Gold*, an earlier version of *StatPac for Windows*.[38]

Hernon and Richardson have identified, evaluated, and compared more than 70 statistical analysis software programs, many of which are intended for use with microcomputers.[39] A Web site created and maintained by Stephenson includes numerous Web-based sources for statistical data sets and quantitative statistical analyses.[40] The site also includes links to information about visual statistics and free ware statistical calculation programs.

In using computers for statistical analysis, one should be careful that the ease of doing so does not result in too many so-called fishing expeditions. With the possible exception of some exploratory research, the investigator should avoid indiscriminately generating all sorts of analyses without any consideration of relevant concepts, theories, and hypotheses. As is the case with manual analyses, the researcher should be certain that he or she has a thorough understanding of the statistical procedures used. Computers cannot think; they will merely do what they are told to do, or, as the saying goes, "garbage in, garbage out."

ANALYSIS OF NONQUANTIFIED DATA

It is worth noting briefly at this point that not all research data are susceptible to quantification, and such data do not lend themselves to statistical analysis. Yet they may still have a contribution to make to the analysis and interpretation of the results of a study, and should not be dismissed perfunctorily. Indeed, studies intended to gather qualitative type data have been enjoying a resurgence, and there are research methods and techniques specifically designed to gather non-quantitative or qualitative data.

The analysis of qualitative data differs from the analysis of quantitative data not only in the nature of the data but also in the nature of the process. For example, qualitative analysis is not perceived as a separate phase as in quantitative research. In fact, "qualitative researchers have frequently suggested that research design, data collection and analysis are simultaneous and continuous processes."[41]

One of the major objectives of qualitative data analysis is the generation of concepts. The general process typically involves immersing oneself in the data, looking for patterns, identifying surprising events, and being sensitive to inconsistencies. One of the key activities of qualitative analysis is the coding of data. Coding, which is similar to indexing, is a critical process since it serves to organize the raw information that has been collected and because it represents the first step in the conceptualization of the data.

As has been noted elsewhere in this text, it may well be desirable to combine quantitative and qualitative methods in a single study. Doing so would, of course, also necessitate combining quantitative and qualitative data analysis techniques. Chapter 7 of this book presents additional information about qualitative research methods and data analysis, including statistical software packages. A book edited by Glazier and Powell provides an introduction to qualitative research and gives examples of qualitative research studies in library and information management.[42]

SUMMARY

Statistical methods are generally used for descriptive purposes and for statistical inference. Descriptive statistics deal with the tabulation of data; their presentation in tabular, graphical, or pictorial form; and the calculation of descriptive measures. Inferential statistics are used for making inductive generalizations about populations, based on sample data, and for testing hypotheses. Both types of statistics permit interpreting quantitative data in such a way that the reliability of conclusions based on the data may be evaluated objectively by means of probability statements.

The typical basic steps in statistical analysis are categorizing the data, coding the data, and calculating the appropriate statistics. Descriptive statistics, if calculated, can characterize what is typical in a group, indicate how widely cases in the group vary, show the relationships between variables and groups, and summarize the data. Inferential statistics can estimate population parameters and test the significance of relationships between and among variables.

Certain inferential statistics are classed as parametric statistics, and they require the assumption of a normal population. Others are considered nonparametric or distribution-free statistics. The requirements for using specific statistics of either kind tend to vary somewhat, and the researcher should carefully avoid using statistical tests inappropriately.

There are cautions that one should heed in utilizing statistics. Perhaps the most important principle to keep in mind is that statistics, whether generated manually or by a computer, cannot substitute for early, sound conceptual development of the research design and statistical analysis. Even the most sophisticated, comprehensive computer statistical packages simply "crunch" numbers, with no real regard for the underlying theories and hypotheses. It is left to the researcher to determine which statistical techniques represent valid methods of analyzing the data. The final interpretation of the analysis must be done by the investigator; statistics can only facilitate the process.

NOTES

[1]D. P. Wallace, "The Use of Statistical Methods in Library and Information Science," *Journal of the American Society for Information Science* 36 (November 1985): 403.

[2]Geoffrey R. Norman and David L. Streiner, *PDQ Statistics*, 3d ed. (Hamilton, Ontario: B. C. Decker, 2003).

[3]Herbert F. Spirer, Louise Spirer, and A. J. Jaffe, *Misused Statistics*, 2d, rev. exp. ed. (New York: M. Dekker, 1998).

[4]D. Rowntree, *Statistics Without Tears: A Primer for Non-Mathematicians* (New York: Charles Scribner's Sons, 1981).

[5]Richard M. Jaeger, *Statistics: A Spectator Sport*, 2d ed. (Newbury Park, CA: Sage Publications, 1990).

[6]I. S. Simpson, *Basic Statistics for Librarians*, 3d ed. (London: Library Association, 1988).

[7]Arthur Wayne Hafner, *Descriptive Statistical Techniques for Librarians*, 2d ed. (Chicago: American Library Association, 1998).

[8]Peter Hernon, et al., *Statistics for Library Decision Making: A Handbook* (Norwood, NJ: Ablex Publishing, 1989).

[9]Peter Hernon, *Statistics: A Component of the Research Process*, rev. ed. (Norwood, NJ: Ablex Publishing, 1994).

[10]Bert R. Boyce, Charles J. Meadow, and Donald H. Kraft, *Measurement in Information Science* (San Diego: Academic Press, 1994).

[11]Peter Stephen and Susan Hornby, *Simple Statistics for Library and Information Professionals*, 2d ed. (London: Library Association, Publications, 1997).

[12]W. Paul Vogt, *Dictionary of Statistics and Methodology: A Nontechnical Guide for the Social Sciences*, 2d ed. (Thousand Oaks, CA: Sage Publications, 1999): xiii.

[13]Paul D. Leedy, *Practical Research: Planning and Design*, 2d ed. (New York: Macmillan, 1980): 141.

[14]Chava Frankfort-Nachmias and David Nachmias, *Research Methods in the Social Sciences*, 4th ed. (New York: St. Martin's Press, 1992): 339.

[15]John H. Fennick, *Studies Show: A Popular Guide to Understanding Scientific Studies* (Amherst, NY: Prometheus, 1997).

[16]Gary Golden, *Survey Research Methods* (Chicago: ACRL, 1982).

[17]Annie S. Barnes, ed., *Social Science Research: A Skills Handbook* (Bistol, IN: Wyndham Hall Press, 1985).

[18]Hernon, *Statistics*.

[19]Liwen Vaughan, *Statistical Methods for the Information Professional: A Practical, Painless Approach to Understanding, Using, and Interpreting Statistics*, ASIST Monograph Series (Medford, NJ: Information Today, 2001).

[20]Wallace, "The Use of Statistical Methods," 402–10.

[21]Edward Tufte, *Envisioning Information*, 2d ed. (Cheshire, CT: Graphics Press, 1997); Edward Tufte, *The Visual Display of Quantitative Information*, 2d ed. (Cheshire, CT: Graphics Press, 2001).

[22]Barnes, *Social Science Research*.

[23]David V. Huntsberger and Patrick Billingsley, *Elements of Statistical Inference*, 4th ed. (Boston, MA: Allyn and Bacon, 1977): 71.

[24]Hubert M. Blalock, Jr., *Social Statistics*, rev. 2d ed. (New York: McGraw-Hill, 1979): 183.

[25]Ibid., 187.

[26]Ibid., 451.

[27]Frank M. Andrews, Laura Klem, Terrence N. Davidson, Patrick M. O'Malley, and Willard L. Rodgers, *A Guide for Selecting Statistical Techniques for Analyzing Social Science Data*, 2d ed. (Ann Arbor: Survey Research Center, Institute for Social Research, University of Michigan, 1981).

[28]David Gerhan, "Statistical Significance: How It Signifies in Statistics Reference," *Reference & User Services Quarterly* 40, no. 4 (2001): 361–74.

[29]Eric Trahan, "Applying Meta-Analysis to Library Research and Information Science Research," *Library Quarterly* 63 (January 1993): 81–82.

[30]David Lopez-Lee, "Indiscriminate Data Aggregations in Meta-Analysis: A Cause for Concern Among Policy Makers and Social Scientists," *Evaluation Review* 26, no. 5 (2002): 520–44.

[31]Siu L. Chow, "Meta-Analysis of Pragmatic and Theoretical Research: A Critique," *Journal of Psychology* 121 (May 1987): 259–71.

[32]Gene V. Glass, Barry McGaw, and Mary L. Smith, *Meta-Analysis in Social Research* (Beverly Hills, CA: Sage Publications, 1981).

[33]Claire Selltiz, Lawrence S. Wrightsman, and Stuart W. Cook, *Research Methods in Social Relations*, rev. ed. (New York: Holt, Rinehart & Winston, 1959): 424.

[34]Andrews, et al., *A Guide for Selecting Statistical Techniques*, 1.

[35]Earl R. Babbie, *The Practice of Social Research*, 10th ed. (Belmont, CA: Wadsworth/Thomson Learning, 2004): 396.

[36]*SPSS 11.0 Syntax Reference Guide* (Chicago: SPSS Inc., 2001).

[37]*SPSS 11.5 Brief Guide* (Chicago: SPSS Inc., 2002).

[38]Hernon, *Statistics*, 48–58.

[39]Peter Hernon and John V. Richardson, eds., *Microcomputer Software for Performing Statistical Analysis: A Handbook Supporting Library Decision Making* (Norwood, NJ: Ablex Publishing, 1988).

[40]Mary Sue Stephenson, 2003 September 1. Available, *http://www.slais.ubc.ca/resources/research_methods/quantita.htm*.

[41]Alan Bryman and Robert G. Burgess, eds., *Analyzing Qualitative Data* (London: Routledge, 1994): 217.

[42]Jack D. Glazier and Ronald R. Powell, eds. *Qualitative Research in Information Management* (Englewood, CO: Libraries Unlimited, 1992).

Chapter 10

Writing the Research Proposal

VALUE OF RESEARCH PROPOSALS

The best research is well planned, and a key step in carrying out such planning is the preparation of a research proposal. The development of the proposal can help to reduce wasted effort and provide a more efficient, problem-free study by encouraging the researcher to clarify the exact nature of the investigation. In developing the research proposal, the investigator should specify the procedures which he or she expects to follow; and in doing so, the researcher will be better prepared to carry out all of the necessary, relevant steps. It is also useful, at this time, to indicate the progress to be expected at various stages of the project. While the deadlines indicated by such a timetable will not always be met, the attempt to meet them should result in a more punctually conducted study. Also, the proposal can provide the basis for discussing the strengths and weaknesses of the proposed project, facilitate the identification of conceptual and theoretical errors, and help to point out weaknesses in selected designs and methods.

In addition, the research proposal is useful for announcing one's research intentions and therein providing enough detail about the proposed project to prevent misinterpretations about the research goals and techniques to be employed. Research proposals are required of doctoral students as an indication that they are prepared to conduct the research properly, and that the topic is worthy of investigation. Last, but not least, proposals are usually necessary for applying for outside funding or grants for research projects.

ORGANIZATION AND CONTENT OF A TYPICAL PROPOSAL

The format of a research proposal will vary somewhat according to the purpose of the proposal and the institutions involved, but the major components are generally the same and are presented below in the order in which they usually occur.

Title Page

Most sponsoring agencies specify the format for the title page, and may even provide a special form. Likewise, universities usually specify the format to be followed by doctoral students. Regardless of the format used, the title of the proposal should accurately reflect the contents and the scope of the suggested study.

Abstract

Most research proposals, with the possible exception of dissertation proposals, should provide a short summary or abstract of about 200 words. The abstract should touch on every major component of the proposal except the budget, if there is one. Some readers read only the abstract and others rely on it for a quick overview of the proposal. Some sponsoring agencies use the abstract to weed out unsuitable proposals and to disseminate information. Consequently, the writing of the abstract should be done with care.

Table of Contents

A table of contents is not always deemed necessary, especially for brief proposals, but it is useful for presenting an overview of the organization of the proposal. In addition to outlining the major components of the proposal, it may provide lists of illustrations, tables, appendices, and so on.

Introduction and Statement of the Problem

An introduction is not always considered necessary, as it tends to duplicate information that follows. But an opening statement characterizing what is being proposed can help to introduce the subject to the reader. Some authors use introductions to outline the major components of the proposal. If included, it should be brief and avoid unnecessary redundancy.

The first section of the typical proposal, if there is not a separate problem section, also introduces the problem to be studied and provides a brief historical background for the problem where appropriate. If the problem warrants being divided into subproblems, they are identified at this point. This section also should indicate the importance of the proposed study, or why a solution is needed, and identify anticipated benefits and their significance.

To obtain the background provided in this section, and possibly elsewhere in the proposal, a variety of sources of information may be consulted. The following list includes some of the types of background information often needed for writing a research proposal. Examples of common sources of such information in the field of library and information science are also included below.

1. Terminology: *ALA Glossary of Library and Information Science*, edited by Heartsill Young (American Library Association, 1983); *Observer's Dictionary of Library Science Information and Documentation in Six Languages* (Observer Scientific, 1973); *Harrod's Librarian's Glossary and Reference Book*, 9th ed., edited and compiled by Ray Prytherch (Gower Publishing, 2000); *Dictionary of Information Science and Technology*, Carolyn Watters (Academic Press, 1992); *Concise Dictionary of Library and Information Science*, 2nd ed., Stella Keenan and Colin Johnston (Bowker-Saur, 2002); and *ODLIS Online Dictionary of Library and Information Science*, Joan M. Reitz (2002) http://www.wesu.edu/library/odlis.html.

2. Brief background: *Encyclopedia of Library and Information Science*, 2nd ed., edited by Miriam A. Drake, vol. 1–4 (Dekker, 2003), also available on-line, with the purchase of the print version; *Encyclopedia of Library and Information Science*, vol. 1–73 (Dekker, 1968–2003), also available on-line, with the purchase of the print version; *Encyclopedia of Librarianship*, 3d ed., edited by Thomas Landau (Hafner, 1966); and the *ALA World Encyclopedia of Library and Information Services*, 3d ed. (American Library Association, 1980).

3. Trends: *Library Trends* (1952–, quarterly) and the *Annual Review of Information Science and Technology* (ASIST, 1966–).

4. Statistics
   (a) Agencies regularly gathering and publishing statistics about libraries or librarians:
      i) Association for Library and Information Science Education— *Library and Information Science Education Statistical Report*, 1980–, annual.
      ii) Association of Specialized and Cooperative Library Agencies— *The State Library Agencies*, 10th ed., 1993; *The Report on Library Cooperation*, 7th ed., 1990.
      iii) American Library Association (ALA). A number of units within ALA are concerned with collecting and reporting library-related statistics. The Office for Research and Statistics has issued several statistical reports. The Public Library Association has published the *Public Library Data Service Statistical Report* on an annual basis since 1988. The Association of College and Research

Libraries regularly compiles and publishes *Academic Library Trends and Statistics*.

iv) Association of Research Libraries—*ARL Statistics*, 1974–, annual (published under a different title from 1964); *ARL Annual Salary Survey*, 1973–.

v) Bowker Company—*American Library Directory*, 1923–, biennial; *Bowker Annual of Library and Book Trade Information*, 1956–.

vi) National Center for Education Statistics (NCES), U.S. Department of Education—periodically collects statistics from school, public, and academic libraries. The frequency and titles of the reports vary. Originally they were referred to as LIBGIS reports (statistics on public libraries and public school libraries) and HEGIS reports (statistics on academic libraries). The HEGIS reports are now known as IPEDS (Integrated Postsecondary Education Data System). The IPEDS data are available on-line at http://nces.ed.gov/pubsearch/pubsinfo.asp?pubid=2003397. ALS, the Academic Library Survey, was once part of IPEDS but became a separate survey in 1999. LIBGIS essentially became FSCS— the Federal-State Cooperative System for public library data. The NCES program for collecting data on schools and their libraries is the Schools and Staffing Survey (SASS).

vii) Special Libraries Association—results of its salary survey are published every two years with annual updates.

viii) American Association of School Librarians—collects data on school library media centers.

(b) Other sources of statistics

i) State library agencies—most state libraries collect statistics on public libraries. The Library Research Service (LRS) of the Colorado State Library gathers and reports statistics on libraries of that state. The LRS and the University of Denver, Library and Information Science Program, maintain a Web site (http://www. lrs.org/) which includes information on research and statistics.

ii) Individual libraries—a few libraries collect data on a regional or national level. Reports of individual libraries can be useful also, but the lack of standardization presents some problems for analysis.

iii) Library research centers—the Library Research Center (LRC) of the University of Illinois Graduate School of Library and Information Science. Its Web site (http://www.lis.uiuc.edu/gslis/research/lrc.html) includes information about the Center's current projects.

5. Biographical information—*ALA Membership Directory* (1950–, annual— combined with the *ALA Handbook of Organization* since 1980); *Who's Who in Library and Information Services* (ALA, 1982); *Dictionary of American Library Biography*, edited by Bohdan S. Wynar (Libraries Unlimited, 1977); and *Directory of Library and Information Professionals* (Research Publications, 1988).

6. Directory-type information—*American Library Directory; The ALA Handbook of Organization* (annual); *Directory of Special Libraries and Information Centers*, 3 vols. (Gale Research, 1996); and the Web sites of some organizations that list their members.
7. Bibliographical data—see the indexes cited in the Review of Related Research section of this chapter.

Other miscellaneous resources include ALA's *Library Technology Reports*, reports of the Council on Library and Information Resources, ARL *SPEC Kits*, and *CLIP Notes*, published by ACRL.

Review of Related Research

The review of related research, or literature review, is in effect an expansion of the historical background presented in the problem section. It cites and briefly reviews the related research studies that have been conducted. Nonresearch reports and "opinion pieces" should generally be excluded from consideration unless they are particularly insightful or represent all that have been written on the problem. It is desirable, if not essential, that related research in other fields be cited as well. In some cases, the research done in other fields will be all that exists of any real importance. In other words, this section of the proposal describes the foundation on which the proposed study will be built by discussing work done by others, evaluating their methodologies and findings, and stating how the proposed research will differ. The literature review should be selective (the final report often contains additional works or information) and should group the cited studies in some logical fashion.

It is in this section that the theoretical or conceptual framework is established for the subsequent stages, particularly the development of the hypothesis. The literature review helps to suggest the best approach to seeking a solution to the problem. Before continuing with the research study, it is essential to know what has already been done. Unfortunately, bibliographic control of LIS research, particularly research in progress, is not what it could be, but there are several publications that identify some current research. A selective list follows:

1. *The Bowker Annual of Library and Book Trade Information*, New York: Bowker, 1956–. Annual. Includes sections on funding and grants and research and statistics.
2. *Library Literature & Information Science*, previously titled *Library Literature*, New York: Wilson, 1934–. Bimonthly. Cites journal articles, books, and other published research studies. Available electronically and in paper.
3. *Library & Information Science Abstracts (LISA)*. London: Library Association, 1969–. Bimonthly. Another basic index. Available in electronic and paper formats.
4. *Resources in Education (RIE)*, Washington D.C.: U.S. Department. of Education, 1966–2002. Monthly. An important source of unpublished research

reports in the areas of education and library science. Together with the *Current Index to Journals in Education*, it constitutes the printed equivalent of the ERIC computer data base. However, the clearinghouse has been reorganized, and these publications ceased in 2002.

5. *Dissertation Abstracts International*, Ann Arbor, MI: UMI ProQuest, 1938–. Monthly. Available in electronic format.

6. *Masters Abstracts International*, Ann Arbor, MI: UMI ProQuest, 1962–. Quarterly. Available in electronic format.

7. "Doctoral Dissertation Topics Accepted in Library and Information Science." An irregularly published section of the "Research Record" in the *Journal of Education for Library and Information Science*.

8. *Information Research Watch International*, London: Bowker-Saur, 2000–. The print equivalent is published six times per year, and the electronic version is updated monthly. This journal is intended for those who need to keep abreast of research and development work in librarianship, information science, archives, documentation, and the information aspects of other fields. Its coverage is international. Each entry provides an overview of a research project and information about personnel, duration, funding, and references. Formerly *Current Research in Library and Information Science* and before that *RADIALS Bulletin*, London: Bowker-Saur, 1981–1999. Quarterly. An annual compilation titled *Current Research for the Information Profession* is distributed by the American Library Association.

9. *Library and Information Science Annual*, Littleton, CO: Libraries Unlimited, 1987–1999. 7 vols. Documents developments in the library and information science field. Includes evaluative reviews of professional titles and an annotated listing of doctoral dissertations.

10. *Library and Information Research* (formerly *Library and Information Research News*), Loughborough, Leicestershire: Library and Information Research Group, 1970s–. A quarterly publication that includes papers, news, and book reviews. It is available on the Web at http://www.lirg.org.uk/lirn/directory.htm.

11. "Research News," a column in the *Canadian Journal of Information and Library Science (CJILS)*. Reports news on LIS research in Canada, including work being done by Canadians abroad and LIS work that relates to Canada. The column also announces winners of Canadian research awards.

12. *New Review of Information and Library Research*. An annual publication that promotes current research of interest to information professionals.

Professional associations are also possible sources of information about research in progress or recently completed research. Within the American Library Association, the Library Research Round Table (LRRT) is particularly concerned with research. Its objectives are to extend and improve library research; to offer programs aimed at describing, criticizing, and disseminating library research findings; and to educate ALA members about research techniques and their usefulness in obtaining information with which to reach administrative decisions and solve problems. ALA's Office for Research and Statistics can also serve as a source of information about current research in progress. It appears that a growing percentage of the papers presented at professional conferences are reports of research. ALISE (Association for Library and Information Science Education) sponsors a research grant award that requires that recipients present progress reports at ALISE conferences, a research paper competition, and a doctoral forum for the exchange of research ideas.

An on-line database, *Federal Research in Progress*, is available through several on-line database providers and occasionally includes records of library-related research being performed under the sponsorship of U.S. government agencies. All records include title, principal investigator, performing organization, and sponsoring organization. Most records also include a description of the research, progress reports, and subject descriptors. Many reports of completed research and research in progress are available on the Web. Some reports of funded research projects are available only on the Web.

Research Design

Returning to the outline of a typical research proposal, the next section usually is devoted to a description of the proposed research. Almost always written for the specialist rather than the layperson, it includes the following elements:

1. Goals and objectives—A goals and objectives section, identified as such, is not always included at this point. If it is, a few statements emphasizing the major purposes of the research method to be employed should suffice.
2. Hypothesis—At this time, the major research hypothesis, or hypotheses, should be stated. This section also will include minor or secondary and alternative hypotheses, if any have been developed. As discussed earlier, the researcher may have concluded that the development and testing of formal hypotheses is not feasible at this stage of the research. Thus, he or she may decide instead to pose one or more research questions to be answered.
3. Assumptions—Basic assumptions are usually given after the hypothesis statement. These are needed to help support the hypothesis and, therefore, logically occur at this point. They should directly relate to the hypothesis and build the case for the hypothesis, not the methodology.
4. Definitions—The operational or working definitions for key terms and terms that are used in a unique way logically follow the hypothesis and assumptions. There is some disagreement as to how much detail should be provided here, rather than in the section describing the data collection instrument, but the operational definitions should at least tell what is to be observed and imply how. For example, an operational definition of library use may specify that external circulations are to be measured by analyzing circulation records. Many researchers prefer to incorporate the hypothesis, assumptions, and definitions in the problem section but may repeat them here.

5. Methodology—The next large section in the typical proposal describes the research methodology. In brief, this is where the researcher describes how the study will be organized and the situation in which the hypothesis will be tested.

   The researcher also should provide details in this section on the techniques and tools that will be used to collect data. This should include a description of the kind of data that will be collected to test the hypothesis, including the criteria for admissibility of data; whether it will be limited to primary or secondary data; the likely sources of these data; and the type(s) of data collection methods or tools (e.g., questionnaire, interview, etc.) to be used to gather the data. If a pretest is to be made, it too should be described at this point. Readers interested in analyses of methodologies used by previous researchers may wish to consult articles by Lundeen,[1] Peritz,[2] Nour,[3] Feehan et al.,[4] and Powell.[5]

6. Treatment of the data—Next, the researcher should describe how he or she proposes to analyze the data to be collected. This part of the proposal generally does not need to be very specific; for example, the specific statistical tests, if any, to be employed in the analysis probably do not need to be itemized here. But at least the general kinds of analysis to be used (e.g., descriptive, bivariate, multivariate, inferential, etc.) should be specified along with the rationales for using them. "Dummy tables" may be provided at this point to illustrate how the data will be categorized and analyzed. If computer statistical packages are to be utilized in the analysis, it probably is advisable to specify them.

Institutional Resources

It may be useful to describe relevant institutional resources that are available to support the proposed research project. Such a section is particularly advisable for grant proposals requesting external funding. Items in this section may include computer facilities, library resources, and survey research personnel and facilities.

Personnel

A section describing personnel to be employed in the study may be necessary only for grant proposals, or for projects involving a relatively large number of people. A personnel section is rarely needed for individual research projects, such as dissertation research, though funding agencies often require the submission of a resume for the principal investigator (PI). If a personnel section is included, it should provide relevant background information about the research staff, emphasizing their qualifications and what they can contribute to the project. Costs relating to personnel will be covered in the following discussion of the budget.

Budget

The budget has two main functions. First, it estimates, as realistically as possible, the costs of completing the objectives of the proposed research. The reader will use the budget details to determine whether the proposal is economically feasible and realistic. Second, the budget provides a means to monitor the project's financial activities over the life of the project. In this way, it is possible to determine how closely the actual progress in achieving the objectives is being made relative to the proposed budget.

Before considering some of the specific items that should be included in a proposed budget, there are several general points or guidelines worth mentioning, keeping in mind that only grant proposals are likely to have a budget section. Regarding time and personnel, the most common approach to estimating these factors is to list the various stages of the project (developing the data collection tools, data analysis, etc.) and to calculate how much time and how many staff hours will be required for each. Such estimates usually are based on experience and similar studies, but it should be remembered that almost every operation takes longer than expected. In fact, some researchers argue that the estimates should provide additional time for snags or problems, up to an additional 50% of the initial estimates.

Budgets are more likely to be underestimated than overestimated, because the researcher may not realize how much work is actually involved. In addition, researchers tend to get carried away with collecting data or following new leads and, in the process, collect too much irrelevant data. Also, the researcher is anxious to receive approval of the budget and proposal and is prone to underestimating for that reason. A certain amount of budget flexibility is desirable, and underestimating costs reduces that potential.

In order to decrease the likelihood of underestimating the budget, it is advisable for the researcher to check the currentness of the figures at the last minute. It is also desirable to build in a hedge against inflation, or to increase the figures for subsequent years of a multiyear proposal by a reasonable percentage. Explanations for how the major budget figures were calculated should be provided.

Another guideline or rule of thumb worth noting is that the budget should be fitted to the research project, not vice versa. In other words, one should not decide how much money he or she has available or is likely to obtain, and then design a study within those constraints. Instead, the researcher should design the study to investigate the problem as well as possible, and then determine how much such an investigation will cost. The project can then be reduced, if necessary. Determining the budget before designing the study is comparable to selecting a methodology before identifying the problem to be studied. Also, the amount of time and personnel needed for the different stages of a research project will depend to some extent on the type of study being proposed. For example, an exploratory study typically requires a relatively greater amount of time for data analysis than does a more focused study where the researcher has a better defined notion of what he or she is examining.

A typical budget will usually contain at least the following items:

1. Salaries and wages—Personnel costs are determined essentially by translating the time and staffing into appropriate salaries and wages. Usually included here are fringe benefits, if paid, and the costs of any contractual services, such as a consultant's fee.
2. Space—Itemized here are the costs, if any, of providing space for the project. For example, the rental of an office would be included here.
3. Equipment—Equipment costs, whether purchased or rented.
4. Materials and supplies—Provided here are the costs for consumable materials and items such as miscellaneous office supplies.
5. Travel expenses.
6. Support services—Expenses related to the use of services and facilities such as computers and photocopiers.
7. Miscellaneous expenses—Additional costs related to telephone service, purchase of books, postage, and so on.
8. Indirect costs—Costs that cannot directly be identified with a particular project, such as library services, utilities, accounting, maintenance, secretarial support, and so on. These are often figured as a percentage of salaries and wages or of modified total costs. This figure is usually somewhere between 30% and 70% of direct costs. The exact percentage, and the basis for figuring it, usually is established or negotiated by the institution with which the researcher is affiliated and the funding agency.
9. Budget summary—If the budget is relatively long, it may be advisable to provide a summary of the budget, listing major items only.

A sample of a typical 12-month budget is presented in Table 10.1. In this example, the first column represents the proposed contribution of the funding agency; the second column, the support to be provided by the researcher's organization; and the third column, the total. (Usually, the greater the proportion the parent organization is prepared to provide, the greater are the chances of obtaining outside funding.)

Anticipated Results

Returning to the outline of the research proposal, the next common section is an evaluation of expected project results, or the likely impact of the study. This information is particularly important for grant proposals, as the potential funding agency must be convinced of the value of the research project.

Limitations of the Study

Typically, the last section of the text of a research proposal points out the limitations of the project. While the researcher does not want to be negative at this point, it is important to note, in a few concise statements, the limitations imposed

TABLE 10.1
Sample 12-Month Budget

	Sponsor	U-M	Total
Personnel			
Project Director, 25%, Academic Year	$ 15,000	$ 0	$ 15,000
Project Associate, 10%	0	3,000	3,000
Research Assistant, 50%	9,000	0	9,000
Clerk-Typist, 50%	7,000	0	7,000
Subtotal	$ 31,000	$ 3,000	$ 34,000
Staff Benefits (31% of S & W)	$ 9,610	$ 930	$ 10,540
Subtotal	$ 40,610	$ 3,930	$ 44,540
Consultants			
John Smith, $200/day, 2 days	$ 400	$ 0	$ 400
Equipment			
Methometer	$ 2,000	$ 0	$ 2,000
Materials and supplies			
Glassware	$ 200	$ 0	$ 200
Chemicals	200	0	200
Subtotal	$ 400	$ 0	$ 400
Travel			
Project Director consultation with sponsor, Ann Arbor to Washington, D.C., and return. 1 person, 2 days			
Airfare	$ 700	$ 0	$ 700
Per Diem @ $100/day	200	0	200
Local Transportation	25	0	25
Subtotal	$ 925	$ 0	$ 925
Total Direct Costs	$ 44,335	$ 3,930	$ 48,265
Indirect costs			
(52% of modified total direct costs)	$ 22,014	$ 2,044	$ 24,058
Grand Total	**$ 66,349**	**$ 5,974**	**$ 72,323**

Reprinted from *Proposal Writer's Guide* by Donald E. Thackrey (Ann Arbor: University of Michigan, Division of Research Development and Administration, 1996, page 8.)

by the research method, setting, and so on. In essence, the researcher is stating what the research can and cannot do; he or she is not denigrating the value of the study.

Back Matter

Immediately following the text, the writer usually provides the list of references or cited works. If there are fewer than six, they often are inserted in the text; if more, a separate section is probably warranted. After the list of references, the writer may choose to provide a bibliography which will list all the works consulted in writing the proposal and possibly other suggested readings. In a short proposal this is usually unnecessary.

If the author wishes to provide the reader with additional information that is not crucial to the text, then he or she may wish to include one or more appendices. This should not be overdone, however, especially in grant proposals. If there is any doubt about the need to include some information in an appendix, then it is probably best to omit it.

At this point, or perhaps earlier, the researcher may elect to provide a timetable outlining the dates by which he or she expects to have completed certain stages of the proposed study. Or, if not given in a separate section, this information may be integrated throughout the text or even provided as a separate document. Regardless of how it is presented, the development of a timetable is an important exercise in that it sets deadlines for the project and thereby helps to keep it on schedule.

CHARACTERISTICS OF A GOOD PROPOSAL

As Leedy and Ormrod state, "Research demands that those who undertake it be able to think clearly, without confusion."[6] Therefore, it is important that a research proposal be a straightforward document that includes only that information which contributes to an understanding of the problem and its proposed solution. While it should be well written, its primary purpose is to communicate clearly, not to be a literary masterpiece. To that end, the language should be clear and precise and represent conventional prose; the proposal should be clearly and logically organized, and it should make ample use of headings and subheadings.

The general format should be attractive, conform to external mechanics of good form (margins, pagination, etc.), and should be neat and free of typographical errors. The proposal should represent a high level of scholarship, as evidenced by insight into the problem, imagination in the design of the study, adequate grasp of research and statistical tools, and display of a scientific attitude. An increasing number of funding agencies are accepting electronic proposals, and some require electronic submissions.

FEATURES THAT DETRACT FROM A PROPOSAL

Unfortunately, numerous features of a proposal may diminish its effectiveness. Such weaknesses are always to be avoided, but they are particularly crucial when applying for funding. Some of these deficiencies are obvious, though still surprisingly common. For example, proposals are sometimes guilty of not conforming to the guidelines of the funding or approving agency, or of not addressing the research area or interests of the agency. (That is not to say the researcher should not be creative, however, in identifying possible sources of funding.) Proposals also suffer if they are not complete. It is not unusual for research proposals to lack a clear and explicit budget, for example. It is essential, of course, that grant proposals meet the submission deadline if there is one.

The National Institute of Child Health and Human Development, part of the National Institutes of Health (NIH), listed the most common reasons for the rejection of research proposals:

a. Lack of new or original ideas
b. Diffuse, superficial, or unfocused research plan
c. Lack of knowledge of published relevant work
d. Lack of experience in the essential methodology
e. Uncertainty concerning the future directions of the research.[7]

There are many other characteristics that may weaken a proposal, some as minor as the font size. A list of the reasons for grant proposals having been rejected by the NIH is presented in Table 10.2.

TABLE 10. 2
Why Grant Proposals Are Unsuccessful

The National Institutes of Health (NIH), a major provider of project grants to colleges and hospitals, approves less than half of the grant applications it receives. [The NIH Web site, www.nih.gov, includes grant guidelines and funding opportunities.] A study of applications rejected by the NIH includes more than 50 categories for the rejection of proposals. The figure to the right in the listing below indicates the percentage of proposals for which that specific reason for rejection was cited. Since proposals are normally turned down on more than one ground (in this study, an average of four reasons were cited), the percentages add up to more than 100 percent. The most often cited reasons for rejection were questionable project designs, inadequate explanation of the research in the proposal, and the competence of the investigator. Budgets were seldom a problem.

Class I: Nature of Research

The problem is of insufficient importance or biologically irrelevant	11.8
Proposal is repetitive of previous work	9.6
Theory is outmoded or questionable	1.0
Experimental purpose or hypothesis is vague	12.7
Problem is more complex than investigator realizes	1.7
Research based on hypothesis that is doubtful or unsound	4.0
Proposed research based on conclusions that may be unwarranted	2.7
Too little science: problem is more developmental than research	2.3
Problem is scientifically premature and warrants at most a pilot study	7.7

Class II: Approach

Assumptions are questionable; evidence for procedures is questionable	14.6
Approach is not rigorous enough, too naive, too uncritical	11.6
Approach is not objective enough	2.7
Validity questionable; criteria for evaluation are weak or missing	0.6

(Continued)

TABLE 10. 2 (Continued)
Why Grant Proposals Are Unsuccessful

Approach poorly thought out	6.1
Application is poorly prepared or poorly formulated	15.5
Proposal is not explicit enough, lacks detail, or is too vague or general	32.8
Rationale for the approach is poorly presented	3.9
Methods or scientific procedures unsuited to stated objective	16.5
The design is too ambitious or otherwise inappropriate	13.1
The approach lacks scientific imagination	13.1
Some administrative or practical problems are unsolved	1.9
Unethical or hazardous procedures will be used	1.6
Controls are either inadequately conceived or inadequately described	6.5
The procedure is not well enough organized, coordinated, or planned	6.7
Some problems are not realized or dealt with adequately	16.9
The overall design is unsound, or some techniques are unrealistic	35.5
Approach will not produce useful new insights	3.5
The results will be confusing, difficult to interpret, or meaningless	14.4
The emphasis is on data collection rather than on data interpretation	5.3
Class III: Investigator	
Investigator does not have adequate experience for this research	31.6
Investigator is unskilled in scientific method	4.0
Investigator has produced too few publications during the research	6.4
Articles are of generally low quality	3.5
Results from previous year's support are inadequate	9.3
The investigator's knowledge or judgment of literature is poor	20.2
The investigator is spreading himself too thin	1.5
Class IV: Other	
The investigator needs more liaison with colleagues in this field	10.5
The project will rely on insufficiently experienced associates	0.5
The institutional setting is unfavorable	2.4
The overall budget is too high	7.5
The budget for personnel is too high	2.4
The budget for equipment is too high	0.7
The budget for other items is too high	0.6
The overall budget is too low	1.2

Source: National Institutes of Health. Reprinted from *Federal Grants and Contracts Weekly*, March 31, 1981.

OBTAINING FUNDING FOR LIS RESEARCH

If one is planning to seek external funding for his or her research project, there is a variety of resources to which the researcher can turn for guidance.

If the proposal has been written at the request of a specific funding agency (i.e., in response to a RFP, or request for proposal) or in response to a clear indication that a funding agency is interested in proposals on a topic, seeking funds is relatively easy. The agency should be contacted at an early stage and asked for whatever advice they are able to give as the proposal develops. In most cases the agency will send material describing what it wants and appropriate application forms. In some cases, an agency will refer you to previous projects they have funded and/or volunteer to critique drafts of your proposal. The amount of help an agency is willing to give varies widely. In any case it is important to be aware that assistance in developing a proposal is not a promise that the proposal will be funded. Agencies may deliberately encourage several people to prepare requests so that they can pick the one they judge to make the best use of available funds.[8]

In lieu of a relatively firm commitment from a funding agency, it is necessary to identify likely sources of support. As Lynch notes, both informal and formal sources should be used to get ideas. Individuals working in the same subject area are possible sources of suggestions for funding.[9] Professional organizations may also be able to give useful advice. In considering and applying to potential funding agencies, it is important to identify organizations that would appear to have an interest in, and something to be gained from, one's proposed research. On the other hand, one should be imaginative in identifying such agencies and not restrict efforts to only the most obvious organizations.

For those persons needing information about granting foundations and agencies and about specific grants, there are numerous standard works available. These include the *Catalog of Federal Domestic Assistance, Annual Register of Grant Support, The Foundation Directory, The Foundation Grants Index, The Grants Register, Directory of Research Grants*, the daily *Federal Register, The Foundation 1000* (formerly *Source Book Profiles*), the *Foundation Reporter* (formerly *Taft Foundation Information System*), and the *Commerce Business Daily*. DIALOG offers a computer database titled "GRANTS," an abstract file of sources of grants in a wide range of subject areas. It lists active grant offerings from associations, private foundations, commercial agencies, and government agencies. "GRANTS" is produced by Oryx Press and corresponds to the printed work, *Directory of Research Grants*. Other databases include the *Foundation Grants Index Online*, the *Sponsored Programs Information Network (SPIN), The Foundation Directory*, and the *Illinois Researcher Information System (IRIS)*. Indeed, an increasing amount of information about grants can be found on the Internet. Among other resources found there are documentation for grant applications; subject guides to funding agencies and, in many cases, their home pages; and various discussion lists. There is a listserv called GRANTS-L, which includes information on sources of government and nonprofit funding for scholarly research. Various workshops and seminars on obtaining grants are regularly held throughout the country.

One article, "Library Grant Money on the Web: A Resource Primer," published in *Searcher*, provides descriptions and URLs for grant funding agencies and resources.[10] Bauer not only describes how to seek grant funding proactively and to develop a grant proposal, but also describes the various government and private funding sources and their differences.[11] Waters lists grant sources and foundations that have funded libraries, thereby identifying potential sources for future funding.[12] Other publications with information about grants and funded research in library and information science include the following:

1. *The Big Book of Library Grant Money: Profiles of Private and Corporate Foundations and Direct Corporate Givers Receptive to Library Grant Proposals, 2004–2005*, Taft Group, Detroit, MI/Chicago: American Library Association, 2004.
2. *National Guide to Funding for Libraries and Information Services*, by Jeffrey A Falkenstein. 7th ed., New York: Foundation Center, 2003.
3. "Research on Libraries and Librarianship" (annual report of the Office for Research and Statistics, American Library Association), *Bowker Annual Library and Book Trade Information*, New York: R. R. Bowker.
4. D. Kight and E. Perry, "Grant Resources on the Web," *C&RL News* (July/August 1999): 543–45.
5. Penny Kyker, "Selected World Wide Web Sites for Library Grants and Fund-Raising," *Library Administration & Management* 12 (Spring 1998): 64–71.

After identifying possible research agencies, Lynch and others recommend gathering as much information as possible about the agencies' interests and what they have supported in the past.[13] In addition, it is usually advisable to contact the potential grantors at an early date to inform them of one's intent to apply for support and to provide the agency with a brief, written description of the proposed research. Feedback gained at this stage can help to assess the interest of the organization, refine the project, and expedite consideration of the formal proposal to follow. Personal contact at this point can be especially beneficial.

According to an article published in the *Chronicle of Higher Education*, grant officers are in agreement that foundations look at three basic qualities when reviewing grant proposals: the significance of the problem proposed for investigation, the quality of the proposed solution, and the research records of the persons planning to carry out the research. The article includes a list of reference collections operated or coordinated by the Foundation Center, a nonprofit organization established in 1956.[14] According to the Grantsmanship Center, reviewers of proposals are most interested in the purpose and definition of the project, the priority of the project, the financial information, the background of the requesting organization, personnel, and evaluation of the project. A workshop document prepared by the University of Michigan's Division of Research Development and Administration listed nine questions that a foundation is likely to ask when reviewing a proposal:

1. Is the proposal problem solving?
2. Is the problem important?
3. Is this the appropriate foundation?
4. Is the proposal innovative?
5. Will the project become self-supporting?
6. Can the proposing group do the work?
7. Is the project demonstrative (i.e., can it be used as a model)?

8. How will the program be evaluated?
9. Is the amount of money requested sufficient?

Another key to obtaining funding is identifying research areas that are considered timely. From time to time, "inventories" of needed research studies have been produced and may be of some assistance in the identification of topics likely to be seen as relatively high priorities by funding agencies. Though dated now, a good example of such a document was published in 1981 by Cuadra Associates, for the U.S. Department of Education Office of Libraries and Learning Technologies. Titled *A Library and Information Science Research Agenda for the 1980's*, it reflected the input of 26 library and information science researchers and practitioners.[15] More recent research agendas include "Research Agenda for College Librarianship,"[16] "A Research Agenda for Libraries,"[17] "A Research Agenda for YALSA,"[18] "In Search of Practical Applications: A Public Services Research Agenda for University Libraries,"[19] "Research Agenda for Library Instruction and Information Literacy,"[20] "SLA Research Statement,"[21] "ARL 2000 Program Plan," which outlines eight objectives for the ARL agenda,[22] *The Digital Reference Research Agenda*,[23] and the "Council on Library and Information Resources (CLIR) Agenda."[24] The Spring 2003 issue of *Library Trends*, titled "Research Questions for the Twenty-first Century," identifies problems and questions that need to be addressed by research and considers how they might be approached.[25]

SUMMARY

The proposal is as essential to successful research as the outline is to good writing. It represents what should be the careful planning that precedes a well-conceived research study. The proposal should spell out, to a reasonable degree, the details of a proposed research project and serve as a guide to which the researcher may refer as he or she carries out the study.

In terms of format, most research proposals are essentially the same. The elements generally included are the title page, abstract, literature review, hypothesis and assumptions, definitions, research design, data analysis, a budget if appropriate, anticipated results, limitations, and references. A timetable, which can be quite useful in keeping the research project on schedule, may be appended or may be integrated throughout the text of the proposal.

There is a variety of characteristics that can increase the attractiveness of a proposal. Most of these attributes simply result from the proposal's being well written and from the author's using an appropriate, attractive format. Perhaps most important, the proposal should be clear, straightforward, and succinct.

There is also a variety of features that may detract from a research proposal. They range from unsound hypotheses to excessive budgets, with the most common problems being inexplicit proposals, unsound designs, and unqualified investigators. It is important for any research proposal to be as free of detracting features as possible, but this is particularly crucial for proposals for sponsored research.

NOTES

[1]Gerald W. Lundeen, "Research Record," *Journal of Education for Librarianship* 24 (Winter 1984): 206–7.

[2]Bluma C. Peritz, "The Methods of Library Science Research: Some Results from a Bibliometric Survey," *Library Research* 2 (Fall 1980): 251–68.

[3]Martyvonne M. Nour, "A Quantitative Analysis of the Research Articles Published in Core Library Journals of 1980," *Library and Information Science Research* 7 (July 1985): 261–73.

[4]Patricia E. Feehan et al., "Library and Information Science Research: An Analysis of the 1984 Journal Literature," *Library and Information Science Research* 9 (July 1987): 173–85.

[5]Ronald R. Powell, "Recent Trends in Research: A Methodological Essay," *Library and Information Science Research* 21, no. 1 (1999): 91–119.

[6]Paul D. Leedy and Jeanne E. Ormrod, *Practical Research: Planning and Design*, 7th ed. (Upper Saddle River, NJ: Merrill Prentice Hall, 2001): 123.

[7]"National Institute of Child Health and Human Development, Quick Tips: Most Common Reasons for Disapproval," Sep 4, 2002. Available, *http://www.nichd.nih.gov/about/cpr/dbs/tip4.htm*.

[8]Mary Jo Lynch, "Proposal Procedures: Guidelines for ALA Units," (Chicago: ALA Office for Research, 1981): 15.

[9]Ibid., 16.

[10]Bill Becker, "Library Grant Money on the Web: A Resource Primer," *Searcher* 11, no. 10 (November/December, 2003): 8–14.

[11]David G. Bauer, *"How To" Grants Manual: Successful Grantseeking Techniques for Obtaining Public and Private Grants*, 4th ed. (Phoenix, AZ: American Council on Education/Oryx Press, 1999).

[12]Richard L. Waters, "Fund Raising: Grants and Other Bits of Information," *Public Library Quarterly* 17, no. 3 (1999): 51–54.

[13]Lynch, "Proposal Procedures."

[14]Suzanne Perry, "Getting a Foundation Grant Takes More Than a Good Idea, Program Officers Say," *Chronicle of Higher Education* 25 (October 1982): 25–28.

[15]*A Library and Information Science Research Agenda for the 1980's* U.S. Department of Education Office of Libraries and Learning Technologies, (Los Angeles: Cuadra Associates, 1981).

[16]"Research Agenda for College Librarianship," *College & Research Libraries News* 56, no. 7 (July/August, 1995): 470–71, 485.

[17]"A Research Agenda for Libraries," *Publishing Research Quarterly* (Fall 1994): 78.

[18]"A Research Agenda for YALSA," *Youth Services in Libraries* (Spring 1995): 267–71.

[19]Barbara A. Dewey, "In Search of Practical Applications: A Public Services Research Agenda for University Libraries," *Journal of Academic Librarianship* (September 1997): 371–79.

[20]"Research Agenda for Library Instruction and Information Literacy; the Updated Version," *College & Research Libraries News* (February 2003): 108–13. Available, *www.ala.org/Content/ContentGroups/ACRLI/IS/ISCommittees/Web_pages/Research/Research_Committee.html*

[21]Special Libraries Association. "Putting our knowledge to work: A New SLA Research Statement." Web page, June 2001. Available *http://ww.sla.org/content/memberservice/researchforum/rschstatement.cfm*.

[22]"ARL 2000 Program Plan." Available, *http://www.arl.org/arl/pplan00.html*.

[23]*The Digital Reference Research Agenda* (Chicago: Publications in Librarianship, Association of College and Research Libraries, no. 55, 2003).

[24]"Council on Library and Information Resources (CLIR) Agenda." Available, *http://www.clir.org/about/about.html* - agenda.

[25]M. J. Lynch, ed. "Research Questions for the Twenty-first Century," *Library Trends* 51, no. 4 (Spring 2003): 499–686.

Chapter 11

Writing the Research Report

Regardless of how well a research project is conceived and conducted, if its findings are not disseminated in some fashion, its value will be negligible. The research report, whether it is an unpublished document or a journal article, in print or electronic, remains an important vehicle for the dissemination of research results. The researcher should not consider his or her task complete until the research results have been made available to the appropriate audience, and in the best form possible. Meadows, in his book *Communicating Research*, states, "Communication lies at the heart of research."[1] Newman goes so far as to say, "Original scholarship and the publication that emerges from it are the moral obligations of those who accept public money to perform as intellectuals."[2] The Committee on Research and Statistics of ALA, in a June 2001 brochure, points out "that unless the implications of research are communicated to practitioners, the results are of little value."[3]

GENERAL OBJECTIVES OF THE RESEARCH REPORT

The general objectives of the research report are to acquaint the reader with the problem that has been investigated and to explain its implications or importance. The report should present the data fully and adequately; the data should support

269

the report's interpretations and conclusions. The report should interpret the data for the reader and demonstrate how the data help to resolve the problem.

In meeting these objectives, the research report should be as well structured and logical as possible. It should be a straightforward document that sets forth clearly and precisely what the researcher has done to solve, or at least to investigate, the research problem. It need not be a literary masterpiece, but it should be readable.

GENERAL OUTLINE OF THE RESEARCH REPORT

What follows is an outline of a relatively typical, thorough research report. Not all reports will present these items in exactly this order, or even include all of them. Others may include additional points. Most of these items were discussed in some detail earlier and therefore are basically listed here.

The Preliminaries/Front Matter

1. Abstract—A brief summary which restates the problem, the procedures, the main findings, and the major conclusions. It is usually about 200 words or less in length. It is considered optional unless the report or journal format specifically calls for it.
2. Title—The title, in effect, serves as part of the abstract and should, within a reasonable length, be descriptive of the study.
3. Copyright notice—U.S. copyright protection is effective for the life of the author plus seventy years. All U.S. publications automatically receive U.S. copyright protection, but there are possible advantages to be gained from actually registering a publication with the U.S. Copyright Office.
4. Acknowledgments (optional).
5. Table of contents—this is particularly important if the report is relatively long.
6. List of tables (where needed).
7. List of figures (graphic illustrations other than tables).

The Text

1. Introduction and problem
   a. Brief introduction—This is not always considered desirable as it usually summarizes the report and therefore becomes somewhat redundant. It can help to express the purpose of the study at an early point in the report.
   b. Statement of the problem—This section also typically includes a brief review of documents relevant to the problem.
   c. Identification of subproblems, if any.
   d. Delimitations of the study.

   e. Conceptual definitions of key terms.
   f. Abbreviations, if needed.
   g. Statement of the need for the study.
   h. A note on the organization of the remainder of the report.
2. Review of related literature—This review will build on the briefer literature review provided for the problem statement. It should provide the conceptual basis for the hypothesis to follow. It may also draw on related subject fields. If individuals are cited, their authority should be indicated.
3. Conceptual framework of the study—As is true for the proposal, many researchers prefer that this section precede the literature review and often include it in the introductory or problem section.
   a. Hypothesis(es) and/or research questions.
   b. Assumptions—These basic assumptions help to support the logic of the hypothesis.
   c. Operational definitions of important concepts.
4. Design of the study—The design of the study is broader than the basic research method (e.g., survey), which should already be apparent at this point. The description of the design should be clear and precise about what was done and how it was done.
   a. The population and sample, if any—This section should include a description of the research locale or setting if important.
   b. Sources of relevant data, including criteria for admissibility.
   c. Data collection techniques and instruments.
   d. Data analysis techniques.
5. Results
   a. Descriptive statistics, if utilized.
   b. Inferential statistics—The section where hypotheses, if any, are tested.
   c. Other findings—An optional section of miscellaneous findings or results not directly related to the hypothesis.
   d. Summary of results.
6. Summary and conclusions
   a. Summary of the study.
   b. Interpretations and conclusions.
   c. Limitations of the results.
   d. Recommendations, if any, for future research.

Back Matter

1. References—The list of citations or footnotes, if not provided at the appropriate locations in the text.
2. Bibliography—A list of other "classic" studies and highly relevant items; it also will include the references, if not listed separately.
3. Appendix—The appendix or appendices should include only supplementary material not essential to an understanding of the text.

GUIDELINES FOR ORGANIZING
AND PRESENTING THE RESEARCH REPORT

Organization of the Report

In organizing a research report of any length, it is always a good idea to develop and follow a detailed outline. In writing the report, it helps to organize the information by employing appropriate headings. Several manuals of style can be used for guidance in selecting headings.[4] One common approach is to utilize centered headings for the major division (all upper case letters), followed in a logical, hierarchical order by free-standing sideheads (capitals and lower case, underscored); paragraph sideheads (underscored, first word only capitalized, followed by a period); and fourth-level headings (capitals and lower case, underscored).

Footnotes and Documentation

In citing information borrowed from other works, it is again important to use accepted guidelines or manuals of style. The specific style to be employed may be left up to the author, though many journals and book publishers do prescribe a certain format. Regardless of who determines the style to be used, it is important to be consistent throughout the report.

Another general guideline is that, if material is borrowed from any source, whether it be a direct quotation or a paraphrase, then both the author and the work should be cited. If the quotation, or borrowed data, is extensive, and the report may be published or copyrighted, the writer should secure in writing from the holder of the copyright (usually the publisher) permission to reprint the material. In addition to the footnote or reference, the words "Reprinted by permission of the publisher (or author)" should be placed in an appropriate location or added to the footnote. Plagiarism is, of course, unethical and should be avoided at all costs.

Prose Style of the Report

It is generally recommended that a research report be written in the past tense, as it is a report of events which have already occurred. It is usually suggested that the writer employ the passive voice, which means that no identifiable subject is performing an act, and avoid the first person (see Losee and Worley[5] and Creswell[6] for a differing opinion as well as some other suggestions for writing and presenting the results of research).

The prose itself should be clear, exact, and efficient, and should reflect simple English. Regarding efficiency, Hillway argues that every statement that the writer makes should fall into one of the following four categories: (a) a direct statement of fact, (b) a basic assumption, (c) an expression of expert opinion, or (d) the author's personal opinion. It may be advisable to consider eliminating any other type of statement.[7]

Text Preparation

In preparing the text for the research report, it is again advisable to adhere to standard guidelines. Needless to say, general standards for neatness, accuracy, punctuation, and so on should be met. Aesthetics are also worth considering; for example, ample space should be left for margins and between the headings and text. Word processing and electronic publishing software facilitate the revision process. Electronic dictionaries and spell checkers are useful to identify misspellings, and electronic thesauri are helpful in selecting alternative words.

Graphic Presentation of Data

Graphics can in some cases present information more clearly and succinctly than can prose. At the very least, graphic presentations can help to supplement explanations and data presented in the text. There is a whole host of types of graphic presentations available, including statistical tables, line graphs, bar charts, pie charts, flowcharts, pictographs (simple pictures or cartoons), and maps. In using graphic representations, the researcher should remember, however, that they should be used only to facilitate the understanding of data. They are not intended to entertain and should not distract from the purpose of the text. Graphic representations should be kept as simple as possible, and they should be clear and accurate.

When designing graphic representations, the writer should see that each one is referred to in the text. It is also important that they be self-contained. In other words, each graphic should contain a title, an explanation of any symbols used, instructions on how to read or use the graphic, a brief description of what it is intended to show, and an indication of the sources of the data. Graphics should be placed as close as possible to the points in the text where they are first discussed.

EVALUATING THE RESEARCH REPORT

When reading a report of research, the informed, critical reader will generally look for the following: (a) adequacy of documentation, (b) accuracy of sources, (c) correctness of interpretation of sources, (d) appropriateness of data analysis, (e) basis for conclusions, (f) format and style, and (g) evidence of creativity. But there are many specific criteria worth considering, and they may be categorized according to the major sections of a typical research report. A checklist of such criteria, many of which were taken from Wynar, follows.[8]

SUGGESTED CRITERIA FOR JUDGING
A RESEARCH REPORT

1. Background
   a. Is the title descriptive, accurate, and of a reasonable length?
   b. Does the introduction give a clear indication of the general scope of the research?
   c. Is the reason or purpose for the research sufficiently indicated?
   d. Is the problem clearly stated and analyzed into definite subordinate questions or issues where appropriate?
   e. Is the logic of the analysis of the problem sound? In other words, have the critical factors been identified, relationships properly identified, and so on?
   f. What is the hypothesis or research question?
   g. Is the hypothesis of social or theoretical significance, and is it stated so that it can be resolved or tested?
   h. Are the variables clear? Have they been designated as independent and dependent variables where appropriate? Any logical consequences or implications?
   i. Are the basic assumptions needed to support the hypothesis made clear?
   j. Are adequate operational or working definitions provided?
   k. Is the coverage of previous, related research adequate? Is the report related to the earlier studies?
2. Design of the study
   a. Does the research design seem adequate and logical for the solution of the problem?
   b. Are the reasons for its choice adequately explained?
   c. Was the methodology explained in an understandable way so that it can be replicated?
   d. If important terms are used in an unusual sense, are they defined?
   e. Are the data collected adequate for the solution of the problem? In other words, do we have satisfactory measurements of the relevant variables?
   f. Are the data sufficiently quantitative (when appropriate) for the solution of the problem?
   g. Are the instruments used by the investigator adequate reflections of the conceptual variables of the study (i.e., do they measure the variables in a reliable and valid manner)?
   h. If sampling procedures were used, were they adequately explained?
   i. If the sample was supposedly random, was it in fact chosen so that each member of the population had an equal chance of being selected?
   j. If the researcher used the sample for generalizing, was it adequate for doing so?
   k. How reliable and valid is the design overall?
3. Treatment of the data
   a. Are the data presented as an integral part of the logical solution of the problem?

   b. What techniques were used to analyze the quantitative (or qualitative) data? Do they seem to be appropriate and effective?

   c. Were graphical and/or tabular formats appropriately used to display pertinent data?

   d. Is there evidence of care and accuracy in the collection and treatment of the data?

   e. Is irrelevant material or information excluded?

   f. Do the inferences based on the data seem to be sound?

4. Summary and conclusions

   a. Do the conclusions actually serve to answer questions or issues raised in the study?

   b. Are all conclusions based essentially on data made known to the reader?

   c. Are conclusions free from mere unsupported opinions?

   d. Are the limitations or qualifications of the conclusions clearly and concisely expressed?

   e. Are applications and recommendations, when included, judiciously made?

   f. Can the conclusions be generalized to a larger population?

   g. Did the researcher appear to be aware of the theoretical implications, if any, of the research?

   h. Did the researcher make recommendations for future research?

5. Appendices

   a. If there is an appendix, is it supplementary in nature, rather than essential to an understanding of the text?

   b. Does it include all original data?

6. Bibliography

   a. Does it appear that one style manual was followed (i.e., is the bibliographic style consistent)?

Other authors have developed similar checklists for evaluating research reports, including Mouly,[9] Busha and Harter,[10] Marchant and Smith,[11] Robbins,[12] and Isaac and Michael.[13] Leedy, in a useful work titled *How to Read Research and Understand It*, guides the reader through the evaluation of actual research reports.[14] A book by Hittleman and Simon is a useful guide for the consumer of research.[15] Entire books devoted to the evaluation of research articles include those written by Pyrczak[16] and Girden.[17]

In reading and evaluating a research report, the reader would be well advised to be particularly watchful for certain faults commonly exhibited by reports. Among these weaknesses are the following:

1. Broad, sweeping statements without sufficient evidence or documentation to support them.

2. A lack of precision in statements, or a tendency to state ideas vaguely.

3. A weak organization and arrangement.

4. A failure to describe fully and clearly the method by which the hypothesis was tested, or even a failure to test the hypothesis.
5. A lack of direct linking of the problem to the hypothesis. As was discussed earlier, the hypothesis should represent at least a partial solution to the problem, and therefore must be related to it.
6. A failure to distinguish adequately between the problem and the purpose of the study. In essence, the problem represents what was studied, and the purpose reflects why it was studied.
7. Incorporating information or materials from some source without clearly indicating how they were derived from the source.
8. Bringing new elements, concepts, or ideas into the summary and/or conclusions without having introduced them earlier in the study.
9. Writing the final report as originally conceived rather than as the findings dictate. In other words, the researcher must be sensitive to the results of the research and not be hesitant to reflect them in the conclusions, even when they are contrary to expectations.[18]

PUBLISHING RESEARCH RESULTS

"Librarians have a fundamental responsibility to contribute to professional communication."[19] "The research process is *not* complete until it has been reported."[20] Libraries cannot benefit from the results of research if they are not published.[21] Or, as Hillway stated, "To make his discoveries known to the world, the scholar must accept the task of publication as one of his essential responsibilities."[22] Unfortunately, according to a study conducted by Powell, Baker, and Mika, only 26% of librarians publish research results.[23]

Early in the process of "getting published," the would-be author must decide on the format to be employed, the report vehicle, and the likely audience. Among the most common formats are monographs, scholarly articles in journals, papers delivered at professional meetings (often appearing in conference proceedings), unpublished reports such as those collected by ERIC, and dissertations. The last two are not publications in the conventional sense; but unpublished reports sometimes, and dissertations almost always, represent original research.

Researchers who have decided to publish their research results in the journal article format must know the journals (vehicles) in which they might publish; select a subject for a manuscript (essentially done when the research was initiated); determine the methodology and style of writing to employ; write the manuscript; prepare the manuscript for submission (as dictated by the journal's instructions to authors); work with the editor in the review of the manuscript; and, if accepted for publication, tend to the final editing and proofreading of the manuscript and galley proofs.[24]

Regarding the selection of a vehicle and audience, Busha and Harter have a useful section in their book on research methods.[25] They discuss the major types of outlets for written research reports and cite numerous examples. As Busha and Harter note, "the selection of a publication vehicle in which to communicate a research report should depend upon the topic of the study, the nature of the material presented, and the desired audience."[26] Electronic journals are becoming an increasingly common option.

O'Connor and Van Orden report on the results of a survey of 33 national library periodicals.[27] They focus on identifying an author's chances of having an unsolicited manuscript published and on the review process for selecting manuscripts for publication. They point out the importance of journal editors' publishing the purpose and scope of their periodicals and their methods and criteria for reviewing manuscripts and the importance of prospective authors' being aware of them. More recent articles updating and supplementing the analysis done by O'Connor and Van Orden were published in 1988[28] and 1996.[29]

When journal referees evaluate manuscripts, they generally address criteria similar to those used to evaluate research reports (see the criteria provided earlier in this chapter). A referee's report used by the *Library Quarterly* asks the referee to answer the following questions:

1. Does the study address a significant problem, topic, or issue?
2. Does the work offer fresh insights or original treatment of the problem?
3. Does the author demonstrate a command of the relevant literature?
4. Are the research methods appropriate to the problem?
5. Are there flaws in the methods, arguments, or data analyses?
6. Are the conclusions justified by the results of the analysis?
7. Do the findings confirm, expand, revise, or challenge conventional knowledge or professional consensus?
8. Is the paper well organized and clearly written?
9. Is the paper interesting to read?

Would-be authors wishing to report their research results in book format must follow a procedure not much different from that for publishing a journal article. "The author's major responsibility is to develop the idea, to write the manuscript, and to deliver it to the publisher in an acceptable and readable form."[30] Just as one should take care to select the most appropriate journal, one should shop around for a book publisher. Factors to consider in selecting a publisher include pricing, design, marketing, editorial assistance, production schedule, review process, and royalty arrangements. Those wishing to know more about the book contract may wish to refer to the work by Schuman just quoted. Morris highlights the fundamentals of writing and publishing books and journal articles from the perspective of the school library media specialist.[31]

A book by Schroeder and Roberson provides listings of library-related periodicals, electronic journals and newsletters, publications of state library associations, and refereed journals.[32] St. Clair provides a useful article on publishing library research.[33] Giesecke, former editor of *Library Administration & Management*, describes the different types of publications and journals and the most effective methods for preparing the report based on the type of publication.[34] She also includes information on common mistakes made by authors, which provides a helpful checklist. Labaree provides a practical list of tips for academic librarians for getting published in scholarly journals.[35] ACRL's *InPrint: Publishing Opportunities for College Librarians* provides descriptive information about submitting manuscripts and journal data for library and information science journals and related journals.[36] A description of the publication and sample entries are available at http://acrl.telusys.net/epubs. "How to Get Published in LIS Journals: A Practical Guide," is included in its entirety in Appendix B. Gordon provides pertinent information on how to integrate writing with practice, how to develop ideas for writing, and how to handle rejections for submitted papers.[37] The New Members Round Table of ALA provides a discussion group, NMRTWriter, dedicated to supporting librarians wishing to write and publish articles and books.

Graduates of doctoral programs are encouraged to publish their dissertations as books and/or to summarize them for publication in a journal. In doing so, they should remove much of the redundancy typical of dissertations, decrease some of the details regarding previous research and methodology, and relate the work to the concrete world as much as possible. The *Publication Manual of the American Psychological Association* addresses converting a dissertation into an article.[38]

SUMMARY

Unless the results of research are properly communicated, all of the efforts that went into the research are, to a great extent, for naught. The first basic step required for disseminating the results of research is the writing of the report. This report should be a straightforward document that clearly, precisely, and efficiently describes what the researcher has done to investigate a problem.

The research report should be well organized and generally follow a standard, recommended format. The researcher should exercise care in the documentation for and writing of the report. It should be neat and error free. Graphic presentations should be used where appropriate. The writer should be aware of what the informed reader would be looking for and be careful to avoid the common faults of research reports.

In writing the report and looking ahead to its publication, the researcher should keep in mind the audience that it should reach and the method of publication or dissemination likely to be used. It is important to be aware of the review mechanisms of journals and to tailor manuscripts to their criteria and interests. In conclusion, the importance of reporting research results should not be underestimated. The research report, regardless of format, is what communicates specific information to an audience, adds to the general body of knowledge, and hopefully stimulates further research.

NOTES

[1] A. J. Meadows, *Communicating Research* (San Diego: Academic Press, 1998): ix.

[2] John Newman, "Academic Librarians as Scholars," *College & Research Libraries News* (January 1998): 19.

[3] "Dissemination of Research in LIS: a statement by the American Library Association Committee on Research and Statistics." Webpage, June 2001. Available *http://www.ala.org/orscommittes/ dissemination/dissemination.htm.*

[4] Paul D. Leedy and Jeanne E. Ormrod, *Practical Research: Planning and Design*, 7th ed. (Upper Saddle River, NJ: Merrill Prentice Hall, 2001): 285–86.

[5] Robert M. Losee, Jr., and Karen A. Worley, *Research and Evaluation for Information Professionals* (San Diego: Academic Press, 1993): 217.

[6] John W. Creswell, *Research Design: Qualitative and Quantitative Approaches* (Thousand Oaks, CA: Sage Publications, 1994): 201.

[7] Tyrus Hillway, *Introduction to Research*, 2d ed. (Boston, MA: Houghton Mifflin, 1964): 265.

[8] Dan Wynar, *Syllabus for Research Methods in Librarianship* (Denver, CO: Graduate School of Librarianship, 1962): 129–30.

[9] George J. Mouly, *Educational Research: The Art and Science of Investigation* (Boston, MA: Allyn & Bacon, 1978): 343–44.

[10] Charles A. Busha, and Stephen P. Harter, *Research Methods in Librarianship: Techniques and Interpretations* (New York: Academic Press, 1980): 28.

[11] Maurice P. Marchant and N. M. Smith, "Research Thrust of Brigham Young University's Library School," *Journal of Education for Librarianship* 20 (Fall 1979): 132.

[12] Jane B. Robbins, "The Quality of Published Library and Information Science Research," *Library and Information Science Research* 13 (Spring 1991): 315–17.

[13] Stephen Isaac and William Burton Michael, *Handbook in Research and Evaluation: A Collection of Principles, Methods and Strategies Useful in the Planning, Design, and Evaluation of Studies in Education and the Behavioral Sciences*, 3d ed. (San Diego: EdITS, 1995): 238.

[14] Paul D. Leedy, *How to Read Research and Understand It* (New York: Macmillan, 1981).

[15] Daniel R. Hittleman and Alan J. Simon, *Interpreting Educational Research: An Introduction for Consumers of Research*, 3d ed. (Upper Saddle River, NJ: Merrill, Prentice Hall, 2002).

[16] Fred Pyrczak, *Evaluating Research in Academic Journals: A Practical Guide to Realistic Evaluation* (Los Angeles: Pyrczak Publishing, 1999).

[17] Ellen R. Girden, *Evaluating Research Articles from Start to Finish*, 2d ed. (Thousand Oaks, CA: Sage Publications, 2001).

[18] Hillway, *Introduction to Research*, 274–75.

[19] James G. Neal, "Editorial: The Librarian Research and Publication Imperative," *Library and Information Science Research* 17 (Spring 1995): 199.

[20] Jane B. Robbins, "Affecting Librarianship in Action: The Dissemination and Communication of Research Findings," in *Applying Research to Practice*, edited by Leigh L. Estabrook (Urbana-Champaign: University of Illinois, Graduate School of Library and Information Science, 1992): 78.

[21] Larry N. Osborne, "Research Record," *Journal of Education for Library and Information Science* 25 (Spring 1985): 318.

[22] Hillway, *Introduction to Research*, 156.

[23] Ronald R. Powell, Lynda M. Baker, and Joseph J. Mika, "Library and Information Science Practitioners and Research," *Library and Information Science Research* 24 (2002): 49–72.

[24] Richard D. Johnson, "The Journal Article," in *Librarian/Author: A Practical Guide on How to Get Published*, edited by Betty-Carol Sellen (New York: Neal-Schuman Publishers, 1985): 21–35.

[25] Busha and Harter, *Research Methods in Librarianship*.

[26] Ibid., 374.

[27] Daniel O'Connor and Phyllis Van Orden, "Getting into Print," *College and Research Libraries* 39 (September 1978): 389–96.

[28]John Budd, "Publication in Library and Information Science: The State of the Literature," *Library Journal* 113 (September 1988): 125–31.

[29]Barbara J. Via, "Publishing in the Journal Literature of Library and Information Science: A Survey of Manuscript Review Processes and Acceptance," *College and Research Libraries* 57 (July 1996): 365–76.

[30]Patricia G. Schuman, "From Book Idea to the Contract," in *Librarian/Author: A Practical Guide on How to Get Published*, edited by Betty-Carol Sellen (New York: Neal-Schuman Publishers, 1985): 37.

[31]Betty J. Morris, "Getting Published: What Every Library Media Specialist Needs to Know," *Knowledge Quest* 26, no. 3 (March/April 1998): 16–17.

[32]Carol F. Schroeder, and Gloria G. Roberson, *Guide to Publishing Opportunities for Librarians* (New York: Haworth Press, 1995).

[33]Gloriana St. Clair, "Improving Quality: An Editor's Advice to Authors," *College and Research Libraries* 54 (May 1993): 195–97.

[34]Joan Giesecke, "Preparing Research for Publication," *Library Administration and Management* 12, no. 3 (Summer 1998): 134–37.

[35]Robert V. Labaree, "Tips for Getting Published in Scholarly Journals: Strategies for Academic Librarians," *College & Research Libraries News* 65, no. 3 (March 2004): 137–39.

[36]Alice Harrison Bahr, Michael J. McLane, and Lynn W. Livingston, *InPrint: Publishing Opportunities for College Librarians* (Chicago: Association of College and Research Libraries, 1997).

[37]Rachel Singer Gordon, "Getting Started in Library Publication," *American Libraries* 35, no. 1 (January 2004): 66–69.

[38]*Publication Manual of the American Psychological Association*, 5th ed. (Washington, DC: American Psychological Association, 2001): 326–29.

Appendix A

Domain Assumptions of Research

by Jack D. Glazier

BASIC DOMAIN QUESTIONS

While there are many elements and aspects of the research process that are important to the production of valid and reliable research results, there is one general aspect that tends to be overlooked. That aspect has to do with the domain assumptions that individuals carry into any research project. Domain assumptions are those assumptions that are the most basic and serve to structure individuals' belief systems as well as their lives in general. In structuring belief systems and lives, domain assumptions and the modern concept of research intersect.

Research is a complex undertaking because, whether basic or applied, it is the pursuit of knowledge. The ancient Greeks classified knowledge in two forms, "doxa" or opinion and "episteme" or knowledge or truth. The early Greek philosophers and historians, for the most part, generated "doxa" or opinion. They did so because they relied on speculation and myth as opposed to sensation or experience for their knowledge. This did not mean that they accepted "doxa" as the only legitimate means for knowing the world around them as evidenced by

281

the fact that the Greeks had a separate word, "episteme," that they used for "knowledge or truth." This means that two problems that existed for the ancient Greeks are still relevant for modern researchers. The first problem has to do with the epistemological and ontological assumptions that all researchers carry into their work. The second one is concerned with the metatheoretical organization, dynamics, and linkages among theories, paradigms, and disciplines.

Before researchers can begin designing research projects, deciding on the methods and methodologies to be employed, and making decisions relative to sample size or strategies, they must first reflect upon their basic epistemological and ontological assumptions. These are the personal assumptions that all researchers and most individuals encounter in the process of figuring out who one really is, what is accepted as knowledge or "episteme," what is opinion or "doxa," and how persons come to know what they think they know. What one believes comprises both how reality is ascertained and the content of such a reality.

These philosophical questions are fundamental to learning and discovery. They are questions that are as old as learning itself. But they are also questions to which mankind has been unable to find a single correct answer. They are part of each individual's world view (Weltanschauung) or belief system that is taken for granted as one goes about his or her daily activities. However, when it comes to research, one's belief system takes on greater significance because it provides the domain assumptions upon which the work and knowledge of research are based.

Before one examines the nature of epistemology and ontology, consideration must be given to how individuals acquire their belief systems and knowledge. This has implications for researchers in terms of what Camic refers to as the predecessor-selection processes.[1] It also has implications for the formulation of what Mullins[2] calls theory groups and the ultimate emergence of new disciplines.

Individuals acquire knowledge and belief systems from parents, teachers, experiences, and other sources too numerous to list here. Some of this knowledge and the bases for one's value and belief system appear early in life as a result of conditioning and role imitation of our parents and siblings and link all phases of one's upbringing (Cooley,[3] Baldwin,[4, 5] Freud,[6] Mead[7]). Most of this early knowledge and training is formative and not gained by the choice of the receiver. However, as people grow older they are able to select, within limits, what to learn and from whom.

This selection process is a topic considered in the works of Mullins[8] and Camic.[9] Mullins documents how individuals choose the theories they adopt and how they carry and transmit these to others who in turn carry on the traditions of their predecessors.[10] Camic articulates with more specificity the processes by which scholarly knowledge is transmitted.[11] This transmission, he argues, is driven by rational linkages between concepts and cumulative growth. It is contingent on a "content-fit" that brings together, according to Maines, Bridger, and Ulmer, "scholars [who] purposely select predecessors whose work fits their own intellectual purposes."[12] This relates directly to the development and transmission of theories, paradigms, and disciplines discussed later in this chapter.

UNDERSTANDING THEORIES OF KNOWLEDGE

Etymology, Nature, and Role of Epistemology and Ontology

The study of knowledge has been referred to since the time of the ancient Greeks as epistemology. The Greek root word for this term is "episteme," the word used earlier meaning "knowledge or truth." The suffix "ology" comes from the Greek "logos" meaning "the principle of reason or theory." These elements come together to form the concept of epistemology as "theory of knowledge." Runes formally defines epistemology as "[t]he origin, structure, methods, and validity of knowledge."[13] However, understanding the etymology and formal definition of the term conveys only limited information about the role of epistemology, the historical and modern range of theories of knowledge, and their impact on research.

Grounding our epistemological perspective is our ontological perspective. The term ontology comes from the Greek words "ontos" meaning "being" and "logos" meaning "theory." "Being" is the extended term with the concept of existence subsumed under it. Together, the word ontology is formed which means "theory of being or existence." Aristotle argued that this was the First Philosophy—the study of the nature of things. Runes defines ontology as "[t]he science of fundamental principles."[14]

The role of ontology is to serve as the basis for all things including the nature of knowledge. The role of epistemology is to serve as the foundation upon which to build one's knowledge of the world. An individual's ontological perspective must come first, then followed by her or his epistemological position. However, as is frequently the case, to articulate one requires simultaneously considering the other. In this case, as epistemology is discussed, by necessity so is ontology. This is especially true when the subjective/objective continuum is examined. Ontology not only encompasses the fundamentals of knowledge but also has implications for our understanding of being.

However, it is epistemology that is the foundation of the assumptions that ground the research methodologies that we employ to gather data and that supplies the basis for the means of analysis from which we interpret our data and draw our conclusions. These assumptions are not universals. They can and frequently do differ from individual to individual. As a result, there may be as many interpretations of the meaning of data as there are individuals doing the analysis and interpretation. As McNall observes, "Just because someone has grown up in society, he is not a qualified interpreter of human experience."[15] And so it is in libraries and library and information science. The very fact that one has been socialized in or is intimately familiar with libraries and their ways brings with it certain assumptions and biases that can impede rather than facilitate research related to libraries and those associated with them.

Subjective/Objective Continuum

The subjective/objective continuum encompasses a broad range of ontological perspectives on knowledge. At one end of the continuum there is pure or radical subjectivism. A radical subjectivist, if there is such a person, believes in a world that is entirely phenomenal (see Figure A.1). That is, a person understands that a world of objects is a mere projection of the mind and there is no truly external or objective world. The world of reality exists in the mind of the individual. This position is often referred to as "idealism." It is the position of radical subjectivists who pose problems in terms of empirical data gathering for several reasons. First, in an entirely subjective world, how do minds communicate since there is no independent existence? If all a person can know is what is in her or his own mind and everything else is an extension of individual minds, are individuals not truly "islands unto ourselves?" Such isolation, according to Runes, is solipsistic to the extent that the individual self is viewed as the whole of reality while others and the external world are only representations of the self with no independent existence.[16] What this implies is that there can be no independent, external sense data to gather and analyze. This is a problem with which philosophers historically have struggled—the question of a mind/matter duality. In fact, the question becomes, how do we even know that we as individuals exist? This was the question that provoked the famous aphorism by the seventeenth-century philosopher Rene Descartes: "Cogito ergo sum" (I think, therefore I am).

Second, at the other end of the spectrum, is the view of pure or radical objectivism. An individual who would be labeled a radical objectivist is one who believes in a world that is entirely nominal and empirically accessible. This position is often referred to as "materialism." This is a world in which individuals are able to perceive sense data directly and objectively without the interference of personal values or opinions.

However, most modern researchers fall somewhere between the two poles of radical subjectivism and radical objectivism. Most individuals recognize the existence of an external world that can be perceived in the form of sense data. Sense data are data that can be empirically gathered and analyzed, and from which conclusions can be drawn. Still, most also recognize that when a researcher gathers data and begins the process of analysis, that researcher must be

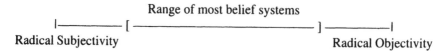

Range of most belief systems

|—————— [———————————————————] ——————|
Radical Subjectivity   Radical Objectivity

FIGURE A.1.   The Subjective/Objective Continuum

aware that he or she carries within himself or herself sets of values and beliefs that influence perception. In other words, what we perceive is filtered through our systems of values and beliefs and to that extent loses some degree of objectivity.

It is this filtering system of which the researcher must first be aware. By understanding personal dynamics and being reflexive (aware of one's self and what is going on in the general proximity and broader contexts which might influence perception), the researcher attempts to limit the extent to which sense data are colored by these personal and proximal influences. Hence, the degree of objectivity that the researcher is able to achieve depends largely on his or her skill at recognizing and limiting subjective or outside influences. As the renowned social psychologist/philosopher Campbell notes,[17]

> the goal of objectivity in science is a noble one, and dearly to be cherished. It is in true worship of this goal that we remind our selves that our current views of reality are partial and imperfect.

The second point that must concern the researcher is the transition from sense data to words and concepts. This has to do with what Maines and Chen call "human symbolization."[18] In essence the process begins with the assignment of a symbol or set of symbols to perceived sense data.[19] The symbols become a representation in communication of the elements in sense data. Representations are interpretations by the observer calling for, once again, care in their application. Such representations are a form of communicative action within the context of the social process in what has been described as "structuration."[20] These are first-order symbols that later are translated into second-order symbols in the form of printed or electronic words and concepts and thereby become critical elements in Habermas' "theory of communicative action."[21] In other words, the assignment of symbols (first-order) to sense data and the later transfer of those symbols to words and concepts (second-order symbols) becomes an important link in the process of social action, an important end for research and society.

However, research by itself is of little value until it is communicated by means of print or other media. Understanding the communication processes is, therefore, an important part of understanding the research process. The application of symbols to sense data supports Maines and Chen's contention that consciousness is a result of social interaction.[22] The assignment of symbols is an important part of the communication process for, without symbols, mankind has nothing with which to communicate. Accordingly, Maines and Chen argue that "referential symbols designate objects, events, qualities, and sequences."[23] While not limited to vocalizations, referential symbols begin at that point but are further extended to print and other forms of communication relative to research results and processes. It is the pursuit of this goal that is the point of our meticulous efforts to design good research and select appropriate methods and methodologies. It is to this end that the sciences, natural and social, must be committed.

METHODS AND METHODOLOGIES

Etymology and Role of Methods and Methodologies

Understanding what is meant by methods and methodology and the difference between the two is found again in the examination of each term. Method comes from the Greek words "meta" meaning "from or after" and "hodos" meaning "journey." These terms can be understood to mean the "journey or pursuit after or of" some end. Runes defines method as "[a]ny procedure employed to attain a certain end."[24] In this case, the end is the data to be gathered and the method is the means. However, the habit of referring to research methods and methodologies as interchangeable is misleading.

The term methodology originates with the same Greek terms as the word method. This enables individuals to use the term method as the root word in understanding the intricacies of the broader term methodology. Adding the now familiar Greek suffix "logos" meaning "study, theory, or principle of reason" to the root word "method" leaves the word methodology meaning "a study of the plans which are used to obtain knowledge" as defined by Polkinghorne.[25] Thus, while the term method refers to specific means of collecting data, methodology refers to the strategies surrounding the use of multiple methods of data collection as required by different types of attempts to achieve higher degrees of reliability and validity. The topics of triangulation and the various types of validity and reliability are covered in more detail elsewhere in this book.

Methods, Methodologies, and Theories of Knowledge

The methodological selection of particular data collection methods relies on various criteria. At this juncture, the concern is with the epistemological bases for selection. Earlier, the discussion centered on the extremes of the subjective/objective continuum. However, these only represent theoretical polar extremes and have few operational implications for day-to-day research design and implementation. Now consideration will be extended to both the actual role, historical and present, of epistemological perspectives and the research process.

Historically, arguments concerning what constituted acceptable research centered on the degree of empiricism required. Some ancient Greeks chose to speculate hypothetically on objects of interest to scholars of the time. The subjective aspect of the speculative arts became suspect, tainted by an individual's values and beliefs. Others, particularly Aristotle, attempted to forge links between the more objective empiricism of science and the more subjective speculation of philosophy through the process of systematizing the knowledge of their predecessors. Aristotle accomplished this by utilizing empirical observation, conceptual categorization, and analysis through the development and use of categorical logic.

Many philosophers relied upon what Francis Bacon later formalized as the inductive method for the means of studying nature. It was a method grounded in empiricism and in search of increased objectivity, through empirical data gathering and generalization or extrapolation. Extrapolation, then, became a key element in the reemergence of a predictive natural science that relies upon strict objectivity. This was the deductive method. Many natural and social scientists now rely on the scientific method (i.e., deductive research as discussed in more detail in this book).

The pursuit of objectivity became reified as the scientific method became widely used, leaving its proponents little tolerance for other, more subjective methods of gathering data. This was the position of the positivists who sought to rely on the most objective methods available and the logic that converted language into a mathematical form, abandoning emotion as subjective, noninformative, and purely emotive.

Positivism with its formal origins in the works of Comte in the mid-19th century emerged in the 20th century as modernism. It is characterized as structured, rigid, and highly rational. It revered the natural sciences for their certainty and rationality. However, the modernist tradition was marked by the emergence of multiple, rival paradigms to challenge the hegemony of positivism. Out of this came a theoretical, multidisciplinary synthesis that became known as postmodernism. It is characterized by its theoretical flexibility and pluralistic paradigms.

The differences among the belief systems and methodological debates involving positivism, modernism, and the postmodern movement occur within the framework of the distinction between the Greek terms "episteme" and "doxa." The term "episteme" comes from two terms "epi" meaning "upon" and "(hi)stanai" meaning "to stand, or something on which we can stand, certainty and knowledge." The second term, "doxa," means "opinion or belief." In other words, "doxa" is "What we believe is true" and "episteme" is "What we know is true." "Episteme" is representative of positivism just as "doxa" is representative of postmodernism. In addition, the change in emphasis from a more positivist orientation to a more postmodern orientation involves a return to more inductive approaches to research.

It is the objectivity that preoccupied the positivists, and the more subjective perspectives were increasingly prevalent during the modern and postmodern periods from which many of the newer methodological approaches have emerged. First, keep in mind that when trends regarding the legitimacy of various types of knowledge (objective/subjective) are considered, it is not the continuum's extremes being discussed. The methodological implications being considered here are to be viewed from a more generalist perspective. Second, if a theoretical exemplar of postmodernism were to be held up, constructionism might be a key. Constructionism is consistent with more subjective paradigms and methodological approaches. And, as in the case of symbolic interactionism, both qualitative (i.e., more subjective) and more quantitative approaches (i.e., more objective

288 APPENDIX A: DOMAIN ASSUMPTIONS OF RESEARCH

or less subjective) emphasize that the same theoretical paradigm can spawn multiple methodologies. Both quantitative (e.g., surveys, experiments) and qualitative (e.g., participant observation, interviews) methods are discussed in detail in this text.

DISCIPLINES, PARADIGMS, AND THEORIES

History and Context of Paradigmatic Change

Disciplines, paradigms, and theories are social constructions. They are not epiphenomenal in their origins. They are creations of scholars and theorists. They are not independent beings with a life independent of their creators. It is the reification of these concepts and the processes by which they are created and perpetuated that capture our attention here.

Numerous historians and sociologists of science have addressed these issues. Among the better known have been Thomas Kuhn, Nicholas Mullins, Charles Camic, and, most recently, Stephen J. Gould. It is, however, Kuhn's formulation that has been more widely discussed over the past several years, and he is best known for his views on paradigmatic revolution.[26] While Kuhn's position is not consistent with the one proposed here, he makes some important observations and is a good example of the dialectical process that occurs through intellectual exchanges.

Kuhn argues that paradigmatic revolutions are episodes "in which a scientific community abandons one time-honored way of regarding the world . . . in favor of another, usually incompatible approach to its discipline."[27] He suggests that it is these "revolutionary episodes" that advance science. The process, he argues, is a competition for domination of a particular discipline. His argument begins with the acknowledgement that scholars tend to congregate in ideological communities or, as Mullins noted, "theory groups." These are communities/groups in which members define themselves and are defined by others as being uniquely responsible for a specific set of shared goals, values, methods, and means of socialization.[28] The socialization processes include training their predecessors by passing on the rituals, myths, heroes, and traditions of the community. Thus, Kuhn's view that "[p]aradigms are something shared by members of such groups" becomes significant.[29]

In essence, Kuhn argues that paradigms are ways of collecting and understanding the nature of sense data. This process comprises the collection, understanding, and translation of sense data into theories and theories into paradigms that become a structuring device for understanding future data. This process is what he called the maturation of a paradigm. For Kuhn, "What changes with the transition to maturity is not the presence of a paradigm but rather its nature."[30]

When change comes for a mature paradigm, it does not come incrementally but in the form of a radical change—a revolution. Kuhn defines a revolution as "a special sort of change involving a certain sort of reconstructing of group commitments."[31] For example, Kuhn would argue that Einstein's theory of relativity was a revolutionary paradigmatic change within physics. This type of change is defined as revolutionary because it involves a sudden, unexpected change in the basic assumptions and theories grounding what was then Newtonian physics. The situation was that while extraordinary, Einstein's discovery was preceded by various theories regarding quantum mechanics and other foundational work in the general area of relativity that prepared the scientific community for Einstein's formulation. Hence, the ensuing reconstruction was less radical than we tend to recognize.

The processes associated with innovation tend to be dialectical in nature. Innovation builds on existing knowledge. New ideas are combined with existing belief systems resulting in a synthetic concept. This is an incremental process with new ideas being introduced in cloistered intellectual environments until a new paradigm and the public are ready for its introduction.

In actuality, the dynamics of innovation tend to be incremental for utilitarian reasons. The process itself is gradual in nature. Discoveries tend to be limited in scope because researchers work in narrow environments. Next is the dialectical stage in which the new discoveries are interpreted in light of existing facts and circumstances producing innovation. Finally, if people are not prepared for an innovation, if they cannot imagine it as possible, they will not intellectually invest in it. It will be simply viewed as an anomaly. Acceptance comes much more readily if people are prepared for change.

A familiar example of change that is slow to be accepted is the introduction of the on-line public access catalog (OPAC). The technology was available long before it was introduced in libraries on a large scale. In those communities that were gradually prepared for the move from the card catalog to the OPAC, the introduction was more easily accepted. It also helped that most communities operated both systems until patrons became familiar with using the new technology and that the International Standard Bibliographic Description (ISBD) record structure was familiar to patrons. Those who moved too fast with the introduction of the technology encountered much more resistance from patrons and others than those who were more deliberate.

While innovation is viewed here as dialectical and incremental, it may appear to the public as revolutionary at first. It is also defined by most as progress. This is a value judgment that Gould argues is a bias of our species.[32] His argument begins with a criticism of the view that Darwinism is evolutionary in an upward cycle with homo sapiens at the top of the hierarchy. This, he argues rightly, is an egocentric tendency that allows our bias to influence the interpretation of sense data. The data indicate that there are numerous species that change at their own rate and according to their needs without an innate natural order that favors mankind. Change is change for its own sake and out of necessity for survival based on its environment. This is the case with disciplines, paradigms, and theories. They change in response to their environments which are socially constructed. The idea that the dynamic of change is progress implies an egocentric social construction. Change is the response to environmental variables and whether it betters our situation is a value judgment.

Another Perspective on the Emergence of New Paradigms and Disciplines

One way of looking at disciplinary development and change that is less value laden is to understand it as an incremental social process that can be analyzed and understood in terms of social theory. The following formulation has emerged out of the works of Kuhn,[33, 34] Mullins[35] Grover and Glazier,[36] Powell and DiMaggio,[37] Glazier and Hall,[38] and Glazier and Grover.[39] However, Mullins' seminal work on theory and theory groups, as well as Powell's and DiMaggio's work on the new institutionalism, were central in formulating the general thesis presented here.

To begin, theories, paradigms, and disciplines, though reified, are merely labels we place on individuals so we can categorize their interests and beliefs.[40] Theories are no more than the people who develop them and believe in them. As with theories, paradigms are no more than those individuals who construct and subscribe to them. They each comprise people interacting with others. The unit of analysis is people and their social relationships. They are not some ethereal phenomena that can be studied and understood as abstract entities. This having been said, we will now begin what will at the outset appear to be an abstract analysis of the dynamics of disciplines, paradigms, and theories. However, we should again remember that what we will actually be talking about are people, their relationships, and the social constructions that structure them.

The process of structuring the social constructions which enable research is referred to as "structuration" by Giddens.[41] This process of structuring phenomena in the form of the self, society and individual knowledge, society and social knowledge, and discovered and undiscovered knowledge produces the context for the work of individuals as they endeavor to explain the conceptualization of the sense data they encounter as they go about both their daily activities and their specialized activities in the form of research. Glazier and Grover further argue that theories, paradigms, and eventually disciplines emanate from a context of these socially constructed arenas of knowledge discovery and production.[42]

As these dynamics work themselves out, often in the form of scholarly research which results in the theories that scholars come to represent, they are drawn together into what Mullins calls theory groups.[43] It is these theories which are the seeds of new divergent paradigms. Divergent paradigms are the products of initial research which is sporadic and yields loosely coupled, disorganized, and often inconsistent theories.[44] This is referred to as internal divergence (see Figure A.2) .

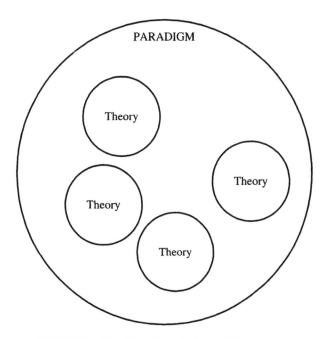

FIGURE A.2.   Paradigm Internal Divergence

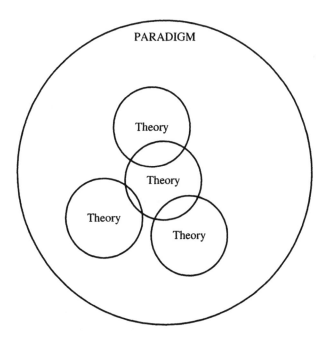

FIGURE A.3.   Paradigm Internal Convergence

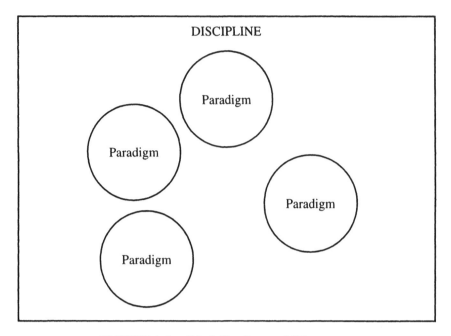

FIGURE A.4.   Discipline Internal Divergence

As research proceeds, the theories that make up each paradigm become more consistent, more organized, and more tightly coupled. This is referred to as internal convergence (see Figure A.3) .

Convergence yields planned research agendas and broader ranges of theorizing resulting in the emergence of new paradigms. The more theories converge, the more consistent are the paradigms. Again, initially these paradigms are externally divergent. The relations between divergent paradigms can be characterized as loosely coupled, accompanied by a high degree of environmental ambiguity, and generally lacking external consistency (see Figure A.4) . These relations also reflect the internal structure of divergent paradigms relative to their constituent theories discussed above.

It is important to keep in mind at this point that a paradigm is "a framework of basic assumptions with which perceptions are evaluated and relationships are delineated and applied to a discipline or profession."[45] The danger of studying paradigms is that they tend to become reified and treated as though they had a life of their own. They have a life only in the sense that their proponents use them to orient and direct their work.

Internal and external divergence and convergence of theories and paradigms are not the result of "natural law" or mystical force. Theoretical and paradigmatic change and organization are the result of the work of individual researchers and teachers working collectively or privately. Organizations are created between

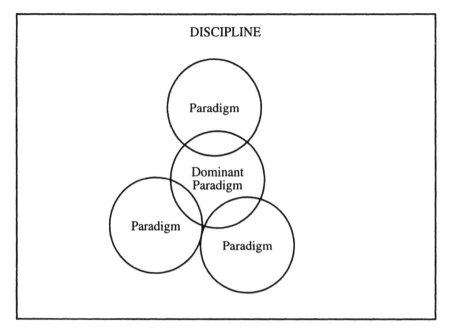

FIGURE A.5.   Discipline Internal Convergence

these loosely knit individuals and groups through both formal and informal communication. As a result, many of the same principles that we apply to the study of organizations and collectives are applicable here. In this case, the organizations and collectives are identified by the paradigms they employ. Dynamics such as power, resource allocation and dependency, socialization, environmental ambiguity, values, negotiated order, and dialectical relations are useful concepts in understanding the political and social aspects of paradigms as organizational entities.

The internal convergence of a paradigm is characterized by increased political and intellectual influence in the discipline in question (see Figure A.5). Fully internally and externally convergent paradigms are what Kuhn refers to as mature paradigms.[46]

This convergence is based on the perceived degree of higher internal consistency and its increased ability to gain agreement to explain a given state of affairs or set of variables. The increase in influence of a paradigm means an increase in the power of the proponents of the paradigm to control vital resources, disciplinary norms, and definition of disciplinary and paradigmatic boundaries. When this level of influence is achieved and a paradigm has achieved its maximum degree of maturity, it is said to be the dominant paradigm in a discipline.

At this point in the development of a discipline, the emergence of a dominant paradigm tends to coincide with a general external convergence of other paradigms such as the information transfer paradigm in the discipline around that dominant paradigm. Such a state of general convergence can be methodological, ideological, or both. While, in this case, the dominant paradigm tends to be more quantitatively oriented, emphasizing a systems perspective, subordinate paradigms tend to be more qualitatively oriented (though not exclusively) emphasizing the individual needs of the patrons. Most paradigms within the discipline do not give up their own identities. Subordinate paradigms continue to work out their theoretical inconsistencies through increased research while acknowledging the superordinate position of the dominant paradigm in the discipline. These processes relative to subordinate paradigms are characteristic of a state of internal divergence, that is until they are able to achieve internal convergence.

Disciplinary Dynamics Components

The tendency of external convergence can be best explained by viewing the discipline in social organizational terms. The discipline can be viewed as analogous to an organizational field, and the various paradigms in the discipline would be viewed as one might view the organizations in an organizational field.

Organizational behavior under situations of stress that tend to be present when environmental ambiguity is present cause some notable patterns of organizational field structuration. In other words, divergent paradigms in a discipline behave in a fashion similar to organizations in an organizational field in which there is little leadership to assure lines of needed resources. As convergence takes place over time, a dominant paradigm will frequently emerge that promotes disciplinary stability by bringing other paradigms in the discipline into conformity with the dominant paradigm.

Conformity is facilitated by resource dependency of subordinate paradigms to the dominant paradigm (in some cases multiple dominant paradigms). Resource dependency stems from dominant paradigms having proponents serving as editors and referees of important disciplinary journals, having proponents in control of key departmental positions at universities, and having proponents in positions in the foundations that supply grant monies for research. All of these are resources that lend legitimacy and power to the dominant paradigm.

When applied to a discipline, the result is that proponents of alternative paradigms in the discipline are forced into conformity with the dominant paradigm. This is based on a perceived asymmetry of power favoring the proponents of the dominant paradigm. This power differentiation can be the result of inequities in the distribution and control of resources as well as other perceived power structures favoring proponents of the dominant paradigm. Hence, if one wants to get articles published in mainstream journals, or gain faculty and research positions at top universities and foundations, or get the grants that are the lifeblood of research, he or she must conform by acknowledging the gatekeeper role of proponents of the dominant paradigm.

Conformity is usually voluntary and frequently unconscious since most of those in the discipline have been socialized in light of the ideologies of the dominant paradigm. To resist conforming yields environmental ambiguity and uncertainty within the discipline. Conformity occurs when other paradigms echo the dominant paradigm by adopting similar methodologies and ideologies in order to receive favorable treatment in resource allocations or institutional appointments and so forth.

The final component of conformity to be discussed here is the socialization of discipline members. Socialization occurs when the values, norms, and standards of the other paradigms are brought into conformity with the perceived definitions of values, norms, and standards of the dominant paradigm. This is evidenced in the control of the processes of socialization through the education of a majority of the members of a discipline. These are the dynamics and processes in which member paradigms in a discipline conform to the dominant paradigm's definitions of the appropriate values, ideologies, and individual boundaries.

Conformity is viewed as the external convergence of the various paradigms in a discipline. However, the dominance of any individual paradigm is not necessarily assured for an indefinite length of time. This is because other variables besides internal convergence affect the dominance of any given paradigm. Those variables can include the perceived dominance of one discipline over another, the amount of ambiguity and environmental turbulence between disciplines, and the values acknowledged by disciplines. When definitions cease to be shared, external convergence is likely to dissolve into external divergence between member paradigms.

Divergence will tend to remain until another paradigm asserts its dominance. Theoretically, all paradigms in a discipline could be convergent to such a degree that zero growth is being experienced by the paradigm or the discipline as a whole. Zero growth, however, seems highly unlikely because of the number of variables involved. It is conceivable that when a dominant paradigm is experiencing zero growth, it is in such a strong position of dominance that the discipline as a whole may experience paradigmatic divergence yet not be able to gain dominance. If multiple, highly divergent paradigms continue to vie for disciplinary dominance, structural conditions develop that require one to give way to the other, or more likely, one will split from the existing discipline to establish a new discipline (for example, the separation of the natural sciences from philosophy).

SUMMARY

In our efforts to gain increasingly higher levels of objectivity, we must remain vigilant relative to our own inner subjective selves. We accomplish this by being as aware and reflexive as possible. We cannot deny our own belief and value systems, but we can control for them. We are aware of the role of epistemology and ontology to help locate ourselves ideologically with respect to the selection of research methodologies and specific methods as ways of controlling outside variables. This is supplemented by sampling strategies and other strategies for methodological selection discussed elsewhere in this book.

Finally, we began by locating the role of research in the process of theorizing. The role of theorizing is also dealt with in other sections of this book. However, we found that research is a part of the context of paradigms and disciplines which tend to be self-structuring and self-reproducing. We also discovered that as paradigms change so too do disciplines. These changes frequently come in the form of observable behaviors that can be studied using social science technologies. Theories, paradigms, and disciplines present observable behaviors because they are represented by individuals and groups which socially interact and, hence, have observable behaviors. These behaviors can be studied using social science methods and frequently understood using social science concepts and theories.

This appendix is about change and innovation, which are the basis and reason for research in general. However, it is important to remember that change does not mean progress but only that some degree of difference is discernible. To make judgments beyond the fact that change has taken place is, as Gould reminds us, "egregiously biased."[47]

NOTES

[1]Charles Camic, "Reputation and Predecessor Selection: Parsons and the Institutionalists," *American Sociological Review* 57 (1992): 421–45.

[2]Nicholas Mullins, *Theories and Theory Groups in Contemporary American Sociology* (New York: Harper and Row, 1973).

[3] Charles H. Cooley, *Human Nature and the Social Order* (New York: Schocken, 1964).

[4]James M. Baldwin, *The Mental Development in the Child and the Race* (New York: Macmillan, 1906).

[5]James M. Baldwin, *Social and Ethical Interpretations in Mental Development* (New York: Macmillan, 1907).

[6]Sigmund Freud, *The Future of an Illusion* (Garden City, NY: Doubleday Anchor, 1961).

[7]George H. Mead, *Mind, Self, and Society* (Chicago: University of Chicago Press, 1962).

[8]Mullins, *Theories and Theory Groups.*

[9]Camic, "Reputation and Predecessor Selection," 421–45.

[10]Mullins, *Theories and Theory Groups.*

[11]Camic, "Reputation and Predecessor Selection," 421–45.

[12]David R. Maines, Jeffery C. Bridger, and Jeffery T. Ulmer, "Mythic Facts and Park's Pragmatism: On Predecessor-Selection and Theorizing in Human Ecology," *Sociological Quarterly* 37 (Summer 1969): 521.

[13]Dagobert D. Runes, ed., *The Dictionary of Philosophy* (New York: Citadel Press, 2001): 167.

[14]Ibid., 388.

[15]Scott G. McNall, *The Sociological Experience* (Boston: Little, Brown and Company, 1969): 3.

[16]Dagobert D. Runes, ed. *Dictionary of Philosophy* (Totowa, NY: Littlefield, Adams and Company, 1962).

[17]Donald T. Campbell, "Evolutionary Epistemology," in *The Philosophy of Popper*, edited by P. A. Schilpp (LaSalle, IL: Open Court, 1974): 447.

[18]David R. Maines and Shing-Ling Chen, "Information and Action: An Introduction to Carl Couch's Analysis of Information Technologies," *Information Technologies and Social Orders*, edited by Carl J. Couch (New York: Aldine De Gruyter, 1996).

[19]Jack D. Glazier and Robert Grover, "A Multidisciplinary Framework for Theory Building," *Library Trends* 50 (Winter 2002): 317–29.

[20]Anthony Giddens, *The Constitution of Society* (Cambridge, England: Polity, 1984).

[21]Jurgen Habermas, *The Theory of Communicative Action*, Vol. 1, *Reason and the Rationalization of Society* (Boston: Beacon, 1984).

[22]Maines and Chen, "Information and Action."

[23]Ibid.

[24]Runes, *The Dictionary of Philosophy*, 346.

[25]Donald Polkinghorne, *Methodology for the Human Sciences: Systems of Inquiry* (Albany: State University of New York Press, 1983): 5.

[26]Thomas S. Kuhn, *The Structure of Scientific Revolutions* (Chicago: University of Chicago Press, 1970).

[27]Kuhn, *The Essential Tension: Selected Studies in Scientific Tradition and Change* (Chicago: University of Chicago Press, 1977): 226.

[28]Mullins, *Theories and Theory Groups*.

[29]Kuhn, *The Structure of Scientific Revolutions*, 178.

[30]Ibid., 179.

[31]Ibid., 180–81.

[32]Stephen J. Gould, *Full House* (New York: Harmony Books, 1996).

[33]Kuhn, *The Structure of Scientific Revolutions*, 180–81.

[34]Kuhn, *The Essential Tension*, 226.

[35]Mullins, *Theories and Theory Groups*.

[36]Robert Grover and Jack D. Glazier, "A Proposed Taxonomy of Theory: A Conceptual Framework for Theory Building in Library and Information Science," *Library and Information Science Research* 8 (July/September 1986): 237–42.

[37]Walter W. Powell and Paul J. DiMaggio, *The New Institutionalism in Organizational Analysis* (Chicago: University of Chicago Press, 1991).

[38]Jack D. Glazier and Peter M. Hall, "Constructing Isomorphism in an Interorganizational Network," *Humboldt Journal of Social Relations* 22 (1996): 47–62.

[39]Glazier and Grover, "A Multidisciplinary Framework for Theory Building," 317–29.

[40]Ibid.

[41]Giddens, *The Constitution of Society*.

[42]Grover and Glazier, "A Proposed Taxonomy of Theory," 234.

[43]Mullins, *Theories and Theory Groups*.

[44]Glazier and Grover, "A Multidisciplinary Framework for Theory Building," 317–29.

[45]Grover and Glazier, "A Proposed Taxonomy of Theory," 234.

[46]Kuhn, *The Structure of Scientific Revolutions*.

[47]Gould, *Full House*, 14.

Appendix B

How to Get Published in LIS Journals: A Practical Guide*

Daria DeCooman
Managing Editor
Library Connect Pamphlets

* Reprinted with permission of the publisher.

pamphlet #2

How to Get Published in LIS Journals:
A Practical Guide

Guest Editors

LISA JANICKE HINCHLIFFE

Editor, Research Strategies, *and Coordinator for Information Literacy Services and Instruction and Associate Professor of Library Administration at the University of Illinois at Urbana-Champaign*

JENNIFER DORNER

Editor, Research Strategies, *and Social Sciences and Humanities Librarian and Assistant Professor at Portland State University*

2003

Writing for the LIS Profession: Introductory Comments and Questions

Dear Library and Information Science Colleagues,

Research and publishing in our profession are quite interesting phenomena. Research in library and information science (LIS) appears to be uneven, fragmentary, and non-cumulative, and is becoming more oriented toward current practices. Due to heavier work loads, practicing librarians have less time to engage in reflection, research, and publishing; consequently, they are writing more "how we did it good in our library" pieces. These best-practices articles and books are displacing publications based on research and intellectual inquiry. How will this change impact the theoretical foundation of the profession?

Most LIS research falls into one of two different types: basic or action/applied. Furthermore, quantitative research is more popular than qualitative research. It is regrettable that LIS research does not contain more qualitative measures. We tend to be mesmerized by measuring everything with numbers, and place too little emphasis on the meanings of words and feelings provided via qualitative research.

Why should we conduct research in LIS? The reasons for doing so include contributing to the profession; gaining a better understanding of the research process, thus, enabling librarians to assist researchers; discovering new knowledge; and personal growth.

Donald E. Riggs, Vice President for Information Services and University Librarian at Nova Southeastern University, discussing a journal article with Mou Chakraborty, Distance and Instructional Technology Librarian at Nova Southeastern University. Photo courtesy of Nova Southeastern University.

With fewer LIS schools teaching courses in basic research methods, librarians generally do not understand the research process. Research begins with a problem: no problem, no research! One common reason reviewers give a manuscript a negative assessment is that the author failed to clearly identify the problem of the research.

After the research is completed, the next step is to find a home for its findings. The author should first find a journal that is a good match for the contents of the manuscript; one should not write the manuscript, then try to find a journal to carry it. Such a decision could result in a large amount of work for naught. Normally, a research journal article should include the following components: 1. introduction, 2. statement of the problem, 3. justification of the study, 4. review of the literature, 5. methodology (research techniques), 6. collection, analysis, and interpretation of data, and 7. conclusion.

Academic librarians and LIS faculty are the two major contributors to LIS literature. Academic librarians who are on a tenure track publish more than those who are not. Thus, it can be assumed that much of the publishing in research publications is the result of tenure and promotion pressures. Unfortunately, librarians working in public, school, and special libraries contribute less to the literature. Though some of the best minds in the profession work in these types of libraries, their librarians are not encouraged to conduct research and publish.

Librarians, especially librarians with fewer than 10 years of experience, are rather anxious about learning more about the research process and how to get their findings published. Many opportunities exist for research and publishing in LIS. These vary from publishing in refereed journals (both paper and electronic formats) to publishing current practices online. If one has not had prior experience in writing and publishing, one could "test the water" by submitting an article to a state library association journal. Writing and publishing a book chapter is another avenue to see if what you have to share with others is publishable.

Getting one's work published depends on various factors and can take different routes. As this booklet demonstrates, seasoned advice differs regarding how to get one's article or research findings published. There is no one correct or right or foolproof way.

Conducting research and writing about it constitute one of the purest forms of creativity in LIS. Appropriate incentives, support, and rewards must be provided for this very important function, especially if we want LIS to continue with a solid theoretical foundation of understanding.

Regards,

Donald E. Riggs

Dr. Donald E. Riggs, Vice President for Information Services and University Librarian, Nova Southeastern University

Donald E. Riggs has served as president of three state library associations — in Arizona, Colorado, and West Virginia, and as president of LAMA (The Library Administration and Management Association). Riggs' publishing record includes eight books, 43 book chapters, and 92 journal articles. He has been editor of *College & Research Libraries*, founding editor of *Library Administration & Management*, and editor of *Library Hi Tech*. In 1991, Riggs received the Hugh C. Atkinson Memorial Award for his leadership and risk taking in library technology.

Seeking to Publish? Prepare for Success!

By Lisa Janicke Hinchliffe, Editor, *Research Strategies*, and Coordinator for Information Literacy Services and Instruction and Associate Professor of Library Administration at the University of Illinois at Urbana-Champaign; and Jennifer Dorner, Editor, *Research Strategies*, and Social Sciences and Humanities Librarian and Assistant Professor at Portland State University

Preparing a manuscript for publication is a multi-faceted and, sometimes, anxiety-ridden task. Tips presented here should help you keep track of issues you need to think about and complete your work successfully.

At each stage of your writing, there are elements to have in place as you plan to submit your manuscript to a journal. For simplicity's sake, we have grouped the elements into three categories: developing your project, manuscript organization and components, and technical preparation.

Developing Your Project

Thinking about your final manuscript begins when you start thinking about your project — whether it is a pure research project or a new library service you are developing. Setting the stage is an important element in writing a successful manuscript.

> "Thinking about your final manuscript begins when you start thinking about your project..."

Almost any project in a library will reasonably begin with a literature search to learn what others have done on the topic. From this review flows your thinking about your own project, its publishable elements, and the context for your findings. Where does your article fit in with the literature of the field? Rarely is a research project or program idea so unique that it is without supporting literature in the discipline. If you describe your project without placing it in the context of other work that has been done, your audience might take this as ignorance of the field or, worse, hubris. Searching the literature in related fields, such as education or computer science, may also be helpful if your project is interdisciplinary or cross-disciplinary in scope. Putting your research or program in the context of other work already done will assure your audience of your understanding of the issues and your expertise on the topic.

In addition to the general literature review, it is important to think carefully about your topic and its relevance. Will what you say be of use to the audience of the journal? Are you sharing your experience or your research in a way that is meaningful to others? For example, how could research conducted in the library of a small private liberal arts college be of interest to librarians at a mid-sized urban public university? To make an article meaningful to librarians whose institutions do not mirror your own in size and user population, the manuscript must describe how the environmental context did or did not contribute to the success of the project or influence your research findings.

Thinking early on about the audience for which you are writing will shape the development of your thinking and the project.

Manuscript Organization and Components

Different types of manuscripts are organized in different ways and contain different components. Though one does not have to follow a rigid outline, following generally accepted and expected practices can help the reader understand what you are saying.

In their book *Research and Writing in the Disciplines* (Fort Worth: Harcourt Brace Jovanovich, 1992), Donald Zimmerman and Dawn Rodrigues have a helpful chapter titled "A Look at Research Reports in Different Disciplines." The chapter outlines the elements and organization of research reports in the humanities, social sciences, natural sciences, and engineering. Though all contain similar components, the order and relationships of the components vary. *MLA Style Manual and Guide to Scholarly Publishing* and the *Publication Manual of the American Psychological Association* also provide useful advice on manuscript organization.

Because of the interdisciplinary and cross-disciplinary approaches used in many areas of library and information science, the particular organizational structure and components you use will depend on your research methods and your intended audience. You can get some sense of what is commonly used by browsing past issues of the journal to which you plan to submit your manuscript and by examining the structure of articles identified in your literature review.

Technical Preparation

Technical preparation of the manuscript is perhaps the easiest and the most tedious stage of the process. Obvious advice here includes careful proofreading for typographical errors and adherence to standard grammar and style. The most important document to reference in this stage of manuscript preparation is the Guide to Authors for the particular journal to which you are submitting your manuscript. Author guidelines often include directions about the submission process; title page; tables, figures, and illustrations; and references/bibliography. Follow this guide very carefully. It is best understood as a set of rules rather than guidelines!

In addition to preparing the manuscript itself, you will need to write a cover letter to the editor to accompany your submission. In the letter you should indicate that the enclosure is a submission, provide a succinct summary of the work and its relationship to literature on the topic, and provide your mail, email, phone, and fax contact information. If you will soon be out of contact for a lengthy period of time, indicate that as well — as a heads-up in case the editor needs to contact you.

Having prepared your manuscript — submit it! Your attention to detail in the preparation stage of publication will serve you well as your manuscript makes its way through the reviewing, revising, and publication processes.

Lisa Janicke Hinchliffe (left), Editor, Research Strategies, discussing how to publish in LIS journals with attendees at ACRL's 2003 conference in NC, and Daviess Menefee, Elsevier's Director of Library Relations, Americas. Photo by Nancy Stevenson.

Questions to Ask When Selecting a Journal

By Susan E. Searing, Library & Information Science Librarian and Associate Professor of Library Administration at the University of Illinois at Urbana-Champaign

You have a finished draft of your article. Now you're wondering which journal to send it to. First, do your homework. Examine recent journal issues (or their tables of contents on the web) to identify those that cover the subject of your article. Then ask five questions about each journal you're considering.

■ *Is this journal peer-reviewed?*

If you're an academic librarian who must produce quality scholarship for promotion and tenure, publishing in peer-reviewed journals is critical. Look at the journal's front matter or author submission guidelines to determine if it's peer-reviewed, or consult a standard guide like *Ulrich's Periodicals Directory*. Many online indexes now indicate whether journals are peer-reviewed, too.

■ *Is this a prestigious journal?*

Everyone wants to publish in a journal with a good reputation, but opinion varies. Research shows, for example, that practicing librarians and LIS faculty rank journals differently. Ask your colleagues and mentors which journals they value most. Information on rejection rates, when available, may be a clue. (The theory runs that the more prestigious a journal is, the choosier it can be.) Another clue is the journal's impact factor, as measured by ISI's *Journal Citation Reports*. Remember that some tenure committees still look down their noses at upstart electronic-only journals.

■ *Who is this journal's audience?*

Some journals are aimed at specialists; others reach a broader audience. Some are regional, others national, and still others international. Is your article of interest primarily to readers with pre-existing expertise — in cataloging, say, or archives — or do you seek wide exposure for your ideas and research findings? Journals published by professional organizations often reach more readers than commercial journals.

■ *How long will it take to see your article in print?*

There are two critical time periods: the time it takes from submission to acceptance or rejection; and the time it takes from acceptance to publication. Journals vary widely in both regards, but solid information about turn-around time is hard to come by. A few LIS journals have begun to print this information along with each article, while other journals note typical time frames in their author guidelines. And remember, the time to publication will be much longer if your first choice rejects you, and you start the submission cycle over.

■ *What role has this journal played in improving scholarly communication?*

Librarians bemoan rising journal prices and the proliferation of new, narrowly specialized titles. As you consider which journal to submit your work to, ask yourself: Has this publisher dealt fairly with librarians? Is it committed to working on issues that matter to libraries, like long-term access to electronic content? What options will you have to retain intellectual property rights?

> Want to know more? See "Publishing in LIS: A Few Useful Sources" at http://www.library.uiuc.edu/lsx/lispubguide.html

Start Small — Think Big

By Jeff Slagell, Assistant Director of Library Services, Delta State University

It can be a daunting task to try to publish when you're new to any profession and I think this is especially true for newly-minted librarians. Typically, LIS programs don't emphasize research and writing as much as other fields. The simplest advice that I can pass along to you is to start small and think big.

Your first published article doesn't have to be an earth-shattering research study in a refereed publication. Another common misconception is that you need a finished product in hand before you contact an editor. In actuality, most of my publications were the result of submitting a brief abstract or contacting the editor directly with only an idea. I would go even further to say that there are many editors that would actually prefer that you contact them early in the writing process. This allows them to make comments and ensure your article and style are appropriate for their publication.

"One article somehow magically leads to the next."

I have consistently seen the publishing "domino effect" take place with myself and a number of my colleagues. One article somehow magically leads to the next. Perhaps your library or institution has a regular newsletter. A brief report could lead to an article in a state/regional library association publication, eventually leading to national and refereed titles. Yes, there are a few core refereed titles that are quite competitive, but it's important to keep in mind that there are many editors constantly trolling librarian waters for new talent and ideas.

Once you have your foot in the door, it's essential that you follow through with the publication's established guidelines. Think of this as the "mechanics" of the process. Be mindful of their writing style, your draft deadlines, and appropriate citation methods. Nothing will annoy an editor more than if you miss deadlines and create extra work during an already tight publication schedule. However, you can also use the above considerations to your advantage. I have received invitations to write simply based on the fact that I was easy to work with and turned everything in on time.

"Ultimately, the key is to just start."

After you think you have a finished product, always pass it along to a trusted colleague for proofreading before you submit it. Regardless of the article type, it's always possible to become too close to the material and miss typographical mistakes and other errors. Your proofreader could be one of your peers or a mentor with significant writing experience. You might also want to take this process a step further and collaborate with one or more people in creating an article. It splits up the workload and allows for different perspectives on your topic.

Ultimately, the key is to just start. I have witnessed several colleagues with great ideas that never reached fruition because they were afraid to take that first step. I think you'll find that, once you have that initial article under your belt, you'll gain confidence and create networking opportunities that will prove invaluable in the future. The library science publishing environment is wide open. Write about what you know or what you have a passion for and watch your small ideas evolve into something big.

Lessons Learned as Author and Editor

By Connie Foster, Editor, *Serials Review*

Writing and editing are dynamic, creative processes. At some point both author and editor must release the finished product and submit to the production process (more copyediting, proofing and queries). To offer the best manuscript possible, keep in mind the following points.

1. Surround yourself with current, concise reference resources. A good dictionary, style manual, thesaurus and, for occasional moments of inspiration, a book on effective writing, such as William Zinsser's *On Writing Well* or Strunk and White's *The Elements of Style*. Select topics which interest you. Seek ideas from discussions on electronic lists, in-house studies that can be placed in a broad context with a literature review, or hot topics at conferences.

2. Organize, organize, organize. Revise, revise, revise. The process of revision is more important than the initial writing. How many revisions? While strictly up to you, I suspect that even the best of authors probably average five, six, or ten revisions, minimum!

3. Know the finer points of grammar that drive editors crazy: where to place punctuation when using quotation marks, how to use quotations appropriately, and avoiding first person narrative and passive voice.

4. Read the instructions to authors before you begin so that you can establish font, type, and spacing. Refer to the recommended style manual for endnotes or footnotes, citation of electronic sources, spelling conventions, and formats for graphs, figures, tables, and charts.

5. Avoid co-authoring. Why? Only the lead author gets proofs, only one author gets first citation, and only very dedicated personalities working alike can carry equal responsibilities in the process and emerge still speaking to each other.

Connie Foster, Editor, Serials Review. Photo by Hanwang Yuan, Web Site & Virtual Library Coordinator, Western Kentucky University Libraries.

> "*Writing is a challenge and a satisfaction.*"

6. Have a colleague or someone not in the profession read your manuscript. Although this process bares your professional soul and seems awkward, it is one way of soliciting valuable criticism.

7. Submit accurate figures, tabulations, and consistencies between text and figures. Triple check these! Document pages, volumes, issues, and dates of sources correctly the first time, so that you do not have to backtrack later.

An editor's delight is receiving a carefully prepared manuscript. If you are uncertain whether your manuscript fits the scope of the journal, discuss your thesis with the editor.

Guidelines for the submission process not covered above are the following.

- Only submit your article to one journal at a time. Never play off one journal against the other. Peer review and editorial comments require significant time and analysis.

- Contact the editor if you have not had a response within a reasonable time. Usually an editor will inform you of the status (being peer reviewed, ready to return with comments, etc.). If you feel the delay is unworkable, talk to the editor!

Learn from rejections. Learn from acceptances. I have never had anyone refuse to revise, even more than once. While your ego may be temporarily deflated, taking a deep breath and pounding the keyboard is well worth producing a strong, quality article.

Writing is a challenge and a satisfaction. The more you write the more comfortable you will become in creating a niche in the information universe and sharing research and experiences with a community of scholars and industry professionals.

> "Over the years, I've found that these four publishing tips work. First, select your desired readers. Choosing a seldom-targeted audience, such as trustees, upped the interest in my article 'Advocacy ABCs for Trustees' (American Libraries, September 2001). Second, have something important to share, whether it's avoiding lawsuits or getting more funding. Third, mix theory with practical case histories and quotes; readers love to hear from real people. Finally, be ready to rewrite often so your publication is engaging, informative and memorable."
>
> — **Ellen G. Miller, founding president of the Kansas Library Trustee Association, and president of Ellen Miller Group in Lenexa, Kansas**
>
> (For further information, check out http://www.ellenmillergroup.com)

Peer Review

By Peter Hernon, Co-editor, *Library & Information Science Research*

Peter Hernon, Co-editor, Library & Information Science Research.

Scholarship and research in library and information studies most often appear in journals, monographs, annual reviews, and conference proceedings. Those journals, especially the ones operating at the national and international levels, tend to be subject to editorial peer review — prepublication review.

The concept of a refereeing system can be traced back more than 300 years to the *Philosophical Transactions of the Royal Society*, when some members of the Society Council reviewed papers for publication. The purpose of this system of review was (and remains) to ensure a certain level of quality to published works, with those knowledgeable about the issue or problem being analyzed or studied judging the work on its merits and making a recommendation (favorable or not) to the editor. Peer reviewing means that one's "peers" shape the editorial decision and that the editor operates within that context; if this situation is altered and the editor disregards reviewer recommendations, peer reviewing becomes compromised.

> "*The concept of a refereeing system can be traced back more than 300 years...*"

For many journals their editorial boards serve as the reviewers. However, journals may invite others to review and, when they do so, these journals likely acknowledge these supplementary reviewers in the final issue of a volume. Editors ascertain the areas of reviewer expertise so that those individuals passing judgment have the necessary background and knowledge of the literature to make valid judgments. Some journals use "double blind" peer reviewing, meaning that the reviewers do not know the names, affiliations, or positions of the authors of the manuscripts they are judging, and the authors do not know who reviewed their work. Editors might even remove some references from papers if those references might reveal an author's identity. The purpose of such an action is to ensure that a name or affiliation does not influence the judgment and that any contact between author and reviewer goes through the editor.

How the Process Works

Someone — not necessarily within the profession — might write a paper that reflects either scholarship (analytical) or research. Here research is defined as an investigation that applies the components of the inquiry process: reflective inquiry, procedures (research design and methodology), reliability and validity, and presentation. That paper would be submitted to the editor, who selects the reviewers (most typically two or three). Those reviewers judge the paper on its merits. The problem statement must explain the value of the research or scholarship and demonstrate that the paper does not deal with an insignificant issue or problem. The literature review must demonstrate a command of relevant readings, regardless of discipline and nationality of authors. (Fortunately, today, publishers have the means to ensure that published papers appear in databases such as ScienceDirect that bring together works of different disciplines and fields of study for easy retrieval and use.)

> "*Peer reviewing means that one's 'peers' shape the editorial decision and that the editor operates within that context...*"

The reviewers make a recommendation and call for: 1. acceptance without any changes or with minor changes, 2. outright rejection, or 3. revision. Upon completion of revision the paper should be accepted. Otherwise, needed revision might be so extensive that the reviewers recommend additional review by themselves or others. Sometimes the reviewers make the same recommendation and other times they do not. If they do not, some editors call on different reviewers to break any tie in vote, others might cast a vote themselves, and others might return the manuscript to the author, sharing the differences of opinion and asking the author to revise the paper to address the concerns raised. In such instances, the paper should be resubmitted for formal review.

In the case of the journals that I have edited, I copyedit all manuscripts and review all references for consistency with the editorial style manual — before the manuscripts go to peer review. Once the review decision has been rendered, that decision, together with the copyedited manuscript, is returned to the author. If the review outcome was favorable, the author is encouraged to make the changes quickly and to return the paper so that it can be scheduled for an upcoming issue. The final paper should be accompanied with a disk containing the paper and any tables/figures.

Prior to submission of the paper, it is best to review a recent issue of the journal, the author instructions, and any material at the journal's Web site. The peer review process itself might be handled electronically. It might be completed within a short time (a couple of weeks), a month, or longer depending on the editorial practice. *Library & Information Science Research* does the reviewing and copyediting within three weeks, and the other journals I have edited did these within one month.

Conclusion

The prestige of a journal is associated with the quality of its contents. Evidence of that quality comprises the journal's impact factor (the extent of distribution of citations and "downloading" to all the articles appearing in the journal), rejection rate (the assumption is that a healthy rejection rate demonstrates that the journal separates "the wheat from the chaff"), the number of subscriptions, the extent of downloading of articles, and, most importantly, whether or not the journal is peer reviewed.

I know of numerous cases in which faculty members only gained institutional recognition for works that appeared in peer reviewed journals. Note that within peer reviewed journals, an institute or department may recognize a hierarchy of journals. I am fortunate to have always been associated with the higher tier of those journals. Clearly, prestige is associated with editorial peer review and the quality of those reviewers and their judgments.

Peter Hernon is Professor at Simmons College's Graduate School of Library and Information Science, where he teaches courses on academic libraries, research methods, evaluation of library services, and government policy, services, and resources. He has authored 40 books and approximately 200 articles. He is the founding and past editor of *Government Information Quarterly*, past editor-in-chief of *The Journal of Academic Librarianship*, and co-editor of *Library & Information Science Research*. His co-authored book, *Assessing Service Quality*, received the 1999 Highsmith Award from the American Library Association.

Writing from Presentations

By Scott Walter, Washington State University

The most difficult part of getting published is finding an idea about which you and your colleagues are concerned, and presenting it in a way that makes your thoughts on the subject clear, cogent, and persuasive. If you have already written something up for presentation, you may be well on your way to publication in a professional or scholarly journal. That said, there are some points to remember to help make your journey to publication a smooth one.

First, remember that conferences, like peer-reviewed journals, have an acceptance rate. At a national conference such as the biennial meeting of the Association of College & Research Libraries, the acceptance rate for papers may be as low as 30%. If you have had a paper or poster session accepted for presentation at a professional conference, you have already:

- effectively articulated a topic of interest to your colleagues;
- demonstrated that you can organize your thoughts on this topic in a meaningful way; and,
- conducted some measure of research that informs your conclusions on the topic.

In other words, you have just outlined your future article.

Second, remember that journal editors are always surveying conference programs and poster session descriptions for ideas. My first LIS article (Walter, 2000) started out as a 3-slide poster session that caught the eye of a journal editor. Choose your presentation topic carefully and treat its completion seriously, and you will almost certainly find a potential patron who can help you bring your idea to press. If not, remember that it is appropriate to make contact with an editor in order to gauge her interest in your study. Knowing that most editors are always keen to locate solid work, you should feel free to alert selected colleagues to the fact that you have recently made a successful presentation and ask if an article on your topic would be of interest to readers of their journals. Just remember not to promise the same article to more than one journal!

Finally, remember that not all presentations are appropriate for all publications. Ask yourself the following questions as you move from presentation to publication.

- Is there is enough substance to your project to turn it into an article?
- Will you have to engage in further research to flesh it out (e.g., if your presentation was in the form of a panel discussion, are you ready to do the extra work necessary for the write-up)?
- Have you prepared a literature review that places your work in the context of past research and practice (and, if so, does your piece still stand as a valuable contribution to the literature)?
- Have you prepared a conclusion that summarizes what was learned in your research project, and points the way toward further research on this topic?
- Can your PowerPoint presentation (or poster slides) serve as an effective outline, or do you need more?
- If your presentation was a simple report of a successful initiative in your library, are there journals that are more likely to publish a purely descriptive piece, as opposed to a research-based piece?

Scott Walter, Washington State University.

The answer to that final question is "Yes!," but, even so, there are few conference presentations — posters, panel discussions, or even papers — that are immediately ready for publication. What almost all presentations will do is provide you with an opportunity to lay the groundwork for publication: articulating a significant question for research or practice; proposing an answer to that question; finding an audience interested in hearing your answer; and, effectively outlining your argument. From there, the trip to the printer is relatively short.

Reference: Walter, S. (2000). "Engelond: A model for faculty - librarian collaboration in the information age." *Information Technology and Libraries,* 19:1, 34-41.

LIS Publications from Elsevier

Journals on ScienceDirect at
http://www.sciencedirect.com

Government Information Quarterly
Information Processing & Management
Information & Organization
International Information & Library Review
International Journal of Information Management
Journal of Academic Librarianship
Journal of Government Information
Journal of Strategic Information Systems
Library and Information Science Research
Library Collections, Acquisitions and Technical Services
Research Strategies
Serials Review
World Patent Information

Book Series
Advances in Librarianship
Advances in Library Administration and Organization
www.elseviersocialsciences.com/libraryscience/books

Find out more about publications
in the Social & Behavioral Sciences

www.elseviersocialsciences.com

For Library and Information Sciences
www.elseviersocialsciences.com/libraryscience

SCIENCE DIRECT*

Additional Resources

BOOKS:

First Have Something to Say: Writing for the Library Profession, by Walt Crawford. American Library Association Editions, 2003. ISBN: 0838908519.

Jump Start Your Career in Library and Information Science, by Priscilla K. Shontz, Steven J. Oberg, and Robert R. Newlen. Scarecrow Press, 2002. ISBN: 0810840847.

Basic Statistical Analysis: 7th Edition, by Richard C. Sprinthall. Pearson, Allyn & Bacon, 2002. ISBN: 0205360661.

How to Succeed in Academics, by Linda L. McCabe and Edward R.B. McCabe. Academic Press, 2000. ISBN: 0124818331.

How To Write & Publish a Scientific Paper: 5th Edition, by Robert A. Day. Oryx Press, 1998. ISBN: 1573561657.

Methods of Educational and Social Science Research: An Integrated Approach: 2nd Edition, by David R. Krathwohl. Allyn & Bacon, 1997. ISBN: 0801320291.

Basic Research Methods for Librarians, 3rd Edition, by Ronald R. Powell. Greenwood Publishing Group, 1997. ISBN: 1567503381.

ARTICLES:

"Problem statements in seven LIS journals; An application of the Hernon/Metoyer-Duran attributes," by Mary C. Stansbury. *Library & Information Science Research,* 24:2. Elsevier, 2002.

"The Peer Review Process: Acceptances, Revisions, and Outright Rejections," by John V. Richardson, Jr. *The Library Quarterly,* 72:1. The University of Chicago, 2002.

"Keeping track: Librarians, composition instructors, and student writers use the research journal," by Trixie G. Smith. *Research Strategies,* 18:1. Elsevier, 2001.

"Getting Research Published," by Donald E. Riggs. *College & Research Libraries,* 62:5. Association of College & Research Libraries, 2001.

"Let Us Stop Apologizing for Qualitative Research," by Donald E. Riggs. *College & Research Libraries,* 59:5. Association of College & Research Libraries, 1998.

ONLINE RESOURCES:

Newsletter of Library and Information Science Journals Section
From International Federation of Library Associations and Institutions (IFLA)
http://www.ifla.org.sg/VII/s45/slisj.htm

Journals for LIS Research
From Library and Information Science Library, University of Illinois at Urbana-Champaign
http://www.library.uiuc.edu/lsx/Serial.html

NMRTWriter
ALA's electronic discussion list for librarians seeking to write and publish.
To subscribe, send a message saying "subscribe NMRTWRITER Firstname Lastname" to:
listproc@ala1.ala.org

The Informed Librarian Online
Monthly compilation of the most recent tables of contents from over 250 library and information-related online and print journals, magazines, and newsletters published in the US and other countries.
By Infosources Publishing
http://www.infosourcespub.com/book4.cfm

BUBL LINK/5:15 Catalogue of Internet Resources: Publishing Studies
By Centre for Digital Library Research, Strathclyde University
http://www.bubl.ac.uk/link/p/publishingstudies.htm

libraryconnect@elsevier.com

CONTACTS

ELSEVIER
Library Connect Editorial Office
525 B Street, Suite 1900
San Diego, CA 92101, USA
Phone: +1.619.699.6379
libraryconnect@elsevier.com

ELSEVIER
Library Connect Pamphlets Editor
Daria DeCooman
Global Account Development &
Channel Marketing Manager
525 B Street, Suite 1900
San Diego, CA 92101, USA
libraryconnect@elsevier.com

ELSEVIER
LIS Publications
Chris Pringle
Publisher, Social Sciences
Langford Lane
Kidlington, Oxford OX5 1GB, UK
Phone: +44.1865.843712
c.pringle@elsevier.com

References

Adler, Patricia, and Peter Adler. "Observation Techniques." In *Handbook of Qualitative Research*, edited by Norman Denzin and Yvonne Lincoln, 377–92. Thousand Oaks, CA: Sage Publications, 1994.

Altman, Ellen, and Peter Hernon, eds. *Research Misconduct: Issues, Implications, and Strategies*. Greenwich, CT: Ablex Publishing, 1997.

American Library Association. *Policy Statement on the Role of Research in the American Library Association*. Chicago: American Library Association, 1970.

American Society for Information Science and Technology. "Vision." Web page, 2001. Available, *http://www.asis.org/AboutASIS/asis-mission.html*.

Aminzade, Ron, and Barbara Laslett. In *The Practice of Social Research*. 10th ed., by Earl Babbie, 336. Belmont, CA: Wadsworth/Thomson Learning, 2004.

Anderson, James A. *Communication Research: Issues and Methods*. New York: McGraw-Hill, 1987.

Andrews, Frank M., Laura Klem, Terrence N. Davidson, Patrick M. O'Malley, and Willard L. Rodgers. *A Guide for Selecting Statistical Techniques for Analyzing Social Science Data*. 2d ed. Ann Arbor; Survey Research Center, Institute for Social Research, University of Michigan, 1981.

Argyris, Chris. "Creating Effective Relationships in Organizations." *Human Organization* 17 (1958): 34–40.

"ARL 2000 Program Plan." Web page. Available, *www.arl.org/arl/pplan00.html*.

Babbie, Earl R. *The Practice of Social Research*. 2d ed. Belmont, CA: Wadsworth, 1979.

———. *The Practice of Social Research*. 8th ed. Belmont, CA: Wadsworth, 1998.

———. *The Practice of Social Research*. 9th ed. Belmont, CA: Wadsworth, 2001.

———. *The Practice of Social Research*. 10th ed. Belmont, CA: Wadsworth/Thomson Learning, 2004.

Bahr, Alice Harrison, Michael J. McLane, and Lynn W. Livingston. *InPrint: Publishing Opportunities for College Librarians*. Chicago: Association of College and Research Libraries, 1997.

Bakeman, Roger. "Behavioral Observations and Coding." In *Handbook of Research Methods in Social Personality Psychology*, edited by Harry Reis and Charles Judd. Cambridge, England: Cambridge University Press, 2000.

Baldwin, James M. *The Mental Development in the Child and the Race*. New York: Macmillan, 1906.

Baldwin, James M. *Social and Ethical Interpretations in Mental Development*. New York: Macmillan, 1907.

Banks, Julie. "Are Transaction Logs Useful? A Ten-Year Study." *Journal of Southern Academic and Special Librarianship* (2000). Available, *http://www.icaap.org/iuicode?62.01.03.04*.

Banks, Julie. "Can Transaction Logs Be Used for Resource Scheduling? An Analysis." *Reference Librarian* 63 (Special Report, 1999): 95–108.

Bao, Xue-Ming. "An Analysis of the Research Areas of the Articles Published in *C&RL* and *JAL* Between 1990 and 1999." *College & Research Libraries* 66 (2000): 536–44.

Bar-Ilan, Judit, and Bluma C. Peritz. "Informetric Theories and Methods for Exploring the Internet: An Analytical Survey of Recent Research Literature." *Library Trends* 50 (Winter 2002): 371–92.

Barnes, Annie S., ed. *Social Science Research: A Skills Handbook*. Bristol, IN: Wyndham Hall Press, 1985.

Bartlett, Richard A. "The State of the Library History Art." In *Approaches to Library History*, edited by John D. Marshall, 13–23. Tallahassee: Florida State University Library School, 1965.

Bauer, David G. *"How To" Grants Manual: Successful Grantseeking Techniques for Obtaining Public and Private Grants*. 4th ed. Phoenix, AZ: American Council on Education/Oryx Press, 1999.

Becker, Bill. "Library Grant Money on the Web: A Resource Primer." *Searcher* 11, no. 10 (2003): 8–14.

Benard, Russell H. *Social Research Methods: Qualitative and Quantitative Approaches*. Thousand Oaks, CA: Sage Publications, 2000.

Benson, Dennis K., and Jonathan L. Benson. *A Benchmark Handbook: A Guide to Survey Research Terms*. Columbus, OH: Academy for Contemporary Problems, 1975.

Berger, Kenneth W., and Richard W. Hines. "What Does the User Really Want? The Library User Survey Project at Duke University." *Journal of Academic Librarianship* 20 (November 1994): 306–9.

Bertot, John Carlo, Charles R. McClure, and Joe Ryan. *Statistics and Performance Measures for Public Library Networked Services*. Chicago: American Library Association, 2001.

Bertot, John Carlo, Charles R. McClure, William E. Moen, and Jeffrey Rubin. "Web Usage Statistics: Measurement Issues and Analytical Techniques." *Government Information Quarterly* 14, no. 4 (1997): 373–95.

Bishoff, Liz. "Public Access to the Library of Congress Subject Headings." Paper presented at the Annual Conference of the American Library Association, 1987.

Bixrud, Julia C. *The Association of Research Libraries Statistics and Measurement Program: From Descriptive Data to Performance Measures*, ED459726, Washington, D.C.: Association of Research Libraries, 2001.

Blalock, Hubert M., Jr. *Social Statistics*. Rev. 2d ed. New York: McGraw-Hill, 1979.

Bogdan, Robert. "Foreword." In *Naturalistic Inquiry for Library Science: Methods and Applications for Research, Evaluation, and Teaching*, edited by Constance Ann Mellon. New York: Greenwood Press, 1990.

Bogdan, Robert, and Sari Knopp Biklen. *Qualitative Research for Education: An Introduction to Theory and Methods*. Boston: Allyn and Bacon, 1982.

Bogdan, Robert, and Sari Knopp Biklen. *Qualitative Research for Education: An Introduction to Theory and Methods*. 4th ed. Boston: Allyn and Bacon, 2003.

Bok, Derek. *Higher Learning*. Cambridge, MA: Harvard University Press, 1986.

Bookstein, Abraham. "How to Sample Badly." *Library Quarterly* 44 (April, 1974): 132.

———. "Questionnaire Research in a Library Setting." *Journal of Academic Librarianship* 11 (March 1985): 24–28.

———. "Sources of Error in Library Questionnaires." *Library Research* 4 (1982): 85–94.

Bowers, Fredson. *Principles of Bibliographical Description*. New Castle, DE: Oak Knoll Books, 1994.

Boyce, Bert R., Charles J. Meadow, and Donald H. Kraft. *Measurement in Information Science*. San Diego: Academic Press, 1994.

Bradley, Jana. "Methodological Issues and Practices in Qualitative Research." *Library Quarterly* 63 (1993): 431–49.

Braxton, John M., and Alan E. Bayer. "Perceptions of Research Misconduct and an Analysis of Their Correlates." *Journal of Higher Education* 65 (1994): 351–72.

Bruyn, Severyn. "The Methodology of Participant Observation." In *Reader in Research Methods for Librarianship*, edited by Mary Lee Bundy, Paul Wasserman and Gayle Raghi, 172–85. Washington DC: Microcard Editions, 1970.

Bryman, Alan, and Robert G. Burgess, eds. *Analyzing Qualitative Data*. London: Routledge, 1994.

Buchanan, Elizabeth. "Ethics, Qualitative Research and Ethnography in Virtual Space." *Journal of Information Ethics* 9, no. 2 (2000): 82–87.

Budd, John. "Publication in Library and Information Science: The State of the Literature." *Library Journal* 113 (1988): 125–31.

Budd, John M. "An Epistemological Foundation for Library and Information Science." *Library Quarterly* 65, no. 3 (1995): 295–318.

———. *Knowledge and Knowing in Library and Information Science: A Philosophical Framework*. Lanham, MD: Scarecrow Press, 2001.

Burke, Mary et al. "Editorial: Fraud and Misconduct in Library and Information Science Research." *Library & Information Science Research* 18 (1996): 199–203.

Burkell, Jacquelyn. "The Dilemma of Survey Non-response." *Library & Information Science Research* 25 (Autumm 2003): 239–63.

Busha, Charles A. "Library Science Research: The Path to Progress." In *A Library Science Research Reader and Bibliographic Guide*, edited by Charles A. Bush. Littleton, CO: Libraries Unlimited, 1981.

Busha, Charles A., and Stephen P. Harter. *Research Methods in Librarianship: Techniques and Interpretations*. New York: Academic Press, 1980.

Buttlar, Lois, "Information Sources in Library and Information Science Doctoral Research." *Library & Information Science Research* 21 (1999): 227–45.

Camic, Charles. "Reputation and Predecessor Selection: Parsons and the Institutionalists." *American Sociological Review* 57 (1992): 421–45.

Campbell, Donald T. "Evolutionary Epistemology." In *The Philosophy of Popper*, edited by P. A. Schilpp. LaSalle, IL: Open Court, 1974.

Campbell, Donald T., and Julian C. Stanley. *Experimental and Quasi-Experimental Designs for Research*. Chicago: Rand McNally, 1963.

Carlin, Andrew P. "Disciplinary Debates and Bases of Interdisciplinary Studies: The Place of Research Ethics in Library and Information Science." *Library & Information Science Research* 25 (2003).

Case, Donald O. *Looking for Information; A Survey of Research on Information Seeking, Needs, and Behavior* (London: Academic Press, 2002).

Charmaz, Kathy. "Grounded Theory." In *Approaches to Qualitative Research: A Reader on Theory and Practice*, edited by Sharlene Nagy Hesse-Biber and Patricia Leavy. New York: Oxford University Press, 2004.

Chatman, Elfreda. *The Information World of Retired Women*. Westport, CT: Greenwood Press, 1992.

Cherry, Joan M. "Improving Subject Access in OPACs: An Exploratory Study of Conversion of Users' Queries." *Journal of Academic Librarianship* 18 (1992): 95–9.

Chow, Siu L. "Meta-Analysis of Pragmatic and Theoretical Research: A Critique." *Journal of Psychology* 121 (May 1987): 259–71.

Ciliberti, Anne C., Marie L. Radford, and Gary P. Radford, "Empty Handed? A Material Availability Study and Transaction Log Analysis Verification" *The Journal of Academic Librarianship* 24 (July, 1998).

Citro, Constance, Daniel Ilgen, and Cora Marrett. "Panel on Institutional Review Boards, Surveys, and Social Science Research; Committee on National Statistics and Board on Behavioral, Cognitive, and Sensory Sciences, Division on Behavioral and Social Sciences and Education, National Research Council of the National Academies." *Protecting Participants and Facilitating Social and Behavioral Sciences Research*. Washington DC: National Academies Press, 2003.

Clark, Herbert, and Michael Schober. "Asking Questions and Influencing Answers." In *Questions About Questions: Inquiries into the Cognitive Bases of Surveys*, edited by Judith Taylor, 15–48. New York: Russell Sage Foundation, 1992.

Coffey, Amanda, and Paul Atkinson. *Making Sense of Qualitative Data: Complementary Research Strategies*. Thousand Oaks, CA: Sage Publications, 1996.

Cohen, Jacob. *Statistical Power Analysis for the Behavioral Sciences.* 2d ed. Hillsdale, NJ: Lawrence Erlbaum Associates, 1988.

Collings, Dorothy G. "Comparative Librarianship." In *Encyclopedia of Library and Information Science,* vol. 5, 492–502. New York: Marcel Dekker, 1971.

Connaway, Lynn Silipigni. "Focus Group Interviews: A Data Collection Methodology for Decision Making." *Library Administration & Management* 10 (Fall 1996): 231–39.

Connaway, Lynn Silipigni. "The Levels of Decisions and Involvement in Decision-Making: Effectiveness and Job Satisfaction in Academic Library Technical Services." (University of Wisconsin-Madison, 1992).

Connaway, Lynn Silipigni, John M. Budd, and Thomas R. Kochtanek. "An Investigation of the Use of an Online Catalog: User Characteristics and Transaction Log Analysis." *Library Resources and Technical Services* 39:2 (April 1995): 142–52.

Converse, W. R. "Research: What We Need, and What We Get." *Canadian Library Journal* 41 - (October 1984): 235–41.

Cooley, Charles H. *Human Nature and the Social Order.* New York: Schocken, 1964.

"Council on Library and Information Resources (CLIR) Agenda." Web page. Available, *http://www. clir.org/about/about.html - agenda.*

Couper, Mick P., and Sue Ellen Hansen. "Computer-Assisted Interviewing." In *Handbook of Interview Research: Context & Method,* edited by Jaber F. Gubrium and James A. Holstein, 557–75. Thousand Oaks, CA: Sage Publications, 2002.

Covey, Denise Troll. *Usage and Usability Assessment: Library Practices and Concerns.* Washington, DC: Digital Library Federation and Council on Library and Information Resources, 2002.

Cox, Allan B., and Fred Gifford. "An Overview to Geographic Information Systems". *Journal of Academic Librarianship* 23, no. 6 (1997): 449–61.

Crawford, Gregory A. "The Research Literature of Academic Librarianship: A Comparison of College & Research Libraries and Journal of Academic Librarianship". *College & Research Libraries* 60 (May 1999): 224–30.

Creswell, John W. *Research Design: Qualitative and Quantitative Approaches.*" Thousand Oaks, CA: Sage Publications, 1994.

Dalrymple, Prudence W. "A Quarter Century of User-Centered Study: The Impact of Zweizig and Dervin on LIS Research." *Library & Information Science Research* 23 (2001): 155–65.

Danton, J. Periam. *The Dimensions of Comparative Librarianship.* Chicago: American Library Association, 1973.

Darlington, Yvonne, and Dorothy Scott. *Qualitative Research in Practice: Stories from the Field.* Philadelphia: Open University Press, 2002.

Davis, Charles. "On Qualitative Research." *Library and Information Science Research* 12 (1990): 327–28.

Davis, Charles H. "Information Science and Libraries: A Note on the Contribution of Information Science to Librarianship." In *The Bookmark* 51, 52: 84–96. Chapel Hill: The University Library and the Friends of the Library, University of North Carolina, 1982.

Davis, Charles H., and James E. Rush. *Guide to Information Science.* Westport, CT: Greenwood Press, 1980.

Davis, Donald G., Jr. "Ebla to the Electronic Dream: The Role of Historical Perspectives in Professional Education." *Journal of Education for Library and Information Science* (Summer 1998): 229–35.

Davis, Donald G., Jr., and John M. Tucker. *American Library History: A Comprehensive Guide to the Literature.* Santa Barbara, CA: ABC-Clio, 1989.

Denzin, Norman. *The Research Act: A Theoretical Introduction to Sociological Methods.* 3d ed. Englewood Cliffs, NJ: Prentice Hall, 1989.

Dervin, Brenda, Lois Foreman-Wernet, and Eric Lauterbach, eds. *Sense-Making Methodology Reader: Selected Writings of Brenda Dervin.* New York: Hampton Press, 2003.

Dewdney, Patricia. "Recording the Reference Interview: A Field Experiment." In *Qualitative Research in Information Management,* edited by Jack D. Glazier and Ronald R. Powell, 122–50. Englewood, CO: Libraries Unlimited, 1992.

Dewdney, Patricia, and Roma Harris. "Community Information Needs: The Case of Wife Assault." *Library and Information Science Research* 14 (1992): 5–29.

Dewey, Barbara A. "In Search of Practical Applications: A Public Services Research Agenda for University Libraries." *Journal of Academic Librarianship* (September, 1997): 371–79.

Dickson, Jean. "An Analysis of User Errors in Searching an Online Catalog." *Cataloging & Classification Quarterly* 4:3 (1984): 19–38.

Dieing, Paul. *Patterns of Discovery in the Social Sciences.* London: Routledge & Kegan Paul, 1972.

The Digital Reference Research Agenda. Chicago: Publications in Librarianship Association of College and Research Libraries, 2003.

Dimitroff, Alexandra. "Research Knowledge and Activities of Special Librarians: Results of a Survey." *Special Libraries* 87 (Winter 1996): 1–9.

"Dissemination of Research in LIS: A Statement by the American Library Association Committee on Research and Statistics." Web page, June 2001. Available, *http://www.ala.org/orscommittees/dissemination/dissemination.htm.*

Drabenstott, Karen Markey. "Focused Group Interviews." In *Qualitative Research in Information Management,* edited by Jack D. Glazier and Ronald R. Powell, 85–104. Englewood, CO: Libraries Unlimited, 1992.

Duff, Wendy M., and Joan M. Cherry. "Use of Historical Documents in a Digital World: Comparisons with Original Materials and Microfiche." *Information Research* 6, (October 2000). Available, *http://informations.net/ir/6-1/paper86.html.*

Eaton, Thelma. "Bibliographical Research." *Library Trends* 13 (July 1964): 42–53.

Eisenberg, Michael B. "The State of Research Today." *School Library Media Quarterly* 21 (Summer 1993): 241.

Ely, Margot, Margaret Anzul, Teri Friedman, Diane Garner, and Ann McCormack Steinmetz. *Doing Qualitative Research: Circles Within Circles.* London: Falmer Press, 1991.

Engle, Michael. "Creativity and the Research Process in Academic Libraries." *College & Research Libraries News* 48 (November 1987): 629–31.

Erdos, Paul L. *Professional Mail Surveys.* Rev. ed. Malabar, FL: Robert E. Krieger Publishing, 1983.

Feehan, Patricia E. et al. "Library and Information Science Research: An Analysis of the 1984 Journal Literature." *Library and Information Science Research* 9 (July 1987): 173–85.

Fennick, John H. *Studies Show: A Popular Guide to Understanding Scientific Studies.* Amherst, NY: Prometheus, 1997.

Ferrante, Barbara Kopelock. "Bibliometrics: Access in Library Literature." *Collection Management* 2 (Fall 1987): 199–204.

Fidel, Raya. "The Case Study Method: A Case Study." *Library and Information Science Research* 6 (July 1984): 273–88.

———. "Qualitative Methods in Information Retrieval Research." *Library and Information Science Research* 15 (1993): 219–47.

Fink, Arlene. *How to Ask Survey Questions.* Thousand Oaks, CA: Sage Publications, 1995.

———. *The Survey Handbook.* Thousand Oaks, CA: Sage Publications, 1995.

Fink, Arlene, and Jacqueline Kosecoff. *How to Conduct Surveys; A Step-by-Step Guide,* 2nd ed. (Thousand Oaks, CA: Sage Publications, 1998).

Fisher, William. "When Write Is Wrong: Is All Our Professional Literature on the Same Page." *Library Collections, Acquisitions, & Technical Services* 23 (Spring 1999): 61–72.

Fontana, Andrea, and James Frey. "Interviewing: The Art of Science." In *Handbook of Qualitative Research,* edited by Norman Denzin and Yvonna Lincoln, 361–76. Thousand Oaks, CA: Sage Publications, 1994.

Fortner, Robert, and Clifford Christians. "Separating Wheat from Chaff in Qualitative Studies." In *Research Methods in Mass Communications,* edited by Guido Stempel and Bruce Westley. Englewood Cliffs, NJ: Prentice Hall, 1989.

Fowler, Floyd J., Jr. *Survey Research Methods.* 2d ed. Newbury Park, CA: Sage Publications, 1993.

————. *Survey Research Methods*. 3d ed. Newbury Park, CA: Sage Publications, 2001.

Frankfort-Nachmias, Chava, and David Nachmias. *Research Methods in the Social Sciences*. 4th ed. New York: St. Martin's Press, 1992.

Freud, Sigmund. *The Future of an Illusion*. Garden City, NY: Doubleday Anchor, 1961.

Froehlich, Thomas J. "Ethical Considerations of Information Professionals." in *Annual Review of Information Science and Technology*, vol.27, edited by Martha E. Williams (Medford, NJ: American Society for Information Science, 1992).

Frey, James H. *Survey Research by Telephone*. Beverly Hills, CA: Sage Publications, 1983.

Garrison, Guy. "A Look at Research on Public Library Problems in the 1970's." *Public Libraries* 19 (Spring 1980): 4–8.

Gatten, Jeffrey N. "Paradigm Restrictions on Interdisciplinary Research into Librarianship." *College & Research Libraries* 52 (November 1991): 575–84.

Gay, L. R. *Educational Research; Competencies for Analysis and Application*. 2d ed. Columbus, OH: Charles & Merrill, 1981.

Gay, L. R. *Educational Research: Competencies for Analysis and Application*. 5th ed. Englewood Cliffs, NJ: Charles E. Merrill, 1996.

Gay, L. R., and Peter W. Airasian. *Educational Research: Competencies for Analysis and Application*. 7th ed. Upper Saddle River, NJ: Merrill/Prentice Hall, 2003.

Geertz, Clifford. *The Interpretation of Cultures: Selected Essays*. New York: Basic Books, 1973.

Gerhan, David. "Statistical Significance: How It Signifies in Statistics Reference." *Reference & User Services Quarterly* 40, no. 4 (2001): 361–74.

Giddens, Anthony. *The Constitution of Society*. Cambridge, England: Polity, 1984.

Giesecke, Joan. "Preparing Research for Publication." *Library Administration & Management* 12, no. 3 (1998): 134–37.

Gilbert, Linda. "Going the Distance: 'Closeness' in Qualitative Data Analysis Software." *International Journal of Social Research Methodology* 5, no. 3 (2002): 215–28.

Girden, Ellen R. *Evaluating Research Articles from Start to Finish*. 2d ed. Thousand Oaks, CA: Sage Publications, 2001.

Glaser, Barney. "The Constant Comparison Method of Qualitative Analysis." *Social Problems* 12 (Spring 1965): 436–45.

Glaser, Barney G., and Anselm L. Strauss. *The Discovery of Grounded Theory: Strategies for Qualitative Research*. New York: Aldine de Gruyter, 1967.

Glass, Gene V., Barry McGaw, and Mary L. Smith. *Meta-Analysis in Social Research*. Beverly Hills, CA: Sage Publications, 1981.

Glazier, Jack D., and Robert Grover. "A Multidisciplinary Framework for Theory Building." *Library Trends* 50 (Winter 2002): 317–29.

Glazier, Jack D., and Peter M. Hall. "Constructing Isomorphism in an Interorganizational Network." *Humboldt Journal of Social Relations* 22 (1996): 47–62.

Glazier, Jack D., and Ronald R. Powell, eds. *Qualitative Research in Information Management*. Englewood, CO: Libraries Unlimited, 1992.

Gold, Raymond. "Roles in Sociological Field Observation." In *Issues in Participant Observation*, edited by George McCall and J. L. Simmons, 30–39. Reading, MA: Addison-Wesley, 1969.

Golden, Gary. *Survey Research Methods*. Chicago: ACRL, 1982.

Goldhor, Herbert. *An Introduction to Scientific Research in Librarianship*. Urbana: University of Illinois, Graduate School of Library Science, 1972.

Goldman, Alfred E., and Susan S. McDonald. *The Group Depth Interview*. Englewood Cliffs, NJ: Prentice-Hall, 1987.

Goodall, Deborah. "It Ain't What You Do, It's the Way That You Do It: A Review of Public Library Research with Special Reference to Methodology." *Public Library Journal* 11 (1996): 69–76.

Gorden, Raymond. "Dimensions of the Depth Interview." In *Reader in Research Methods for Librarianship*, edited by Mary Lee Bundy, Paul Wasserman, and Gayle Araghi. Washington, DC: NCR, 1970, 166–171.

Gordon, Rachel Singer. "Getting Started in Library Publication." *American Libraries* 35, no. 1 (2004): 66–69.

Gorman, G. E., and Peter Clayton, with contributions from Mary Lynn Rice-Lively and Lyn Gorman. *Qualitative Research for the Information Professional: A Practical Handbook*. London: Library Association Publishing, 1997.

Gould, Stephen J. *Full House*. New York: Harmony Books, 1996.

Grazier, Margaret H. "Critically Reading and Applying Research in School Library Media Centers." *School Library Media Quarterly* 10 (Winter 1982): 135–46.

Grotzinger, Laurel. "Methodology of Library Science Inquiry—Past and Present." In *A Library Science Research Reader and Bibliographic Guide*, edited by Charles H. Busha, 38–50. Littleton, CO: Libraries Unlimited, 1981.

Grover, Robert, and Jack D. Glazier. "A Proposed Taxonomy of Theory: A Conceptual Framework for Theory Building in Library and Information Science." *Library and Information Science Research* 8 (July-September 1986): 227–42.

Grover, Robert, and Martha L. Hale. "The Role of the Librarian in Faculty Research." *College & Research Libraries* 49 (January 1988): 9–15.

Grover, Robert J., and Jack Glazier. "Implications for Application of Qualitative Methods to Library and Information science Research." *Library and Information Science Research*. 7 (July 1985) 247–60.

Habermas, Jurgen. *The Theory of Communicative Action*, Vol. 1, *Reason and the Rationalization of Society*. Boston: Beacon, 1984.

Hafner, Arthur Wayne. *Descriptive Statistical Techniques for Librarians*. 2d ed. Chicago: American Library Association, 1998.

Hagler, Ronald. "Needed Research in Library History." In *Research Methods in Librarianship: Historical and Bibliographical Methods in Library Research*, edited by Rolland E. Stevens, 128–37. Urbana: University of Illinois, Graduate School of Library Science, 1971.

Harmon, Robert B. *Elements of Bibliography: A Guide to Information Sources and Practical Applications*. 3d ed. Lanham, MD: Scarecrow Press., 1998.

Harris, Michael H., ed. *Reader in American Library History*. Washington, DC: NCR Microcard Editions, 1971.

Harrison, Michael L. *Diagnosing Organizations* (Newbury Park, CA: Sage, 1987).

Hauptman, Robert. *Ethics and Librarianship* (Jefferson, NC: McFarland, 2002).

Hayes, R. M. *Use of the Delphi Technique in Policy Formulation: A Case Study of the "Public Sector/Private Sector" Task Force*. Los Angeles: University of California, Graduate School of Library and Information Science, 1982.

Hernon, Peter. "Determination of Sample Size and Selection of the Sample: Concepts, General Sources, and Software." *College & Research Libraries* 55 (March 1994): 171–79.

———. "Editorial: Components of the Research Process: Where Do We Need to Focus Attention?" *Journal of Academic Librarianship* 27 (March 2001): 81–89.

———. "Editorial: Publishing Research." *Journal of Academic Librarianship* 22 (January 1996): 1–2.

———. "Editorial: Research in Library and Information Science—Reflections on the Journal Literature." *Journal of Academic Librarianship* 25 (July 1999): 263–66.

———. "Library and Information Science Research: Not an Island unto Itself." *Library and Information Science Research* 14 (January-March 1992): 1–3.

———. "LIS Extends to the Research Frontier." *College & Research Libraries* 53 (January 1992): 3–5.

———. *Statistics: A Component of the Research Process*. Rev. ed. Norwood, NJ: Ablex Publishing, 1994.

———. "Library and Information Science Research: Is It Misunderstood?" *Library and Information Science Research* 15 (Summer 1993): 215–17.

Hernon, Peter, and Candy Schwartz. "Can Research Be Assimilated into the Soul of Library and Information Science?" *Library and Information Science Research* 17 (Spring 1995): 101.

————. "Editorial: We Will Not Rest on Our Laurels!" *Library and Information Science Research* 25 (2003): 125–26.

Hernon, Peter, and Cheryl Metoyer-Duran. "Problem Statements: An Exploratory Study of Their Function, Significance, and Form." *Library and Information Science Research* 15 (Winter 1993): 71–92.

Hernon, Peter, and Ellen Altman. *Service Quality in Academic Libraries.* Norwood, NJ: Ablex Publishing, 1996.

Hernon, Peter, and Ellen Altman. *Assessing Service Quality: Satisfying the Expectations of Library Customers* (Chicago: American Library Association, 1998).

Hernon, Peter, and John V. Richardson, eds. *Microcomputer Software for Performing Statistical Analysis: A Handbook Supporting Library Decision Making.* Norwood, NJ: Ablex Publishing, 1988.

Hernon, Peter, and John R. Whitman. *Delivering Satisfaction and Service Quality: A Customer-Based Approach for Librarians* (Chicago: American Library Association, 2001).

Hernon, Peter, and Robert E. Dugan. *An Action Plan for Outcomes Assessment in Your Library* (Chicago: American Library Association, 2002).

Hernon, Peter et al. *Statistics for Library Decision Making: A Handbook.* Norwood, NJ: Ablex Publishing, 1989.

Hesse-Biber, Sharlene Nagy. "Unleashing Frankenstein's Monster? The Use of Computers in Qualitative Research." In *Approaches to Qualitative Research: A Reader on Theory and Practice*, edited by Sharlene Nagy Hesse-Biber and Patricia Leavy. New York: Oxford University Press, 2004.

Hillway, Tyrus. *Introduction to Research.* 2d ed. Boston: Houghton Mifflin, 1964.

Hisle, W. Lee. "Top Issues Facing Academic Libraries: A Report of the Focus on the Future Task Force." *College & Research Libraries News* 63 (November 2002): 714, 715, 730.

Hittleman, Daniel R., and Simon Alan J. *Interpreting Educational Research: An Introduction for Consumers of Research.* 3d ed. Upper Saddle River, NJ: Merrill, Prentice Hall, 2002.

Hogan, Sharon A., and Mary W. George. "Cropping Up: Librarians' Desire to Conduct Serious Research." *Research Strategies* 4 (Spring 1986): 58–59.

Holliday, Adrian. *Doing and Writing Qualitative Research.* London: Sage Publications, 2002.

Hsu, Jeffrey. "The Development of Electronic Surveys: A Computer Language-Based Method." *The Electronic Library* 13, no. 3 (1995): 195–202.

Hunter, Rhonda N. "Successes and Failures of Patrons Searching the Online Catalog of a Large Academic Library: A Transaction Log Analysis." *RQ* 30 (1991): 395–402.

Huntsberger, David V., and Patrick Billingsley. *Elements of Statistical Inference.* 4th ed. Boston: Allyn and Bacon, 1977.

Ikpaahindi, Linus. "An Overview of Bibliometrics: Its Measurements, Laws, and Their Implications." *Libri* 35 (June 1985): 163–77.

Irwin, Raymond. *The Golden Chain: A Study in the History of Libraries.* London: H. K. Lewis, 1985.

Isaac, Stephen, and William B. Michael. *Handbook in Research and Evaluation: A Collection of Principles, Methods and Strategies Useful in the Planning, Design, and Evaluation of Studies in Education and the Behavioral Sciences.* 3d ed. San Diego: EdITS, 1995.

Jackson, S.L. "Environment: Research." In *A Century of Service: Librarianship in the United States and Canada*, edited by S. L. Jackson, E. B. Herling, and E. J. Josey. Chicago: American Library Association, 1976. 341–54.

Jacobson, Marilyn D. *New York State Education Information Centers Program: Summative Evaluation Report.* Albany: New York State Education Department, 1984. E0250542

Jaeger, Richard M. *Statistics: A Spectator Sport.* 2d ed. Newbury Park, CA: Sage Publications, 1990.

Jansen, Bernard J., and Udo Pooch. "A Review of Web Searching Studies and Framework for Future Research." *Journal of the American Society for Information Science* 52:3 (2001): 235–46.

Jansen, B.J., Amanda Spink, and Tefko Saracevic. "Real Life, Real Users, and Real Needs: A Study and Analysis of User Queries on the Web." *Information Processing and Management* 36 (2000): 207–77.

Johanson, Graeme. "Ethics in Research." In *Research Methods for Students, Academics and Professionals: Information Management and Systems.* 2d ed., edited by Kirsty Williamson. Wagga Wagga, Australia: Charles Sturt University, Centre for Information Studies, 2002.

Johnson, Debra Wilcox, and Lynn Silipigni, Connaway. "Arrowhead Library System, the Older Adult in Rock County: Implications for Library Service." Unpublished consultants' report, 1991.

———. "Cataloger as Decision Maker." Paper presented at the annual meeting of the Wisconsin Library Association, Appleton, WI, November 14, 1990.

———. "Use of Online Catalogs: A Report of Results of Focus Group Interviews." Unpublished consultants' report, 1992.

Johnson, R. Burke. "Examining the Validity Structure of Qualitative Research." *Education* 18, no.2 (1997): 282–92.

Johnson, Richard D. "The Journal Article." In *Librarian/Author: A Practical Guide on How to Get Published*, edited by Betty-Carol Sellen, 21–35. New York: Neal-Schuman Publishers, 1985.

———. *Writing the Journal Article and Getting It Published.* 2d ed. Chicago: ACRL, 1983.

Jones, Robert A. "The Ethics of Research in Cyberspace." *Internet Research: Electronic Networking Applications and Policy* 4 (1994): 30–5.

Jorgensen, Danny. *Participant Observation: A Methodology for Human Studies.* London: Sage Publications, 1989.

Judd, Charles M., Eliot R. Smith, and Louise H. Kidder. *Research Methods in Social Relations.* 6th ed. Fort Worth, TX: Holt, Rinehart, and Winston, 1991.

Jurow, Susan R. "Tools for Measuring and Improving Performance." In *Integrating Total Quality Management in a Library Setting*, edited by S. Jurow and S. B. Bernard, 1–14. New York: Haworth, 1993.

Kalin, Sally W. "The Searching Behavior of Remote Users: A Study of One Online Public Access Catalog (OPAC)." In proceedings of the 54th Annual Meeting of the American Society for Information Science (1991).

Kalton, Graham. *Introduction to Survey Sampling.* London: Sage Publications, 1990.

Kaplan, Abraham. *The Conduct of Inquiry: Methodology for Behavioral Science.* San Francisco: Chandler Publishing, 1964.

Kaser, David. "Advances in American Library History." In *Advances in Librarianship*, edited by Michael H. Harris, vol. 8, 188–99. New York: Academic Press, 1978.

Kaske, Neal K. "Studies of Online Catalogs." In *Online Catalogs/Online Reference*, edited by Brian Aveney and Brett Butler, 20–30. Chicago: American Library Association, 1984.

Kaske, Neal K. "Research Methodologies and Transaction Log Analysis: Issues, Questions, and a Proposed Model." *Library Hi Tech* 11 (1993).

Kaske, Neal K., and N. P. Sanders. "Online Subject Access: The Human Side of the Problem." *RQ* 19 (Fall, 1980): 52–58.

Keily, L. "Improving Resources Discovery on the Internet: The User Perspective." in Proceedings of the 21st International Online Information Meeting (Oxford: Learned Information, 1997): 205–212.

Keppel, G. *Design and Analysis: A Researcher's Handbook.* 3d ed. Englewood Cliffs, NJ: Prentice-Hall, 1991.

Kidder, Louise H. *Research Methods in Social Relations.* 4th ed. New York: Holt, Rinehart & Winston, 1981.

Kidder, Louise H., and Charles M. Judd. *Research Methods in Social Relations.* 5th ed. New York: Holt, Rinehart and Winston, 1986.

Kidston, James S. "The Validity of Questionnaire Responses." *Library Quarterly* 55 (April 1985): 133–50.

Kimmel, Allan J. "Ethics and Values in Applied Social Research." in *Applied Social Research Methods*, vol. 12 (Newbury Park, CA: Sage Publications, 1988).

King, David N. "Evaluation and Its Uses." In *Evaluating Bibliographic Instruction: A Handbook*, 5–21. Chicago: ACRL, 1983.

Kracker, Jacqueline, and Wang Peiling, "Research Anxiety and Student's Perceptions of Research: An Experiment Part II. Content Analysis of Their Writings on Two Experiences Using Kuhlthau's Information Search Process at a Large Southeastern University," *Journal of the American Society for Information Science and Technology* 53 (February 2002): 295–307.

Kraemer, Helena C., and Sue Thiemann. *How Many Subjects? Statistical Power Analysis in Research.* Newbury Park, CA: Sage Publications, 1987.

Kraft, Donald H., and Bert R. Boyce. *Operations Research for Libraries and Information Agencies: Techniques for the Evaluation of Management Decision Alternatives.* San Diego: Academic Press, 1991.

Krathwohl, David R. *Methods of Educational and Social Science Research: An Integrated Approach.* 2d ed. New York: Longman, 1998.

Krippendorf, Klaus. *Content Analysis: An Introduction to Its Methodology.* London: Sage Publications, 1980.

Krueger, Richard A. *Focus Groups: A Practical Guide for Applied Research.* Beverly Hills, CA: Sage Publications, 1988.

Kuhlthau, Carol Collier. *Seeking Meaning: A Process Approach to Library and Information Services.* 2d ed. Norwood, NJ: Ablex, 2003.

Kuhn, Thomas S. *The Essential Tension: Selected Studies in Scientific Tradition and Change.* Chicago: University Of Chicago Press, 1977.

———. *The Structure of Scientific Revolutions.* Chicago: University of Chicago Press, 1970.

Kvale, Steinar. *InterViews: An Introduction to Qualitative Research Interviewing.* Thousand Oaks, CA: Sage Publications, 1996.

Labaree, Robert V. "Tips for Getting Published in Scholarly Journals: Strategies for Academic Librarians." *College & Research Libraries News* 65, no.3 (2004): 137–39.

Lakner, Edward. "Optimizing Samples for Surveys of Public Libraries: Alternatives and Compromises." *Library and Information Science Research* 20, no.4 (1998): 321–42.

Lance, Keith Curry "What Research Tells Us About the Importance of School Libraries." *Knowledge Quest* 31 Supplement (September–October, 2002). 17–22.

LeCompte, Margaret, Judith Preissle, and Renata Tesch. *Ethnography and Qualitative Design in Educational Research.* 2d ed. New York, Academic Press, 1993.

Lee, Raymond, and Lea Esterhuizen. "Computer Software and Qualitative Analysis: Trends, Issues, and Resources." *International Journal of Social Research Methodology* 3, no.6 (2000): 231–43.

Leedy, Paul D. *How to Read Research and Understand It.* New York: Macmillan, 1981.

———. *Practical Research: Planning and Design.* 2d ed. New York: Macmillan, 1980.

———. *Practical Research; Planning and Design.* 4th ed. New York: Macmillan, 1989.

Leedy, Paul D., and Jeanne E. Ormrod. *Practical Research: Planning and Design.* 7th ed. Upper Saddle River, NJ: Merrill Prentice Hall, 2001.

A Library and Information Science Research Agenda for the 1980's. U.S. Department of Education, Office of Libraries and Learning Technologies. Los Engeles, CA: Cuadra Associates, 1981.

Library History Round Table. "Statement on History in Education for Library and Information Science." Chicago: American Library Association: 1989.

Liebscher, Peter. "Quantity with Quality? Teaching Quantitative and Qualitative Methods in an LIS Master's Program." *Library Trends* 46, no.4 (1998): 668–80.

Lincoln, Yvonna. "Insights into Library Services and Users from Qualitative Research." *Library and Information Science Research* 24 (2002): 3–16.

Lincoln, Yvonna S., and Egon G. Guba. *Naturalistic Inquiry.* Newbury Park, CA: Sage Publications, 1985.

Lofland, John, and Lyn Lofland. *Analyzing Social Settings: A Guide to Qualitative Observation and Analysis.* 2d ed. Belmont, CA: Wadsworth, 1984.

Lopez-Lee, David. "Indiscriminate Data Aggregations in Meta-Analysis: A Cause for Concern Among Policy Makers and Social Scientists." *Evaluation Review* 26, no.5 (2002): 520–44.

Losee, Robert M., Jr., and Karen A. Worley. *Research and Evaluation for Information Professionals.* San Diego: Academic Press, 1993.

Lucas, Thomas A. "Time Patterns in Remote OPAC Use." *College & Research Libraries* 54 (1993): 439–45.

Lundeen, Gerald W. "Research Record." *Journal of Education for Librarianship* 24 (Winter 1984): 206–7.

Lynch, Mary Jo. *Libraries in an Information Society: A Statistical Summary.* Chicago: American Library Association, 1987.

———. "Proposal Procedures: Guidelines for ALA Units." Chicago: *ALA Office for Research*, 1981.

———. "Research and Librarianship: An Uneasy Connection." *Library Trends* 32 (Spring 1984): 367–83.

Lynch, M. J., ed. "Research Questions for the Twenty-First Century." *Library Trends* 51, no.4 (2003): 499–686.

Maines, David R., and Shing-Ling Chen. "Information and Action: An Introduction to Carl Couch's Analysis of Information Technologies." In *Information Technologies and Social Orders*, edited by Carl J. Couch. New York: Aldine De Gruyter, 1996.

Maines, David R., Jeffery C. Bridger and Jeffery T. Ulmer. "Mythic Facts and Park's Pragmatism: On Predecessor-Selection and Theorizing in Human Ecology." *Sociological Quarterly* 37 (Summer 1969): 521–49.

Mann, Chris, and Fiona Stewart. "Internet Interviewing." In *Handbook of Interview Research: Context and Method*, edited by Jaber F. Gubrium and James A. Holstein, 603–27. Thousand Oaks, CA: Sage Publications, 2002.

Marchant, Maurice P., and N. M. Smith. "Research Thrust of Brigham Young University's Library School." *Journal of Education for Librarianship* 20 (Fall, 1979): 129–35.

Markey, Karen. *Subject Searching in Library Catalogs: Before and After the Introduction of Online Catalogs*. Dublin, OH: OCLC, 1984.

Marshall, Joanne G. *An Introduction to Research Methods for Health Sciences Librarians*. Chicago, Medical Library Association, Courses for Continuing Education 1989.

Martyn, John, and F. Wilfrid Lancaster. *Investigative Methods in Library and Information Science: An Introduction*. Arlington, VA: Information Resources Press, 1981.

Mathews, Anne J. "An Overview of Issues, Proposals, and Products in Library/Information Research." *Journal of Education for Library and Information Science* 29 (Spring 1989): 251–61.

Matthews, Joseph R., Gary S. Lawrence, and Douglas K. Ferguson. *Using Online Catalogs: A Nationwide Survey, A Report of a Study Sponsored by the Council on Library Resources* (New York: Neal-Schuman, 1983).

Maxwell, Joseph. "Understanding and Validity in Qualitative Research." In *Qualitative Researcher's Companion*, edited by Michael Huberman and Matthew Miles, 37–64. Thousand Oaks, CA: Sage Publications, 2002.

Maylone, Theresa, ed. "Qualitative Research." *Library Trends* 46, no.4 (1998): 597–768.

McClure, Charles R. "Increasing the Usefulness of Research for Library Managers: Propositions, Issues, and Strategies." *Library Trends* 38 (Fall 1989): 280–94.

———. "Management Data for Library Decision Making: The Role of the Researcher." *Library Lectures*, edited by Robert S. Martin, vol. 56. Baton Rouge: Louisiana State Univercity Libraries, 1988.

McClure, Charles R., and Ann Bishop. "The Status of Research in Library/Information Science: Guarded Optimism." *College & Research Libraries* 50 (March 1989): 127–43.

McClure, Charles R., and Peter Hernon, eds. *Library and Information Science Research: Perspectives and Strategies for Improvement*. Norwood, NJ: Ablex Publishing, 1991.

McCracken, Grant. *The Long Interview*. Newbury Park, CA: Sage Publications, 1988.

McGrath, William E. "Introduction." *Library Trends* 50, no.3 (2002), 309–316.

McGrath, William E. ed. "Current Theory in Library and Information Science." *Library Trends* 50 (Winter 2002), 309–569.

McKechnie, Lynne (E. F.), and Karen E. Pettigrew. "Surveying the Use of Theory in Library and Information Science Research: A Disciplinary Perspective." *Library Trends* 50, no.3 (2002): 406–17.

McNall, Scott G. *The Sociological Experience*. Boston: Little, Brown and Company, 1969.

Mead, George H. *Mind, Self, and Society*. Chicago: University of Chicago Press, 1962.

Meadows, A. J. *Communicating Research*. San Diego: Academic Press, 1998.

Mellon, Constance A. "Library Anxiety: A Grounded Theory and Its Development." *College & Research Libraries* 47 (March 1986): 160–65.

———. *Naturalistic Inquiry for Library Science: Methods and Applications for Research, Evaluation, and Teaching*. New York: Greenwood Press, 1990.

Miles, Matthew, and Michael Huberman. *Qualitative Data Analysis: A Sourcebook of New Methods.* Beverly Hills, CA: Sage Publications, 1984.

Miller, Delbert C., and Neil J. Salkind. *Handbook of Research Design and Social Measurement.* 6th ed. Thousand Oaks, CA: Sage Publications, 2002.

Millsap, Larry, and Terry Ellen Ferl. "Research Patterns of Remote Users: An Analysis of OPAC Transaction Logs." *Information Technology and Libraries* 12 (1993): 321–43.

Morgan, David L. *Focus Groups as Qualitative Research.* Newbury Park, CA: Sage Publications, 1988.

Morris, Betty J. "Getting Published: What Every Library Media Specialist Needs to Know." *Knowledge Quest* 26, no.3 (1998): 16–17.

Morse, Janice. "Designing Funded Qualitative Research." In *Handbook of Qualitative Research*, edited by Norman Denzin and Yvonna Lincoln, 220–35. Thousand Oaks, CA: Sage Publications, 1994.

Moukdad, Haidar, and Andrew Large. "Users' Perceptions of the Web as Revealed by Transaction Log Analysis." *Online Information Review* 25:6 (2001): 349–59.

Mouly, George J. *Educational Research: The Art and Science of Investigation.* Boston: Allyn & Bacon, 1978.

Mudrock, Theresa. "Revising Ready Reference Sites: Listening to Users Through Server Statistics and Query Logs." *Reference and User Services Quarterly* 42 (Winter 2002): 155–63.

Muller, Robert H. "The Research Mind in Library Education and Practice." *Library Journal* 92 (March 1967): 1126–29.

Mullins, Nicholas. *Theories and Theory Groups in Contemporary American Sociology.* New York: Harper and Row, 1973.

Nachmias, David, and Chava Nachmias. *Research Methods in the Social Sciences.* 2d ed. New York: St. Martin's Press, 1981.

———. *Research Methods in the Social Sciences.* 3d ed. New York: St. Martin's Press, 1987.

"National Institute of Child Health and Human Development, Quick Tips: Most Common Reasons for Disapproval." Web page, September 2002. Available, *http://www.nichd.nih.gov/about/cpr/dbs/tip4.htm.*

Neal, James G. "Editorial: The Librarian Research and Publication Imperative." *Library & Information Science Research* 17 (Spring 1995): 199–200.

Nelson, Janet L. "An Analysis of Transaction Logs to Evaluate the Educational Needs of End Users," *Medical Reference Services Quarterly* 11:4(1992): 11–21.

Newman, John. "Academic Librarians as Scholars." *College & Research Libraries News* (January 1998): 19–20.

Nicholls, William L. II, Reginald P. Baker, and Jean Martin. "The Effect of New Data Collection Technology on Survey Data Quality." In *Survey Measurement and Process Quality*, edited by P. Biemer, M. Collins, C. Dippo, N. Schwarz, D. Trewin, and L. Lyberg. New York: Wiley, 1996.

"NIH Proposal Review: Key Words to Watch." *Federal Grants & Contracts Weekly* 12 (1988): A47–48.

Nielsen, Brian. "What They Say They Do and What They Do: Assessing Online Catalog Use Instruction Through Transaction Log Monitoring." *Information Technology and Libraries* 5 (1986): 28–33.

Norden, David J., and Gail Herndon Lawrence. "Public Terminal Use in an Online Catalog: Some Preliminary Results." *College & Research Libraries* 42 (1981): 308–16.

Norman, Geoffrey R. and David L. Streiner. *PDQ Statistics.* 3d ed. Hamilton, Ontario: B. C. Decker, 2003.

Nour, Martyvonne M. "A Quantitative Analysis of the Research Articles Published in Core Library Journals of 1980." *Library and Information Science Research* 7 (July 1985): 261–73.

O'Connor, Daniel, and Phyllis Van Orden. "Getting into Print." *College & Research Libraries* 39 (September 1978): 389–96.

O'Connor, Daniel O., and Soyeon Park. "Guest Editorial: Crisis in LIS Research Capacity." *Library and Information Science Research* 23 (2001): 103–6.

O'Neill, Edward T. "Operations Research." *Library Trends* 32 (Spring 1984): 509–20.

Osareh, Farideh. "Bibliometrics, Citation Analysis and Co-Citation Analysis: A Review of Literature I." *Libri* 46 (1996): 149–58.

Osborne, Larry N. "Research Record." *Journal of Education for Library and Information Science* 25 (Spring 1985): 316–19.

Ottensmann, John R. "Using Geographic Information Systems to Analyze Library Utilization." *Library Quarterly* 67 (1997): 373–95.

Paris, Marion "Thoughts on the Case Study." *Journal of Education for Library and Information Science* 29 (Fall 1988): 138.

Patton, Michael Quinn. *Qualitative Evaluation and Research Methods*. 2d ed. Newbury Park, CA: Sage Publications, 1990.

Peischl, Thomas M. "Benchmarking: A Process for Improvement." *Library Administration & Management* 9 (Spring 1995).

Peritz, Bluma C. "The Methods of Library Science Research: Some Results from a Bibliometric Survey." *Library Research* 2 (Fall 1980): 251–68.

———. "Research in Library Science As Reflected in the Core Journals of the Profession: A Quantitative Analysis (1950–1975)." Berkeley: University of California Press, 1977.

Perrault, Anna H., and Ron Blazek. "Transforming Library Services through Action Research." *Florida Libraries* 40, no.3 (1997): 60–61.

Perry, Suzanne. "Getting a Foundation Grant Takes More Than a Good Idea, Program Officers Say." *Chronicle of Higher Education* 25 (1982): 25–28.

Peters, Thomas. "When Smart People Fail: An Analysis of the Transaction Logs of on Online Public Catalog." *Journal of Academic Librarianship* 15 (1989): 267–73.

Peters, Thomas A. *The Online Catalog: A Critical Examination of Public Use*. Jefferson, NC: McFarland, 1991.

Peters, Thomas. "Using Transaction Log Analysis for Library Management Information." *Library Administration & Management* 10 (Winter 1996): 20–5.

Pettigrew, Karen E., and Lynne E. F. McKechnie. "The Use of Theory in Information Science Research." *Journal of the American Society for Information Science and Technology* 52 (2001): 62–73.

Polkinghorne, Donald. *Methodology for the Human Sciences: Systems of Inquiry*. Albany: State University of New York Press, 1983.

Poole, Carolyn E. "Guest Editorial: Importance of Research and Publication by Community College Librarians." *College & Research Libraries* (2000): 486–89.

Poole, Herbert L. *Theories of the Middle Range*. Norwood, NJ: Ablex Publishing, 1985.

Powell, Ronald R. "Recent Trends in Research: A Methodological Essay." *Library and Information Science Research* 21 (1999): 91–119.

———. "Research Competence for Ph.D. Students in Library and Information Science." *Journal of Education for Library and Information Science* 36 (Fall 1995): 319–29.

Powell, Ronald R., Lynda M. Baker, and Joseph J. Mika. "Library and Information Science Practitioners and Research." *Library and Information Science Research* 24 (2002): 49–72.

Powell, Walter W., and Paul J. DiMaggio. *The New Institutionalism in Organizational Analysis*. Chicago: University of Chicago Press, 1991.

Publication Manual of the American Psychological Association. 5th ed. Washington, DC: American Psychological Association, 2001.

Pyrczak, Fred. *Evaluating Research in Academic Journals: A Practical Guide to Realistic Evaluation*. Los Angeles: Pyrczak Publishing, 1999.

"Questions and Answers." *ISR Newsletter* (Spring-Summer 1982): 6–7.

Reis, Harry, and Shelly Gable. "Event-Sampling and Other Methods for Studying Everyday Experience." In *Handbook of Research Methods in Social and Personality Psychology*, edited by Harry Reis and Charles Judd. New York: Cambridge University Press, 2000.

"Research Agenda for College Librarianship." *College & Research Libraries News* 56, no.7 (July/ August 1995): 470–71, 485.

"A Research Agenda for Libraries." *Publishing Research Quarterly* (Fall 1994): 78.

"Research Agenda for Library Instruction and Information Literacy; The Updated Version." *College & Research Libraries News* (February 2003): 108–13.

"A Research Agenda for YALSA." *Youth Services in Libraries* (Spring 1995): 267–71.

Riggs, Donald E. "Losing the Foundation of Understanding." *American Libraries* 25 (May 1994): 449.

Robbins, Jane B. "Affecting Librarianship in Action: The Dissemination and Communication of Research Findings." In *Applying Research to Practice*, edited by Leigh L. Estabrook, 78–88. Urbana-Champaign: University of Illinois, Graduate School of Library and Information Science, 1992.

―――. "The Quality of Published Library and Information Science Research." *Library and Information Science Research* 13 (Spring 1991): 315–17.

―――. "Research in Information Service Practice." *Library and Information Science Research* 12 (April 1990): 127–28.

Robbins, Kathryn and Ruth Holst. "Hospital Library Evaluation Using Focus Group Interviews." *Bulletin of the Medical Library Association* 78:3 (July 1990). 311–3.

Robinson, A. M. *Systematic Bibliography*. London: Clive Bingley, 1979.

Robinson, Barbara M. *A Study Reference Referral and Super Reference in California* (Sacramento, CA: California State Library, 1986).

Roselle, Ann, and Steven Neufeld. "The Utility of Electronic Mail Follow-Ups for Library Research." *Library and Information Science Research* 20, no.2 (1998): 153–61.

Rowntree, Derek. *Statistics without Tears: A Primer for Non-Mathematicians*. New York: Charles Scribner's Sons, 1981.

Rubin, Herbert, and Irene Rubin. *Qualitative Interviewing: The Art of Hearing Data*. Thousand Oaks, CA: Sage Publications, 1995.

Runes, Dagobert, ed. *Dictionary of Philosophy*. Totowa, NY: Littlefield, Adams and Company, 1962.

Runes, Dagobert D, ed. *The Dictionary of Philosophy*. New York: Citadel Press, 2001.

Ryan, Kenneth J. "Scientific Misconduct in Perspective: The Need to Improve Accountability." *Chronicle of Higher Education* (1996): B1–B2.

Scharf, M. K., and Jean Ward, "A Library Research Application of Focus Group Interviews," in Association of College and Research Libraries National Conference, Energies for Transition (Chicago: ACRL, 1986): 191–3.

Schonlau, Matthias, Ronald D. Fricker, and Marc N. Elliott. *Conducting Research Surveys via E-Mail and the Web*. Santa Monica, CA: Rand, 2002.

Schroeder, Carol F., and Gloria G. Roberson. *Guide to Publishing Opportunities for Librarians*. New York: Haworth Press, 1995.

Schuman, Patricia G. "From Book Idea to the Contract." In *Librarian/Author: A Practical Guide on How to Get Published*, edited by Betty-Carol Sellen, 36–49. New York: Neal-Schuman Publishers, 1985.

Schutt, Russell K. *Investigating the Social World; The Process and Practice of Research*, 2nd ed. (Thousand Oaks, CA: Pine Forge Press, 1999).

Schwartz, Morris, and Charlotte Schwartz. "Problems in Participant Observation." *American Journal of Sociology* 60 (1955): 343–56.

Schwerzel, Sharon W., Susan V. Emerson, and David L. Johnson. "Self-Evaluation of Competencies in Online Searching by End-Users After Basic Training." In Proceedings of the *Forty-Fifth ASIS Annual Meeting*, edited by Robert S. Kohn, Anthony E. Petrarca, and Celianna I. Taylor, 272–75. White Plains, NY: Knowledge Industry, 1982.

Selltiz, Claire, Lawrence S. Wrightsman, and Stuart W. Cook. *Research Methods in Social Relations*. Rev. ed. New York: Holt, Rinehart & Winston, 1959.

Shafer, Robert J., ed. *A Guide to Historical Method*. 3d ed. Homewood, IL: Dorsey Press, 1980.

Shaughnessy, Thomas W. "Library Research in the 70's: Problems and Prospects." *California Librarian* 37 (July 1976): 44–52.

Shenton, Andrew, and Pat Dixon. "Youngsters' Use of Public Libraries for Information: Results of a Qualitative Research Project." *New Review of Children's Literature and Librarianship* 8 (2002): 33–54.

Shera, Jesse H. "Darwin, Bacon, and Research in Librarianship." *Library Trends* 3 (July 1964): 141–49.

―――. "On the Value of Library History." *Library Quarterly* 22 (July 1952): 240–51.

Sheridan, Judson D. "Perspectives from 202 Jesse Hall; the Research Continuum." Graduate School and Research Note 14 (February 1988): 1–2.

Shiflett, Lee. "Sense-Making and Library History." *Journal of Education for Library and Information Science* (Summer 2000): 254–59.

Shiflett, Orvin L. "Clio's Claim: The Role of Historical Research in Library and Information Science." *Library Trends* 32 (Spring 1984): 385–406.

Sieber, Joan. *Planning Ethically Responsible Research: A Guide for Students and Internal Review Boards*. Newbury Park, CA: Sage Publications, 1992.

Silverstein C., M. Henzinger, H. Marais, and M. Moricz, "Analysis of a very Large Web Search Engine Query Log." *SIGIR Forum* 33:1 (1999): 6–12.

Simpson, I. S. *Basic Statistics for Librarians*. 3d ed. London: Library Association, 1988.

Simpson, J. A., and E.S.C. Weiner, preparers. *The Oxford English Dictionary*. 2d ed. Oxford, England: Clarendon Pr, 1989.

Simpson, Charles W. "OPAC Transaction Log Analysis: The First Decade," in *Advances in Library Automation and Networking*, edited by Joe Hewitt (Greenwich, CT: JAI Press, 1989): 35–67.

Smith, T., A. Ruocco, and Bernard Jansen. "Digital Video in Education." in Proceedings of the 30th ACM SIGCSE Technical Symposium on Computer Science Education (New Orleans, LA. 1998).

Smith, Charles. "Content Analysis and Narrative Analysis." In *Handbook of Research Methods in Social Personality Psychology*, edited by Harry Reis and Charles Judd. Cambridge, England: Cambridge University Press, 2000.

Smith, Linda C. "Citation Analysis." *Library Trends* 30 (Summer 1981): 83–106.

Smith, Martha M. "Survival and Service: The Ethics of Research on the Uses of Information Provided by Librarians." *North Carolina Libraries* (1994): 64–67.

Special Libraries Association. "Putting OUR Knowledge to Work: A New SLA Research Statement." Web page, June 2001. Available, *http://www.sla.org/content/memberservice/researchforum/rschstatement.cfm*.

Spink, Amanda, Dietmar Wolfram, B. J. Jansen, and Tefko Saracevic, "Searching the Web: The Public and Their Queries." *Journal of the Americal Society for Information Science and Technology* 52:3 (2001).

Spink, Amanda, and Jack L. Xu, "Selected Results from a Large Study of Web Searching: The Excite Study." *Information Research* 6:1 (2000)

Spirer, Herbert F., Louise Spirer, and A. J. Jaffe. *Misused Statistics*. 2d rev., and exp. ed. New York: M. Dekker, 1998.

SPSS 11.0 Syntax Reference Guide. Chicago: SPSS Inc., 2001.

SPSS 11.5 Brief Guide. Chicago: SPSS Inc., 2002.

St. Clair, Gloriana. "Improving Quality: An Editor's Advice to Authors." *College & Research Libraries* 54 (May 1993): 195–97.

Steffen, Nicolle O., Keith Curry Lance, and Rochelle Logan. "Time to Tell Who Story: Outcome-Based Evaluation and the Counting on Results Project." *Public Libraries* 41 (July–August 2002): 222–8.

Stempel, Guido. "Content Analysis." In *Research Methods in Mass Communication*. 2d ed., edited by Guido Stempel and Bruce Westley, 124–36. Englewood Cliffs, NJ: Prentice Hall, 1989.

Stephen, Peter, and Susan Hornby. *Simple Statistics for Library and Information Professionals*. 2d ed. London: Library Association Publication, 1997.

Stephenson, Mary Sue, "WELCOME TO RESEARCH METHODS RESOURCES ON THE WWW." Web page, [accessed 2003]. Available at: *http://www.slais.ubc.ca/resources/research_methods/index.htm*.

Stevens, G. Ruggeri, and J. McElhill. "A Qualitative Study and Model of the Use of Email in Organizations." *Internet Research* 10, no.4 (2000): 271–83.

Stevens, Rolland E., ed. *Research Methods in Librarianship: Historical and Bibliographical Methods in Library Research*. Urbana: University of Illinois, Graduate School of Library Science, 1971.

Strauss, Anselm. *Qualitative Analysis for Social Scientists*. Cambridge, England: Cambridge University Press, 1987.

Sullivan, Peggy A. "Research in Librarianship: Achievements, Needs, and Prospects." *Illinois Libraries* 60 (May 1978): 510–14.

Swisher, Robert. "Focus on Research." *Top of the News* 42 (Winter 1986): 175–77.

Talja, Sanna. "Analyzing Qualitative Interview Data: The Discourse Analytic Method." *Library and Information Science Research* 21, no.4 (1999): 459–77.

Taylor, Steven, and Robert Bogdan. *Introduction to Qualitative Research Methods.* 2d ed. New York: John Wiley and Sons, 1984.

Tibbo, Helen R. "How Do Historians Find Primary Resources?" Paper presented at the Second National Library Research Seminar College Park, University of Maryland, November 3, 2001.

Tolle, John E. *Current Utilization of Online Catalogs; A Transaction Log Analysis,* vol. 1 (Dublin, OH. OCLC Office of Research, 1983).

Tosh, John. *The Pursuit of History: Aims, Methods and New Directions in the Study of Modern History.* 2d ed. London: Longman, 1991.

Townley, Charles T. "Developing Relationships between Academic Libraries and the State Library of Pennsylvania: A Report of the Research Recommendations." unpublished consultant's report, Report No.: ED250542, August 1984.

Trahan, Eric. "Applying Meta-Analysis to Library Research and Information Science Research." - *Library Quarterly* 63 (January,1993): 73–91.

Tufte, Edward R. *Envisioning Information.* 2d ed. Cheshire, CT: Graphics Press, 1997.

————. *The Visual Display of Quantitative Information.* 2d ed. Cheshire, CT: Graphics Press, 2001.

Turner, Barry. "Some Practical Aspects of Qualitative Data Analysis: One Way of Organizing the Cognitive Processes Associated with the Generation of Grounded Theory." *Quality and Quantity* 15 (1981): 225–47.

Van House, Nancy A. "Assessing the Quantity, Quality, and Impact of LIS Research." In *Library and Information Science Research: Perspectives and Strategies for Improvement,* edited by Charter R. McClure and Peter Hernon, Norwood, NJ: Ablex, 1991.

Vaughan, Liwen. *Statistical Methods for the Information Professional: A Practical, Painless Approach to Understanding, Using, and Interpreting Statistics.* ASIST Monograph Series. Medford, NJ: Information Today, 2001.

Verny, Roger, and Connie Van Fleet. "Conducting Focus Groups." In *Library Evaluation: A Casebook and Can-Do Guide,* edited by Danny P. Wallace and Connie Van Fleet, 43–51. Englewood, CO: Libraries Unlimited, 2001.

Via, Barbara J. "Publishing in the Journal Literature of Library and Information Science: A Survey of Manuscript Review Processes and Acceptance." *College & Research Libraries* 57 (July 1996): 365–76.

Vickery, B. C. "Academic Research in Library and Information Studies." *Journal of Librarianship* 7 (July 1975): 153–60.

Vogt, W. Paul. *Dictionary of Statistics and Methodology: A Nontechnical Guide for the Social Sciences.* 2d ed. Thousand Oaks, CA: Sage Publications, 1999.

von Ungern-Sternberg, Sara. "Teaching Bibliometrics." *Journal of Education for Library and Information Science* 39, no.1 (1989): 76–80.

Wagner, Mary M., and Suzanne H. Mahmoodi. *A Focus Group Interview Manual.* Chicago: American Library Association, 1994.

Wallace, Danny P. "Bibliometrics and Citation Analysis." In *Principles and Applications of Information Science for Library Professionals,* edited by John N. Olsgaard. Chicago: American Library Association, 1989.

————. "The Use of Statistical Methods in Library and Information Science." *Journal of the American Society for Information Science* 36 (November 1985): 402–10.

Wallace, Patricia M. "How Do Patrons Search the Online Catalog When No One's Looking? Transaction Log Analysis and Implications for Bibliographic Instruction and System Design." *RQ* 33 (1993): 239–352.

Walter, Suzanne. *Focus Groups: Linkages to the Community.* Denver Public Library (Denver: US West Communications, 1988).

Wang, Chih. "A Brief Introduction to Comparative Librarianship." *International Library Review* 17 (1985): 107–15.

Ward, Jean, Kathlen A. Hansen and Douglas M. McLeod, "The News Library's Contribution to Newsmaking." *Special Libraries* 79:2 (Spring 1988): 143–47.

Waters, Richard L. "Fund Raising: Grants and Other Bits of Information." *Public Library Quarterly* 17, no.3 (1999): 51–54.

Wayne State University Policy and Procedures Regarding Scientific Misconduct. Executive Order 89–4, December 21, 1989. Detroit, MI: Wayne State University, 1989.

Weber, Robert Philip. *Basic Content Analysis*. 2d ed. Newbury Park, CA: Sage Publications, 1990.

Weick, Karl. *Sensemaking in Organizations*. Thousand Oaks, CA: Sage Publications, 1995.

Westbrook, Lynn. *Identifying and Analyzing User Needs* (New York: Neal-Schuman Publishers, 2001).

White, Emilie C. "Bibliometrics: From Curiosity to Convention." *Special Libraries* 76 (Winter 1985): 35.

Whyte, William. "On Making the Most of Participant Observation." *American Sociologist* 14 (1979): 56–66.

Widdows, Richard, Tia A. Hensler, and Marlaya H. Wyncott, "The Focus-Group Interview: A Method for Assessing User's Evaluation of Library Service," *College & Research Libraries* 52 (July 1991): 352–9.

Wiedenbeck, Susan, Robin Lampert, and Jean Scholtz. "Using Protocol Analysis to Study the User Interface." *Bulletin of the American Society for Information Science* 15 (1989): 25–26.

Wiegand, Wayne, comp. *Libraries in the U.S. Timeline*. Published by the American Library Association and the ALA Public Information Office, December 1999. Inserted in *American Libraries* Vol. 30, No.11, (December 1999).

Williams, James F. II, and Mark D. Winston. "Leadership Competencies and the Importance of Research Methods and Statistical Analysis in Decision Making and Research and Publication: A Study of Citation Patterns." *Library & Information Science Research* 25 (2003): 387–402.

Wilson, T. D., and D. R. Streatfield. "Structured Observation in the Investigation of Information Needs." *Social Science Information Studies* 1 (1981): 173–84.

Wilson, Tom. "Electronic Resources for Research Methods; Research Methods; Action Research." Web page (accessed December 12, 2002). Available, *http://informationr.net/rm/RMeth6.html*.

Winkler, Karen J. "'Disillusioned' with Numbers and Counting, Historians Are Telling Stories Again." *Chronicle of Higher Education* 28 (June 1984): 5–6.

Wolcott, Harry. *Writing Up Qualitative Research*. Thousand Oaks, CA: Sage Publications, 2001.

Wurzburger, Marilyn. "Conducting a Mail Survey: Some of the Things You Probably Didn't Learn in Any Research Methods Course." *College & Research Libraries News* 48 (December 1987): 697–700.

Wynar, Bohdan S. *Introduction to Bibliography and Reference Work*. 4th ed. Rochester, NY: Libraries Unlimited, 1967.

Wynar, Dan. *Syllabus for Research Methods in Librarianship*. Denver, CO: Graduate School of Librarianship, 1962.

Xu, Jack L. "Internet Search Engines: Real World IR Issues and Challenges." Presentation to CIKM99 (Kansas City, MO. 1999).

Yin, Robert K. *Case Study Research: Design and Methods* (Beverly Hills, CA: Sage, 1984).

Yin, Robert K. *Case Study Research: Design and Methods*, rev. ed. (Newbury Park, CA: Sage, 1989).

Young, Heartsill, ed. *The ALA Glossary of Library and Information Science*. Chicago: American Library Association, 1983.

Young, Victoria L. "Focus on Focus Groups." *College & Research Libraries News* 7 (July-August 1993): 391–94.

Zink, Steven D. "Monitoring User Search Success Through Transaction Log Analysis: The WolfPAC Example." *Reference Services Review* 19:1 (1991): 49–56.

Zweizig, Douglas L. "Measuring Library Use." *Drexel Library Quarterly* 13 (July 1977): 3–15.

———. "With Our Eye on the User: Needed Research for Information and Referral in the Public Library." *Drexel Library Quarterly* 12 (Jan–Apr 1976): 48–58.

Author Index

Subject Index*

Accidental sample *see* Sampling
Action research *see* Applied research
Alpha error, 239
Analysis of variance (ANOVA), 240
Applied research
  action research, 54–55
  defined, 2, 53
  evaluative research, 55–58
Associational relationships
  descriptive surveys, 87, 91
Associational studies *see* Correlational studies
Assumptions, 36, 257
Attitude scales *see* Questionnaires
Attitudinal survey, 127
Availability samples *see* Sampling
Axial coding *see* Data, coding

Basic research
  cyclical nature, 20–21
  defined, 2
  general criteria, 20–25
  rationale, 6–9
    benefit to management, 7
    growth of profession, 6–7
    improved service to researchers, 8–9

    personal growth, 9
    reading research reports, 8
Benchmarking, 56
Beta error, 239
Bias
  defined, 88
  experimental research, 171, 173
  interviews, 148–149
  questionnaires, 125, 126
    closed, 129
    content, 135
    differential scales, 133
    organization, 139
    types, 138
    wording, 136–137
  research design, 84
  sampling, 111
Bibliographic coupling, 63
Bibliographical research
  descriptive bibliography, 221–222
  process, 222–223
  systematic bibliography, 221
Bibliometrics
  applications, 63
  Bradford's Law of Scatter, 63
  citation analysis, 63
  Internet-based research, 64

*Index compiled by Regina K. Manning and Katherine E. Seeburger.

Human symbolization, 285
Hypotheses
  causality, 40
  compatibility, 40
  conceptual definitions, 39–40
  constructs, 39
  defined, 34–35
  development, 36
  generalizability, 40
  historical research, 217–218
  null, 34, 237–238
  operational definitions, 39–40, 42
  research design, 257
  sources, 35
  spurious definitions, 40
  testability, 40
  testing, 41–43, 245–246
  theory, grounded, 40
  types, 34–35
  universality, 40
  variability, 40
  variables, 36–38
  working definitions, 39–40

Incomplete sample *see* Sampling
Independent variable *see* Variables
Indexes *see* Questionnaires
Inductive reasoning, 17, 18
Inferential statistics
  nonparametric, 242–243
    chi-square test, 242
    defined, 237–238
    Kruskall-Wallis test, 243
    level of significance, 242
    Mann-Whitney U-test, 242–243
    sample size, 242
    Spearman rank-order correlation, 243
    Wilcoxon Sign test, 243
  parametric, 238–242
    alpha error, 239
    analysis of variance (ANOVA), 240
    beta error, 239
    difference of means, 240
    multiple analysis of variance (MANOVA), 240
    normal curve, 239

Pearson product-moment correlation coefficient, 240
    power, 239
    regression, 241–242
    sample size, 239
    scattergram, 240–241
    student's t-test, 240
    Tukey HSD (Honestly Significant Difference) test, 240
    Z test, 239–240
Informetrics *see* Bibliometrics
Institutional Review Boards (IRB), 69
  ethics, 69
  misconduct, 73–74
Intensity sampling *see* Sampling
Internal consistency, 47–48
Internal convergence *see* Paradigms
Internal criticism *see* Historical research
Internal divergence *see* Paradigms
Internal validity *see* Validity
Internet surveys *see* Questionnaires
Internet-based research *see* Bibliometrics; Research
Interval estimates *see* Sampling
Interval scale *see* Scales
Interviews
  advantages, 150, 193–194
  bias, 148, 149
  computer-mediated communication (CMC), 149
  conducting, 147–149
  development, 147
  disadvantages, 149–150
  focus groups, 150–155
  Internet, 149–150
  personal, 147–149
  recording, 152–153
  schedule, 147
  standardized, 147
  structured, 147, 193
  telephone, 155–157
    computer-assisted personal interviewing (CAPI), 155
    computer-assisted telephone interviewing (CATI), 155
  unstructured, 150, 152
Invariability, 40
Item validity *see* Validity

About the Authors

RONALD R. POWELL is professor in the Library and Information Science Program at Wayne State University. Prior to becoming a library and information science educator, he served as a university librarian and college library director. Powell has taught, conducted research, and published in the areas of research methods, collection development, bibliographic instruction, academic libraries, the measurement and evaluation of library resources and services, and education for librarianship. His other books include *Basic Reference Sources* (with Margaret Taylor), *Qualitative Research in Information Management* (with Jack Glazier), and *The Next Library Leadership* (with Peter Hernon and Arthur Young).

LYNN SILIPIGNI CONNAWAY is a Consulting Research Scientist at the OCLC Office of Research. Her current research projects include the identification and comparison of circulation and interlibrary loan patterns and library collections and WorldCat data mining to facilitate library decision making. She is a co-investigator on an IMLS-funded project to investigate the information-seeking behaviors of faculty, graduate students, and undergraduates from 44 central Ohio colleges and universities. She was formerly the Vice President of Research and Library Systems at netLibrary, a Division of OCLC, served as the Director of the Library and Information Services Department at the University of Denver, and was on the faculty of the School of Library and Informational Science at the University of Missouri, Columbia.